Print,
Manuscript,
& Performance

Print, Manuscript, & Performance

THE CHANGING RELATIONS OF THE MEDIA IN EARLY MODERN ENGLAND

Edited by
Arthur F. Marotti and
Michael D. Bristol

Ohio State University Press
Columbus

An earlier version of Alexandra Halasz's essay was published as part of her book *The Marketplace of Print: Pamphlets and the Public Sphere in Early Modern England* (Cambridge: Cambridge University Press, 1997). Reprinted with permission of Cambridge University Press.

Copyright © 2000 by The Ohio State University.
All rights reserved.

Library of Congress Cataloging-in-Publication Data

Print, manuscript, and performance: the changing relations of the media in early modern England / edited by Arthur F. Marotti and Michael D. Bristol.
    p. cm.
  Includes bibliographical references and index.
  ISBN 0-8142-0845-2 (alk. paper) — ISBN 0-8142-5049-1 (pbk. : alk. paper)
    1. English literature—Early modern, 1500–1700—History and criticism. 2. Literature and society—England—History—16th century. 3. Literature and society—England—History—17th century. 4. Performing arts—England—History—16th century. 5. Performing arts—England—History—17th century. 6. Printing—England—History—16th century. 7. Printing—England—History—17th century. 8. Manuscripts, Renaissance—England. 9. Transmission of texts—History. I. Marotti, Arthur F., 1940– II. Bristol, Michael D., 1940–
PR428.S64P752000
302.2'244'094209031—dc21

                                                          99-047596

Text and jacket design by Paula Newcomb.
Type set in Minion by Graphic Composition, Inc., Athens, Georgia.
Printed by McNaughton & Gunn.

The paper used in this publication meets the minimum requirements of the American National Standard for Information Sciences—Permanence of Paper for Printed Library Materials.
ANSI Z39.48–1992.

9 8 7 6 5 4 3 2 1

Contents

Acknowledgments   vii

Introduction
Michael D. Bristol and Arthur F. Marotti   1

PART ONE   PRINT AND CULTURAL CHANGE

1. From Oral Delivery to Print in the Speeches of Elizabeth I
   Leah S. Marcus   33

2. The Structural Transformation of Print in Late Elizabethan England
   Douglas Bruster   49

3. Pamphlet Surplus: John Taylor and Subscription Publication
   Alexandra Halasz   90

4. Wither and Professional Work
   Joseph Loewenstein   103

PART TWO   MANUSCRIPT AND PRINT: COMPETITION, OVERLAP, AND MUTUAL INFLUENCE

5. "The Merit of a Manuscript Poem": The Case for Bodleian MS Rawlinson Poet. 85
   Randall Anderson   127

6. Manuscript Transmission and the Catholic Martyrdom Account in Early Modern England
   Arthur F. Marotti   172

7. The Rapes of Lucina
   Harold Love 200

8. Ann Halkett's Morning Devotions:
   Posthumous Publication and the Culture of Writing in
   Late Seventeenth-Century Britain
   Margaret J. M. Ezell 215

PART THREE SPECTACLE, THEATER, AND THE CULTURE OF PRINT

9. Reforming Resistance: Class, Gender, and Legitimacy
   in Foxe's *Book of Martyrs*
   Steven Mullaney 235

10. Staging the News
    F. J. Levy 252

11. Shamelessness in Arden: Early Modern Theater and
    the Obsolescence of Popular Theatricality
    Michael D. Bristol 279

    Contributors 307
    Index 309

Acknowledgments

The essays in this collection grew out of a three-session 1995 Modern Language Association forum organized by Arthur F. Marotti, a project in which he was greatly assisted by Michael D. Bristol. Six of the papers from that occasion were developed into the essays included in this volume: those by Margaret J. M. Ezell, Alexandra Halasz, Joseph Loewenstein, Leah S. Marcus, Michael Bristol, and Steven Mullaney.

Introduction

Michael D. Bristol and Arthur F. Marotti

Printing with moveable type is a remarkable invention that has been credited with bringing about rapid and massive social change from the time of its introduction in early modern Europe. At times it has been suggested that these changes in the way society is organized and in the way people think about themselves are somehow immanent in the technology of print itself. For many thinkers, printing is the hero in a triumphal narrative of the emergence of individuality, personal freedom, and the democratic institutions of liberal society. Alvin Gouldner argues that print is fundamental to the "democratization of writing."[1] Alvin Kernan treats printing as fundamentally synonymous with the institution of literature and high culture.[2] Elizabeth Eisenstein describes printing as the catalytic agent for both religious reformation and modern science.[3] A significant contrast to these basically affirmative accounts of the social meaning of print technology can be found in the work of Walter Ong. Writing from a very different ideological perspective, Ong thinks that the transformations brought about by the expansion of print culture have been, on the whole, regrettable. For Ong, the ever-expanding authority of the written word entails an irretrievable loss in the experience of personal intimacy, presence, and immediacy in social interactions.[4] Interestingly, what all these thinkers share is an apparent belief in the causal force of print technology.[5]

While it is true that the invention of printing caused important social changes to take place, it might be worthwhile to ask what social changes could have caused the invention of printing. The arguments of technological determinism, widely popularized in their most extreme form in the writings of Marshall McLuhan, insist that "the medium is the message."[6] This punchy but essentially dogmatic aphorism states that every medium of communication, from cuneiform tablets to the telephone and the Internet, has an underlying logic that permanently alters the way people relate to their own sensory organs. Although the claim that a communications medium can fundamentally change the way the human nervous system is organized is probably incapable of empirical demonstration, to suggest that social habits and epistemological relations change when radios or telephones or fax machines come into general use is not a particularly controversial argument. In any case, what the arguments of technological determinism occlude is the role of social intentions, implemented through plans, projects, and lucid reflection in the development of any technological infrastructure. For one thing, to speak of "invention" in this context is a misleading usage. People "invent" things because they are looking for a solution to some kind of practical problem. Even the legendary "accidental discoveries" are made because someone is deliberately trying to find out how to accomplish some well specified aim or purpose. Technological determinism also tends to ignore the historical importance of unintended consequences and opportunism in the elaboration of a communications technology. People hit on ways to use technology that could hardly be apparent to its inventors. Michael Warner's critique of technological determinism is powerfully germane here. He rejects the view that "technology has an ontological status prior to culture."[7] Instead, he maintains that the development and the deployment of any technology follows from the articulation of social desire as manifested in politics, economics, and works of the imagination.

In his massive history of the social effects of technology, Lewis Mumford insists over and over that machines in the sense of hardware or complex engineering are decidedly secondary in importance to the techniques of administration. The most important technical invention is not any particular machine but what he calls "the human machine" or simply "the machine" or, in other words, the complex division of social labor.[8] In this view the secret of the pyramids is just a lot of people working very hard for a very, very long time. What the pharaohs had was not only powers of policing and surveillance; they also knew the arts of scheduling, logistics, and the design of critical paths. This knowledge is what enabled them to use the techniques of stonecutting and of moving heavy objects to make the things they wanted to make. A technology in this sense corresponds to what Harold Innis calls a monopoly of knowledge. Innis (whom Marshall McLuhan cites often in his work) argues that the development of civilization has been influenced by the means of communication that predominate in different historical moments.[9] Each medium has its own particular "bias" that significantly affects the "character of knowledge," and so technological innovation is not a direct cause of social change, but it is highly correlated with the formation of new social and political institutions. The establishment of these new institutions will eventually consolidate important shifts in the distribution of wealth and power.

Printing may have been a highly significant invention, but in a sense nobody really saw its consequences until it was too late. Technologies actually become significant only after they have reached the point of "lock-in," the point at which the propagation of a particular technique or device through the population reaches a critical number. The utility to us of fax machines and e-mail is a simple function of the number of other people who have such devices. This notion is what explains the overpowering dominance of Microsoft's operating systems among computer users. Similarly, the social power of print can only be felt when large numbers of people know how to read and write. But the mere availability of printed material is no guarantee that anyone will be able to read it or even to see the point of reading, as any teacher of English literature knows all too well. A technology "takes hold" if and only if a number of collateral techniques are in place. The Chinese had gunpowder, but all they did with it was to make fireworks. To build long-distance artillery you need not only gunpowder but also advanced techniques of metallurgy and precision casting, which are of course also necessary for the development of printing. But long-range artillery, like printing, is not merely the blind convergence of various mechanical techniques. Both are attempts to solve problems of action at a distance.

Technology, then, is not just ingenious hardware or even systematic modes of social administration. The material and social aspects of technology are perhaps best understood as the expression of a characteristic social desire. Albert Borgmann, in his recent study *Technology and the Character of Contemporary Life*, describes this as the "device paradigm."[10] What's important for Borgmann is not the machinery of technology but rather the commodity that the machinery has been designed to procure. He uses the example of mechanically reproduced music to illustrate his argument.

> What are the gains and losses in the rise of technologically recorded and reproduced music? .... In the pursuit of an answer to these questions, we will have to pay attention to the sharp division between the commodious availability of music that a stereo set procures and the forbiddingly complex and inaccessible character of the apparatus on which that procurement rests. It is the division between the commodity, e.g., music, and the machinery, e.g., the mechanical and electronic apparatus of a stereo set, that is the distinctive feature of a technological device.[11]

Technology, then, is not simply an ensemble of means and instrumentalities. It is, more fundamentally, a relationship between means and ends governed by a desire for a maximum yield in commodities in return for a minimum expenditure of skilled engagement or effort.

In one sense Borgmann's arguments are linked to attitudes of nostalgia reflected in the work of Walter Ong and Harold Innis. There is an obvious sympathy here for the values that inhere in the oral tradition and with forms of political organization designed to human scale. Like Thoreau, Borgmann evidently believes that men and women should be able to define their own goals and to pursue them under their own power. The implied social norms here are "pedestrian" in the sense that they oppose the distortions of time and space introduced by high-speed, mechanized transport and communication. But Borgmann is not a reactionary technophobe and nay-sayer. His argument is simply that the question of technology has been badly and misleadingly posed. Technology is most often debated in terms of ease or freedom of access—access to the word of God through the medium of the printed word, access to the masterpieces of classical music through the medium of recorded music, access to universal knowledge through the medium of the Internet. Borgmann is skeptical about the saliency of notions of access, and he focuses instead on what we might call the social content of technology. The disburdening promise of technology is deceptive more often than not: a device that makes things easier for some people can make things harder for others.

The media investigated in this collection of essays involve not only different sociologies and modes of production but also, of course, different epistemological relations between the perceiver and the object of perception, different involvements of the human sensory-neural systems, and different forms of consciousness. Spectacle and theater belong more to a communally shared world of sound[12] and visuality (if not also, in the aroma-soup of the physically compacted audience or crowd, of smell and

INTRODUCTION 5

touch as well): they belong to a world of orality, of immediacy, and of human social presence. Manuscript communication, which as scholars have pointed out is close to the world of orality,[13] exploits the connection between what Harold Love has called "chirography and presence"[14] to create an intimate, and interactive, bond between writer and reader. In one of his verse letters, John Donne said "letters mingle Soules"[15]—or, at least, they create the illusion of such contact. The world of manuscript communication, like that of contemporary Internet and e-mail communication, is one in which the roles of reader and producer are fused: if not "interactive" in the late twentieth-century meaning of the term, it is certainly participatory—a system in which "separates,"[16] small gatherings, and even large collections of texts (in, for example, commonplace-book miscellanies and poetical anthologies) are modified and supplemented by those who receive them in the lines of transmission, the whole environment being one in which texts are malleable and social rather than fixed and possessively individualistic. Early modern print culture fostered processes of abstraction and textual fixity. With its utilization of diagrams, charts,[17] catalogs, and indexes,[18] it encouraged the spatialization and disciplinary partitioning of knowledge: it was a "hypervisualized noetic world,"[19] creating, as Marshall McLuhan has put it, "a new ratio of the senses."[20] Print culture's features, according to Elizabeth Eisenstein, include the dissemination, standardization, reorganization, compilation, preservation, and amplification and reinforcement of knowledge.[21] Print arrested "linguistic drift,"[22] facilitated the achievement of "fame,"[23] led to the segregation of the realm of the aesthetic, and fostered possessive individualism.[24] Paradoxically, print both reinforced social hierarchy and democratically opened up texts to potentially broad and heterogenous readerships. On the one hand, through situating published books in a system of patronage, through different levels of pricing, through varying formats—from the broadsheet to the quarto pamphlet and up to the expensive, prestigious folio—print culture involved economic and social discriminations; on the other hand, knowledge was liberated from the control of a social (and academic) literate elite for an increasingly literate general populace whose access to texts entailed politically charged rights of interpretation and use. Print furthered processes of linguistic and political nationalism[25] even as it facilitated international communication—the latter especially in texts written in the still vital international language of learning, Latin. Whereas oral tradition, manuscript transmission, and, to an extent, spectacle and theater were centripetal forces, dispersed throughout a nation and active on the local level, print culture was—in England, for example, through its centralization in London and regulation by the government—a politically centrifugal force, designed to serve the core interests of the politically centralized nation-state.

The various media, of course, interacted and overlapped in interesting ways. Some genres and collections of texts circulated in manuscript form were swallowed whole by the print medium. Print both affected and was affected by the other media. For example, the oral orientation of rhetorical training shaped the ways some materials were presented in print and the manner in which printed texts, such as play texts, were used to evoke the memory of the oral performance.[26] Since the early modern period was one in which texts were read or performed for live audiences,[27] oral (memorized) texts, manuscripts, and printed materials all could serve as resources for this activity. In the theater, play texts regularly passed from authorial manuscript (by way of revisions and censorship) to oral performance, to further revisions (often by writers other than the original authors), to (authorized or unauthorized) print version(s), or, in a case like Thomas Middleton's *A Game at Chess,* to manuscript circulation.[28] In the printing shop, following a practice used for manuscript copying, a manuscript text would be memorized line by line as the compositor set type. Printed texts could find their way back into manuscript and even, through memorization, into oral transmission, just as the process could run from oral performance to manuscript to print.[29] Printed texts sometimes would deliberately invite manuscript additions.[30] It was, of course, also assumed that readers would annotate by hand the books that they owned, thus preserving one of the interactive features of oral and manuscript culture. In the period of interesting overlap of manuscript and print transmission, certain features of the printed book—such as the entitling, numbering, sequencing, and generic arrangement of poems and the poetic or prose dedication and presentation of a work to a patron or patroness—could be incorporated in the production of manuscripts. On-demand (snob-appeal) publication of manuscript works and collections by booksellers and publishers in modern "scriptoria" testifies to the extension of marketing practices from the book trade into the manuscript system (though the process originally worked, as in the case of the early publisher William Caxton, in the opposite direction).[31]

The essays in this volume explore the complex interactions between a technologically advanced culture of the printed book and a still powerful traditional culture based on the spoken word, spectacle, and manuscript. They consider not only various aspects of the "history of the book" but also the protracted overlap of manuscript and printed forms of publication, along with the tensions between the new public media of the book and the commercial theaters. Looking back from our own transitional moment as we attempt to negotiate the shift from typographic to electronic and visual media, the contributors here address such questions as the social character of texts, historical changes in notions of literary authority and intellectual property, and the epistemological and social implications of various communications technologies. Scholars who work on manuscript culture, the history of printing, cultural history, historical bibliography, and the institutions of early modern drama and theater have been brought together for this project to deal with the large cultural and historical issues involved.

These essays offer fine-grained analysis of the messy and difficult history of print in relation to other social practices in the early modern period. The focus here is on the articulation of social norms and the advancement of specific political agendas through the medium of the printed words. For the most part these essays are built on a fairly robust conception of social agency, stressing both the strategic initiatives and the ethical orientation of those who used print media or who contributed to its institutional codification. Not surprisingly, the authors of these essays display some real sympathy with notions of individualized authorship and with the standards of civil society that underwrite the concept of authorial rights. And, for the most part, the authors avoid any kind of nostalgia for those traditional forms of collective expression that tend to be displaced or occluded by the advent of universal literacy and the printed book. But these are not conventionally "Whiggish" discussions of the progressive or emancipatory character of print and its sibling technology in the commercial theater. All of these essays reveal a much more thoughtful concern for the larger implications of printing and the circulation of books in shaping deeper aspirations for personhood and for collective life as these are redefined in early modern England.

Print and Cultural Change

One of the most notable features of print as a communications technology is that it makes possible unprecedented economies of scale. Setting type by hand is a laborious and exacting task, though a skilled typesetter can work with surprising speed. Once the type has been set, however, multiple copies can be produced quickly and cheaply using mostly unskilled labor to operate the press. In this sense printing is a crucially important example of what Harold Innis describes as a "space-binding" technology. Innis argues that heavy, durable media like cuneiform tablets or the stained glass windows and stone carvings in Gothic cathedrals are "time-binding." Ideas that are literally carved in stone appear in societies that possess great long-term stability but only a limited capacity to govern and administer widely dispersed territory. The most significant innovation brought about by printing was not simply the use of moveable type but the application of that technology to the mass production of the codex form. The codex is a remarkable and mostly unappreciated invention, light in weight, cheap to produce, and extremely portable. Books and pamphlets lend themselves much more readily to propagation in space, but are probably less well suited to maintaining long-term social stability. It is the mobility of the book and its general indifference to the social status of its readers that accounts for the role of printing in the acceleration of social change.

The essays here most centrally concerned with print and cultural change all tend to reveal the mobile and space-binding character of print. But the uniform and centralized administration of geographical space is not the primary interest here. More important is the circulation of books and pamphlets throughout a complex and diversified social space. As these essays make clear, early modern England was neither a simple nor an idyllic society. The history of early modern printing is a fascinating example of what Marx has called "uneven development." Printing was carried out under the close supervision of the Stationers' Company, itself an outgrowth of much older trades that actually preceded the invention of printing. As a traditional livery company, this institution was generally more concerned with the defense of "ancient" privilege than it was with encouraging any kind of social change or mobility. Printing as a trade was thus a fundamentally contradictory practice, with inherent conflicts of interest between the members of the Stationers' Company and the newly emerging practice of individualized authorship. Books and pamphlets were also key weapons in the protracted religious struggles of the period. And books were used to debate virtually all of the many questions of the allocation of social and political authority. Printing had no strongly determinative or autonomous role in any of this but rather reflected the larger dispositions of power, wealth, and symbolic capital by which it was constituted as a distinctive set of practices.

In the accounts that follow, printing is never represented as the singular agent of important social change. For one thing, printing itself was neither

INTRODUCTION 9

an isolated nor an unforeseen technology. Printing was a novel solution to a problem of duplication already encountered in the older scriptoria. More important, print technology depended on the collateral development of auxiliary technologies such as papermaking, the manufacture of inks, metallurgy, woodblock and metal engraving, and the science of precise measurement. In this sense printing was simply one of the more vivid and obvious manifestations of a more general reconfiguration of the technological infrastructure, or "the machine" in Mumford's terms. Furthermore, printing had to compete from the outset with other media, including the more socially prestigious forms of manuscript circulation. And toward the end of the sixteenth century an even more powerful rival in the field of communications appeared, in the newly popular commercial theaters of London. Finally, it is crucial to remember that the commercial trade in printed books is perhaps most important as a strategy for the deployment of capital. Printing, of course, is about the circulation of ideas, just as Elizabeth Eisenstein and other historians of print maintain. But in another sense printing is fundamentally indifferent to what gets printed; the important thing is the way printing secures the circulation of capital.

Leah S. Marcus's essay, "From Oral Delivery to Print in the Speeches of Elizabeth I," considers the relations and interactions between the spoken word and its representation in written form. She professes to feeling "impatience" with scholars who privilege the immediacy of speech over the more alienated forms of writing and who invest face-to-face communication with "an almost mystical integrity." Instead, she argues for a much more complex distribution of authority and of meaning across the various media that were available to the queen. Elizabeth evidently composed her speeches in her mind, using the classical arts of composition and of memory. The full and official weight of the queen's authority was thus registered "in person" when she pronounced the royal word. She used colorful and very direct language to create a forceful impression of an extemporaneous monologue. But although these addresses were in fact scripted rather than extemporaneous, they were not actually (like John Donne's sermons, for example) committed to paper until after their performance. This is why, according to Marcus, the various manuscripts of Queen Elizabeth's public oratory are probably not an altogether reliable record of what she actually said. What the manuscript versions represent is not the "original text" of speeches composed ahead of time for oral delivery. The manuscripts were edited transcripts, often considerably moderated in tone, intended for public circulation among members of the court.

Even more editing was done before the speeches were committed to print. Marcus presents evidence to show that inflammatory words and phrases that appear in some of the manuscript versions of speeches are often replaced by more circumspect language in the printed texts. The queen's self-censorship is interesting, as we see her following the advice of her "spin doctors" and adjusting her communications to suit the temper of public opinion, the printed versions intended as the record of the queen's pronouncements suitable to a general audience. Writing cannot be as authoritative as the oral *prototypon*, but by printing her speeches Elizabeth had a way to propagate her words through the increasingly expansive social space of a general readership. There is, however, no such thing as a single "best text" of the queen's speeches. There is rather a "bewildering array" of alternative forms, each composed with a particular audience and a particular political agenda in mind. But if the oral *prototypon* is the only genuinely authoritative form, why bother committing these speeches to print at all? The very existence of the printed texts suggests a monarch who not only is fully aware of the existence of something like a public sphere in early modern England but also is highly sensitive to both the dangers and the opportunities of print as a powerful form of publicity.

The implications of the early-modern public sphere are the focus of Douglas Bruster's essay, "The Structural Transformation of Print in Late Elizabethan England." Bruster begins his discussion by observing that English books became increasingly personal toward the end of the sixteenth century, especially in the proliferation of the various genres of satire, invective, and public ridicule. These abusive texts, which named names and often bordered on slander, identified their targets by very detailed descriptions of the body. The personalization of texts coincided with a new kind of social status for their authors. Writers became celebrities and their books became "best-sellers"; this new form of public visibility then provoked and encouraged the publication of more of the same. The technology of print was not new in the late sixteenth century. In fact, as Bruster points out, by the end of Elizabeth's reign scarcely anyone living would have been able to remember a time when books were not readily available and widely distributed. What was new, however, was the rapid acceleration of a mass market in books together with a growing emphasis on "contemporary authors and their works." According to Bruster, this made "authorship . . . an essential category for Elizabethan readers and writers."

The new and growing celebrity of authors made it possible for all sorts of people to find out "how the other half lived." To understand what courtiers were really like, it was no longer necessary to be invited to visit the court. You could read about it in a book. This was equally true, of course, of the Elizabethan underworld. But there is much more to this development than simply an increased "circulation" of topical information about those neighborhoods one hears about but never visits. The appearance of best-selling authors and their textual celebrity contributed powerfully to an increased social fluidity between persons (authors and readers) and things (books and other artifacts of print technology). For Bruster this fluidity amounted to a "nascent public sphere" in late sixteenth-century England. Print thus eroded what Habermas has described as the system of "representative publicity" in the early modern period. The queen was no longer the sole representative of public life, despite the vigor of her speech and the magnificence of her triumphal processions. Printed books created a new kind of virtual space in which the voices of ordinary private citizens could articulate a public identity. The initiatives created by this personalization of writing were not, however, confined to the private, interiorized world of the reader vis-à-vis the printed page. As Bruster points out, the public playhouses of London provided a venue for vivid and sustained enactment of private persons engaged in public discourse. The social significance of these new theaters is fully understood only against the background of printing, with its expansion of the sphere of publicity and market relations.

Market relations and the manifold forms of commodity exchange are the main concern of Alexandra Halasz's "Pamphlet Surplus: John Taylor and Subscription Publication." John Taylor, "The Water Poet," actually could well stand as the exemplary case of an early modern best-seller along the lines described by Douglas Bruster. An unbelievably productive writer of pamphlets and occasional pieces, he was perhaps best known for his ability to remain in the public eye rather than for anything particularly interesting or noteworthy he had to say. A true celebrity, he was well-known mostly for being well-known. According to Halasz, the one strand of consistency in his otherwise diverse output of texts is the continual reappearance throughout his writing of what she calls "the subscription scenario." In this narrative scheme Taylor represents himself as having written a particular text at the request of a number of subscribers, who then refuse to pay him for his labor on their behalf. This endlessly repeated story of broken promises and bad debts is for Halasz a fascinating record of the economic contradictions of authorship and of book production during the early modern period.

In one sense the author of a text is simply an exploited laborer protesting that his "wage" is less than the value of the object produced on behalf of the owners of capital, who in this case are the members of the Stationers' Company who "make impressiones of Bookes in [his] name" and place him in the position of giving away his labor for nothing. But the author is at the same time an entrepreneur who "theoretically controls both the conditions of his work and the distribution of the product of that labor." The expectation of profit from the activity of writing is supposed to offset the losses entailed in the wage relationship. But according to Halasz, the "subscription scenario" always breaks down, Taylor is always cheated, and he always suffers an "existential loss" in his writing, which, though done in good faith, always turns out to be more trouble than it was worth. Writing can create celebrity, but you can't take that to the bank, or so it would appear. Why then did Taylor persist in the publication of one pamphlet after another? Halasz claims that Taylor "gets it right"; the solution to the equations of the "subscription scenario" was to be found in the recognition of discourse as a commodity. The "rationality and civic highmindedness" of the public sphere were simply new forms of currency in the market for cultural goods and services.

John Taylor understood the métier of authorship as a form of small-time entrepreneurship, where the main problem is with customers who refuse to pay their bills. George Wither, by contrast, conceived of authorship as a profession. In "Wither and Professional Work," Joseph Loewenstein describes Wither's career as a series of attempts to articulate and defend the rights of authorial labor against the entrenched power of the Stationers' Company. For Wither the chief problem in writing is not with people refusing to honor their debts but with outright theft of literary property through various forms of plagiarism. The assertion of an exclusive right in "original material" had already become a familiar aspect of early seventeenth-century literary culture, as authors attempted to assert their individual identity as creators of texts.[32] Wither was less concerned with competitors' stealing his ideas than he was with the expropriation of authorial labor by a monopolistic guild. He became an activist in the defense of "the poet's rights" and eventually succeeded in obtaining an ad hoc patent or grant of authorial copyright for his *Hymns and Songs of the Church*. Patents that assigned a direct financial interest to individual authors in the publication of their work were not altogether new. What made Wither's patent so unusual was that it required the stationers to include the *Hymns and Songs of the Church* in every copy of every book of Psalms, including those already bound and held in booksellers' inventories. This promised to be an extremely lucrative deal for Wither, but the various trades within the Stationers' Company were extremely unhappy with the development.

One of the interesting points Loewenstein develops in his essay is the relationship between two contrasting notions in Wither's career of the "professional man of letters." Some of Wither's arguments for authorial rights anticipate the language of modern economic libertarianism. Wither claimed a natural entitlement as the creator of certain works to bring those works to the market without the encumbrances created by antiquated institutions like the Stationers' Company, which obstructed the natural flow of commerce between producers and consumers of texts. But Wither's patent was not earned simply because he had convincing legal and economic arguments. In fact, it was his "profession" in the religious, rather than the economic, sense of this term that really accounted for the success of his initiative. Wither had been jailed for his writing on at least two separate occasions, and thus represents both sides of most current notions of professional authorship. An author gets paid for the value of his work, but he is also legally accountable for what he writes. Loewenstein uses the example of Wither's career to argue that the ideology and the practice of possessive individualism are perhaps first worked out in the sphere of literary production and distribution. Ironically, however, Wither's defense of individual liberty and of the rights of labor is asserted under the protection of royal authority.

Manuscript and Print: Competition, Overlap, and Mutual Influence

In the first two and a half centuries after Gutenberg's invention began to affect European culture, the older system of manuscript transmission of texts retained a remarkable vitality and importance, adapting itself to the newly reconfigured multimedia world as it both opposed and interacted with the print medium. From the private letter, to the personal manuscript commonplace-book miscellany or poetical anthology, to the group collecting efforts that took place in aristocratic social circles, universities, the Inns of Court, and the court, manuscript transmission belonged to a culture that valued personal intimacy, sociality, and participation, if not also intellectual and social exclusivity—all features that generally distinguished it from print transmission. Closer to the world of orality and its sociological assumptions, the manuscript medium could be used to foster familial and kinship ties, group solidarity, local identity, and factional or partisan interests.[33]

Texts circulated in manuscript and often collected into larger units included occasional poetry,[34] plays,[35] and other sorts of literary works (some, like Sidney's *Arcadia,* quite lengthy); music and songs;[36] news reports and regular newsletters (like those of Sir Robert Sidney's agent at court, Rowland Whyte);[37] transcripts or reports of speeches and proceedings in Parliament;[38] letters by prominent political figures like the Earl of Essex and Sir Walter Ralegh; descriptions of trials and executions; censorable political and religious manifestos and tracts;[39] and satiric prose and poetry directed against notable public personages, some of which were (prosecutable) libels, some actually posted in public places.[40]

Compared to many intellectually ambitious studies of early modern print culture, broad studies of manuscript production and transmission have been relatively few. Recent books by Mary Hobbs, Harold Love, Arthur F. Marotti, Peter Beal,[41] and H. R. Woudhuysen, however, have signaled a new interest in the late stages of manuscript culture, sparked, certainly, by Peter Beal's volumes in the ambitious *Index of English Literary Manuscripts.*[42] Whereas previously scholars of the early modern period mainly examined literary manuscripts textually in order to produce modern critical editions of major authors, now scholars are beginning to study these documents in a broader sociocultural matrix to discover the ways manuscript production and transmission are implicated in a set of social practices with far-reaching implications. Since the manuscript medium continued to serve important sociopolitical purposes through at least the first two and a half centuries of the post-Gutenberg era, and since it interacted in revealing ways with a developing print culture, it is a rich subject for investigation.

Harold Love has distinguished three kinds of "scribal publication" in the early modern period: "author publication, entrepreneurial publication, and user publication."[43] The first kept maximum control in the hands of the author, the second put the commercial copier or vendor of a text in control, and the third allowed recipients down the line of manuscript transmission of texts to appropriate, reproduce, and change what they obtained. Clearly, the question of ownership of textual property was very complex in such a system, especially given the fact that both editors and collectors felt free to supplement, revise, censor, or answer the originals they received, sometimes changing them quite drastically.[44] Love refers to the way in which, even for authors, the manuscript medium encouraged "incessant revision," so that our (print-culture-based) notion of an author's "final intention" is really inappropriate for writing produced under such conditions.[45]

In "'The Merit of a Manuscript Poem': The Case for Bodleian MS Rawlinson Poet. 85," Randall Anderson selects for special attention one of the richest and most interesting of the sixteenth-century manuscript poetical anthologies.[46] He uses this collection to deal with issues of personal and group literary tastes, practices of competitive versifying and literary exchange, and the links of manuscript transmission to particular social and institutional environments (the court and St. John's College, Cambridge). He also raises the question of anthologizing—first, both in relation to the late Tudor printed poetical miscellanies and to modern poetical collections. He argues that surviving manuscript collections suggest that modern anthologies of the aesthetically best or canonical tests are not really "representative" of the literary culture of the period, because they do not adequately reflect the "full range" of verse available in the manuscript system (and in print publication).

Although, as Anderson notes, some few anthologies draw heavily on poems found in the surviving manuscript documents—especially the recent ones by David Norbrook and H. R. Woudhuysen[47] and by Emrys Jones[48]—for the most part modern literary anthologizing and the related literary histories have created a distorted image of the body of poetical writing of the period.[49] The examples of unknown or lesser-known poems that Anderson quotes from the Rawlinson manuscript give a good sense of the kinds of texts that lie outside the familiar corpus of canonical verse.

Manuscript communication was a refuge for texts whose publication state censorship prevented. In "Manuscript Transmission and the Catholic Martyrdom Account in Early Modern England," Arthur F. Marotti examines a neglected literary subgenre. Catholic martyrdom accounts were intended to cement bonds in a persecuted minority community, to complement the printed Catholic polemics and propaganda, and generally, by encouraging firm adherence to the faith and nonaccommodation to English Protestantism, to counter the government's efforts to eradicate native Catholicism. Like other manuscript-circulated Catholic texts, the martyrdom narratives were disseminated through established networks of transmission within England. Moreover, because such texts were involved in reporting and news-transmission within Rome-centered Catholicism and because they were needed by a Continental martyrology industry that published a series of propagandistic texts addressed both to English and Continental readerships, they circulated also in an international environment.

Focusing on a selection of the documentary remains of the practice of circulating these texts—some in late nineteenth- and early twentieth-century compendia, some still in manuscript collections like the Westminster Diocesan Archives—Marotti analyzes some of the features of this subgenre that exploit the connections of the manuscript medium to human presence and communal involvement, including the narratological techniques and thematic preoccupations that highlight confessional differences between Catholicism and Protestantism. He relates the circulation of martyrdom accounts, for example, to the circulation of martyrs' relics[50] (both often finding Continental resting places). Finally, he discusses the interesting case of how one of these texts, containing the gallows speech of John Southworth, who was executed during the Interregnum, could be included in a Restoration print publication to make a political point relevant to internecine religio-political conflict among English Protestants.

In his essay, "The Rapes of Lucina," Harold Love examines an interesting case of a Jacobean play, John Fletcher's *Valentinian,* and its radical revision by the Earl of Rochester as *Lucina's Rape* (1675), to trace "an unusual but not unique odyssey through the media, moving from print, to the stage, then to manuscript circulation, then to print again, then back to manuscript, then to the stage again, and finally back to print." He argues that "significant aspects of the artistic handling are modified to meet the expectations of each new mode of transmission and its public." Starting with the "Histoire d'Eudoxe, Valentinian, et Ursace" from Honoré D'Urfé's prose romance *Astrée,* a work aimed originally at a female readership, Love demonstrates how the change of media (and of genre) from page to stage forced the dramatist John Fletcher to use a different form of characterization for the story and to compress a great variety of incidents in a dramatic work that draws on the features of Shakespeare's and Jonson's Roman plays and on the conventions of Jacobean revenge dramas. Love sees in the Restoration radical revision of this play by the Earl of Rochester an attempt to desensationalize its ending and to eliminate some of the diffuse material to focus more clearly on the major characters—in effect, to complete the changes needed to make a leisurely prose-romance narrative into an effective drama (effective, at least, for a neoclassical sensibility different from the Jacobean one).

Love finds the "media history" of *Valentinian* revealing. Unpublished during the life of its author and withheld from publication by the theater company that owned the text, it went through the typical process of revision before revival for performance at other opportune moments, when the political circumstances made the play newly relevant. Once published in the massive 1647 folio of Beaumont and Fletcher's works and thus canonized as a work of literature, the play became a fixed (though newly politically relevant) reading text that encouraged "reading practices more suitable for poems and romances." When Rochester revised the play for a court theater that had an audience able to make fresh topical applications of its characters and content, he made changes specifically designed to use the resources and limitations of the indoor play-space; but his literary execution, revealing "an invasion of performance by print values," made the text more appropriate for reading than for stage presentation. When the dangerous political relevance to the circumstances surrounding the Titus Oates "Popish Plot" of the late 1670s prevented its stage presentation, Rochester released the text into manuscript circulation, the medium in which he felt literarily most comfortable, the play remaining unpublished until after his death.

Love, who has studied the transmission of Rochester's texts more thoroughly than any other scholar, demonstrates the ways the manuscript medium encouraged the characteristic features of that writer's art—"the subversive, seditious, and indecent." Given the censorship of the stage and of print publication, Rochester found in scribal publication an environment offering the kind of freedom of expression that was exploited by writers of politically pointed satires and lampoons—the possibility also of breaking a taboo such as the one preventing "open discussion and representation on the stage of homosexuality." The scenes of homosexual eroticism, which were included in the posthumous 1685 printing of the play, were deemed scandalous; and when the play was performed, the erotically charged scene between Valentinian and a eunuch, for example, was altered to replace the eunuch with a female character. In sum, Love demonstrates how the Fletcher and the Fletcher-Rochester plays register the effects of the various media in which they were transmitted, and he sheds light on some of the ways that the media themselves changed in relation to one another. Finally, he concentrates on an author, the Earl of Rochester, whose decided preference for manuscript circulation makes him perhaps the last canonical English author to write primarily for this medium.

Given the restrictions on their public activity, it is not surprising that the manuscript medium was more frequently utilized by women than was print.[51] In her essay, "Ann Halkett's Morning Devotions: Posthumous Publication and the Culture of Writing in Late Seventeenth-Century Britain," Margaret J. M. Ezell examines the writing of a woman who did not, however, like many other early modern women, use scripted texts to communicate with others in her network of social relations, but who composed a massive body of noncirculating manuscript writing that registered "the impact of reading print texts and ... the conventions of writing for print" on the practices of an author who could only envision posthumous print publication. In her enormous body of writing, "an astonishing twenty-one folio and quarto manuscript volumes composed between 1644 and the late 1690s" (only a small portion of which has been printed), Halkett "was consciously shaping her own manuscript writings for a print readership rather than a manuscript one." Ezell highlights Halkett as an interesting example of the ways "protocols of authorship" in the early modern period were "affected by the writer's response to print technology as well as issues involving gender and geographical region."

Ezell argues that Halkett's incorporation of some of the features of print publication in her manuscript works—for example, titles, tables of contents, page numbers, marginal glosses—are a sign not only of the textual environment of published works in which she situated her writing intellectually, but also of her preparation of her texts for possible posthumous publication. The whole question of the "private" and "public" in such a case is quite ambiguous, since the private woman author, who had a history and reputation as an active public person, both withheld her texts from manuscript or print publication and deliberately designed them for later entry into the public sphere. Ezell offers a combination of financial, religio-political, geographical, and gender factors to explain Halkett's decision not to try to have her writings printed in her own lifetime. "[T]he perfect example of the private or 'closet' writer," Halkett envisioned a public life for her texts after her death.

Spectacle, Theater, and Performance in the Age of Print

The medium of live oral performance in the early modern period was a highly diversified practice that embraced formal public oratory, sermons, and speeches by prisoners before execution, along with participatory forms of folk festivity and improvised social drama. It also included more formal, scripted "playing" in municipal guild cycles, universities, and aristocratic households.[52] The commercial theaters that began to do business in London in the early 1570s exhibited significant continuities between traditional plebeian culture and the new public theaters of Elizabethan London.[53] The playhouses were built as a way to accommodate and also to exploit popular traditions of conviviality. The plays that were performed borrowed extensively from the symbolic vocabulary of carnival and popular festive form. They also created new possibilities for the articulation of popular resistance to unwanted or unwelcome forms of political authority.[54] The institution of early modern theater was, finally, an alternative agential space. The playhouse became a permanent and commercially profitable form of carnival, with its tradition of masquerade, social inversion, and the general derangement of social identity.

Notwithstanding their ancestry in traditional popular culture, the public theaters of Elizabethan London were a radically innovative technology for the production of cultural goods and services. The social impact of live performance is, of course, significantly multiplied by the possibility of mechanical reproduction in the form of printed quartos of popular plays. More fundamentally the plays themselves were read and memorized as texts by the members of the acting companies before they could be performed. Even the "rude mechanicals" of *A Midsummer Night's Dream* know how to read their parts, and this example suggests the existence of a broad social base of literacy in early modern cities and towns. Plays in manuscript were also read by officials in the Revels Office before they could be licensed for production in the public theaters.[55] Finally, copies of plays circulated among members of the Stationers' Company, who exploited an important secondary market for dramatic performances. Theatrical performance is fundamentally reoriented by these changes, in the discursive structure of dramatized narrative and in its orientation to a new kind of social addressee.

The capacity of theatrical performance to put into question entrenched social norms of hierarchy, patriarchal authority, and gender difference provoked a violently intense antitheatrical protest in sixteenth- and seventeenth-century England.[56] A general mistrust of the seductive allure of the playhouse can be found much earlier in the writings of the early church, most notably in Augustine's *Confessions*. The games, spectacles, and carnivalesque irreverence typical of popular culture were vigorously denounced in many of the antitheatrical treatises, beginning in 1577 with Lord Northbrooke's *A Treatise wherein Dicing, Daunsing, Vaine Plays or Enterluds . . . Are Reproved*. The appearance of an organized professional theater in London created even greater anxiety about the alleged effects of the new medium, not unlike contemporary protests against the evils of comic books, television, and rock music. For the most part the antitheatrical literature stressed the link between the commercial playhouse and the excesses of popular festive form. But the real threat to social stability was not the theater's links with traditional popular culture. The greater danger was the way theater linked up with new social constituencies and new forms of public space created by the culture of the printed book.[57] Despite intermittent efforts to suppress it, the institution of show business founded in the major cities of early modern Europe has continued to expand and flourish while the ancestral forms of popular festivity have on the whole declined in importance. The reasons for this are complex, but part of the explanation is that traditional plebeian culture simply did not have the resources at its disposal to match the pace of technical innovation initiated by the early modern playing companies.

The cultural institution created by Marlowe, Shakespeare, and Jonson was in a number of important ways already very distant from its formal and thematic sources in traditional popular culture. Popular culture and popular theatricality are fundamentally parochial in their outlook, concerned mostly with maintaining a settled way of life over the *longue durée* of social time. The playhouses of London, by contrast, were largely urban and cosmopolitan, broadly oriented to a newly expanded sense of social space.[58] They also, crucially, exhibited a radically new relationship with the risks and opportunities of commodity exchange. The performance of a play is a commodity not only in the sense of a cultural service available for purchase but also in Albert Borgmann's sense of "the device paradigm." Theater organized along the lines of commodity exchange was a technical innovation that made a desired social good available without the effort or burden of direct participation. This describes quite precisely what the commercial theater of Elizabethan and Jacobean London had to offer as an alternative to popular culture. The playhouses provided an experience of spectacle, recreation, and conviviality that was not bound to the seasonal calendar and did not require elaborate or time-consuming preparation. The kind of fun available to the new constituency of cultural consumers in the early modern playhouses was perhaps impersonal and deficient in social immediacy, but the quality of the performances was higher than what could be obtained through the traditional forms of popular celebration.

Attending the first performance of *The Tempest* at the Globe would certainly have been a very different kind of social experience than planning and performing in one of the Corpus Christi plays with other members of your guild. In that sense the "business of playing" in early modern London was already an alienated form of cultural expression, though this was perhaps what made it an "art form."[59] It could even be argued that organizations like the King's Men have more in common with institutions like the Disney Corporation than they do with the local community associations that performed in theatrical and festive events like the Hocktide plays at Coventry. The commercial theaters were a radically new form of publicity that would eventually make it possible to coordinate the beliefs and the actions of very large numbers of people over a broad and irregular social topography.

The social character of the early modern theaters was first worked out in the research of Alfred Harbage.[60] In Harbage's account, the early modern theaters appealed to a socially diverse public because playwrights like Shakespeare and Jonson found ways to articulate a widely shared common culture. Important variants of this view have been developed in studies by Raymond Williams, Robert Weimann, and Walter Cohen.[61] The idea that the early modern theater could adequately represent the broader interests of many different groups has been seriously challenged in other recent work, much of which suggests that Elizabethan and Jacobean society was deeply divided between urban and rural interests, and along lines of factional, class, and gender divisions. The problem that has emerged from these accounts is that a number of widely diverging narratives can be supported by existing evidence with equal cogency.

The theater was "subversive"; the theater "served the interests of domination."[62] Elizabethan and Jacobean drama was in complicity with patriarchal domination;[63] Elizabethan and Jacobean drama contested and undermined patriarchal domination.[64] Shakespeare's plays articulated the "popular voice";[65] the plays show that he was "the king's playwright" writing for a "privileged playgoer."[66] These obviously conflicting analyses have been extremely useful in setting out important hypotheses about the early modern theater and in developing a range of extremely useful research programs for testing these proposals. However, many of the recent general accounts of early modern theatricality or the purpose of playing have been somewhat coarse-grained and crudely sketched. Robert Weimann's account of the emergence of an ideological apparatus in early modern England can help to clarify the political and social meaning of the new theater:

> It is only with the advent of the printing press, the subsequent explosion of discursive activities, and as a consequence of the more highly abstract

and self-authorized types of discourse associated with the Reformation, that modern forms and effects of ideology came to be widely appropriated in more easily accessible texts and through more highly variegated uses of language.... From now on the representation and delegation of power find themselves confronted with a new (ideological) power of representation, in the sense that the discursive acts of writing and reading attain to a greater degree of autonomy. The relationship of signifier and signified becomes more dynamic, less predictable, and more indeterminate. Hence there is more space for ambivalence, in which ideology can be either hidden or undetermined.[67]

Weimann's account suggests that the theater's relationship to the hegemony of dominant classes was much more complex than the idealized picture of a common national culture described by Alfred Harbage. In this account the Elizabethan theater clearly had the same degree of independence from the ruling classes as the new commercial enterprises of the booksellers and printing trades.

Paul Yachnin has recently argued that Shakespeare's theater was, for all intents and purposes, powerless. In the decades of its most notable creative productivity, the theater prospered by advancing an idea of the "disinterestedness of art."[68] *Stage-Wrights* shows that theater was able to survive as an institution by keeping its head down, so to speak, and concentrating on avoiding the scrutiny of state censors. Yachnin also draws attention to the strong links between the aesthetic ideal of disinterestedness and the exigencies of the cultural marketplace. Aesthetic goods and services exploit the possibilities of market crossover, so that success in the commercial theater is achieved by fence-sitting opportunism. Huston Diehl, on the other hand, is convinced that the theater was a proactive force in advancing the cause of the Protestant Reformation. The theater was a primary instrument of reform, one that often made paradoxical use of the iconoclastic tradition represented most powerfully in John Foxe's *Book of Martyrs:* "Renaissance dramatists replicate his [i.e., Foxe's] plots of demystification, appropriate his metaphors of stranger and whore, rehearse the eucharistic controversy he explores, and grapple with the questions he raises about the nature and function of their art."[69]

Steven Mullaney's essay for this volume, "Reforming Resistance: Class, Gender, and Legitimacy in Foxe's *Book of Martyrs,*" is also concerned with the relationship between the printed text of *Actes and Monuments* and the oral texts performed in the early modern commercial theaters. He is concerned with the power of spectacle to help articulate and even bring into being a sense of belonging to an imagined community, in this case the community of "true-hearted Christians" who make up the population of Protestant England. Paul Connerton, in *How Societies Remember,* has suggested that the language of commemorative ceremonies has a crucial significance for communities in the affirmation of their social and historical identity.[70] In this sense the narratives of martyrdom recorded by Foxe have the same function for English Protestants as the defeat of Hussein might have for Shi'ite Muslims. But of course the real force of the martyrdoms described by Foxe is not actualized through performance and participation, as is true of the Shi'ite ritual of *Ta'ziyeh.* Even the martyrdoms that actually happened the way Foxe describes them would have been seen only by the relatively small number of local witnesses. However, the circulation of vivid written accounts and graphic illustrations through the medium of the printed book had a tremendous multiplier effect. What the printed record lacks in dramatic immediacy is powerfully offset by the way books propagate the experience of a remembered martyrdom through an extensive social space.

The imaginary community Mullaney describes is constituted through the "affective power" generated through the depiction of carefully delineated and highly particularized contemporary individuality. What is important in Foxe's relentlessly gruesome stories is their ability to give shape to distinctive patterns of feeling. Mullaney argues that an important, though unintended, effect of Foxe's book was to "help the popular stage think its way beyond the morality tradition of indigenous drama, with its abstract personification of states of being, and toward the particular, discursive, and theatrical embodiment of affective characters." The social and psychological complexity of dramatic characters in the early modern commercial theaters is beautifully illustrated in Mullaney's account of Elizabeth Young, a lower-class woman arrested in 1558 for selling Protestant books. Young did not just sell books; she also read them, baffling her interrogators with her learning and her wit. She represents a "living contradiction to the class and gender systems of the age." Even Foxe seems in the end unable to grasp the real meaning of her character. It is only in the theater, Mullaney suggests, that the powerful social contradictions of widespread literacy are fully grasped and actualized.

Efforts to realize the national community of Protestant England through new, space-binding media like print and theater did not always proceed very smoothly. In some ways the new forms of publicity were often better at fomenting controversy and division than they were at consolidating any kind of cultural, religious, or political hegemony. F. J. Levy's essay analyzes the parallel methods of news dissemination in theatrical performances, manuscript newsletters, and printed broadsheets. "Staging the News" shows how a pervasive fascination with discussing what we now call "current events" is evident in all available channels of communication in early modern society. Levy begins with the Privy Council proclamation of 1620 that distinguished between "convenient freedome of speech" and "a more licentious passage of lavish discourse, and bold Censure in matters of State." What the Privy Council was referring to here was the practice of circulating news about the royal family, and about various matters of national and international policy. According to Levy, the circulation of news in both printed and manuscript form was a firmly established practice both in London and in the provinces as early as the 1630s. Not surprisingly, manuscript circulation was mostly aimed at the high-end market of influential and wealthy "opinion leaders" while print was directed at a much larger and diffuse "mass audience." The existence of both news-gathering organizations and a news-consuming public tends to support Douglas Bruster's claims that the basic institutions of a political and literary public sphere already existed in early seventeenth-century England.

Levy does not consider the arguments of technological determinism in his account of early modern interest in news and current events. Technology does not determine social attitudes or social behavior. In fact the reverse may be true: social attitudes determine how various technologies will be used. What matters here seems to be not the various techniques of communication but rather the *habitus* of becoming well-informed about what's going on. The medium is not the message, and in fact messages tend to flow freely through many different media including word of mouth, handwritten letters, printed pamphlets, and even theatrical performances. Leah Marcus, in *Puzzling Shakespeare*, has already shown how topical interests might be encoded in dramatic fictions.[71] Levy takes this notion one step further, arguing that in at least a few plays of the period the governing intention seems to be an explicit concern with "broadcasting" the news. Despite the Privy Council interdiction against "bold censure in matters of state," plays like *Sir John Van Olden Barnavelt* and Middleton's *A Game at Chess* were successful in their evasion of official censorship. Jonson's *The Staple of News* commented on the public fascination with news itself and satirized the idea, evidently ludicrous at the time, that news might actually be bought and sold as a commodity.

Commodity form is in the background of Michael Bristol's essay,

"Shamelessness in Arden: Early Modern Theater and the Obsolescence of Popular Theatricality." Bristol's essay is not directly concerned with the relationship of theatrical performance to the printed book. It is included here because of its wider interest in the relationship between new communications media and the process of social change. His argument begins with the observation that Shakespeare's *As You Like It* shares a number of elements with traditional forms of popular theatricality. The playhouse differs from street performance, however, in its ability to participate in the distinctively modern public space established by the circulation of printed books. This is a space characterized by alienation, increased social distance, and the appearance of an ideological apparatus. But it is also a space where social interactions can be based on notions of disengagement, conscience, and consent rather than on parochial authority and subordination. Using evidence from James Stokes's volume for Somerset in the *Records of Early English Drama,* Bristol describes a series of improvised "social dramas" that erupted when traditional festive celebrations got out of hand.[72] These events were typically motivated in large part by personal animosity or chronic factional rivalries, though these were often assimilated to contemporary religious controversies. The discussion of *As You Like It* then attempts to distinguish between the social space defined by commodity, disengagement, and social distance in the commercial theaters and the popular forms of social discipline based on shame and intimidation characteristic of traditional theatricality.

In making this argument, Bristol does not simply shift his allegiances from the party of "subversion" to the party of "containment." Part of the aim here is to move beyond the vocabulary of domination, power, complicity, and resistance that has now begun to outlive its usefulness as a way to account for the early modern theater as a social institution. What emerges from Bristol's discussion, as it does from those of Mullaney and Levy, is a strong sense of the contemporary modernity of this theater. The theater of Shakespeare and Jonson represented a striking and unprecedented emergence from the traditions of popular festivity from which it borrowed so much of its symbolic vocabulary. The theater was a form of commerce rather than a form of communal celebration. In that way it represented a profound alienation of a collective social tradition. At the same time theater articulated conditions of possibility for a new way of being-together-in-the-world. Bristol's essay distances itself from the aims and methods of historicism, with its characteristic emphasis on what is most distinctive or distant about the early modern period. His approach points to the striking continuities between the early modern playhouse and the equally ambiguous contemporary institution of commercial show business.

This collection of studies, then, invites scholars and students of the early modern period to attend not only to the media through which texts and performances were communicated and disseminated but also to the interplay of the media themselves with the changing material and sociocultural conditions within which both authors and audiences, writers and readers, and producers and consumers functioned. As archival work into the rich documentary remains of the period continues, others will contribute to this continuing scholarly dialogue.

Notes

1. Alvin Gouldner, *The Dialectic of Ideology and Technology* (New York: Oxford University Press, 1982), 40.

2. Alvin Kernan, *The Death of Literature* (New Haven: Yale University Press, 1990).

3. Elizabeth Eisenstein, *The Printing Press as an Agent of Change: Communication and Cultural Transformation in Early-Modern Europe*, 2 vols. (Cambridge: Cambridge University Press, 1979).

4. Walter Ong, *Orality and Literacy* (London: Methuen, 1982).

5. For an excellent discussion of technological determinism, see Michael Warner, *The Letters of the Republic: Publication and the Public Sphere in Eighteenth Century America* (Cambridge, Mass.: Harvard University Press, 1990), 1–34.

6. Marshall McLuhan, *The Gutenberg Galaxy: The Making of Typographical Man* (Toronto: University of Toronto Press, 1962).

7. Warner, *Letters of the Republic*, 7.

8. Lewis Mumford, *Technics and Civilization* (New York: Harcourt Brace and Co., 1934), esp. 9.

9. Harold Innis, *The Bias of Communication* (Toronto: University of Toronto Press, 1951), 33–61.

10. Albert Borgmann, *Technology and the Character of Contemporary Life: A Philosophical Inquiry* (Chicago: University of Chicago Press, 1984), 9.

11. Ibid., 4.

12. See Bruce Smith, *The O Factor: Voice, Media, and Community in Early Modern England* (Chicago and London: University of Chicago Press, 1999).

13. Ong, *Orality and Literacy*, 119.

14. See Harold Love, *Scribal Publication in Seventeenth-Century England* (Oxford: Clarendon Press, 1993), 141–48.

15. "To Sir Henry Wotton" ("Sir, more then kisses, letters mingle Soules"), in John Donne, *The Satires, Epigrams, and Verse Letters*, ed. W. Milgate (Oxford: Clarendon Press, 1967), 71.

16. Harold Love explains that this term refers to "an individually circulated short manuscript which was written as a unit, and not assembled from elements

INTRODUCTION

copied at varying times and places," the "most common format . . . the whole or half-sheet bifolium with the first three pages written on and the last left blank for addressing" (*Scribal Publication*, 13).

17. See Walter Ong, *Ramus, Method, and the Decay of Dialogue* (Cambridge, Mass.: Harvard University Press, 1958), 80, 81, 202.

18. Ong, *Orality and Literacy*, 123–26.

19. Ibid., 127.

20. McLuhan, *Gutenberg Galaxy*, 227.

21. Eisenstein, *Printing Press as an Agent of Change*, 1:117.

22. Ibid.

23. Ibid., 1:121. Cf. Leo Braudy, *The Frenzy of Renown: Fame and Its History* (New York: Oxford University Press, 1986), 264–312.

24. Eisenstein, *Printing Press as an Agent of Change*, 1:121.

25. See Benedict Anderson, *Imagined Communities: Reflections on the Origin and Spread of Nationalism*, rev. ed. (London and New York: Verso, 1991).

26. See the forthcoming essay by Harold Love, "Oral and Scribal Texts in Early Modern England," in *The Cambridge History of the Book in Britain*, vol. 4.

27. See Roger Chartier, "Leisure and Sociability: Reading Aloud in Modern Europe," trans. Carol Mossman, in *Urban Life in the Renaissance*, ed. Susan Zimmerman and Ronald F. E. Weissman (Newark: University of Delaware Press, 1989), 103–20.

28. See Harold Love's commentary in the forthcoming Oxford edition of Middleton.

29. Love, *Scribal Publication*, 65–70; H. R. Woudhuysen, *Sir Philip Sidney and the Circulation of Manuscripts 1558–1640* (Oxford: Clarendon Press, 1996), 50, suggests that "Booksellers and stationers may . . . have been prepared to lend books to customers for transcription."

30. Woudhuysen notes that "documents—forms, broadsides, notices—were printed with spaces to be filled. Plague bills, leases, indentures, and trading documents had to be completed by hand; Church of England or heralds' visitation articles were left conveniently blank; almanacs were designed to leave space for notes and occasional memoranda; in single-sheet folio newsbooks the blanks may have been reserved for manuscript additions of domestic news whose circulation was otherwise forbidden by the government" (*Sir Philip Sidney*, 20).

31. See Woudhuysen on "Manuscripts for Sale" (*Sir Philip Sidney*, 174–203); Love, *Scribal Publication*, 124–33, 231–83; W. J. Cameron, "A Late Seventeenth-Century Scriptorium," *Renaissance and Modern Studies* 7 (1963): 25–52.

32. See Loewenstein's "The Script in the Marketplace," *Representations* 12 (fall 1985): 101–14.

33. See Love, *Scribal Publication*, 177–230, on "scribal communities" and "The Social Uses of the Scribally Published Text," and Arthur F. Marotti, *Manuscript, Print, and the English Renaissance Lyric* (Ithaca: Cornell University Press, 1995), 30–48, on the different environments for manuscript production and circulation. Woudhuysen states, "The attraction of manuscript circulation lay in the medium's social status, its personal appeal, relative privacy, freedom from government control, its cheapness, and its ability to make works quickly available to a select audience" (15).

34. See Marotti, *Manuscript*, 1–208, and Mary Hobbs, *Early Seventeenth-Century Verse Miscellany Manuscripts* (Aldershot, Hampshire: Scolar Press, 1992).

35. For a discussion of manuscripts of plays and play plots, including versions of play texts sold to wealthy patrons, see Woudhuysen, *Sir Philip Sidney*, 134–45, 389–90.

36. See Hobbs, *Verse Miscellany Manuscripts*, 93–95, 105–15, and Love, *Scribal Publication*, 23–31.

37. See F. J. Levy, "How Information Spread among the Gentry, 1550–1640," *Journal of British Studies* 21 (1982): 11–34; Richard Cust, "News and Politics in Early Seventeenth-Century England," *Past and Present* 112 (August 1986): 60–90; and Love, *Scribal Publication*, esp. 9–22, 124–26.

38. Love, *Scribal Publication*, esp. 15–22, 134–37.

39. Ibid., 184–91.

40. Ibid., 82–83. As Love notes, regular postal service was not put in place until 1635, so the physical transportation of written material from one place to another was a very slow and chancy business (81).

41. Peter Beal, *In Praise of Scribes: Manuscripts and Their Makers in Seventeenth-Century England* (Oxford: Clarendon Press, 1998).

42. Vols. 1 and 2 (in 4 parts) (London and New York: Mansell, 1980–97). See also Mary Thomas Crane's specialized study of practices of commonplace-book compilation, *Framing Authority: Sayings, Self, and Society in Sixteenth-Century England* (Princeton: Princeton University Press, 1993).

43. Love, *Scribal Publication*, 47.

44. See Marotti, *Manuscript*, 135–208.

45. Love, *Scribal Publication*, 53.

46. This text was edited by Laurence Cummings as "John Finet's Miscellany," Ph.D. diss., Washington University, St. Louis, 1960.

47. *The Penguin Book of Renaissance Verse 1509–1659* (Harmondsworth: Penguin, 1992).

48. *The New Oxford Book of Sixteenth-Century Verse* (Oxford: Oxford University Press, 1991).

49. Marotti, *Manuscript*, has also argued this point, attributing the situation to the biases of modern editors and literary historians caused by their immersion in the assumptions of print culture.

50. Cf. "Southwell's Remains: Catholicism and Anti-Catholicism in Early Modern England," in *Texts and Cultural Change in Early Modern England*, ed. Cedric C. Brown and Arthur F. Marotti (Basingstoke, Hampshire: Macmillan; New York: St. Martin's Press, 1997), 37–65.

51. See Love, *Scribal Publication*, 54–58; Marotti, *Manuscript*, 45–46, 54–56; Margaret Ezell, "'To Be Your Daughter in Your Pen': The Social Functions of Literature in the Writings of Lady Elizabeth Brackley and Lady Jane Cavendish," *HLQ* 51 (1988): 281–96, and "The Myth of Judith Shakespeare: Creating the Canon of Women's Literature," *NLH* 21 (1990): 579–92.

52. Louis Montrose, *The Purpose of Playing* (Chicago: University of Chicago Press, 1996).

53. Michael Bristol, *Carnival and Theater: Plebeian Culture and the Structure of Authority in Renaissance England* (London: Methuen, 1986).

INTRODUCTION

54. Jean E. Howard, *The Stage and Social Struggle in Early Modern England* (London: Routledge, 1994).

55. Some plays, especially in the seventeenth century, were deliberately circulated in manuscript as reading texts. For the argument that Shakespeare participated in this practice, see Richard Dutton, "The Birth of the Author," in Brown and Marotti, eds., *Texts and Cultural Change,* 153–78.

56. Jonas Barish, *The Antitheatrical Prejudice* (Berkeley: University of California Press, 1981).

57. Leeds Barroll, "A New History for Shakespeare and His Time," *Shakespeare Quarterly* 39 (1988): 441, 465.

58. Michael Bristol, *Big-Time Shakespeare* (London: Routledge, 1996).

59. William Ingram, *The Business of Playing: The Beginnings of the Adult Professional Theater in Elizabethan London* (Ithaca: Cornell University Press, 1992).

60. Alfred Harbage, *Shakespeare's Audience* (New York: Columbia University Press, 1941) and *Shakespeare and the Rival Traditions* (New York: Macmillan, 1952).

61. Raymond Williams, *Drama in Performance* (Harmondsworth: Penguin Books, 1974); Robert Weimann, *Shakespeare and the Popular Tradition in the Theater* (Baltimore: Johns Hopkins University Press, 1982); Walter Cohen, *Drama of a Nation: Public Theater in Renaissance England and Spain* (Ithaca: Cornell University Press, 1985).

62. Michael Bristol, *Carnival and Theater: Plebeian Culture and the Structure of Authority in Renaissance England* (London: Methuen, 1986); Leonard Tennenhouse, *Power on Display* (London: Methuen, 1986).

63. Lisa Jardine, *Still Harping on Daughters: Women and Drama in the Age of Shakespeare* (Totowa, N.J.: Barnes and Noble, 1992).

64. Howard, *Stage and Social Struggle* (see n. 54, above).

65. Annabel Patterson, *Shakespeare and the Popular Voice* (Oxford: Basil Blackwell, 1990).

66. Alvin Kernan, *Shakespeare: The King's Playwright in the Stuart Court* (New Haven: Yale University Press, 1995); Ann Jennalie Cook, *The Privileged Playgoers of Shakespeare's London: 1576–1642* (Princeton: Princeton University Press, 1981).

67. Robert Weimann, "Towards a Literary Theory of Ideology: Mimesis, Representation, Authority," in *Shakespeare Reproduced: The Text in History and Ideology,* ed. Jean E. Howard and Marion F. O'Connor (London: Methuen, 1987), 269–70.

68. Paul Yachnin, *Stagewrights: Theater in Legitimation in Shakespeare, Jonson, and Middleton* (Philadelphia: University of Pennsylvania Press, 1997), 2 ff.

69. Huston Diehl, *Staging Reform, Reforming the Stage: Protestantism and Popular Theater in Early Modern England* (Ithaca: Cornell University Press, 1997), 39.

70. Paul Connerton, *How Societies Remember* (Cambridge and New York: Cambridge University Press, 1989); cf. David Cressy, *Bonfires and Bells: National Memory and the Protestant Calendar in Elizabethan and Stuart England* (Berkeley and Los Angeles: University of California Press, 1989).

71. Leah S. Marcus, *Puzzling Shakespeare: Local Reading and Its Discontents* (Berkeley: University of California Press, 1988).

72. James Stokes, *Records of Early English Drama: Somerset,* 2 vols. (Toronto: University of Toronto Press, 1996).

Part One

Print and Cultural Change

CHAPTER ONE

From Oral Delivery to Print in the Speeches of Elizabeth I

Leah S. Marcus

The speeches of Queen Elizabeth I exist in many different versions, both manuscript and print. The variety of forms taken by a single speech is perplexing: not only the words can change from one version to another but whole paragraphs can mysteriously come and go—nay, even the overall political direction of a given speech can alter from one surviving version to another. The one form we most assuredly do not have is the speeches as she actually gave them, with the tone, inflection, and gestures she brought to her delivery of them. Elizabeth speaking is, for us, an absent presence. Indeed, interestingly enough in view of deconstructionist arguments that have long since dismantled a "metaphysic of presence," the area from which she frequently spoke enthroned was called the Presence, in almost a sacramental sense of the term. Like the body and blood of Christ existing in, with, and under the bread and wine in an Anglican communion service, the divine person of the monarch existed "in, with, and under" her physical being in the chamber of Presence. And like the sacramental host, the Presence was moveable, coming into being wherever the queen sat formally enthroned.

Many of us have expressed impatience with assumptions made by students of the orality/writing binary, who are sometimes prone to invest speech as opposed to writing with an almost mystical wholeness, integrity, and "presence" supposedly lost to human communication in our own culture, which—considered over its whole range of oral, written, and secondarily oral forms like TV and the telephone—supposedly permits such great distance between a speaker and his or her audience that meaning becomes opaque and difficult to fathom. Utterance within a primary oral culture can have a similar opacity: the pronouncements of the Delphic oracle provide a good example. It is certainly the case, however, that sixteenth-century speakers often viewed the production of written versions of their oral discourse as a fall into uncertainty rather like that posited as an effect of writing by some modern students of the orality/writing binary; similarly, sixteenth-century audiences frequently lamented that manuscript and printed versions of a speech offered only a pale, obscure reflection, an imperfect copy, of the utterance as communicated orally by its author-speaker. Sixteenth-century English culture—even learned culture—had not quite adjusted to the idea that writing could constitute a primary mode of communication. In their introductions to collections of printed sermon literature or university lectures, for example, preachers and scholars frequently felt compelled to assure their invisible public that despite the lessened immediacy of the medium of communication, their readers should still imagine them as physically present—just as if they stood in the pulpit before their congregation or at a university lectern before their auditors and interacted with them directly. Similarly, men of the theater who published their plays often apologized for the loss of the visual and auditory milieu of the playhouse and what John Marston called, in the course of just such an apology, its "soul of lively action." In such conceptualizations, printed texts are dead bodies that must somehow be reanimated.[1]

We find the same sense of loss articulated in recorded versions of Queen Elizabeth's speeches. No matter how precisely the words were recaptured, her "presence" could never quite be realized on the printed or manuscript page. One parliamentary diarist who had transcribed from memory Elizabeth's "Golden Speech" of 1601 and the speeches that preceded it apologized to his prospective readers: "Many things through want of memory I have omitted, without setting down many her majesty's gestures of honor and princely demeanor used by her. As when the speaker spake any effectual or moving speech from the commons to her majesty, she rose up and bowed herself. As also in her own speech, when the commons, apprehending any extraordinary words of favor from her, did any reverence to her majesty, she likewise rose up and bowed herself, etc."[2] And one of the transcribers of Elizabeth's first speech on the execution of Mary Queen of Scots in 1586 expressed similar frustration: "Whereof the reporter requireth of all that were hearers a favorable interpretation of his intent, because he findeth that he cannot express the same answerable to the original, which the learned call *prototypon*."[3] As another would-be reporter complained of the same speech, it "was uttered with such majesty and contained matter of such rare and singular wisdom that he could not nor would presume to report the same unto them," but contented himself with touching "summarily some few parts thereof."[4] By comparison with other speakers in Parliament, the queen's words carried powerful weight: it was the queen's spoken affirmation of a law (in law French, "La roigne le veult") that brought it into legal force, not the written record of it. And that spoken utterance could only be preserved via the pale reflections of the manuscript and printed texts.

The present study of Elizabeth's speaking in Parliament derives from a new collected edition of *Speeches, Letters, Verses, and Prayers of Queen Elizabeth I*.[5] Both the edition and the present article are based on the contention that we have fundamentally misunderstood the relationship between Elizabeth's speeches as delivered and the manuscript and printed versions in which they have come down to us. I will concentrate here on the 1586 speech for which I have just cited Sir Robert Cecil's apology about the inadequacy of the printed record to the *prototypon*. In fact, Cecil's printed version of the speech is (by the standards of the period) quite faithful to the manuscript copies that circulated at court, one of which shows corrections in the hand of Elizabeth herself. Did his apology over her 1586 speech merely register the loss of the queen's person and voice, or was the version he published lacking in some other way? How might Elizabeth's prototype—the speech as she delivered it—have differed *even in terms of language* from the versions that circulated afterwards?

In working with Elizabeth's speeches heretofore, editors have assumed that she wrote them out before she delivered them: the speech as uttered might depart from the script, but the written script—particularly if it existed in Elizabeth's own hand—would provide a reasonably safe guide to the speech as she delivered it. In some cases, she clearly did write out a speech before delivery, but in those cases, so far as we have been able to determine, the actual speech would be delivered in her name by others, usually Sir Nicholas Bacon or William Cecil, Lord Burghley. Even in such cases, however, if the queen did not feel that the speech as offered by her lord keeper or lord chancellor sufficiently expressed her mind, she was quite capable of offering a stronger version orally herself. One such case was her speech before Parliament on 2 January 1567, responding to earnest petitions that she marry and/or declare the order of those who should succeed her if she died without offspring. Her advance manuscript of the speech, written in her own hand with many revisions and delivered to Sir Nicholas Bacon so that he could offer it before Parliament, begins, "I love so evil counterfeiting and hate so much dissimulation that I may not suffer you depart without that my admonitions may show your harms and cause you shun unseen peril. Two visors have blinded the eyes of the lookers-on in this present session, so far forth as under pretense of saving all they have done none good. And these they be: succession and liberties."[6] This parliamentary session had been tumultuous and, to the queen's mind, at times seditious, since several M.P.'s had asserted their "liberty" to discuss the queen's marriage and succession even after she had expressly forbidden them to do so. But it seems that Bacon's delivery of her reproof was not forceful enough—indeed, he and the queen were in profound disagreement at the time over the issue of her marriage and the naming of a successor—for at the very end of the session, when Elizabeth "had given her royal assent unto nineteen public acts and thirteen private," she stood up to underscore her view of the proceedings through oral delivery of some of the same points that Bacon had delivered earlier. Here is a report of the beginning of the speech as Elizabeth delivered it herself:

> My lords and others, the commons of this assembly, although the lord keeper hath, according to order, very well answered in my name, yet as a periphrasis I have a few words further to speak unto you. Notwithstanding that I have not been used, nor love to do it, in such open assemblies, yet now, not to the end to amend his talk, but remembering that commonly princes' own words be better printed in the hearers' memory than those spoken by her commandment, I mean to say thus much unto you. I have in this assembly found so much dissimulation, having always professed plainness, that I marvel thereat—yea, two faces under one hood and the body rotten, being covered with two visors: succession and liberty.[7]

This introduction clearly demonstrates Elizabeth's recognition of the special resonance created for auditors by her own words in Parliament, better "printed in the hearers' memory" than when spoken in another's voice by her command. There can be no question that Elizabeth spoke impromptu in this instance, albeit basing herself on the same topics covered in her letter to Bacon. Her figure of "two faces under one hood and the body rotten" is far stronger than the image of "two visors" in the version delivered by Bacon, and sardonically elaborates upon Speaker of the House

Richard Onslow's conceit in a long speech earlier the same day, in which he had compared a kingdom without a king to a "monstrous beast" with "many heads."[8]

But in the majority of cases, I would argue, there was no prepared written copy behind the queen's speeches to Parliament and elsewhere. She is reputed to have had a very well trained and capacious memory, and contemporaries frequently commented upon her improvisational skills. Her early Latin speeches at Oxford and Cambridge were apparently coaxed out of her and delivered impromptu. Similarly, we find Sir Robert Cecil commenting in a letter to the earl of Essex on the brilliance of Queen Elizabeth's impromptu riposte to an unexpectedly insolent address by the Polish ambassador, to whom she had offered a sumptuous welcome at court on 25 July 1597: "To this, I swear by the living God that her majesty made one of the best answers extempore in Latin that ever I heard, being much moved to be so challenged in public, especially so much against her expectation."[9] In this instance, even if she had prepared remarks ahead of time, she was forced by circumstances to revise them and answer extemporaneously. But speaking "extempore" was her usual practice. Rather than writing her speeches out verbatim beforehand, she appears, in keeping with techniques taught by the standard sixteenth-century manuals on memory, to have organized what she planned to say in her own mind as a series of rhetorical loci or places that could be amplified and otherwise adjusted during her delivery, so that the speech would respond quite precisely to the circumstances within which it was uttered. Later, she could run through the loci again to produce the speech in written form, which might differ significantly from the speech as actually uttered.

One of the curious facts about Queen Elizabeth's speeches is that reported versions taken down by her auditors at the time of her delivery are often more vivid, vehement, direct, and verbally eloquent than the "official" versions promulgated later by the court. Reported versions often sound more like her direct and pithy style than even the official versions surviving in her own hand. What frequently happened to Elizabeth's speeches, I would suggest, was that she delivered them face to face with her auditors in a language sufficiently colorful and potentially incendiary to make a strong impression upon her immediate public. But this language did not necessarily translate well to the written page, and was not necessarily neutral enough to be suitable for subsequent distribution to a wider spectrum of subjects. The written versions we have in her own hand or corrected in her hand almost invariably show her (and others) in the process of toning down the original vividness of her language and replacing it with more measured, abstract, often (to us) windy and convoluted, but more formal and politically neutral wording and syntax.

In the scenario I am suggesting, the queen's own manuscripts are not a faithful guide to the speech as delivered; rather, they represent a subsequent stage in which the vivid vehemence of the speech was tamed and elaborated into acceptable Tudor bureaucratese. The reviser was not necessarily the queen herself. Lord Burghley, Robert Cecil, and others also assisted in transforming her speeches from oral to written form, and occasionally these revised versions were published. In dealing with Elizabeth's speeches, therefore, we are confronted with a seemingly paradoxical situation in which an on-the-spot transcription by some third party not at all connected with court circles might well be more faithful to the verve and eloquence of the oral *prototypon* than the speech as promulgated in writing by the queen and her ministers themselves! We have ample evidence that her listeners often had sufficiently capacious memories to remember her speeches almost word for word, just as literate Elizabethans were trained as schoolchildren to remember sermons with great fidelity and transcribe them with fair accuracy. A sermon might last an hour or more; most of Elizabeth's speeches lasted no more than ten or twenty minutes, and were therefore easier to capture.

Let me offer some evidence as to the difference between the spoken and the written forms of Elizabeth's speeches from her first reply to the parliamentary petition delivered to her at Richmond on 12 November 1586. This speech is particularly interesting because, as several witnesses insist, she offered it impromptu. Apparently there was no time for her to prepare a response in advance even had she wished to; nevertheless more than one reporter notes the graciousness, self-possession, and wisdom with which she offered her answer to their petition. The subject under consideration was the continuing danger posed by the existence of Mary Queen of Scots, who had languished in prison for many years and was believed to have participated in several ill-advised conspiracies against the life of Elizabeth I. The parliamentary petitioners sought Mary's speedy execution on the authority of the Queen of England; Elizabeth, however, temporized in her first 1586 response and confounded the arguments of the petitioners by imaginatively placing herself rather than Mary in the position of royal victim. I will discuss a few parallel passages from different versions of the speech in order to demonstrate how its language changed over time and according to the specific purpose for which it was intended. The first version—the one which may well be closest to the speech as presented in terms of its liveliness and outspokenness—comes from a copy of a parliamentary diary (presently at Cambridge University Library) by an unidentified M.P. who was probably a member of the delegation to whom the original speech was delivered, since he writes as an eyewitness of the proceedings. The second version is British Library MS Lansdowne 94: a courtly copy of the speech in a highly formal italic hand, possibly that of Robert Cecil, with many corrections, possibly in the hands of both Elizabeth and Burghley but more likely all in the hand of Elizabeth herself. The third version is that published in octavo the same year under the title *The Copy of a Letter to the Right Honorable the Earl of Leicester* and again in the 1587 edition of Holinshed's *Chronicles,* volume 3: both of these published versions follow the Lansdowne revised version quite closely; indeed, it is likely that the queen revised her speech with publication in mind, since she was interested in making widely known her reluctance to assent to Mary's execution.

In the reported Cambridge University parliamentary diary version, Queen Elizabeth's first speech on the execution of Mary Queen of Scots begins:

> When I remember the bottomless depth of God's great benefits towards me, I find them to be so many or rather so infinite in themselves as that they exceed the capacity of all men, much more of any one, to be comprehended. And considering the manifold dangers intended and practiced against me, which through the goodness of almighty God I have always escaped, I must needs say it is admirable and miraculous (if that be a miracle which is beyond and above the reason of man) that now I live.[10]

Further along, as part of an aside, the queen is quoted in this version as saying, "And yet must I needs confess that the benefits of God to me have been and are so manifold, so folded and embroidered one upon another, so doubled and redoubled towards me, as that no creature living hath more cause to thank God for all things than I have."

The British Library Lansdowne copy appears to be based on a reported version of the speech—quite possibly the queen's own reconstruction as transcribed by one of her secretaries and then recopied by Cecil himself.[11] It incorporates the queen's own corrections, and its revised heading reads

"Her majesty's most gracious answer delivered by herself verbally to the petitioners of the lords and commons, being the estates of parliament." In this version of the speech on the execution of Mary Queen of Scots, the beginning is far more formal than the Cambridge version, and the aside from later is brought into the first sentence, creating more consistent organization but much less appearance of spontaneity:

> The bottomless graces and immeasurable benefits bestowed upon me by the Almighty are, and have been such, as I must not only acknowledge them, but admire them, accounting them as well miracles as benefits, not so much in respect of His divine majesty, with whom nothing is more common than to do things rare and singular, as in regard of our weakness, who cannot sufficiently set forth His wonderful works and graces, which to me have been so many, so diversly folded and embroidered one upon another, as in no sort am I able to express them.[12]

Three relatively short sentences in the Cambridge version have been combined into one complex Latinate period that can be read much more easily than it can be delivered orally. All the way through the speech, the revised Lansdowne manuscript and Cecil's published versions are far more formal in wording and syntax than the Cambridge University version.

In some instances the later versions tame the sharp language of the Cambridge version, which I am arguing may well be the closest of the versions we are considering to the speech as actually delivered. In discussing the possibility of proceeding against Mary Queen of Scots via the common law courts, Elizabeth has a few tart words in the Cambridge version for the lawyers:

> But you, my masters of the law, are so fine—you regard so much the words, syllables, and letters thereof more than the true sense and meaning indeed—that oftentimes you make the same to seem absurd. For if I should have followed that course of the common law, forsooth, she must have been indicted by a jury of twelve men in Staffordshire. She must have held up her hand and openly been arraigned at a bar, which had been a proper manner of proceeding with a woman of her quality! (I mean her quality by birth and not by condition.) Yet this way I might have used according to the common course of the law, as I was assured by the judges of the realm who showed it me written in their books. I mean not the pettifoggers of the law, who look more on the outside of their books than study them within.

In this version, the queen comes close to calling common law procedure absurd and superficial pettifoggery, at least in relation to a woman of the "quality" of Mary Queen of Scots. Of course it is possible that her remarks were elaborated upon by the listener out of a desire to amplify the potential impact of her critique of legal practice. As Harold Love has noted, copies of parliamentary speeches sometimes creatively altered the language of the speech in accordance with the copyist's political goals.[13] Another report of the speech now at Exeter College, Oxford, which uses the third person throughout instead of reproducing Elizabeth's words in the form she uttered them, adds an interesting detail about her manner of delivery, but greatly downplays the attack on the lawyers, recording that "presenting herself nearer the Speaker, she told him that the lawyers were so fine that they would not follow the meaning of the laws, but strictly judge according to the letter of the same; and if she should put them to that, then they should see how the case stood." The next passage repeats the scenario of Mary's indictment in Staffordshire, but without any reference to "pettifoggery." But the Exeter College report characteristically neutralizes some of the queen's sharpest language: in other versions she refers to herself as playing the "blab" for sending privately to Mary to have her confess her offenses; in the Exeter College version she instead accuses herself of playing the "fool."[14] Yet another much more abbreviated report has the same vehemence as the Cambridge Library version, having the queen refer to "some carping attorney or caviling lawyer that have studied on the back side of his book rather than looked into the depth of the law."[15] It seems highly likely that Elizabeth's strong language regarding lawyers as represented here and in the Cambridge manuscript was close to that of the speech in its original impromptu delivery.

The Lansdowne version, which is written in a secretarial hand but incorporates Elizabeth's corrections in her own hand, tames some of the language of the passage, but interestingly adds the politically charged term "precise" to describe the lawyers.

> But you lawyers are so nice and so precise in sifting and scanning every word and letter that many times you stand more upon form than matter, upon syllabs than the sense of the law. For in this strictness and exact following of common form she must have been indicted in Staffordshire, and have been arraigned at the bar, holden up her hand, been tried by a jury; a proper course forsooth to deal in that manner with one of her estate!

In the queen's revisions, pettifoggery and insults of similar magnitude against lawyers have left the picture. Cecil's printed version of the passage is yet more cautious, eliminating the word "precise," which might seem to accuse the lawyers of puritan sympathies:

> But you lawyers are so nice in sifting and scanning every word and letter that many times you stand more upon form than matter, upon syllables than sense of the law. For in the strictness and exact following of common form, she must have been indicted in Staffordshire, have holden up her hand at the bar and been tried by a jury—a proper course forsooth, to deal in that manner with one of her estate!

The passage is still quite forceful, but has lost its inflammatory edge.

At another point in the speech, Elizabeth assures her auditors that she does not abhor Mary's treasonous practices out of fear for her own life. In the Cambridge University version, she expresses the matter thus:

> For these horrible treasons and practices, to tell you truly, I must protest that I am not grieved in respect of myself or of mine own life—which for itself I do not regard, knowing that the less life the less sin. And I assure you for mine own part I am so far from desiring to live as that I think that that person to be most happy which is already dead. Wherefore the regard of life which I have is in respect of you and the rest of my good subjects, knowing that my blood could not have been shed but yours and theirs should have been spilled likewise. Whose happy and good estate if I were sure might be redeemed and preserved with my death, I protest before almighty God I would not desire to live.

In the second sentence of this version of the passage, she offers a close paraphrase of the final lines of Sophocles' *Oedipus Rex*, which she had read in Greek in her youth with her schoolmaster Roger Ascham: "Count no man happy till he dies, free of pain at last."

The quote from Sophocles is paraphrased out of recognition in the published version, which also deemphasizes the politically volatile matter of Elizabeth's death (and the deaths of her subjects):

> These former remembrances, present feeling, and future expectation of evils, I say, have made me think an evil is much the better the less while it endureth, and so, them happiest that are soonest hence; and taught me to bear with a better mind these treasons than is common to my sex—yea,

with a better heart, perhaps, than is in some men. Which I hope you will not merely impute to my simplicity or want of understanding. . . .

The speech in this more "public" version mimes a strategy Elizabeth herself had often deliberately exploited during her earlier decades of rule—a disarming expression of womanly weakness that blunts the rhetorical impact of her "masculine" show of strength. In this instance, however, the Cambridge reporter's memory may have failed him, for the Exeter College version includes a similar reference to the queen's fortitude beyond what "commonly women are." Nevertheless, the general direction of the revisions is clear, and many further examples could be adduced to the same effect. The speech in the reported Cambridge University version is rougher, usually more vehement and politically outspoken; the revised versions for wider consumption are smoother, frequently less pithy and more abstract, less potentially divisive in their impact. The Cambridge version is quite frighteningly graphic on the subject of Elizabeth's death; the later versions are more circumspect. Moreover, the Cambridge version is fairly open in its references to Mary and her agency in various plots against Elizabeth; the later versions are more cautious. "Her treasons" becomes "sundry treasons." Direct reference to the "Scottish queen" become more general references to "she" and "her." At the same time that she obscures Mary's crimes through her revisions to the speech, however, Elizabeth also obscures her own responsibility to enforce the parliamentary ordinances that would require Mary's death.[16] The revised speech as it circulated at court and went off to the publisher was loftier, more general, less inflammatory, but also more noncommittal in terms of what it promised to her petitioners.

Similar instances of toning down after the fact can be found in the revision of other speeches. Notoriously, the seemingly official published version of Elizabeth's "Golden Speech" (delivered 30 November 1601) is a brief, pale synopsis of the glowing language of the speech as reproduced in contemporary reports. In the case of the Golden Speech, most later published versions follow the contemporary transcripts far more closely than they do the 1601 published version. Indeed, we can speculate that the appearance of the disappointingly bland published version of the Golden Speech may have prompted some M.P.'s who had been in attendance to search their memories and produce reports that accorded more closely with the speech as they had experienced it. Sometimes, however, the evidence is more difficult to read. We have in Elizabeth's hand a first paragraph of her angry speech of 5 November 1566, in response to a parliamentary delegation of lords and commons who were attempting to pressure her into marrying or at least declaring the order of the succession so that, if she were to die without issue, there could be an orderly transmission of royal authority. Here, as in her answer to the petition on Mary Queen of Scots two decades later, the queen almost certainly spoke impromptu. Nevertheless, there is a copy of the first paragraph of Elizabeth's speech in a version written in her own hand, and presumably after the speech itself had been delivered:

> If the order of your causes had matched the weight of your matter, the one might well have craved reward and the other much the sooner satisfied. But when I call to mind how far from dutiful care, yea, rather how nigh a traitorous trick this tumbling cast did spring, I muse how men of wit can so hardly use that gift they hold. I marvel not much that bridle-less colts do not know their rider's hand, whom bit of kingly rein did never snaffle yet. Whether it was fit that so great a cause as this should have had his beginning in such a public place as that, let it be well weighed. Must all evil bodings that might be recited be found little enough to hap to my share? Was it well meant, think you, that those that knew not how fit this matter was to be granted by the prince would prejudice their prince in aggravating the matter, so all their arguments tended to my careless care of this my dear realm?[17]

In this manuscript version, the queen is short and vehement in condemning the "traitorous trick this tumbling cast" seemingly sprung by advisors close to the throne. Paradoxically, the opening of the speech in a later reported version is considerably calmer and more decorous. Here is the beginning of the same speech as recorded in the Cambridge Library copy, whose transcriber avers that he has taken it down as faithfully "as I could carry away by remembrance":

> If that order had been observed in the beginning of the matter and such consideration had in the prosecuting of the same as the gravity of the cause had required, the success thereof might have been otherwise than now it is. But those unbridled persons whose heads were never snaffled by the rider did rashly enter into it in the common house, a public place, where Mr. Bell with his complices alleged that they were natural Englishmen and were bound to their country, which they saw must needs perish and come to confusion unless some order were taken for the limitation of the succession of the crown.[18]

As we might predict, in this version Elizabeth is more specific about the occasion, singling out "Mr. Bell" and "his [ac]complices," M.P.'s who had negotiated with the lords over the creation of a joint petition, and their inappropriate use of the "common house." And yet the "tumbling cast" and "traitorous trick" have disappeared. How are we to account for the far milder tone of this reported version, which seemingly undoes our earlier generalizations about the relative weight of Elizabeth's own manuscripts versus contemporary transcriptions as records of what Elizabeth actually said? Previous editors have assumed that the first, more inflammatory version is Elizabeth's initial draft of the speech as she was composing it before delivery; and the second version, the speech in a form closer to her actual utterance of it. But under the circumstances of its delivery, she is unlikely to have had time to plan elaborately in advance, even assuming that such was ever her practice. What we may have in this paradoxical instance is a case in which Elizabeth was fairly civil in person to the petitioners, but became increasingly angry in retrospect as she attempted to record her speech afterward on paper. Perhaps she broke off her writing after the initial paragraph because she recognized that her vehemence would not make for a document suitable for wider circulation, much though she might have wished to air her exasperation. The earlier, partial manuscript is endorsed in Lord Burghley's hand as "a part of the beginning of the queen's majesty's speech to thirty lords and thirty commons on Tuesday the fifth of November, 1566. . . . The queen's own hand." But did it represent the queen's spoken words, or her later afterthoughts upon them? Here again, there is an elusive, mysterious dissonance between the queen's own written version of a speech and the speech as reported by an auditor, even though in this case, anomalously, it is the queen's written version after the fact that is most flamboyantly sardonic.

If ever there were a case in which investigation of the documentary evidence leads to uncertainty and *mise en abîme,* the public speaking of Queen Elizabeth I represents such an instance. The situation is somewhat analogous to that encountered by editors of much-revised poems or novels, in which no single exemplar represents the work as the author intended it because the author's purpose changed over time and over the course of multiple revisions. However, in the instance of Elizabeth's speeches we have the additional factor of memorial versions, always differing one from another in important ways, as an important, and sometimes the only, surviving record of her utterance. In editing the speeches of Queen Elizabeth I and making them available to scholars and a wider public, we obviously cannot communicate that elusive original "presence" of which all recorded versions represent copies, even though they differ one from another. All we can hope to do is to communicate some of the complexity of the evidence.

In our forthcoming edition, we frequently print multiple versions of Elizabeth's speeches, both to acquaint readers with the surprising array of forms a given speech could take, depending on the bias of the recorder and the purpose for which the copy was intended, and to give readers a sense of the significant homologies among versions that are in many ways markedly different. Our edition of Elizabeth's writings will be the first that does not combine elements from different manuscript and printed copies of the speeches in order to create a single "best text" in the standard manner of literary critical editions. To edit the speeches thus is to acquire false certainty about what the queen said at the expense of a rich record of revision and varied perception. For many people and purposes in the sixteenth and early seventeenth centuries, as I have suggested above, writing was not authoritative in itself, but only insofar as it served as a record of speech, with the oral *prototypon*, evanescent though it was, retaining primary authority. As John Marston described his own process of composition somewhat later, "'Tis my custom to speak as I think and write as I speak."[19] The thought and the speech come first; the writing follows and serves to record the speaking, albeit most imperfectly. Wherever possible, our edition of Queen Elizabeth's writings respects this sixteenth-century prejudice by reproducing eyewitness accounts of Elizabeth's speeches, distorted though these may be through the lenses of perception and memory. But alongside these early witnesses we reproduce the queen's own manuscripts and printed versions, which show the fascinating process by which she (and sometimes others) rethought and recast her speeches for a wider audience of contemporary readers. The resulting array of textual differences is sometimes readily interpretable through the projection of differing intentionalities at different times on the part of the speech's author or recorder, but sometimes less amenable to interpretation. In the bewildering multiplicity of this manuscript and printed evidence we can catch some of our best glimpses of the brilliant, shape-shifting presence that Queen Elizabeth I was in the perceptions of her subjects.

Notes

1. All of these examples and others are discussed in Leah S. Marcus, *Unediting the Renaissance: Shakespeare, Marlowe, Milton* (London and New York: Routledge, 1996), chaps. 5 and 6, esp. 164–66. See also D. F. McKenzie, "Speech-Manuscript-

Print," in *New Directions in Textual Studies,* ed. Dave Oliphant and Robin Bradford, with introduction by Larry Carver (Austin: Harry Ransom Humanities Research Center, University of Texas at Austin, 1990), 86–109; and Keith Thomas, "The Meaning of Literacy in Early Modern England," in *The Written Word: Literacy in Transition,* ed. Gerd Baumann (Oxford: Clarendon Press, 1988), 97–131.

    2. Cited from British Library [hereafter BL] Harley MS 787, fols. 127r–128v, a later copy of the transcription. Here and throughout, spelling and punctuation are modernized.

    3. R[obert] C[ecil], *The Copy of a Letter to the Earl of Leicester . . . with a Report of Certain Petitions and Declarations Made to the Queen's Majesty at Two Several Times . . . and Her Majesty's Answers Thereunto by Herself Delivered* (London: C. Barker, 1586), sigs. Ci r–Civ v; (STC 6052); rpt. in Raphael Holinshed, *Chronicles* (London, 1587), 3:1582–83.

    4. Cited from the transcription of Hatfield House MS 216/14 in T. E. Hartley, ed., *Proceedings in the Parliaments of Elizabeth I* (Leicester: Leicester University Press, 1995), 2:371–72.

    5. Ed. Leah S. Marcus, Janel Mueller, and Mary Beth Rose (University of Chicago Press, forthcoming). Although the transmission theories offered here (and in the edition) originated with me, I have made use of many labors by my co-editors in writing it and would like to acknowledge their contribution. For full versions of all the materials cited here from manuscript copies and early printed texts, readers are referred to our forthcoming edition.

    6. BL MS Cotton Charter IV.38(2); formerly Cotton Titus F.l, fol. 92.

    7. BL MS Cotton Titus F.1, fols. 121v–122r; a copy. There is another, similar version of this speech printed in Sir Simonds D'Ewes, *The Journals of All the Parliaments of Elizabeth* (London, 1682), 116–17.

    8. Cited from Hartley, ed., *Proceedings,* 2:168–69.

    9. Cited from the secretarial copy of Cecil's letter of 26 July 1597 (United Kingdom, Public Record Office, State Papers Domestic, Elizabeth 12/264/57, fols. 82r–83v).

    10. Here and below, cited from Cambridge University Library MS Gg.III.34, fols. 304–8.

    11. However, this reported version also circulated independently, which suggests that the queen may have had to seek out an independent transcription of the speech in order to make her corrections. See Inner Temple Library Petyt MS 538, vol. 10, fols. 6v–7r, which is almost identical to the precorrection Lansdowne version, except for a missing final paragraph.

    12. Cited from Cecil, n. 3 above. This revised version also circulated in manuscript among the family: there is a copy by Sir Edward Hoby, Lord Burghley's son-in-law, in BL Add. MS 38823, fols. 76r–77r; the printed catalogue terms this volume Sir Edward Hoby's commonplace book, but it is more accurately described as a miscellany.

    13. Harold Love, *Scribal Publication in Seventeenth-Century England* (Oxford: Clarendon Press, 1993; paper ed., Amherst: University of Massachusetts Press, 1998), 9–22.

    14. Cited from Exeter College, Oxford MS 127, as reproduced in Hartley, ed., *Proceedings,* 2:254–58.

15. Cited from BL MS Stowe, 361, in Hartley, ed., *Proceedings,* 2:260.

16. I am indebted to Janel Mueller's talk "Spoken for the Record: Revision, Memory, and Abridgement in Accounts of Elizabeth I's Speech on Executing Mary Queen of Scots, November 12, 1586," which she was kind enough to send me in manuscript and which builds, in turn, on my original version of the present paper, presented at the annual meeting of the Modern Language Association, Chicago, 1995.

17. United Kingdom, Public Record Office, State Papers Domestic, Elizabeth 12/41/5, fol. 8.

18. Cited from Cambridge University Library MS Gg.III.34, fols. 208–12.

19. John Marston, *The Malcontent* (London, 1604), preface.

CHAPTER TWO

The Structural Transformation of Print in Late Elizabethan England

Douglas Bruster

During the closing years of the sixteenth century, English books became remarkably thick with the personal. It is now usual, of course, to evaluate literary works of this period in relation to the self—"personal," in this sense, referring to a new interest in subjectivity and inwardness. Yet beyond this narrow conception of personal selfhood lies a more expansive personalism, one that unfolded textually in the production of books across various modes. From controversial pamphlets to Ovidian erotica, from *à clef* poems to verse satire, an intensively familiar approach to others' bodies and identities—to their *persons* as objects of discourse—became a central feature of late Elizabethan print culture. The strong attraction of personal reference led many writers to ignore Gabriel Harvey's censorious creed of "no Liberty without bounds, nor any Licence without limitation."[1] And whether the liberties they took served political comment, sexual titillation, or social positioning, readers could expect to find everywhere a more sustained and more graphic relation between book and body. Works like *The Faerie Queene* (1590), *Venus and Adonis* (1593), and *Have With You to Saffron-Walden* (1596) offer familiar instances of this relation. We might understand the sense of "personal" in such texts as denoting less the self than the other, and bodies rather than consciousness; it indicates an emphasis on the external, the transpersonal, and that which is between rather than within.

So widespread was this emphasis, in fact, that the works it affected can be seen as belonging to a developing genre that we might call *embodied writing*.[2] Embodied writing can be provisionally defined as a kind of text and a textual practice that, increasingly during the 1590s, put resonant identities and physical forms on the printed page. Embodied writing aggressively drew real and imaginary figures into print for potentially indecorous handling. This writing often described the body in detail, through graphic treatment of physical appearance and body parts. And where its descriptions could involve such mythological personae as Diana, Ganymede, and Corinna, embodied writing also incorporated real bodies under fictional names. Such names as "Stella," "Horace," and "Vanderhulke," for instance, transparently covered those persons whose identities the social relations of the texts betrayed. Granting a bodily presence to fictional characters, and a fictional identity to real bodies, this writing mediated the imaginary and the actual in its bodily address.

We are perhaps most familiar with embodied writing through its appearance, alternately, in the sensuous, "body-wanting" blazons of erotic verse and in the rough handling of antagonists in satirical works.[3] Dissimilar on the surface, these forms possess a common liberty of expression in relation to the body, a liberty that characterizes texts of various modes in this period. While instances of embodied writing are typically explained in relation to classical, Renaissance, and vernacular models—to such forms as Old Comedy, Ovidian narrative, flyting, *effictio*, the *débat*, and the Petrarchan lyric—for a number of reasons late Elizabethan texts share as much with similarly "embodied" works of this time as they do with generic predecessors.[4] Indeed, embodied writing was enabled most strongly not by earlier forms but by the confluence, in the late Elizabethan era, of such factors as the profound reorientation of authority in England following the Reformation; a subsequent and extensive habituation to print; the ambitions of a younger generation of writers eager to ply this familiarity with the printed word; and, perhaps most important, the dynamics of the commercial playhouses, which offered this generation vivid models for the imaginative, and public, representation of persons.

Writing shaped by these forces tended to collapse the traditional distance between bodies and texts, and in doing so brought about important changes in the cultural status of print. Partly through the agency of the late Elizabethan "best-seller," persons merged with characters, and books became entwined with their authors. These authors more openly addressed others' bodies and identities, borrowing various capabilities from the painter, anatomist, mimic, litigator, and barber surgeon. Readers in the last years of Elizabeth's reign came, in turn, to assume a more intimate connection between person and page. With this change in the general horizon of expectations, a significant, more public discursive venue became available in and through the field of print. Thus, what we tend to see primarily as a moment of "golden" or expressive literature emphasizing the self may be better grasped as a period during which literature itself, and print culture generally, underwent a structural change that facilitated the radical expression of otherness. To trace the contours of this shift is to begin to understand not only the role that literature took in the personalization of print but also how a new emphasis on the personal in works of the late Elizabethan era articulated a nascent public sphere.

The rise of embodied writing was roughly circumscribed by a pair of well-known social dramas. The first of these, the Martin Marprelate controversy, began almost accidentally in the late 1580s and soon escalated into a vitriolic pamphlet war concerning the foundations of power in England.[5] Martinist pamphlets harshly criticized the prevailing form of church government, and as part of their critique came to attack specific individuals. Before this unlicensed activity was suppressed, its libertine wit had harassed the Elizabethan church and state to such an extent that it formed, in the words of Robert Weimann, the "greatest popular scandal" of the era.[6] The second of these events is the also scandalous "poetomachia" or satire wars that occupied many poets and playwrights in the years 1598 through 1601. The satire wars took place on stage, in the War of the Theaters, as well as in formal verse satires and epigrams. These satiric exchanges were punctuated by the notorious Bishops' Ban or "Satire Ban" of 1 June 1599, in which the Archbishop of Canterbury and the Bishop of London listed books—some satirical, some obscene, some controversial, some historically oriented—to be variously called in and burned, published no more, or allowed only upon strict examination. Although this essay intends to demonstrate that these two events, the Marprelate controversy and the satire wars, were actually part of a continuum, they offer useful markers for a period that introduced lasting changes to the relations among early modern readers, writers, and texts.

The Marprelate controversy bordered the development of embodied writing and strongly influenced it. Where personal invective had always been a staple of controversial writing, flourishing in the Latin polemics of the Reformation, the vernacular nature of the Marprelate publications ushered in a new era of ad hominem reference.[7] The sharp goads of Marprelate publications like *Hay Any Work for Cooper* (1589) and *An Almond for a Parrot* (1590) made explicit personal address—in the case of these works, address with a political purpose—a more likely quantity for writers of fiction. The personal reference surrounding Falstaff/Oldcastle in Shakespeare's *Henry IV* plays (1597), and Broome/Brook in *The Merry Wives of Windsor* (1597), for example, occurred in the abusive, flyting atmosphere the controversial pamphlets had nurtured. With its street-cry title, *Hay Any Work* lampoons Thomas Cooper, Bishop of Winchester, and in more than one place engages in mocking personal satire: "Parson Gravet, Parson of Sir John Pulchre's in London (one of dumb John's boosing mates) will be drunk but once a week. But what then? Good children should take links in a cold morning, and light them at his nose, to see if, by that means, some part of the fire that hath so flashed his sweet face might be taken away. This were their duty, saith T. C., and not to cry 'Red Nose, Red Nose!'"[8] Such address was often as aggressive as it was explicit: the title page of *A Countercuff Given to Martin Junior* (1589) lauds the success of its author's past retorts and "the clean breaking of his staff upon Martin's face."[9] As the gleeful undertone of this phrase and the mocking details concerning William Gravet's red nose suggest, entertainment proved a powerful weapon on both sides of the exchange. In John Dover Wilson's famous characterization, Martin Marprelate was a "disciple both of Calvin and Dick Tarlton"—having learned, that is, from both the religious reformer and the famous Elizabethan clown.[10]

Yet although the controversy would briefly spill over to the popular stages, an even stronger link with the theaters of the 1590s and after came with its loosening of inhibitions regarding personal satire.[11] So customary had personal reference become by the middle of the first decade of the seventeenth century, for instance, that writers saw fit to inoculate their texts against *à clef* interpretations. In the prologue to *All Fools*, published in 1605, George Chapman speaks of the threat of "personal application" in contemporary stage plays.[12] Likewise, in the epistle prefacing *Volpone*, published two years later, Jonson defensively asks "what publique person" he has provoked—"Where have I been particular? Where personal?"—before indicting those who "care not whose living faces they intrench, with their petulant styles."[13] And Thomas Dekker alludes similarly to dangers associated with embodied writing when *The Gull's Horn-Book* (1609) points to the possibility of a writer "that hath either epigrammed you or hath had a flirt at your mistress, or hath brought either your feather or your red beard or your little legs, etc., on the stage."[14]

Dekker's sentence aligns three experiences: being addressed by an epigram; suffering someone having a "flirt at" one's mistress; and being mocked on stage by actors who represent one's idiosyncracies. At first glance, these might seem different experiences. They are joined, however, by a manipulative, even threatening, relation to the body. The epigram and stage caricature pose threats to the body of Dekker's gull by representing it elsewhere. Someone who has had a "flirt at" one's mistress has insulted her in an obvious way, threatening one whose reputation would reflect upon the gull.[15] Neither mistress nor gull is secure. For even as the mistress's body appears related to, yet dangerously separate from, the gull, so the gull's body seems open to appropriation in both epigram and stage play: it might be flouted on stage with its "red beard" and "little legs, etc." The open nature of the stage made such embarrassment a decidedly public threat. Not coincidentally, then, did statements like Dekker's, and those of Jonson and Chapman, come in the wake of the poetomachia, an episode in which at least two of the former were involved, and which not only increased the license that writers took but itself evolved from an earlier social drama. We can draw a direct line, that is, between the ad hominem of the Marprelate works and the emetics administered to rival writers in the satire wars of the late 1590s and early 1600s. Horace/Jonson's purge of Crispinas/Marston in *Poetaster* (1601) remains only one of a host of violent literary fantasies that, in seeking to remedy the excesses of identifiable persons, found their immediate models in the turmoil of the Marprelate controversy.

As the Bishops' Ban testified by collocating the satiric, the political, and the erotic, in this genre the importance of the body transcended incidentals of domain and mode. Arguments that hold, variously, that the ban concerned itself primarily with satire, or primarily with erotica, or primarily with controversy, miss the point: covering works of controversy, satire, English history, antifeminism, and the erotic, the Bishops' Ban addressed works that took liberties with bodies considered either above mention or above certain kinds of mention.[16] Ian Frederick Moulton observes, in this regard, that "works thought of as ribald or licentious were not differentiated from politically subversive or heretical works, but were included in a broad range of material which could seduce the innocent."[17] What most defined this range of material, and rendered these texts seductive, was an unprecedented openness concerning the body. All the works involved in the ban were seen as transgressive, and they were all transgressive in their embodied familiarity. One might say that the Bishops' Ban "knew" something about the transformation of print culture that we have yet to perceive. During the 1590s, writers and printers alike had experimented with topics and ways of addressing those topics that ignored traditional boundaries, mingling sacred and profane, poetry and politics. Frequently the body itself served as the topic of both statement and objection. For instance, when in his *Virgidemiae* (1597) the Protestant Joseph Hall criticized Robert Southwell for his Catholic poems *Mary Magdalens Funerall Teares* (1594) and *St. Peter's Complaint* (1595), he did so not out of doctrinal differences but on the basis of the alleged profaneness of these poems. What Hall meant to criticize can be seen best, perhaps, in Southwell's Counter-Reformation emphasis on Christ's body. His Peter sensuously blazons Christ's eyes in the manner of a sonneteer of the 1590s: "The matchless eyes matched only each by other / . . . / The eye of liquid pearl, the purest mother"; "These blazing comets, lightning flames of love."[18] Hall objected to Gervase Markham's *The Poem of Poems, or Sion's Muse* (1596) because Markham seemed to make Solomon "a newfound Sonnetist, / Singing his love, the holy spouse of Christ, / Like as she were some light-skirts of the rest."[19] Hall's displeasure here centers on the sheer *familiarity* of Southwell and Markham with their subjects, their lewd and embodied handling of otherwise sacred material.

While Hall assumes that sacred topics should be above the overly personal treatment of literary forms like the blazon, the Marprelate controversy had opened gates that would not soon be closed. Hence Nashe's politically explicit *Almond for a Parrot* gave way, during the 1590s, to his sexually explicit poem *The Choice of Valentines*. And thus did the mild pornography of works like *Hero and Leander* (1593/98) and *Venus and Adonis* (1593) follow the license of the Marprelate publications by exchanging the political for the erotic, replacing its antagonists with arousing mythological bodies, and the stings of controversial satire with a more playful, if equally licentious and satirical, relation to the physical. Although these erotic narratives participated in a tradition springing from Ovid's *Metamorphoses*, poems of the 1590s have an explicitness absent from an earlier Ovidian work like Thomas Lodge's *Scilla's Metamorphosis* (1589). One of the reasons for such a difference is the climate of satire that the Marprelate pamphlets had helped to generate. Satirical works accustomed writers and readers to a sadistic treatment of the body that enabled the bolder erotic, even pornographic, visions of the 1590s. The "witty subversiveness" of late Elizabethan erotic narratives eventually culminated, in fact, in John Weever's *Faunus and Melliflora* (1600), which grafts an account of satire's origins onto a conventional erotic story.[20]

We can see this convergence of satire and sexuality in many of these erotic narratives' blazons. Marlowe's poem, for example, is celebrated for its sensual handling of the myth. He enlivens Leander's swim with a description of an amorous Neptune, who, as a god of water, steals kisses from Leander, and is said to "dive into the water, and there pry / Upon his breast, his thighs, and every limb, / And up again, and close beside him swim, / And talk of love."[21] Shakespeare's Venus is similarly explicit in her equally notorious self-blazon as a "park" in which Adonis, as deer, can graze upon her mountains, dales, the hills of her lips, or lower, "where the pleasant fountains lie."[22] Of this poem Thomas Freeman wrote, in 1614, "Who list read lust, there's *Venus and Adonis* / True model of a most lascivious lecher."[23] Contemporaries gave support to this assessment by focusing on Venus's explicit blazon when quoting this poem in their works and commonplace books.[24] Though Nashe's own pornographic poem would remain in manuscript, others ventured into print such daringly erotic works as *Pygmalion's Image* (1598) and *Salmacis and Hermaphroditus* (1602), texts whose attraction came as much from the scandal of their bodily address— from their indecorum itself—as from the indecency of the bodies they represented. This liberated approach owed its conditions of possibility both to Marlowe and Shakespeare, and to the productive chaos of the Marprelate years before them.

But if the Marprelate controversy served as an instructive episode for writers of this era, authors like Thomas Nashe and John Lyly—enlisted by the authorities to respond to Martin—demonstrate the contributions that imaginative literature made to the rise of embodied writing. Lyly's skills in *à clef* writing had become apparent in such dramas as *Endymion* (1588) and *Midas* (1589), which may have been one reason for his selection as controversialist by the church. Imaginative literature of this era was never distinct from surrounding forms, but it offered inflections on the body that others did not. Thus, while *à clef* poems like *Willoby His Avisa* (1594) and *Caltha Poetarum* (1599) evoke real individuals in their allegorical fictions, including individuals at the highest levels of the Elizabethan church and government, they do so with an often sensual portrayal of the body that readers would not expect in more explicitly political writings. The treatment of the body in such works depends on the hallmark trope of lyric poetry in the late Elizabethan era, the blazon. Along these lines, one might notice Hall's criticism of Markham for resembling a "sonnetist" in his familiar treatment of a decidedly spiritual topic. The mutual influence of, on the one hand, such literary forms and devices as the blazon, satire, epigram, and Ovidian epyllion, and, on the other, more traditionally political forms like controversy and libels, prompts us to see that embodied writing had a number of textual sources even as it connected various domains through the personal.[25]

This emphasis on the personal within texts was accompanied by significant external changes. During the later Elizabethan era, contemporary authors and their works attained a status they had not before enjoyed; this status, in turn, affected the relation between person and print as characters, authors, and books became much closer to each other, and sometimes interchangeable. This is particularly visible in relation to the late Elizabethan "best-seller," a term used here to describe authors and books alike. The 1590s produced a concentration of writers who in any given year had a number of titles printed; the 1590s and early 1600s also produced works that went through five or more editions before Elizabeth's death.[26] To be sure, there had been salient if scattered examples of the best-seller before. We might take Lyly and his *Euphues* texts, and Robert Parsons's *Directory*, as harbingers of this phenomenon in the 1580s. (And, as we will see, Lyly's achievement was significant to the rise of embodied writing in many ways.) In the last decade of the century, however, what before had been confined to isolated books and authors became widespread; even as the total number of imprints remained relatively stable, certain authors and texts experienced a heady popularity.[27] As the examples of Parsons and Lyly might indicate, religious and literary authors and writings formed the bulk of these. And the fact that the "literary" here includes several of Southwell's devotional works speaks to the fact that the early 1590s witnessed the publication of texts by figures—Puritan, Protestant, and Catholic—who would later become involved in larger religious controversies. Correspondingly, best-selling religious texts came from a variety of positions. For instance, Leonard Wright, a participant in the Marprelate controversy on the side of the prelacy, saw his *A Summons for Sleepers* go through five editions from 1589 to 1596, and Thomas Playfere, who eventually became chaplain to King James, also had a work gain five editions: his *A Most Excellent and Heavenly Sermon*, published from 1595 to 1597.

But it would be two Puritan authors, William Perkins and Henry Smith, who would most clearly demonstrate the novel status of selected books and authors. Perkins had three best-sellers during this era: *Armilla Aurea ("The Golden Chain")*, which went through ten editions (English and Latin), from 1590 to 1597; *A Treatise Tending unto a Declaration Whether a Man Be in the Estate of Damnation or the Estate of Grace*, seven editions, 1590[?]–1600; and *The Foundation of Christian Religion*, six editions, 1590–1601. The publication history of Smith's works is even more striking. Spurred, perhaps, by his early death in 1591, the books of "silver-tongued Smith," an extremely popular divine, sold in amazing numbers during the 1590s.[28] Smith had five best-sellers in this period, mainly editions of his sermons: *The Sermons of Henry Smith, Gathered in One Volume*, eight editions, 1592–1601; *A Sermon of the Benefit of Contentation*, seven editions, 1590–91; *Six Sermons Preached by Master H. Smith*, seven editions, 1592–99; *The Wedding Garment*, six editions, 1590–91; and *The Trumpet of the Soul*, five editions, 1591–93. The total number of imprints under each of these authors' names during this period is also extraordinary. While Perkins had a total of fifty-one imprints from 1590 to 1599, Smith had eighty-one imprints published—including twenty-nine during 1591, the year of his death. In this year Smith's works account for over 11 percent of *all* English imprints. And with Perkins's five imprints in 1591, the two authors were responsible that year for over a quarter of all publications of a religious nature, with over three times as many imprints as those of the Bible and the Psalms put together. Clearly this pair of authors enjoyed an astonishing popularity.

That the best-seller was an extensive phenomenon can be seen when one examines, in addition to the status of these religious writers, the prominence of certain literary authors and texts during the 1590s. Best-selling literary texts of this era include Shakespeare's *Venus and Adonis*, seven editions, 1593–1602; Samuel Daniel's *Delia*, five editions, 1592–98; Michael Drayton's *England's Heroical Epistles*, five editions, 1597–1602; Thomas Kyd's *The Spanish Tragedy*, five editions, 1592–1603; Thomas Lodge's *Rosalind*, five editions, 1590–1604; Thomas Nashe's *Pierce Penniless*, five editions, 1592–95; and Robert Southwell's *Mary Magdelans Funerall Teares*, five editions, 1591–1602, and his *Saint Peter's Complaint*, six editions, 1595 to 1602. Like the popularity of Henry Smith's works, the attraction of Southwell's two texts, and of Sidney's *Arcadia*—which saw five editions from 1590 to 1605—must have derived in some part from their authors' early deaths. As Arthur Marotti suggests, during this period the "corpse of the author and the *corpus* of the work were in closer imaginative proximity."[29] The examples of Sidney, Smith, and Southwell hint that this proximity could spur canonization. Such, in any case, had come quickly: Sidney had died in 1586, and Southwell was executed in 1595, during the popularity of *Mary Magdelans Funerall Teares*, but before the success of *Saint Peter's Complaint*. Parallel in another way to Smith's works here were two very popular books: Robert Greene's *Quip for an Upstart Courtier,* which saw six editions in 1592 alone, and John Harington's *Apology,* with five editions in 1596. As is clear from the preceding titles, many of the works that have since achieved canonical status were eagerly received in their own time as well.

Even as such books came to be especially desired by readers of the 1590s, various literary writers also began to experience a new prominence. Beginning in 1591, the year in which Henry Smith's works appeared in such surprising numbers, we find Robert Greene with six imprints of various titles. In 1592, the year of his death, Greene had eighteen editions of twelve different titles in print, and Thomas Nashe, four imprints. In the years 1593 and 1594 Greene again occupied printers with three and four imprints, respectively. Southwell, whose execution had occurred early in 1595, had six imprints brought out that year. The following year, in 1596, Harington had eleven imprints, all entries in his *Ajax* "series": *The Metamorphosis of Ajax, An Anatomy of the Metamorphosed Ajax,* and *An Apology* (to which was joined, also that year, two editions of the pseudonymous *Ulysses upon Ajax,* not by Harington). Lodge, too, had five imprints in 1596. In 1597 Nicholas Breton had four imprints, and in 1598 Shakespeare had seven: six editions of four dramatic titles, and *The Rape of Lucrece.* But 1599 was especially notable for best-selling authors, with John Davies and Shakespeare each having six imprints, and Greene, who had been dead for over half a decade, five imprints. Davies' titles that year included *Nosce Teipsum, Hymns of Astrea,* and the composite *Epigrams and Elegies;* Shakespeare's, *1 Henry IV, Romeo and Juliet, Venus and Adonis,* and the composite *Passionate Pilgrim.*[30] In 1600 Nicholas Breton had seven imprints, six of these consisting of his *Pasquil* series: *Pasquil's Mad-Cap, Pasquil's Fool's-Cap, Pasquil's Mistress,* and *Pasquil's Pass, and Passeth Not.* In 1600 eight imprints by Shakespeare were published: seven editions of six dramatic titles, and *The Rape of Lucrece.* The works of Breton and Shakespeare would again be popular in 1602, when they saw six and five imprints, respectively. By this time, however, the literary "boom" of the 1590s had begun to subside, and hereafter few writers would experience the intensive popularity that many writers had earlier enjoyed.

The titles and publication figures in the preceding paragraphs help establish the outlines of a new development in print culture during the later Elizabethan era. Such numbers describe a popularity new in its extension, and new in its stress on contemporary authors, both alive and recently deceased. In its depth and breadth, this popularity worked to solidify authorship as an essential category for Elizabethan readers and writers. Along with the internal changes that embodied writing had brought about, print culture was shaped by the best-seller's emphasis on contemporary authors and their works, which often put their identities in close focus. These identities were shaped also by writers and printers, who labored to increase the attention given to individual authors and books. R. B. McKerrow has said of John Weever's *Epigrams* (1599), for example, that, "with the exception of the *Palladis Tamia* of Francis Meres, there is, I think, no single work of so early a date which contains references by name to so many Elizabethan writers of the first or second rank."[31] To this E. A. J. Honigmann responds by suggesting that such was hardly an accident: Weever and Meres "belonged to the same group—one that adopted new methods of publicising contemporary writers, and in particular other members of their own group."[32] Such efforts were far from unsuccessful. At the end of Elizabeth's reign, we see for the first time a significant number of readers and publishers placing as much importance on who had written a work as they did on what was in that work. We also see them supporting individual works and clusters of titles in a way that, prior to this time, had been confined to selected works like Lyly's *Euphues* texts.

If these two titles of Lyly's were harbingers to the best-sellers of the 1590s, they also played a part in the rise of embodied writing by inaugurating a textual celebrity. As we will see, this celebrity implied embodied characters and even texts. From 1578, when *Euphues, the Anatomy of Wit* was first published, through 1595, there passed no two years during which either it or its sequel, *Euphues and His England* (1580), was not printed. The immediate effect of these texts can be seen in the rush to "hail" them, evident in such titles as Greene's *Euphues His Censure to Philautus* (1587), and his *Menaphon: Camilla's Alarum to Slumbering Euphues* (1589); Lodge's *Rosalind: Euphues' Golden Legacy* (1590), and his *Euphues' Shadow* (1592); and Arthur Dickenson's *Arisbas: Euphues Amid His Slumbers* (1594). Lyly's texts were so frequently printed and cited that one could see them—one could see "Euphues"—in readers' hands and booksellers' stalls with predictable regularity during this period. So present were these texts and Euphues to the reading public of their day that it remains no exaggeration to call Euphues the first textual citizen of early modern London, an artificial person that one could expect to meet with some frequency in this rapidly expanding metropolis. More than a passing curiosity, this embodiment has serious implications for our understanding of print culture in early modern England, as Lyly's significance comes not in these texts' unprecedented popularity, but in an effect of such popularity.

While the stylistic vogue of "Euphuism" is perhaps too well known to need recounting here, we might consider the context in which Gabriel Harvey first used the term. Harvey coined the word *Euphuism* in his *Four Letters* (1592), whose gossipy subtitle speaks tellingly to the personalism of embodied writing: *Four Letters, and Certain Sonnets: Especially Touching Robert Greene, and Other Parties, by Him Abused; But Incidently of Divers Excellent Persons, and Some Matters of Note.* In the third letter, Harvey turns his full attention to Thomas Nashe—with whom, owing to their energetic, entertaining, and thoroughly regrettable personal feud, he would forever be remembered. Harvey celebrates his chief advantages over Nashe: maturity and discretion. Nashe, he reminds us, was once a student auditor at Cambridge who had beheld Harvey in his full glory as a lecturer. What has Nashe done since, Harvey asks, rhetorically, "excepting his good old *Flores Poetarum*, and Tarlton's surmounting Rhetoric, with a little Euphuism, and Greeneness enough, which were all pretty stale, before he put hand to pen? I report me to the favourablest opinion of those that know his Prefaces, Rhymes, and the very Timpany of his Tarltonizing wit."[33] In this short and vital passage Harvey converts the names of figures—Euphues, Greene, and Tarlton—into, respectively, nouns ("Euphuism," "Greeneness") and an adjective ("Tarltonizing"). But what stands out in addition to this concentration of neologisms is the passage's easy use of identities as things. What are we to make of these strange commodities: Euphuism, Greeneness, and Tarltonizing wit? And by what warrant does Harvey imagine them *as* things?

An initial answer might point to the fact that all three bring to mind popular figures with whom readers and audiences would associate apparently idiosyncratic *styles:* with Euphues, a highly artificial rhetorical pattern; with Greene, a "canicular" scurrility based in the cony-catching pamphlet; and with Tarlton, a libertine wit deriving its energy from familiar address of its object and audience.[34] In this way Harvey's reading of the situation of print in the early 1590s would seem to anticipate Buffon's *Le style est l'homme même*, but with reversed order: L'homme est le style même.[35] What this paraphrase misses, however, and what we elide in calling Euphues, Greene, and Tarlton "figures" is the license Harvey takes in equating a literary character and a text with real individuals. For perhaps even more audacious than his distilling of the human into a thing is his use of a thing—the printed creature of "Euphues," books and character—in parallel with the human. Harvey thus leaves us with a riddle: When is a literary creature like a person? To which our earlier survey of publications figures leads us to respond: When public desire, reading habits, and the printing press combine to make it so. As we have seen, Euphues became so present to the reading public that he, the *Euphues* texts, and the style they fostered were as known to many Londoners as were Greene and Tarlton. Like the "Greene" of countless title pages, and the "Tarlton" of recent and fond memory (he had died in 1588), "Euphues" gained his cultural identity by being dispersed among his admirers. The best-seller gave life to authors, then, and to characters and texts as well.

The slipperiness of identity in Harvey's description relies on a sequence of transactions: if the heavily autobiographical character of Euphues can be said to have translated Lyly's person into fiction, that character was also translated into the narratives condensed in the *Euphues* titles, which in turn came to stand in for a style of rhetoric associated with the character and books—"Euphuism." We might illustrate the chain of metonymy as follows:

$$\text{Lyly} \rightarrow \text{Euphues} \rightarrow \textit{Euphues} \rightarrow \text{"Euphuism"}$$

Shorter patterns of relations take us from a kind of writing to "Greeneness," and from a genre of humor to "Tarltonizing." Motivating these chains of metonymy was the sheer popularity of the figures involved. "Greeneness" could be identified in part because Greene's books existed in great numbers. Harvey accordingly seems to be speaking not to a coterie of readers but to a reading public. That this public was, of course, limited by social position and literacy is apparent in Dekker's reference to "Arcadian and Euphuized gentlewomen."[36] Yet, as the impersonal process of the verbal form ("Euphuized") and the yoking with Sidney's best-selling *Arcadia* might also serve to indicate, it was a public. These adjectives describe readers influenced by texts so widely read that Dekker is under no compulsion to say what he means by "Arcadian" and "Euphuized." Thus where a nineteenth-century critic saw *Euphues* as commencing "the literature of the drawing room" in England, it is more accurate to say that Lyly's texts made "drawing-room" manners and language public, bringing them to an audience larger than Lyly or anyone else had imagined possible.[37]

Given life by the printing press, Euphues haunted the works of Greene and his contemporaries. The historical "moment" of the Harvey passage quoted above was, again, one that hailed *Euphues* in the titles of various books by Greene, Lodge, and Dickenson. Addressing this pattern of reference in his study of Lyly, G. K. Hunter calls it "a completely superficial cashing-in on the manner or the name."[38] It is hard to dismiss this assessment, for these works do deploy "Euphues" in their titles as advertisement, and possibly in a misleading manner. But in seeing such quotation negatively—this remark occurs in a chapter called "The Victim of Fashion"—Hunter fails to notice that it signals one of Lyly's most prominent legacies, and an important contribution to the rise of embodied writing. For, following the success of *Euphues*, best-selling works often featured characters who became, first, independent of, then identified with, their authors.

Among these works were Greene's "cony-catching" pamphlets, Harington's *Ajax* books, and Breton's *Pasquil* sequence (completed in 1602 by *Old Mad-Cap's New Gallimaufry*). Harvey associates the cony-catching pamphlets so closely with Greene that he refers to the latter as "Greene the Conycatcher."[39] Breton, on the other hand, often addresses the readers of his *Pasquil* series in the persona of Pasquil. And because he appeared so frequently in print, Pasquil, like Euphues, acquired a more tangible identity than most literary creations. Some twenty years later the names of Breton and Pasquil would be synonymous with that of Ben Jonson, whose "Execration upon Vulcan" refers to "Nicholas Pasquil."[40] Similarly, when in 1598 Robert Joyner set out to satirize John Harington and the notoriety of his *Ajax* works, he did so by writing an epigram for Harington *as* "Ajax," making little distinction in the poem itself between Harington, his *Ajax* books, and the ever-present privy, or "jakes," lying behind Harington's title.[41] Harington returned the favor by later referring to Joyner as "Itis"—the title of the latter's collection of epigrams and satires.[42] It seems no accident, then, that when John Weever penned "*Ad Gulielmum Shakespear*" in his *Epigrams* (1599), he not only executed it in the form of a fourteen-line sonnet with the "Shakespearean" rhyme scheme (the only poem with this form in the collection) but also mentioned in it both *The Rape of Lucrece* and *Venus and Adonis*, the latter a Shakespearean best-seller.[43] Weever goes on to conclude that although Shakespeare's characters initially seemed "got" by "Apollo . . . and none other," one eventually perceives them to be the writer's own offspring: "They burn in love thy children *Shakespeare* het them, / Go, woo thy Muse more Nymphish brood beget them."[44] "[H]et" means "heated." Shakespeare's creative fire, the image implies, helps to "beget" characters on his personal Muse. Like the other best-selling authors whose characters took on a life outside their texts, Shakespeare is described as responsible for yet separate from his creations.

For persons to merge with characters and for books to be conflated with their authors is perhaps not surprising to readers of this era's texts, for during the 1590s many controversialists ridiculed their opponents by name, and writers of satire would often conceal the objects of their aggression with a nearly transparent disguise. But what we see in the phenomenon of the best-selling author and text goes beyond the satiric and allegorical traditions that the Elizabethans inherited, and, along with embodied writing generally, speaks to a profound, even structural, transformation of print culture. The making of an author's style into a thing (and the naming of that thing after the author); the celebrity of authors, and the textual celebrity of characters who seemed to exist outside their works; the intensive familiarity of recent books and titles; these books' familiarity with bodies and identities: all suggest a personalization of print that changed what and how printed matter meant. Everywhere a new fluidity between person and thing characterized the relation between authors and books, between characters and persons, and between readers and books.

One of the signal results of this fluidity involves what we might call the nascent "public sphere" of late Elizabethan England. The term *public sphere* is usually reserved for later eras, of course, and as such often describes a common space of rational intellectual and political discourse—a space sometimes identified with physical locations such as the German *Tischgesellschaften* (learned "table societies"), French salons, and the coffeehouses of eighteenth-century England.[45] Recently, however, scholars have begun to question the received location of the public sphere, in terms of both place and time. Traditional definitions have stressed bourgeois conversational settings, neutral places in which persons meet to exchange views. But new insights into the role of print as a medium for the articulation of controversial views ask us to see a sphere of public expression that preceded, and in some ways enabled, these later conversational settings. Indeed, where the standard chronology would see the public sphere as a decidedly post-Enlightenment phenomenon, some scholars have posited the existence of a dynamic public sphere in England from at least the 1620s onward, solidifying especially during the Interregnum.[46] David Norbrook, for instance, speaks of the "massively uneven development of the public sphere in the seventeenth century and beyond," observing that "It is not the case that after 1640, or after 1695, there suddenly was a securely established public sphere."[47] Yet while Norbrook is right to call our attention to the public sphere of early seventeenth-century England, even his emphasis on the 1620s is too late to account for the public aspects of print we have witnessed in texts of the 1590s and after. For it was then that the energies of the Marprelate controversy joined with various historical forces to radically expand the discursive limits of print, sounding out the limits of a meaningful public space. Into this space came controversial writers like Nashe and Harvey, explicitly erotic texts, best-selling works such as Greene's cony-catching pamphlets and Harington's *Ajax* books, and such newly embodied characters as Lyly's Euphues and Breton's Pasquil.

But while the personalism connected with such authors, texts, and characters asks us to revise our chronology of the public sphere, the embodied writing of this era compels us to modify inherited notions of the public sphere in qualitative ways. We need to define the public sphere, for instance, in terms of more than physical sites of conversation, rational political discourse, and polemic responding to social and political crises, as the roots of these later formations can be traced in part to the radical, sometimes ludic, expressivity of the 1590s. In vaunting the personal, as we have seen, this expressivity often disregarded conventional notions of status and bodily integrity. If standard accounts of the public sphere see the disregard of rank as one of its constituent features, the leveling aspects of embodied writing—in which a satirist might mock an equal, or even his better, and in which a writer of erotic verse could salaciously emblazon a goddess queen—can be seen as an enabling condition of "social intercourse that . . . disregarded status altogether."[48] The idea of convention is key here, as the events and texts of this period speak to a cultural shift in early modern England that displaced long-standing patterns of respect. This shift involved a general movement from cooperation and the habit of obedience to calculation and competition—a movement, in short, toward modernity. As a phenomenon, this shift was most visible, during the later 1590s and early 1600s, in responses to indecorous practice. The use of the term *public sphere* to describe the directions of print culture at this time, then, is justified not only by the complex ways in which embodied writing prepared for the expressions of the mid- and later seventeenth century and after but by the censoring impulses that printed material of the late Elizabethan era elicited from the political authorities. Subtending the ban on satire, on controversy, on the erotic, and even on unapproved English histories was a response to the putative confusion of spheres: the private had been made public through the medium of print, changing how the space of the public was defined.[49]

The nascent public sphere of the late Elizabethan era involved identity and decorum more than rationality or policy, and was often irreverent rather than somber. Indeed, Habermas's "public sphere" is thoroughly humorless and sober, employing at base what we might see as an epic or tragic model of political discourse. But the public sphere that the late Elizabethan era worked to establish was satirical and comedic, using humor to do "political" work. In providing a space for otherwise ordinary individuals and their voices, the public sphere functioned as a pivotal site for an emergent segment of English society. This public space, again, came into being when writers publicized hitherto private bodies and identities, including their own. Some of these had been out of bounds through the long-standing habit of authority that precluded familiar handling of the aristocracy, others through prudence based on moral decorum. But perhaps more important than the transgression of these boundaries was the unmistakable presence, in print, of individuals from the middle orders of early modern society.[50] Increasingly, the consequential bodies in printed material of this time were from inconsequential origins. Of the hundreds of names that followed the formulaic "To," "Ad," or "On" of the epigram tradition in the 1590s, for instance, many, if not the majority, involve those whose social status would have precluded significant mention in print several decades earlier. The same might be said of the personal allusions to middle-class writers in plays like those of the *Parnassus* trilogy (1599–1603), and in many other topically inclined works.

The public sphere that works of the 1590s began to establish was not only leveling and comedic but also highly theatrical in nature, having at its base a focused playfulness and the public theaters themselves. If Harvey's reference to Euphues and Greene springs from a personalism that licensed readers' attention to paper bodies, his invoking of Tarlton both recalls an older social type, the licensed jester who bonds "lord and clown," and reminds us that the amphitheater playhouses (where the rough music of Tarlton's "Timpany"-wit endeared him to the Elizabethan public) were arenas of celebrity and public discourse. During the 1590s, publishers found that readers were eager to buy the plays they had seen and heard in London's theaters. Beginning in 1593–94, texts of public-theater plays began to make up an increasing percentage of literary publications. By the first decade of the seventeenth century, they would sometimes constitute over 20 percent of all literary publications, and over 5 percent of all titles published. The popularity of this comparatively novel kind of publication has a significant place in the history of embodied writing, for the printing of dramatic scripts made available to the reading public words that it could associate with specific actors, some of them celebrities. However accurate, the anecdote in John Manningham's *Diary* that details Burbage's and Shakespeare's erotic rivalry—Burbage appointed to visit an enamored citizen under the name of "Richard the Third," Shakespeare, anticipating him, sending word that "'William the Conqueror' was before Richard the Third"—testifies to the belief that public playing had generated a "star" system.

What we forget in the coincidence of these names, however, is how closely the jest depends on the recent popularity of the history play. Burbage had doubtless played Richard the Third, and Shakespeare may well have been associated with the one surviving play to feature William the Conqueror.[51] In any case, public playing had made celebrities of certain actors, and the printed play texts that began to appear in great numbers in the 1590s would have offered readers a record of lines they might connect with real bodies on the platform stage. We can see humorous testimony to this effect in Richard Corbett's "Iter Boreale," a poem written shortly before Burbage's death. Describing a journey through England, Corbett relates that one of his hosts, "full of *Ale* and *History*," makes a telling mistake in his rehearsal of the Battle of Bosworth Field:

> Why, he could tell
> The inch where *Richmond* stood, where *Richard* fell:
> Besides what of his knowledge he can say,
> He had Authentic notice, from the Play;
> Which I might guess, by must'ring up the Ghosts
> And policies not incident to Hosts:
> But chiefly by that one perspicuous thing,
> Where he mistook a Player, for a King.
> For when he would have said "King *Richard*" died,
> And call'd "a horse, a horse," he, "*Burbage*" cried.[52]

The Host's confusion of Burbage with Richard is precisely what the Lord Admiral's Men would have hoped for, of course, during any production of the play. But the lingering identification of actor and role was something that the printing of play quartos made especially likely. Those who purchased *Richard III*, for instance, would possess a version (however varied in nature) of what they had heard specific actors speak in London's playhouses: these the lines of Richard Burbage, those the lines of Will Kemp, still others the lines that Shakespeare had spoken on stage. Their voices would have seemed dried in ink.

In much the same way, the bodies of playwrights themselves came to be identified with particular voices or styles. As James Shapiro has argued concerning the question of influence among early modern playwrights, a developing sense of authority, voice, and canonicity formed a prelude to the War of the Theaters at the turn of the century. The sharp parody in such satirical plays as *Cynthia's Revels* (1600), *Satiromastix* (1600), and *Poetaster* (1601) depended on a heightened "sensitivity to the distinctive voices of individual dramatists."[53] Paradoxically, this sensitivity was augmented by the collaborative nature of dramatic authorship. Playwrights became deeply aware of the differences between their own styles and the styles of potential rivals— even, perhaps especially, those with whom they worked most closely—and "struggled to locate themselves relationally" by parodying other dramatists.[54]

Nowhere is this kind of positioning more familiar to modern readers than in the "upstart Crow" passage from *Greene's Groatsworth of Wit* (1592). This "first published notice of Shakespeare in London" comes, the text's most recent editor points out, as "a remarkably bitter outburst . . . apparently provoked by envy at the success of a player turned playwright."[55] Although Henry Chettle is most likely the primary author of this text, its personal satire seems entirely consonant with the atmosphere of embodiment that surrounded Greene, from his citation of Euphues and his self-allegorization as a prodigal poet to his best-selling pamphlets and literary reputation. This well-known passage grounds its general resentment of others in the theatrical business by warning a friend about a particular individual: "Yes trust them not: for there is an upstart Crow, beautified with our feathers, that with his *Tiger's heart wrapped in a Player's hide,* supposes he is as well able to bombast out a blank verse as the best of you: and being an absolute *Johannes fac totum,* is in his own conceit the only Shake-scene in a country."[56] Although much about this notorious passage still occasions debate, it offers several clues as to its primary mystery, the identity of the untrustworthy upstart who has strutted onto the theatrical scene. The more apparent of these clues, though, has overshadowed a less obvious mechanism in the passage. Where "Shake-scene" clearly brings to mind "Shakespeare," the passage has already identified its target by quoting his words. In mentioning this individual's "*Tiger's heart wrapped in a Player's hide,*" that is, our author is revising a line from York's diatribe against Queen Margaret in Shakespeare's *3 Henry VI:* "O tiger's heart wrapped in a woman's hide" (1.4.137). Because a version of this play was first published in 1595, three years after *Groatsworth,* the author of this pamphlet is appealing to what must have been, for many readers, playhouse memories. The chain of associations this quotation depends on, then, involves more than a simple triangulation of pamphlet-author, reader, and object of ridicule. For even if Shakespeare himself acted the part of York, the allusion includes others, and other experiences, in its "embodiment" of Shakespeare.

We might recall Harvey's distillation of "Euphuism" as we trace this process of embodiment. The author of *Groatsworth* points at Shakespeare, and does so to an ideal reader who may have heard Shakespeare's play in person, or had other access to information about the play or quotation. If the former, the *Groatsworth* writer might be seen as assuming the following sequence of agents and events. The diagram charts the "history" of the quotation, from playwright to play, to actor, to audience member, to pamphlet:

(Shakespeare) Playwright ← Play Text ← Actor: "O tiger's heart[!]" ← Playgoer ← *Groatsworth*

But we have to reverse this process to get to the "upstart Crow" the *Groatsworth* author derides, and only when we do so may we realize how complex the allusion is. For although Shakespeare may have acted the part of York, a number of things would still have come between the pamphlet and him: the playhouse, the character (and, assuming another actor, that actor's body in whom the quotation would have been given voice), the paper from which the actor would learn these lines, even the fact that Shakespeare wrote these lines. *Groatsworth* imagines a canny reader who has shared its author's experiences of public spaces in London, and who would recognize the pamphlet's paraphrase as a strategic misquotation of a production in one of the public theaters. *Groatsworth,* further, seems directed toward a reader used to libels, controversial pamphlets, satires, and *à clef* narratives—used to reading as much for the identities on the page as for the plot.

The paper tiger to whom *Groatsworth* points shows how embodied writing licensed readers to imagine licentious authors. Even as others' bodies began to appear more often and more graphically on the page, however, readers began to associate printed matter with authors' bodies. To return to the emetic that Horace administers to Crispinas in *Poetaster*—a transparent fantasy of Jonson's in which he cures Marston of his verbal excesses by making the dramatist vomit his strange words—we see that Jonson locates the problem in Crispinas/Marston's body, and the solution in curing that body. In an age fascinated by neologisms, the deployment of newly acquired words could well prove a mark of distinction. And as Jonson's satire shows us, often these words seemed foreign matter. Yet increasingly during the 1590s, readers considered words and style an integral part of an author's body. In Harvey's distillation of "Greeneness," for example, readers are assumed to have had enough access to and familiarity with a writer's works to identify what Harvey perceived as a quintessential property of Greene's style—to connect Greene's body with the body of his works through some habit of composition, stance, or favorite subject. It is perhaps a combination of these that Shakespeare posits as a personal marker in Sonnet 76, when he asks himself, "Why write I still all one, ever the same, / And keep invention in a noted weed, / That every word doth almost tell my name, / Showing their birth, and where they did proceed?" (lines 5–8). This "noted weed" or familiar garb is the *dispositio* of the poetic speaker's invention, the arrangement in his verse of his material. So familiar is this arrangement, the sonnet relates in an exaggeration meant to show the poet's devotion, that even the poem's words seem to carry birthmarks and to point toward its author.[57] His style, *semper eadem*, gives him away.

Belief in the power of a work to name its author grew during the late Elizabethan era. "Style" came to be seen as only sometimes a conscious decision but "many times natural to the writer," something the author often "holdeth on by ignorance, and will not or peradventure cannot easily alter into any other."[58] The words here are George Puttenham's, from his *Arte of English Poesie,* and it is also in this work that we encounter a revealing myth concerning the identity of authors and their texts. We might call this the *hos ego* myth after the catchphrase by which it would be known during the early modern era. Puttenham tells us that once, when Vergil had composed a distich praising Augustus and had set it upon the palace gate, another writer—a certain "saucy courtier"—saw how much these anonymous lines were admired and took credit for them, receiving a "good reward" from the emperor. Angered at the fraud his modesty had enabled, Vergil returned the following night and "fastened upon the same place this half meter, four times iterated":

Sic vos non vobis
Sic vos non vobis

Sic vos non vobis
Sic vos non vobis

No one could make sense of this, and, having baffled the court, Vergil returned and wrote above these four half-lines "*Hos ego versiculos feci tulit alter honores,*" or "These verses I did make, thereof another took the praise."[59] He then finished the four *Sic vos non vobis* half-lines with corresponding complaints from laboring beasts and insects; "So you not for yourselves," Vergil writes: oxen pull the plow, sheep bear wool, bees gather honey, and birds build nests. Like these toiling creatures, he suggests, poets find themselves robbed of their labor's fruit. Puttenham tells us that, to clinch his case, the poet "put to his name *Publius Virgilius Maro.*" If Vergil's authorship of the earlier distich is implied by the content of his poem, his authority is demonstrated by his ability to finish it when others could not, an authority consolidated with the inscription of his name.

Articulated by Phaer and Twynne in their edition of *The Whole XII Books of the Æneidos* in 1573, the *hos ego* myth was represented in texts with growing frequency toward the end of Elizabeth's reign. After appearing in Puttenham's *Arte of English Poesie* in 1589, it figured also in Joseph Hall's *Virgidemiae* in 1597, and in the second part of *The Return from Parnassus* in 1603. As in this gossipy, satiric play, Hall's use of the phrase calls on the larger story of plagiarism and authority associated with Vergil's rise to cultural notice. In the second satire of book 4, Hall ridicules the embarrassment an aspiring young gentleman feels for his father and their common, laboring-class roots:

> Could never man work thee a worser shame
> Than once to minge thy father's odious name,
> Whose mention were alike to thee as leave,
> As Catch-pol's fist unto a Bankrupt's sleeve;
> Or an *Hos ego* from old *Petrarch's* sprite
> Unto a Plagiary sonnet-wright.[60]

The mere "minge" or mention of his father's name ("Lollio," which is, of course, his own) serves as an uncomfortable reminder to the young gallant of something he would rather forget. But just as the *Groatsworth* passage would have its reader believe that borrowed feathers are recognizably alien to the borrower, so does it seem, to Hall, that debts will out: even as this name returns to remind the young gallant of the source of his money, a "bankrupt" will find himself apprehended, and a "plagiary sonnet-wright" will be admonished by the ghost of Petrarch, who hails the thief with the two words that declare the subject (*ego*) and object (*hos*) of literary ownership.

The *hos ego* myth maintains that an umbilical cord links authors and their writings. In the "original" story Vergil's completion is based on content and style, whereas by Hall's time it seems oriented more toward stylistic borrowing. In this way it illustrates changes in beliefs about what texts were, as during the period under focus a number of readers began to hold that the best way to determine authorship was to search for internal rather than external evidence. That is, where traditionally the political authorities might search for publisher and printer, interrogating individuals to ascertain provenance, during the 1590s and after we see a more forensic approach to the issue of authorship: if authorities had earlier been tempted to coerce those associated with the printing and distribution of dangerous anonymous texts, at the end of Elizabeth's reign readers suggested putting pressure on the *style* of those texts as a way of determining who wrote them. As one might expect, the anonymity of the Marprelate publications figured centrally in this development.

In 1595 the Reverend Matthew Sutcliffe published a pamphlet whose very title indicates the revolving-door progress of that controversy: *An Answer unto a Certain Calumnious Letter Published by Master Job Throckmorton and Entitled "A Defence of J. Throckmorton against the Slanders of Master Sutcliffe" Wherein the Vanity Both of the Defence of Him Self and the Accusation of Others Is Manifestly Declared by Matthew Sutcliffe*. In this pamphlet Sutcliffe, who wrote in support of the system that had rewarded him with multiple benefices, points at Throckmorton as the real author of the Marprelate tracts—or rather, claims that the tracts themselves point at Throckmorton. As Sutcliffe contends, not only did the manuscript of *More Work for Cooper* (in the possession of which the printers Valentine Simmes, Arthur Tomlyn, and John Hodgkins had been arrested in 1589) feature Throckmorton's handwriting and interlinear corrections but "the style is so like to Job Throckmorton's talking and writing, that as children do declare whose they are by the lineaments of their visage and proportion of parts, so these libels do bewray their natural father by the frame of the words and sentences, and such draughts as can proceed from no other author."[61] A few pages later Sutcliffe continues: "the phrase and manner of writing—which are a certain indice and sign of the Author's affections—doth declare from whence the book did come: so scurrilous, wicked and railing stuff could come from no other than Throckmorton." Sutcliffe concludes that Throckmorton is Martin Marprelate: because both his handwriting and his very manner of speaking and writing ("the frame of the words and sentences") confirm his authorship of *More Work*, the boast in that text that its author is Martin Marprelate proves that Throckmorton (and not John Penry or any other of the alleged conspirators) was responsible for the Marprelate tracts.[62]

The warrants for stylistic identification here seem highly subjective. Is there, as Sutcliffe claims, and as modern critics who engage in the statistical analysis of literature maintain, something about "the frame of the words and sentences" of texts that shows a trained eye that a work "can proceed from no other author"? It was Harvey's contention, after all, that however identifiable "Greeneness" and "Euphuism" and "Tarltonizing wit" were, Nashe had been reproducing them in *his* writings. And at another point Harvey accuses Greene of "Tarltonizing," too.[63] A similar irony appears in *Groatsworth*'s borrowing from Shakespeare to claim that Shakespeare had first borrowed from others. Literary identity, like literary property, depends on ownership, and only things that can be stolen can be said to be owned. Ironically, the surest proof of the developing notion of authorship and literary property during this period was its continued discourse of plagiarism. But such a metaphysical approach to authorship misses the realities of writing and politics: the fact that authors, printers, and publishers faced severe punishment for producing certain texts and competed with each other for prestige and money, and that it mattered to readers who had written particular books. Without accepting the basis of Sutcliffe's attribution, then, we can notice the confidence that he displays in his ability to discern an idiosyncratic *style*—and to trace that style to an author's other texts and to a manner of speech. Style is both the man and the text.

Sutcliffe's anatomy of the style of *More Work* offers an understanding of the printed word more forensic than rhetorical. Its relation to empirical method, in fact, might be seen in a story told by Francis Bacon. In his *Apology* for Essex, originally published in 1604, Bacon tells us that once when Queen Elizabeth encountered a particular text and "would not be persuaded, that it was his writing whose name was to it, but that It had some more mischievous Author, and said with great indignation, that she would have him racked to produce his Author, I replied 'Nay Madam, he is a Doctor: never rack his person, but rack his style; let him have pen, ink, and paper, and help of books, and be enjoined to continue the story wherein it breaketh off, and I will undertake, by collecting the styles, to judge whether he were the Author or no.'"[64] Bacon sets himself up as a literary detective able to determine whether two examples of "style" come from the same author. His pride in his ability to "judge" authorship, though, stops short of Sutcliffe's claim of an organic relationship between text and author, for authorship is instead a craft, with pen, ink, paper, and "help of books" all contributing to the final product. But if the author's body is spared the rack his style is not: the physical apparatus of torture gives way to method; and what might once have taken place between bodies, with a book as object, now takes place between a reader and a book, with the author's body as object. Retelling the *hos ego* myth from inside the court, where an Elizabethan Vergil faces another kind of reward, Bacon replicates also Sutcliffe's confidence in stylistic identity.

Their belief remains indicative of the larger reorientation of bodies and print described in the preceding argument. The historical context of Bacon's anecdote reminds us how much print culture had changed in the last few decades of Elizabeth's reign.[65] English citizens who can be imagined as having left their country prior to the Armada would, upon returning after Elizabeth's death, doubtless recognize the basic forms of works published in their absence. But assuming they had had no contact with English publications during the decade and a half they had been away, they just as certainly would be surprised by the profusion of embodied texts greeting them upon their return. As readers, they might be expected to notice a number of things that had happened in and to texts during the last years of Elizabeth's reign. Most remarkable to them might be the way in which print had adopted practices and topics that had before this mainly characterized manuscript forms, like libels and erotic verse.[66] These readers would encounter many explicitly erotic texts, the license behind which had in addition underwritten many of the ad hominem sallies in both the Marprelate controversy and the satire wars. Such readers might have noticed too an emphasis on contemporary authors, something evidenced in a cadre of best-selling authors and texts. These readers may have been surprised to find a closer connection between artificial personae—"paper bodies"—and real ones. The notoriety of personae such as Euphues and Pasquil was accompanied, finally, by an entrenched star system in the public theaters, where actors were enjoying a celebrity that they had not possessed some fifteen years earlier.

How did this situation come about? What lay behind the development of embodied writing described in many of the preceding changes? This kind of writing undoubtedly had many sources, including the changeful political climate under an aging Elizabeth.[67] We should also consider among these sources "the increasingly litigious character of late Elizabethan society and the adversarial bias of contemporary rhetorical training."[68] And to these we could join the ways in which certain literary genres of the 1590s represented "alternative form[s] of ethical innovation in response to the disorienting effects of urbanization on traditional values."[69] But among the overdetermination of sources here, perhaps four in particular stand out. First among these is the momentous change in the roles and sources of authority in England following the Reformation. As Robert Weimann has argued, the Reformation profoundly altered the relations among power, authority, and representation in early modern England, and drastically affected venues and modes of expression. Such authors as Sidney, Nashe, and Lyly "had to cope not only with the wider horizon of international traffic and exchange but also with a largely unsanctioned diffusion of signifying activities."[70] We have already seen that many of the best-selling authors and texts diverged from the middle way of the Elizabethan settlement. From Perkins and Smith to Parsons and Southwell, and from *The Golden Chain* to *St. Peter's Complaint,* print culture of the 1590s bore witness to the Reformation's fragmentation of consensus. The Marprelate controversy, again, proved crucial to what followed, for in the creation of an alternate place for the utterance of deeply held truths it helped form a nascent public sphere for meaningful expression and debate. Texts published in the decades following the Marprelate controversy often took advantage of the license it had extended. Where the Reformation can be said to have multiplied the positions that believers could occupy, embodied writing—including Spenser's *Faerie Queene,* more overtly political allegories like *Caltha Poetarum,* and even devotional works like *Mary Magdalens Funerall Teares*—put many of those positions onto the printed page.

The importance given to reading following the Reformation leads us to the second of the primary sources of embodied writing, the general habituation to print. By the end of Elizabeth's reign, no one living would be able to recall a time when the printing press had not existed, and few would ever have known anyone who could remember such a time. The Elizabethans had become thoroughly familiar with print, and the printed page with them. As Christopher Hill suggests, they were soon to become, if they were not already, "the people of the Book."[71] Thus where the Reformation can be rightly described as "the story of great books," it was also the story of those books' readers, and of the surprising variety of texts (some "great," some not) from which they had to choose.[72] John Foxe prefaced his *Actes and Monuments* with an apology for adding yet another text to what he saw as "an infinite multitude of books," "considering nowadays the world so greatly pestered, not only with superfluous plenty thereof, but of all other treatises, so that books now seem rather to lack Readers, than Readers to lack books."[73] Foxe was not alone in feeling that the "gift of printing" had thoroughly altered English culture. We hear echoes of his sentiment in Spenser's description of Errour in *The Faerie Queene,* for instance, where the monster's vomit is "full of bookes and papers" (1.1.20.6). This would seem to concern more than Catholic propaganda, for Spenser's indictment of this "floud of poyson" displays a reluctance over quantity as well as content. Indeed, the following year, in 1591, the epistle dedicatory of *Martin Mar-Sixtus* believed itself justified in saying, "We live in a printing age," and seven years later John Florio half lamented what he called "this our paper-sea."[74] The flood of books that these authors describe had accustomed people to reading, and during the 1590s writers, printers, and readers began to refashion what had become ordinary. As Matthew Greenfield has argued, the sometimes cacophonous medley of styles in the pamphlet culture of the 1590s developed "as the solution to the *emergence* of a public—a public which read in a new way."[75] Responding to readers who read extensively as well as intensively, writers were forced to adjust their practice in this new era of books and reading.

Many of these writers came from a group that assumed an energetic role in the development of embodied writing. Anthony Esler has identified a "significant younger generation" of Elizabethan subjects who, born in the 1560s, rose to prominence in the 1590s, and it is this generation that remains largely responsible for much of the embodied writing in the later Elizabethan era.[76] Members of this younger generation came to London from Oxford and Cambridge, where satiric revues and epigrams prevailed, and where an emphasis on Latin models (flourishing also in the Tudor grammar schools) and the agonistic forms of humanist controversy helped shape the aggressive style of embodied writing.[77] They came from London's own Inns of Court, where disputation was a keynote, and where explicit literary treatment of the body seemed rather the norm than the exception.[78] Coming also from various English counties, from which London and its "commonwealth of wit" seemed a center of opportunity, members of this younger group both competed among themselves and pushed against the boundaries they had inherited.[79] We can most clearly see this generation, and the generational division it faced, when we examine the disparity of ages of those involved in the Bishops' Ban of 1599. The mean age of the known authors covered by the ban is around thirty (or twenty-seven if Harvey is, as Nashe might prefer, counted an outsider); whereas if we average the ages of the men who issued the ban, Richard Bancroft (Bishop of London) and John Whitgift (Archbishop of Canterbury), along with that of their sovereign, Queen Elizabeth, we get a composite reader over sixty-three years of age.[80] This disparity of ages gives us a hint as to why one may rightly describe the outlook of the Elizabethan younger generation as less "aspiring" (Esler's word) than *despairing*. For not only did a scarcity of patronage and the pressures of the literary marketplace lead to widespread discontent among this group but the apparent hegemony of an older generation—especially as it helped enforce what has been called the "paranoia of the establishment"—seemed a bar to its social progress.[81] Much embodied writing resulted from this generation's frustrations, resentments, and ambitions.

Yet it would be the public playhouses of London that most continually influenced the genre of embodied writing examined in this essay. These theaters can be said to have provided both a space for public expression and a continuing metaphor for its representation. Actors and playwrights alike enjoyed an informal license to represent influential figures, the workings of statecraft, and issues of moment—and all in a venue that used the body to expand received limits on discourse. Actors were indeed "the abstract and brief chronicles of the time," and in their playing testified to an age "grown so pick'd that the toe of the peasant comes so near the heel of the courtier, he galls his kibe."[82] Hamlet prefaces his famous description here by saying it is a phenomenon "this three years I have took note of," a probable allusion to the embodied sallies of the satire wars, if not the War of the Theaters in particular. These theaters were as important conceptually as they were in practice, for the idea of the stage remained central to many notions of community during the early modern era. Nashe's inflection of the *theatrum mundi* trope in his preface to the 1591 edition of *Astrophel and Stella,* for instance, asks its readers to "turn aside into this Theater of pleasure, for here you shall find a paper stage strewed with pearl, an artificial heav'n to overshadow the fair frame, and crystal walls to encounter your curious eyes, whiles the tragicomedy of love is performed by starlight."[83] The "paper stage" he assigns to the following sonnet sequence itself might appear to suggest a private theater or performance place. But the unlicensed movement of Sidney's sequence (hitherto a comparatively private document) from manuscript to print asks us to see this "Theater" as a public space, the relation between its manuscript readers and readers of its printed form analogous to the relation between private- and public-theater audiences. And even as theaters drew on the growing sense of authorship and the embodied writings of the 1590s for some of their energy, so too did print display its indebtedness to the theaters in its representation of the public. Hosting millions of visits by playgoers during the early modern era, purpose-built structures like the Globe, the Rose, the Curtain, and the Swan formed sites of public discourse and offered, through their familiar repertories, a personal celebrity not wholly dependent on the court or connected with the church.

To be sure, the plays performed there seemed to make little happen; they led, that is, to no immediate political action such as a rebellion or the expulsion of an ambassador, and were in this sense "powerless."[84] But they held power of another sort. With their "liberty" and "license" they offered a place for the common handling of otherwise uncommon ideas, and provided models for the familiar representation of identities. As we have seen, the influence was mutual. Presenting historical as well as fictional characters, dramas fostered the kind of personalization that embodied writing would exercise. Thus when we consider Thomas Middleton's 1624 play, *A Game at Chess*—in its intricate though direct allusion to contemporary personages and issues, perhaps the most notoriously embodied text of the early modern era—we will not be surprised to find that Middleton had learned the details of his craft during what he himself had called the "angry satire days" of the late 1590s, when his own *Microcynicon, or Six Snarling Satires* was prohibited by the Bishops' Ban on the first day of June in 1599. The daring, ad hominem politics of *A Game at Chess* might initially seem confined to the theater where the play took life and was, not long after its unprecedented popularity, silenced as a theatrical production. But the following year its clever, embodied satire found new life in print. And during the remainder of the seventeenth century, the license of what an eighteen-year-old Middleton had understood as "satire days" developed into a more mature and enduring liberty.

Notes

This essay has benefited from the generous comments of Joseph Black, W. Scott Blanchard, Mark Thornton Burnett, Stephen Cohen, Roland Greene, Ian Frederick Moulton, John G. Norman, Elizabeth Scala, Jyotsna Singh, Tyler Smith, Elizabeth Spiller, and Douglas Trevor. Any faults that remain are the author's own. In most cases, I have silently modernized spelling and punctuation in quotations from early modern texts. Approximate dates for plays in this essay are given in *Annals of English Drama, 975–1700*, ed. Alfred Harbage, revised by S. Schoenbaum and Sylvia Stoler Wagonheim, 3d ed. (London and New York: Routledge, 1989). All references to Jonson in this essay are from *Ben Jonson*, ed. C. H. Herford, Percy Simpson, and Evelyn Simpson, 11 vols. (Oxford: Clarendon Press, 1925–52); those to Nashe are from *The Works of Thomas Nashe*, ed. R. B. McKerrow, 5 vols. (London: Sidgwick and Jackson, 1904–8); and references to Shakespeare are from *The Riverside Shakespeare*, ed. G. Blakemore Evans, 2d ed. (Boston: Houghton Mifflin, 1997).

1. Gabriel Harvey, from the *Second Letter of Four Letters and Certain Sonnets* (1592; rpt., London: John Lane, 1922), Bodley Head Quartos, 15.

2. My understanding of the relation between print and the body in early modern England has benefited from a number of studies, including the foundational essay by Mary Claire Randolph, "The Medical Concept in English Renaissance Satiric Theory: Its Possible Relationships and Implications," *Studies in Philology* 38, no. 2 (1941): 125–57. I have also profited from John G. Norman's forthcoming study, tentatively titled *Literature after Dissection in Early Modern England*. See, in addition, Gail Kern Paster, *The Body Embarrassed: Drama and the Disciplines of Shame in Early Modern England* (Ithaca: Cornell University Press, 1993); Jonathan Sawday, *The Body Emblazoned: Dissection and the Human Body in Renaissance Culture* (London: Routledge, 1995); and Norman's extended review of Sawday's work in *Medievalia et Humanistica*, n.s., 23 (1996): 176–80. More recently, Kristen Elizabeth Poole has argued that the Marprelate tracts' "polyvalency of competing, overlapping, and interactive voices" opened "a space for the reader's internal participation," thus altering the relations among reader, author, voice, and page (Poole, "Talking Back: Marprelate and His Readers," paper delivered at the annual meeting of the Renaissance Society of America, Vancouver, Canada, 5 April 1997).

3. Nashe uses the coinage "body-wanting" to refer to various "venereal" quotations from Ovid in *The Unfortunate Traveller;* McKerrow, ed., *Works of Thomas Nashe*, 2:271.

4. See, for representative studies along these lines, Douglas Bush, *Mythology and the Renaissance Tradition in English Poetry* (Minneapolis: University of Minnesota Press, 1932), esp. chap. 4, section 2, "The New Ovid," 72–85; et passim. Acknowledging the strong influence of "the dogma *ut pictura poesis*," Bush writes that "mythological poets vied with painters in rich ornamentation and warm flesh tints. The body had come into its own, although in mythological verse it often seems to be under glass" (78). See also Bush's bibliography of English mythological poems to 1680 (301–23). For other approaches to these traditions, see Alvin Kernan, *The Cankered Muse: Satire of the English Renaissance* (New Haven: Yale University Press, 1959); John S. Coolidge, "Martin Marprelate, Marvell, and *Decorum Personae* as a Satirical Theme," *PMLA* 74 (1959): 526–32; Roma Gill, "The Renaissance Conventions of Envy," *Medievalia et Humanistica*, n.s., 9 (1979): 215–30; and Ritchie D. Kendall, *The Drama of Dissent: The Radical Poetics of Nonconformity, 1380–1590* (Chapel Hill: University of North Carolina Press, 1986), who grounds Elizabethan religious satire in a diverse but cohesive aesthetic, a "poetics of dissent" stretching back to the Lollard preachers. For the influence of flyting and the *débat*, see C. L.

Barber, *Shakespeare's Festive Comedy: A Study of Dramatic Form and Its Relation to Social Custom* (Princeton: Princeton University Press, 1959), 5–6, 60, 80, 116. Concerning the influence of Petrarch upon the lyric in early modern England, see Roland Greene, *Post-Petrarchism: Origins and Innovations of the Western Lyric Sequence* (Princeton: Princeton University Press, 1991), 63–108. Greene argues that Sidney's *Astrophel and Stella* "distinctly plays down the temporal process passed on from the *Canzoniere* in favor of a still more person-oriented scope and order" (107). See also Nancy J. Vickers, "Diana Described: Scattered Woman and Scattered Rhyme," *Critical Inquiry* 8 (1981): 265–79, who speaks of Petrarch's "legacy of fragmentation" as it related to "the development of a code of beauty, a code that causes us to view the fetishized body as a norm" (277); and Hannah Betts, who explores the pornographic blazon in the late Elizabethan era ("'The Image of this Queene so quaynt': The Pornographic Blazon 1588–1603," in *Dissing Elizabeth: Negative Representations of Gloriana,* ed. Julia M. Walker (Durham: Duke University Press, 1998), 153–84. P. H. Davison is only one of many critics who have explored the importance of Old Comedy for Jonson and other playwrights of this era; see "*Volpone* and the Old Comedy," *Modern Language Quarterly* 24 (1963): 151–57.

5. Still standard introductions to the issues and chronology of the Marprelate controversy can be found in McKerrow, ed., *Works of Thomas Nashe,* 5:34–65; and William Pierce, *An Historical Introduction to the Marprelate Tracts* (London, 1908). See also the entry by Joseph Black in *The Dictionary of Literary Biography,* vol. 132, "Sixteenth-Century British Nondramatic Writers," 1st ser., ed. David A. Richardson (Detroit: Gale Research, 1993), 240–44; Black's doctoral thesis, *Pamphlet Wars: The Marprelate Tracts and "Martinism," 1588–1688* (University of Toronto, 1996); an essay by Black forthcoming in the *Sixteenth-Century Journal* entitled "The Rhetoric of Reaction: The Martin Marprelate Tracts (1588–1589), Anti-Martinism, and the Uses of Print in Early Modern England" (I am indebted to Black for sharing this with me before its publication); and Leland Carson, *Martin Marprelate, Gentleman* (San Marino: Huntington Library, 1981).

6. Robert Weimann, *Authority and Representation in Early Modern Discourse,* ed. David Hillman (Baltimore: Johns Hopkins University Press, 1996), 90. My remarks in this essay come as a kind of footnote to Weimann's foundational arguments, in the above text and various essays, concerning the changing shapes of authority in early modern England.

7. For insightful surveys of early Tudor polemic, see Louis A. Schuster, "Thomas More's Polemical Career, 1523–1533," in *The Complete Works of St. Thomas More,* ed. Schuster et al., vol. 8, pt. 3 (New Haven: Yale University Press, 1973), 1137–268; and John M. Headley's introduction to More's *Responsio ad Lutherum,* vol. 5, pt. 2 (New Haven: Yale University Press, 1969), 715–831, esp. "Form and Style in the *Responsio,*" 803–23. Headley discusses More's use of Lucian, Horace, Juvenal, Terence, and Plautus in fashioning his abusive satire (814–20). Exploring the intensively ad hominem nature of the controversy between More and Luther, Schuster notices that More's *Confutation of Tyndale's Answer* contains "more than sixty references" to the potentially incriminating fact of Luther's marriage to Katherine von Bora, a former Cistercian nun (1477).

8. In William Pierce, ed., *The Marprelate Tracts 1588, 1589* (London: James Clarke

and Co., 1911), 262–63. This passage refers to William Gravet (d. 1599), vicar of St. Sepulchre in London since 1566, and from the following year prebendary of Willesden in St. Paul's. "[D]umb John" here is John Aylmer (1521–94), Bishop of London; "T. C." is, of course, Thomas Cooper.

9. Thomas Nashe, *A Countercuff Given to Martin Junior: By the Virtuous, Hardy, and Renowned Pasquil of England, Cavaliero* ([London], 1589); in McKerrow, ed., *Works of Thomas Nashe*, 1: 57.

10. John Dover Wilson, "The Marprelate Controversy," in *The Cambridge History of English Literature*, ed. A. W. Ward and A. R. Waller (New York: Macmillan, 1939), 3:436; qtd. in Weimann, *Authority and Representation*, 90.

11. The author of *The Return of the Renowned Cavaliero Pasquill of England* (1589) relates, "Me thought *Vetus Comœdia* began to prick him at London in the right vein, when she brought forth *Divinity* with a scratcht face, holding of her heart as if she were sick." See McKerrow, ed., *Works of Thomas Nashe*, 1:92. For other references to possible stagings of the Marprelate controversy, see McKerrow, *Works of Thomas Nashe*, 4:44, notes to lines 13, 15. See also Kristen Poole, "Saints Alive! Falstaff, Martin Marprelate, and the Staging of Puritanism," *Shakespeare Quarterly* 46 (1995): 47–75. On the influence of Old Comedy (figured, above, in the phrase "*Vetus Comœdia*") as both form and concept, see n. 4, above, and Herford et al., eds., *Ben Jonson*, 8:644, 9:421 n. 232.

12. Allan Holaday, ed., *The Plays of George Chapman: The Comedies* (Urbana: University of Illinois Press, 1970), 235–36, lines 13–19.

13. Herford et al., eds., *Ben Jonson*, 5: lines 52–74. Compare also Marston's prologue to *The Fawn*, published in 1606; there he boasts that in his play "no rude disgraces / Shall taint a public, or a private name" (lines 5–6): John Marston, *The Fawn*, ed. Gerald A. Smith (Lincoln: University of Nebraska Press, 1965). As James P. Bednarz points out, Jonson had a special reason to be concerned over embodied writing, for his "swarthy, pock-marked face afforded his critics an easy and constant opportunity for satire" ("Representing Jonson: *Histriomastix* and the Origin of the Poets' War," *Huntington Library Quarterly* 54 [1991]: 1–30). See pp. 4–5 for various references, usually unflattering, to Jonson's face.

14. E. D. Pendry, ed., *Thomas Dekker: Selected Prose Writings* (Cambridge, Mass.: Harvard University Press, 1968), 101.

15. See *OED* "flirt," *v.* 1–7.

16. Here I disagree with Richard A. McCabe's belief that the terms of the Bishops' Ban "show quite clearly that its primary target . . . was neither eroticism nor lewdness but satire itself" (McCabe, "Elizabethan Satire and the Bishops' Ban of 1599," *Yearbook of English Studies* 11 [1981]: 188–93, 189). The presence of works that were, variously, primarily misogynistic, politically à clef, privately controversial, and satirical, cannot be covered by any current or early modern understanding of "satire." I would argue that satire, eroticism, lewdness, misogyny (of the kind evidenced in *The Fifteen Joys of Marriage* and *Of Marriage and Wiving*) were objectionable because they too openly brought the human body—both generally and particularly—onto the printed page. Lynda E. Boose also departs from McCabe's position, suggesting that to see pornography and satire in an "either-or

context ... is not only unnecessary but misses something vital" ("The 1599 Bishops' Ban, Elizabethan Pornography, and the Sexualization of the Jacobean Stage," in *Enclosure Acts: Sexuality, Property, and Culture in Early Modern England*, ed. Richard Burt and John Michael Archer [Ithaca: Cornell University Press, 1994], 185–200, 196). However, Boose's solution—"as the Muse labored, it brought forth a monstrously hybrid creature that combined the salaciously erotic with the violent, misogynistic excoriations of the Juvenalian satiric speaker" (196)—remains unpersuasive, as it cannot account for the otherwise wide range of materials included in the Ban, including prose controversy and the "English historyes" not allowed by the Privy Council. See Boose, "Bishops' Ban," 199 n. 7. Recently Cyndia Susan Clegg has argued that the Bishops' Ban is not "representative of a widespread, long term, and efficient cultural practice" but is instead "an improvisational play of competing personal interests" related to Essex's activities in the closing years of the century; see Clegg, *Press Censorship in Elizabethan England* (Cambridge: Cambridge University Press, 1997), 217, and chap. 9, "The 1599 Bishops' Ban: 'Shreud suspect of ill pretences,'" 198–207, passim. Obviously my argument would dovetail with Clegg's interest in the intensive personalism of many of the works covered by the Ban—especially those that may be linked with Essex himself.

17. Ian Frederick Moulton, "'Printed Abroad and Uncastrated': Marlowe's Elegies with Davies' Epigrams," in *Marlowe, History, and Sexuality: New Essays on Christopher Marlowe*, ed. Paul Whitfield White (New York: AMS Press, 1997). Moulton continues: "Given an understanding of corruption which does not draw strong distinctions between a 'private' realm of the erotic and a 'public' political realm, I believe that Marlowe's translations of Ovid may well have been perceived as socially disorderly." I am grateful to Moulton for sharing this material with me before its publication.

18. James H. McDonald and Nancy Pollard Brown, eds., *The Poems of Robert Southwell, S.J.* (Oxford: Clarendon Press, 1967), "St. Peter's Complaint," lines 355–57, 361.

19. *Virgidemiae* (1598), in *The Poems of Joseph Hall, Bishop of Exeter and Norwich*, ed. Arnold Davenport, English Texts and Studies (1949; Liverpool: Liverpool University Press, 1969), 1.8.9–11 (p. 19).

20. See William Keach, *Elizabethan Erotic Narratives: Irony and Pathos in the Ovidian Poetry of Shakespeare, Marlowe, and Their Contemporaries* (New Brunswick: Rutgers University Press, 1977), 231. Keach speaks of "the conflict and convergence of satire and erotic poetry at the turn of the century," as evidenced in Weever, and in Marston's *Pygmalion's Image* (188). On the subversive nature of these narratives' Ovidian inheritance, see also Jonathan Bate, "Sexual Perversity in *Venus and Adonis*," *Yearbook of English Studies* 23 (1993): 80–92.

21. Christopher Marlowe, *Hero and Leander*, from *The Complete Poems and Translations*, ed. Stephen Orgel (Harmondsworth, Middlesex: Penguin Books, 1971), lines 175–91, 188–91.

22. *Venus and Adonis*, lines 229–40. With Shakespeare's blazon one might compare Spenser's erotic description of the Temple of Venus in *The Faerie Queene*, 4.10.21 ff.

23. Thomas Freeman, *"To Master W: Shakespeare," Run and A Great Cast* (1614), K2v–K3r, lines 7–8. The *Short-Title Catalogue* cites this work by its first title, *Rub and a Great Cast*; "*Run*" describes a second part subsumed into the first.

24. See Hilton Kelliher, "Unrecorded Extracts from Shakespeare, Sidney and Dyer," *English Manuscript Studies 1100–1700* 2 (1990): 163–87. Kelliher examines a hitherto unnoticed transcription of two stanzas of *Venus and Adonis* (lines 229–40) in the hand of one Henry Colling from around the period 1593–96—what may be "the earliest extract in manuscript yet to be discovered from any poem [of] Shakespeare's" (167). Colling was not the only reader to be especially taken by these stanzas: Kelliher points out that they are also quoted in Thomas Heywood's *Fair Maid of the Exchange* (1602), and in Gervase Markham and Lewis Machin's *The Dumb Knight* (1608).

25. On the early modern libel, see Pauline Croft, "Libels, Popular Literary and Public Opinion in Early Modern England," *Historical Research: The Bulletin of the Institute of Historical Research* 68, no. 167 (1995): 266–85. Croft relates that "The fifteen-nineties saw a proliferation of libels, the result of the strains imposed both by disastrous harvests and by an apparently endless international war which disrupted trade" (269). Libels concerning the Essex uprising, and concerning the trials of Walter Ralegh and those involved in the Bye and Main plots of 1603, demonstrated the continuing unease in the political sphere of early modern England (274–75). For studies of libelous material during the Stuart era, see Alistair Bellany, "'Raylinge Rymes and Vaunting Verse': Libelous Politics in Early Stuart England, 1603–1628," in *Culture and Politics in Early Stuart England*, ed. Kevin Sharpe and Peter G. Lake (Basingstoke: Macmillan, 1994), 285–310; and Tom Cogswell, "Underground Verse and the Transformation of Early Stuart Political Culture," in *Political Culture and Cultural Politics in Early Modern England*, ed. Susan D. Amussen and Mark Kishlansky (Manchester: Manchester University Press, 1995), 277–300.

26. The publication figures in the following paragraphs are derived from research by this writer, using information in *The Short-Title Catalogue*. They form part of a chronological, year-by-year analysis of publications by topic, and by frequency of imprint, tentatively titled "What They Read: Books and Culture in Early Modern England."

27. As Jesse Lander suggests, in a private communication to the author, the fact that the 1590s were a period of retrenchment for London printers and publishers—then feeling the effects of a severe inflation—may have led them to experiment with inexpensive forms like the pamphlet, and to commit themselves to proven texts and authors.

28. The epithet was coined by Nashe in *Pierce Penniless* (1592); see McKerrow, ed., *Works of Thomas Nashe*, 1:192–93.

29. Arthur F. Marotti, "Southwell's Remains: Catholicism and Anti-Catholicism in Early Modern England," in *Texts and Cultural Change in Early Modern England*, ed. Marotti and Cedric C. Brown (New York: St. Martin's Press, 1997), 37–65.

30. Here and with *Greene's Groatsworth of Wit* I follow the attribution of the original title pages in including these texts of divided authorship with the figures for works of less controversial origin. See n. 52, below.

31. John Weever, *Epigrammes—Epigrammes in the Oldest Cut and Newest Fashion*, ed. R. B. McKerrow (Stratford-upon-Avon, 1911; reissued 1922), v.

32. E. A. J. Honigmann, *John Weever: A Biography of a Literary Associate of Shakespeare and Jonson, Together with a Photographic Facsimile of Weever's "Epigrammes" (1599)* (Manchester: Manchester University Press, 1987), 27.

33. Harvey, *Four Letters*, 52. It should be pointed out that Nashe returned the favor here, and did so in kind. In the "Epistle Dedicatorie" to *Have with You to Saffron-Walden,* he mocks Harvey's style with the following: "Spend but a quarter so much time in mumping upon *Gabrielism,* and I'll be bound, body and goods, thou wilt not any longer sneakingly come forth with a rich spirit and an admirable capacity, but *an enthusiastical spirit & a nimble entelechy*" (McKerrow, ed., *Works of Thomas Nashe,* 3:16–17). The italicized phrase—what Nashe calls "Gabrielism"— draws, of course, on Harvey's own works. See McKerrow, ed., *Works of Thomas Nashe,* 4:310, n. to p. 17, line 4.

34. On Tarlton's "celebrity image" in early modern England, see Alexandra Halasz, "'So beloved that men use his picture for their signs': Richard Tarlton and the Uses of Sixteenth-Century Celebrity," *Shakespeare Studies* 23 (1995): 19–38. Halasz charts the development and shapes of Tarlton's celebrity, and explores the "appropriation of [Tarlton's] reputation by the book trade in its effort to expand and create a market for printed texts" (20). See also Robert Weimann, *Shakespeare and the Popular Tradition in the Theater* (Baltimore: Johns Hopkins University Press, 1978), 186–89.

35. Georges Louis Leclerc, Comte de Buffon, *Discours sur le Style* (Paris: Librairie Hachette, 1901), 25. The general sentiment was not new with Buffon, of course (see n. 2 in this edition of the *Discours* for classical precedents), but his has been the most succinct and lasting expression.

36. Dekker, *The Gull's Horn-Book,* in Pendry, ed., *Thomas Dekker: Selected Prose Writings,* 102.

37. J. J. Jusserand, *The English Novel in the Time of Shakespeare* (1894), 105; qtd. in R. Warwick Bond, ed., *The Complete Works of John Lyly,* vol. 1 (Oxford: Clarendon Press, 1902), 160.

38. G. K. Hunter, *John Lyly: The Humanist as Courtier* (Cambridge, Mass.: Harvard University Press, 1962), 259.

39. Harvey, *Four Letters,* 11.

40. Jonson apostrophizes Vulcan after the burning of his library, suggesting that he would have gladly substituted "many a ream / To redeem mine," works that would include "Nicholas Pasquil's *Meddle with your Match,* / And the strong lines, that so the time do catch" (lines 62–63, 77–78). Two manuscript copies of *The Underwood* read "Nicholas *Breton's Meddle with your Match*" (my emphasis): Ben Jonson, "An Execration upon Vulcan," *Underwood,* xliii, in Herford et al., eds., *Ben Jonson,* 11:205–6.

41. Robert Joyner, *Itis, or Three Severall Boxes of Sporting Familiars* (London: Thomas Judson, 1598), A9v–B1r.

42. See epigram 93, "*Against* Itis *a Poet,*" in Norman Egbert McClure, ed., *The Letters and Epigrams of Sir John Harington* (Philadelphia: University of Pennsylvania Press, 1930), 185.

43. On the implications of the unique form here, see Honigmann, ed., *John Weever,* 90–92. Another instance of an author being identified with one of his characters involved Christopher Marlowe, whom Harvey refers to as "Tamber-

laine" in the sonnet ("*Gorgon*, or the wonderfull yeare") appended to *A New Letter of Notable Contents* (London, 1593).

44. Honigmann, ed., *John Weever*, reproduction of E6a of Weever's *Epigrammes* (1599), lines 13–14.

45. "Public sphere" is a phrase and concept advanced by Jürgen Habermas in *The Structural Transformation of the Public Sphere* (1962) to describe the bourgeois sphere of rational political and intellectual exchange that thrived temporarily in the world of the eighteenth-century European "town." The public sphere was demarcated, on one side, by the more intimate realm of private activity that includes the family, commodity exchange, and social labor; and on the other, by the realm of the state, a realm defined by public authority, police, court, and courtly nobility. According to Habermas, places in which the public sphere unfolded had "a number of institutional criteria in common": (1) "they preserved a kind of social intercourse that, far from pre-supposing the equality of status, disregarded status altogether"; (2) "discussion within such a public presupposed the problematization of areas that until then had not been questioned"; (3) "the same process that converted culture into a commodity . . . established the public as in principle inclusive" (*The Structural Transformation of the Public Sphere: An Inquiry into a Category of Bourgeois Society,* trans. Thomas Burger and Frederick Lawrence [Cambridge, Mass.: MIT Press, 1989], 36–37). For later reflections by Habermas on this concept, see "The Public Sphere: An Encyclopedia Article," trans. Sara Lennox and Frank Lennox, in *Critical Theory and Society: A Reader,* ed. Stephen Eric Bronner and Douglas MacKay Kellner (New York: Routledge, 1989), 136–42, and "Further Reflections on the Public Sphere," in *Habermas and the Public Sphere,* ed. Craig Calhoun (Cambridge, Mass.: MIT Press, 1993), 421–61.

46. See, for example, David Norbrook, "*Areopagitica*, Censorship, and the Early Modern Public Sphere," in *The Administration of Aesthetics: Censorship, Political Criticism, and the Public Sphere,* ed. Richard Burt, Cultural Politics 7 (Minneapolis: University of Minnesota Press, 1994). Norbrook works consciously against the cumulative efforts of revisionist and certain new historicist paradigms, which tend to envision "a pre-Enlightenment world of bodily submission" (6–7). Both Steven Pincus (in "'Coffee Politicians Does Create': Coffeehouses and Restoration Political Culture," *The Journal of Modern History* 67, no. 4 [1995]: 807–34) and Sharon Achinstein ("Women on Top in the Pamphlet Literature of the English Revolution," *Women's Studies* 24 (1994): 131–63; and *Milton and the Revolutionary Reader* [Princeton: Princeton University Press, 1994]) join Norbrook in suggesting that a public sphere existed in English political life earlier than Habermas's chronology would allow. Where Pincus might be said to interpret Habermas too literally, however—overidentifying the public sphere with the physical place of the coffeehouse—Achinstein provides a more supple reading of the situation, speaking of "a cultural milieu in which the material conditions were in place for affordable, accessible printing, and an intellectual climate of public debate: all these might be said to anticipate Habermas' scheme by a century or so" ("Women on Top," 155). For a discussion of the ways in which such critics as David Lawton and Anne Middleton have explored a fifteenth-century public sphere, see Joyce Coleman, *Public Reading and the Reading Public in Late Medieval England and France* (Cam-

bridge: Cambridge University Press, 1996), 93–97. This essay was largely completed before I encountered Alexandra Halasz's *The Marketplace of Print: Pamphlets and the Public Sphere in Early Modern England* (Cambridge: Cambridge University Press, 1997). Halasz's argument focuses on pamphlets as a site of public expressiveness in early modern England; although I see such developments occurring across the lines of genre and mode, her emphasis on a particular form allows her to explore these issues in greater detail.

47. Norbrook, "*Areopagitica*, Censorship, and the Early Modern Public Sphere," 7. For a critique of Habermas's idealism that stresses the entrenched hierarchies of early modern Europe, see Robert Darnton's "An Enlightened Revolution?" in *New York Review of Books*, 24 October 1991, 34. For this reference I am indebted to Annabel Patterson's "Rethinking Tudor Historiography," *South Atlantic Quarterly* 92 (1993): 185–208, an essay that contributes to but is not superseded by Patterson's *Reading Holinshed's "Chronicles"* (Chicago: University of Chicago Press, 1994). There Patterson suggests that we can read the *Chronicles* as a "*textual* space ... in which the public's right to information could to some extent be satisfied" (21). My argument with Patterson's claim concerning the public implications of the *Chronicles*—a claim that dovetails in many ways with my own—is that it replicates Habermas's rational emphasis on information and communication. In contrast, I would suggest, the late Elizabethan public sphere often entertained the irrational and the ludic.

48. Habermas, *Structural Transformation of the Public Sphere*, 36.

49. It is something like this pressure on the established order of things that Joseph Loewenstein ascribes to the rogue printer John Wolfe's "tradition of practical assault on control and privilege" in relation to print, and the licensing of print ("For a History of Literary Property: John Wolfe's Reformation," *English Literary Renaissance* 18 [1988]: 389–412, 411).

50. On the shapes of decorum in relation to courtly practice in the Elizabethan era, and the ways in which, as vehicles of exclusion, decorum handbooks were used by these growing ranks of the meritorious to gain power and prestige, see Frank Whigham, *Ambition and Privilege: The Social Tropes of Elizabethan Courtesy Theory* (Berkeley: University of California Press, 1984).

51. That is, Robert Wilson's *Fair Em the Miller's Daughter of Manchester, with the Love of William the Conqueror* (1590), apparently owned by Strange's Men. On Shakespeare's probable connections with this company, see E. A. J. Honigmann, *Shakespeare: The "Lost Years"* (Manchester: Manchester University Press, 1985), 59–76.

52. Richard Corbett, "Iter Boreale," lines 343–52, in *The Poems of Richard Corbett*, ed. J. A. W. Bennett and H. R. Trevor-Roper (Oxford: Clarendon Press, 1955).

53. James Shapiro, *Rival Playwrights: Marlowe, Jonson, Shakespeare* (New York: Columbia University Press, 1991), 8.

54. Ibid.

55. D. Allen Carroll, ed., *Greene's Groatsworth of Wit: Bought With a Million of Repentance* (Binghamton, New York: Medieval and Renaissance Texts and Studies, 1994), preface. For convenience, in what follows I will speak of *Groatsworth* without naming the author; as Carroll indicates in his unpaginated preface, much recent

scholarship shows that "the case for a serious participation by Henry Chettle" in the writing of this text "is much stronger than has been generally thought. Greene *may* have had something to do with the writing of Groatsworth, Chettle *certainly* did."

56. Carroll, ed., *Greene's Groatsworth,* 85, lines 938–43.

57. For an extended meditation on the relation between such intensively self-conscious language—evident in the notorious puns on "Will" in sonnets 135 and 136—and developing forms of poetic subjectivity in the era, see Joel Fineman, *Shakespeare's Perjured Eye: The Invention of Poetic Subjectivity in the Sonnets* (Berkeley: University of California Press, 1986).

58. George Puttenham, *The Arte of English Poesie,* ed. Gladys Doidge Willcock and Alice Walker (1936; rpt., Cambridge: Cambridge University Press, 1970), "Of Stile," 3.5.148.

59. Here I am adopting the translation of Thomas Phaer and Thomas Twynne in *The Whole XII Books of the Æneidos of Virgil* (London, 1573), C4v.

60. Hall, *Virgidemiae,* in Davenport, ed., *The Poems of Joseph Hall,* 4.2.79–84, 57.

61. Edward Arber, ed., *An Introductory Sketch to the "Martin Marprelate" Controversy, 1588–1590,* The English Scholar's Library of Old and Modern Works, no. 8 (London, 1879), 176.

62. Arber, ed., *Introductory Sketch,* 178, 179. At least two other instances of "stylistic" identification came out of the Marprelate controversy. In "The Deposition of Henry Sharpe, a bookbinder at Northampton, on the 15th October 1589," the following is recorded: "When this Second Booke came out, then this Examinate [i.e., Henry Sharpe], as he sayth, began to suspect Penry to be the Author of it and talking with him told him as much, alleging this reason, 'Surely,' sayth this Examinate, 'I think this Book (the *Epitome*) to be of your making, because there are two or three Phrases in the *Epistle* of it, which are yours certainly.' Whereunto Master Penry gave no answer but laughed" (Arber, *Introductory Sketch,* 96). Likewise in "Summary of the information in the hands of the Queen's Government as to the Martinists on the 22nd September 1589," there is related "The author of the written copie [i.e., the manuscript of *More Work for Cooper*], that was taken by the Earl of Derby, taketh upon him to be the same, that made the first. 3. Libels, and the Styl doth not vary. That his last [i.e., *the manuscript work*] was contrived by Penrie besides the former presumptions (gathered of his owne speeches and dealinges in providinge a printer &c after Waldgrave his departure) the two hands used in the same do seem to be, the one Penry's and the other his man's hand; as by a collation of such their writings (as have been heretofore taken) may appear. The style of it and spirit of the man (where he is out of his scoffing vein) doth altogether resemble such his writings, as he hath published with his name to them" (Arber, *Introductory Sketch,* 117). I am grateful to Joseph Black for bringing these instances to my attention.

63. See Harvey, *Four Letters,* 19.

64. Francis Bacon, *Sir Francis Bacon his Apology, In Certain Imputations Concerning the Late Earl of Essex* (1604; London, 1642), 10.

65. Bacon's remembrance of the Elizabethan era also helps place this phenome-

non in its historical context. His anecdote here follows immediately upon similar mention of John Hayward's (Haywood's) politically controversial *The First Part of the Life and Reign of King Henry the IV* (1599)—a work not named in the Bishops' Ban of 1599, yet certainly pertinent to the climate that produced the ban. Elizabeth, according to Bacon, "being mightily incensed with that book which was dedicated to my Lord of *Essex* ... thinking it a seditious prelude to put into the people's heads boldness and faction, said she had good opinion, that there was treason in it, and asked me if I could not find any places in it that might be drawn within case of treason." To which Bacon answered, his *Apology* tells us, "for treason surely I found none, but for felony very many," as "the Author had committed very apparent theft, for he had taken most of the sentences of *Cornelius Tacitus,* and translated them into English, and put them into his text" (Bacon, *Sir Francis Bacon his Apology,* 10).

66. Here I should point out that this essay suggests an earlier chronology to the shift, from manuscript to print, of certain energies connected with political and obscene topics in early modern England than is seen by Marotti (who discusses the emergence of these topics in relation to the 1630s and 1640s) in his *Manuscript, Print, and the English Renaissance Lyric* (Ithaca: Cornell University Press, 1995), esp. chap. 2, "Sex, Politics, and the Manuscript System," 75–133.

67. My argument here about the pivotal nature of the 1590s draws on a number of recent studies, including John Guy, ed., *The Reign of Elizabeth I: Court and Culture in the Last Decade* (Cambridge: Cambridge University Press, 1995); Steve Rappaport, *Worlds within Worlds: Structures of Life in Sixteenth-Century London* (Cambridge: Cambridge University Press, 1989); Peter Clark, ed., *The European Crisis of the 1590s,* (London: George Allen and Unwin, 1985); Eric Mallin, *Inscribing the Time: Shakespeare and the End of Elizabethan England* (Berkeley: University of California Press, 1995); Peter C. Herman, "'O, 'tis a gallant king': Shakespeare's *Henry V* and the crisis of the 1590s," in *Tudor Political Culture,* ed. Dale Hoak (Cambridge: Cambridge University Press, 1995), 204–25; Mark Thorton Burnett, "Apprentice Literature and the 'Crisis' of the 1590s," *Yearbook of English Studies* 21 (1991): 27–38; and Margreta de Grazia, "Fin-de-Siècle Renaissance England," in *Fins de Siècle: English Poetry in 1590, 1690, 1790, 1890, 1990,* ed. Elaine Scarry (Baltimore: Johns Hopkins University Press, 1995), 37–63.

68. See Debra Belt, "The Poetics of Hostile Response, 1575–1610," *Criticism* 33 (1991): 419–59, 436.

69. Lawrence Manley, *Literature and Culture in Early Modern London* (Cambridge: Cambridge University Press, 1995), 372.

70. Weimann, *Authority and Representation,* 10.

71. Christopher Hill, *The English Bible and the Seventeenth-Century Revolution* (London: Penguin Books, 1993), 439.

72. For the Reformation as "the story of great books," see John E. Booty, ed., *The Godly Kingdom of Tudor England: Great Books of the English Reformation* (Wilton, Conn.: Morehouse-Barlow Co., 1981), 8.

73. John Foxe, *Actes and Monuments of the Christian Church* (London, 1576), ii.

74. [R. Wilson?], *Martine Mar-Sixtus* (London, 1591), A3v, and "Address to the

Reader" from Florio's *World of Words* (1598), reproduced in appendix 1 of Frances A. Yates, *John Florio: The Life of an Italian in Shakespeare's England* (Cambridge: Cambridge University Press, 1934), 337.

75. Matthew Greenfield, "The Strange Commodities of Pamphlet Culture," paper delivered at the annual meeting of the Renaissance Society of America, Vancouver, Canada, 5 April 1997.

76. Anthony Esler, *The Aspiring Mind of the Elizabethan Younger Generation* (Durham, N.C.: Duke University Press, 1966), xvi. For more comprehensive accounts of the issue of "age" during the transition to the modern period, see Keith Thomas, "Age and Authority in Early Modern England," *Proceedings of the British Academy* 62 (1977 for 1976): 205–48; Ilana Krausman Ben-Amos, *Adolescence and Youth in Early Modern England* (New Haven: Yale University Press, 1994); and Paul Griffiths, Adam Fox, and Steve Hindle, eds., *The Experience of Authority in Early Modern England* (London: Macmillan, 1996). We still lack a comprehensive study of the University Wits and their influence upon the literary scene of early modern England. But for the marked rise of educational opportunities in sixteenth-century England, see Lawrence Stone, "The Educational Revolution in England 1560–1640," *Past and Present* 28 (1964): 41–80.

77. For the importance of Latin, and Latin literary models, to the late Elizabethan era, see J. W. Binns, *Intellectual Culture in Elizabethan and Jacobean England: The Latin Writings of the Age*, ARCA Classical and Medieval Texts, Papers and Monographs 24 (Leeds: Francis Cairns Publications Ltd., 1990). Binns notes "the pervasive nature of the Latinate culture of Elizabethan England at the zenith of the Queen's reign," and relates that the "age of greatest popularity of the new Latin books is perhaps the fifty-year stretch from 1570–1620" (xv, 3). On the role of the epigram—popular with this generation, and arguably the building block of many larger textual forms—see Hoyt Hopewell Hudson, *The Epigram in the English Renaissance* (1947; rpt., New York: Octagon, 1966); and Mary Thomas Crane, *Framing Authority: Sayings, Self, and Society in Sixteenth-Century England* (Princeton: Princeton University Press, 1993), 136–61. On the relation of humanism's agonistic basis to the activities of its scholar-authorities, see Charles Nisard, *Les gladiateurs de la république des lettres aux XVe, XVIe et XVIIe siècles* (Paris: Michel Levy Freres, 1860). For the roles of discipline in the early modern schoolroom, see Rebecca Bushnell, *A Culture of Teaching: Early Modern Humanism in Theory and Practice* (Ithaca: Cornell University Press, 1996), chap. 2, "The Sovereign Master and the Scholar Prince," 23–72. On the "discipline" of Latin language instruction, see Walter J. Ong, "Latin Language Study as a Renaissance Puberty Rite," *Studies in Philology* 56 (1959): 103–24. Ong sees Latin learning in the Elizabethan grammar schools as a "Renaissance puberty rite"; the sexual segregation of the schools, their strict corporal discipline, insistence upon obedience and imitation, and emphasis on such epic/heroic values, in classical literature, as courage and bravery, led to a hardening of the individual student "for the extra-familial world in which he would have to live" (123).

78. For the influence of the Inns of Court on embodied writing, see Philip Finkelpearl, *John Marston of the Middle Temple: An Elizabethan Dramatist in His Social*

Setting (Cambridge, Mass.: Harvard University Press, 1969), and Arthur F. Marotti, *John Donne, Coterie Poet* (Madison: University of Wisconsin Press, 1986), 3–95, who explores the social conditions of Donne's early verse. More recently, Kenneth Alan Hovey has explored the lingering influence of Francis Bacon's tenure at the Inns of Court, and its hospitality to "parabolic" dramas, for our understanding of his later works and politics. See "Bacon's Parabolical Drama: Iconoclastic Philosophy and Elizabethan Politics," in *Francis Bacon's Legacy of Texts: The Art of Discovery Grows With Discovery,* ed. William A. Sessions (New York: AMS Press, 1990), 215–36.

79. For the early modern "commonwealth of wit" as a "social institution in Vosskamp's and Luhmann's sense," see Eckhard Auberlen, *The Commonwealth of Wit: The Writer's Image and His Strategies of Self-Representation in Elizabethan Literature.* Studies and Texts in English 5 (Tübingen: Narr, 1984).

80. I include in the former number an entry of thirty-five for Marlowe, his age in 1599 had he lived. I follow received estimates of birth dates for Marston (1575?), Middleton (1580?), and Whitgift (1530?).

81. On the decline of patronage during the 1590s, see Alistair Fox, "The Complaint of Poetry for the Death of Liberality: The Decline of Literary Patronage in the 1590s," in Guy, ed., *Reign of Elizabeth I,* 229–57. The "paranoia of the establishment" is described by Guy in the introduction to this study, 11.

82. *Hamlet,* quotations from 2.2.524–25 and 5.1.139–41.

83. Nashe, preface to *Astrophel and Stella* (1591), in McKerrow, ed., *Works of Thomas Nashe,* 3:329.

84. See Paul Yachnin, "The Powerless Theater," *English Literary Renaissance* 21 (1991): 49–74.

CHAPTER THREE

Pamphlet Surplus: John Taylor and Subscription Publication

Alexandra Halasz

John Taylor, who wrote some two hundred pamphlets between 1612 and 1653 on a range of topics that defies classification, is a spectacular example of proliferation in print.[1] Taylor came relatively late to his writing practice (he was in his early thirties when he first published); he was also a waterman, serving in naval expeditions, ferrying passengers across and along the Thames, and occupying positions in the hierarchy of his Company—hence his moniker, The Water-Poet. In traditional literary history Taylor is noted primarily for the 1630 folio edition of his previously published pamphlets and because he apparently arranged for the publication of some of his work by prepublication subscription (an uncommon occurrence in any case and more so among secular pamphleteers).[2]

I want to focus here on the issue of subscription, on the fact that over the years Taylor repeatedly staged what I will call a subscription scenario, in which he claimed that many people had promised to pay him directly upon a pamphlet's appearance and had not done so. The subscription scenario appears in Taylor's pamphlets as early as 1619 and intermittently until the end of his writing life. There are two points that must be made immediately. The first is that it is not at all clear whether the subscription scenario is fact or fiction.[3] Only a handful of Taylor's pamphlets bear an imprint ("printed at the author's charge") that explicitly supports the thesis of subscription publication, and at least one of these titles is nonetheless entered in the Stationers' Register as the Copy of Henry Gosson, the publisher involved with a significant number of Taylor's pamphlets.[4] The second point is that subscription envisions, among other things, a direct relation between writer/producer and reader/consumer.

But the most intriguing aspect of the subscription scenario is that it breaks down, revealing a problem in commensurating production and consumption. I take as a useful metatext here Marx's cryptic formulation in the *Grundrisse* of the relations between production and consumption: "Production mediates consumption; it creates the latter's material; without it consumption would lack an object. But consumption also mediates production in that it alone creates for the products the subjects for whom they are products."[5] In other words, the commodity object is poised between the capacity to produce it and the possibility of its uselessness, its rejection or non-recognition as an object. Here, it might be argued, Marx anticipates the more general critique of use value, that it too, like exchange value, is a socially constructed category. But that would be to argue only one side of Marx's formulation—that production creates consumption, creates both the need for the object and its exchange value. The other side of Marx's formulation, however, suggests that consumption is itself a form of production, that only consumption can make the commodity into an object that has social meaning. Successful subscription might be said to literalize the second half of Marx's formulation. Subscribers invest in the prospect of production, signing on as the subjects for whom the pamphlet is produced and thus insuring that the commodity will not languish between production and consumption. But how can we read unsuccessful subscription and, especially, repeated unsuccessful subscription? What social meaning is carried by a commodity for which subjects have signed on but declined to pay? The subscription scenario is most extensively developed in relation to Taylor's travel pamphlets. In return for the money subscribers promise or give, they receive an account of his journey in pamphlet form. I want to begin, however, by focusing on Taylor's comments in two other pamphlets. In the preface to *Taylors Travels and Circular Perambulations* (1636), Taylor directly addresses the writer's position in the book trade:[6]

> I do request as many as do receive this small Pamphlet to take into their consideration, that I do expect they shall pay me for it. I am sure there hath beene within these 30 years more than 200 impressions of Bookes in my name. For though I have not written above 80. yet some of them hath been printed 10 or 12 times over, 1500 or 2000 every time. Amongst which

number of Pamphlets, I am sure that (first and last) I have given freely for nothing (never expecting anything but thankes) above 30000. books (besides those I have been rewarded for). (*Workes,* 3d collection, 3–4)

The pamphlet itself contains an alphabetical listing of tavern signs and their locations in London, interspersed with epigrams on the symbols used in the signs. The request in the preface that receivers of the pamphlet pay him for it coexists with the recognition that "books in [his] name" are produced and sold far more often without his participation. The preface to *Taylors Travels* envisions a direct monetary exchange between writer and reader, but not, explicitly, subscription. A similar request in a companion pamphlet (listing taverns in the surrounding shires, by town) to those "that are to pay, me money, upon the receiving, or this my publishing my small book" and thereby might "worke a piece of wonder, (which is, to make a Rich Poet)" more strongly suggests a scenario of subscription together with an ironic recognition of its impossibility.[7]

It could be argued that Taylor's invocation of a direct monetary exchange between reader and writer functions as a reminder of the material relations and positions obscured by the channels of production and distribution in the marketplace, which usually preclude any direct contact between writer and reader. I am arguing inter alia that this is indeed the case, that Taylor repeatedly addresses the marketplace-situatedness of his writing and that a certain range of his writing is devoted to describing what might be called the infrastructure of a market-based economy. A pamphlet like *A shilling, or travailes of twelve-pence* (1621), for example, addresses not only the mediating function of the coin—figuring the process of endless exchange in the marketplace—but also thematizes the circulation of discourse as an exchange value. Similarly the pamphlet describing London tavern signs performs a mapping function, gathering the dispersed sites of drink and conversation into the pamphlet, which then circulates, its own conversational exchange figured in the epigrams commenting on the signs.

The subscription scenario, however, is not simply a direct exchange between reader and writer, a payment of money for the book. Not only does the exchange take place outside of the marketplace, as it were, but also the money promised or paid exceeds the market value of the book. The writer promises to execute a certain labor and to produce tangible evidence of that labor in the form of the book. He solicits from the subscriber an investment in the process of production. What Taylor's subscription scenario specifically suggests, then, is an entrepreneurial model of discursive production. He sets himself up as an entrepreneur who undertakes a certain labor and risk and expects a return on his investment of time and energy. In an entrepreneurial model of discursive production, the emphasis falls on labor rather than the object produced. There is no claim of mastery in the shaping of the object, only one of time and energy spent, of what might be called an existential loss.[8] The figure of the entrepreneur occupies the position of laborer and capitalist simultaneously, for he theoretically controls both the conditions of his work and the distribution of the product of that labor. What he loses as a laborer, he hopes to recoup in the form of profit as a capitalist. In the completion of the exchange imagined by the subscription scenario, the reader's task becomes the mirror and continuation of the writer's (traveling from tavern to tavern, engaging time and energy in conversation). Discourse itself becomes a form of labor, a matter of time and energy endlessly reproducing itself, a continual process of loss and surplus. We might say, then, that the subscription scenario affords a means of converting exchange into a relation of continuity between writer and reader in which the reader fulfills and extends the implications of the writer's effort. Yet Taylor is certainly aware that the recognized entrepreneurs of the book trade were the Stationers, those who make "impressions of Bookes in [his] name," and thus place him in the position of "[giving] freely for nothing." The fact that Taylor's subscription scenarios always include a breakdown in the desired relation between writer/producer and reader/consumer might be read as an indirect acknowledgment of the Stationers' role. To do so, however, would foreclose the ways in which the scenario works to implicate the reader too as an entrepreneur.

At the end of a pamphlet called *Kicksey-Winsey: or a Lerry come-twang: wherein J. Taylor hath satyrically suited 800. of his bad debtors* (1619), Taylor appends a "Defence of Adventures upon Returnes" in which he argues that "all men in the world are Adventurers upon Returne" (*Workes*, 202).[9] As its full title might suggest, *Kicksey-Winsey* is the pamphlet most heavily entangled in the question of Taylor's subscription publication. In it he expostulates with those who "will not pay him for his return of his journey from Scotland"(*Workes*, 196). The journey referred to is detailed in *A Pennilesse Pilgrimage* (1618). Taylor undertook to travel from London to Edinburgh without money, depending on the hospitality of those he encountered on his way for subsistence, lodging, and entertainment. That is, the journey consisted of an endless exchange of conversation for the means that would allow continued conversation. According to the pamphlet, the journey was successfully completed in the summer and early fall of 1618. No mention is made in *Pennilesse Pilgrimage* of prepublication subscription. The bad debtors listed in *Kicksey-Winsey* are not named but described by category ("those that have paid," "those that would pay if they could," "those that are fled," etc.). In a second edition of *Kicksey-Winsey* published in 1624, Taylor brings a number of his other travel pamphlets under its address to bad debtors, pamphlets detailing voyages to Germany, Bohemia, York, Salisbury, and a voyage down the Thames in a boat made of brown paper.[10] None of these pamphlets refers to prepublication subscribers. Indeed, in the preface to *Taylors Travels to Prague in Bohemia* (1621), Taylor addresses his reader in a scenario implying that his books were marketed in a bookshop: "I have not given my book a swelling bumbasted title, or a promising inside of newes; therefore if you look for such matter from hence, take this warning, hold fast your money, and lay the booke down" (*Workes*, 574). It is, of course, entirely possible that all (or most) of Taylor's travel pamphlets were printed at his charge, and the fact that only a few so specify results from an absence of standardized procedures.[11] The "bills" detailing the subscription agreement would logically have been printed as separate objects, making their survival unlikely.

It is also possible that the money supposedly paid or promised to Taylor before his journeys was not a subscription per se, but a wager laid on the probability of his completing the journeys according to the particulars set forth in his "bill."[12] Such a wager implicates the potential reader in the speculative venture of the entrepreneur, that is, implicates the reader in the outcome of time and event, in the performance of the writer's labor. The subscription is then not an exchange so much as an elaborate game for which the minimum cost of entry is something above the price of a pamphlet, and greater investments are encouraged. Taylor always "wins" the wager. The subscriber also "wins," for the wagering game is itself a pleasure and, for the subscriber, risk free. Reading the subscription as a bet would allow us to account for both the publication of *Pennilesse Pilgrimage* at the author's charge and for the trade's apparent sponsorship of some of the other titles among Taylor's travel books. Taylor's primary entrepreneurial activity would then consist in setting up the "wagering journey," and the publication of the pamphlet would be a separate but intertwined activity, subject to the usual marketplace practices of buying and selling.

It is also possible to understand the money supposedly paid or promised to Taylor before his journeys specifically in relation to the economy of travel, to the need for an "expense account." Even the "penniless pilgrimage" involved an outlay of cash: Taylor began the journey with a pack animal and a knapsack of provisions. Later journeys involved the expenses of horses, coaches, and boats as well as food and lodging. The money is thus given to enable the journey; those who pay are "sponsors" of the trip, to borrow Bernard Capp's term.[13] Subscribers provide the cash outlay the journey requires and receive in exchange an account of the journey. In this reading, subscription becomes a form of patronage, and it is once again possible to separate Taylor's entrepreneurial activity from the publication of the pamphlet. Reading along these lines and taking Taylor's claims in *Kicksey-Winsey* at face value, Bernard Capp estimates that the publication of *Pennilesse Pilgrimage* brought Taylor a profit of £450, despite the default of a large number of subscribers.[14]

If the subscription is seen as a bet or as a cash fund enabling Taylor's journeys, the money implied by the subscription scenario is not functioning as a means of exchange, for it exists in a disproportionate relation to the value for which it is exchanged. We could say, then, that it functions as a signifier of Taylor's desire to capitalize on his travels, on his work. And both a wagering game and a patronage situation suggest that the capital at stake for Taylor is not simply economic, for he also gains fame and gentlemanly acquaintance, if not companionship. In *Pennilesse Pilgrimage* he reports at length on his inclusion in aristocratic hunting parties, for example, and his meeting with Ben Jonson outside of Edinburgh. So we might say that the money in the subscription scenario signifies both economic and cultural capital. This allows us to make sense of the fact that Taylor may well have received a considerable economic surplus from his subscription ventures and yet still made an issue of the unpaid balance, for in advertising the failure of gentlemen to honor their agreements, Taylor keeps his cultural capital in circulation.

But these readings account only for the side of production, and they do not account at all for Taylor's insistence that production has netted him loss rather than surplus. Let us return then to the idea of subscription as a cash fund enabling the journey. Taylor travels and then writes his travels. On the way he meets local dignitaries and is often well entertained. In what then does Taylor's labor consist? In the traveling or the writing? Taylor gets to take the trip and claim it as work. Is the journey itself a perquisite? Or is the doubled claim of labor—traveling and writing—a justification of his claim for payment in excess of the usual compensation to writers? Is the surplus figured by the excess in his claim for payment a means of exposing the surplus value that, Marx would later argue, is masked in the commodity? In his complaints about unpaid subscriptions, Taylor repeatedly asserts the effort and discomfort of travel, its existential cost to him. The only adequate recompense, he insists, would be all the subscription monies. We can read Taylor's insistence in Marx's terms: the pamphlet is the commodified form of the labor expended, both the outcome of that labor and the means by which the writer is compensated not only for his labor (direct exchange) but also for the value created by the commodity (surplus value). Though I would argue that the subscription scenario does advance an economistic understanding of surplus along the lines Marx later develops, it is not wholly convincing as an explanation of the reiteration of the subscription scenario. So we are left with Taylor's insistence on his losses—losses represented by the unpaid subscription monies and presumably materially present in a surplus of pamphlets available for sale.

We can now begin to see why the subscription scenario always breaks down—indeed, must break down. Taylor's claim that his labor results in a loss tacitly argues that his labor has produced a surplus. That is, the effect of the breakdown is to expose the existence of a surplus. And only the breakdown can expose the side of consumption. At least some readers acquire information or pleasure without having to compensate the writer for the full extent of his effort and without having to work to organize or acquire that information or pleasure. Whether readers subscribe or not, whether subscribers pay as promised or not, readers are, from the side of consumption, the beneficiaries of a condition of surplus created by the writer. Thus the subscription scenario calls attention to a doubled surplus conveyed by the commodity/pamphlet. The producer's loss of time and energy produces both the economic surplus of profit and a cultural one of accumulated information or pleasure and the leisure it implies. In this reading, Taylor becomes an enthusiastic apologist for a developing commodity economy. And we arrive again at a reading of the money in the subscription scenario as a signifier of both economic and cultural forms of surplus, but with a difference, for the unpaid money marks a surplus that does not accrue to the writer/producer. Nor is it linked to the Stationers in the conventional operation of the book trade. In the breakdown of the subscription scenario the money is significant because it is unpaid. It marks, I am arguing, a surplus that is not immediately economic, a surplus that accrues to readers. But if, as I suggested earlier, the subscription scenario works to implicate both writer and reader in an entrepreneurial logic, the unpaid money must be susceptible to an economic reading as well.

In the late pamphlets whose surviving exemplars include a "bill," the bill is an integral part of the pamphlet. Not only does it function as a preface or part of a preface but it is sometimes a continuous part of the object, printed on the same sheet as the title page and the first few pages of text. Often in verse, the bills set out the basic elements of the subscription scenario: that Taylor undertakes a journey upon completion of which he will present a printed account of that journey to those who have signed their names and dwellings. The bill printed at the beginning of *Taylors Travels from London. to the Isle of Wight* (1649), though atypical in its prose and its legalistic language, makes the implied contract of all the bills explicit:

> When John Taylor hath beene from London to the Isle of Wight and returned againe, and that at his returne, he doe give or cause to be given to me, Booke or Pamphlet of true newes and relations of Passages at the Island, and to and fro in his Jorney; I doe promise to give to him or his assignes, the summe of what I please in Lawfull money of England, provided that the sayd summe be not under 6 pence. (*Workes,* Fourth Collection, [1])

The bill establishes a contract between Taylor as creditor and the signer/subscriber as debtor. Moreover, in its allowance for assignment, the bill functions as a partly negotiable instrument; the subscriber's debt may be paid to a third party designated by Taylor. This particular bill, then, could be read as acknowledging the position of the Stationer, but for the fact that the title page on which the bill appears also carries an imprint stating that it was "printed at the author's charge" and is "nowhere to be sold." More to the point, the economic structure created by the bill approximates that of a (inland) bill of exchange. It inscribes the pamphlet not in the visible marketplace sites of commodity sale and purchase but in the financial relations that underwrite the production and circulation of commodities.

The stipulated minimum debt of six pence once again calls attention to a surplus, for it is a highly inflated price for a twelve-page pamphlet. If we assume that the bill circulated separately, prior to the production of the pamphlet, subscribers would be incurring a debt on which they would not realize full value. They would be investing in Taylor and his project(s) rather than in a particular value/good that would return to them. If we assume a breakdown in the subscription relation, or a situation in which the bill and imprint are fictional, and thus that the reader acquires the pamphlet in customary ways at usual prices, then the bill in effect argues that the reader benefits by getting the pamphlet at a "cut rate" price. In either case, Taylor, as the drawer of the bill, occupies the position of the capitalist, and the (potential) reader is willy-nilly inscribed within a logic of capital, either as an investor in Taylor-pamphlet-futures or as the beneficiary of the price reduction enabled by capitalist production.

The breakdown in the subscription scenario secures Taylor's position as creditor. That is to say, it rewrites his "loss" as a situation in which his readership is forever indebted to him. Taylor's position as creditor also paradoxically underwrites the reader's avoidance of loss, for though readers are indebted to him, the circumstances of pamphlet production and circulation compel the writer toward a position of continued production—continuing adventures upon return for the writer and continuing returns for the reader. The ongoing subscription scenario and its repeated breakdown thus figure a continuous effort to bring the positions of writer and reader into some kind of equilibrium. This is the logic of seriality, of journalism. It is a logic that reveals a constitutive disequilibrium between the economic circumstances in which discourse is produced and distributed as a commodity and the social implications of its dissemination as discourse. Produced as commodities, Taylor's pamphlets yield a cultural surplus in the information or pleasure they convey. They also, more generally, yield a dialectic of surplus and loss, or lack, in the desire for or expectation of such discourses. "Consumption," Marx wrote in his notebook, "*ideally* posits the object of production as an internal image as a need, as drive and as purpose."[15]

Taylor's subscription scenario needs to be read, I want to suggest, as presenting a constitutive problematic in what we have come to call the public sphere. The premise of subscription sets up an economic calculus in which production and consumption exist in a predictable balance, a perfect circuit. By disrupting that circuit, breakdown does not so much reinstitute a separation between production and consumption as reveal that they are simultaneously inextricably related and incommensurable. Production cannot be commensurated with consumption because the unfolding of consumption rehearses and creates social meanings not bound by the transactions of sale and purchase in the marketplace. Consumption is always either in excess of production or falling short—in either case, beckoning renewed production and precipitating the reciprocating rhythm of loss and surplus, the pamphlet surplus that Taylor's subscription scenario reveals. Subscription posits a closed system of production and consumption; breakdown, a dissemination that is open-ended, unpredictable, promiscuous.

Both the mix of discourses Taylor's pamphlets contain and their frequent triviality offend the rationality and civic highmindedness associated with the notion of a public sphere. But I would argue that Taylor gets it right, that a public sphere—then or now—cannot be separated from the economic interests invested in the production of discourse as a commodity. But a pamphlet—whether or not printed at its author's charge—becomes a discourse nowhere to be sold precisely because the production of discourse as a commodity precipitates a dissemination beyond the marketplace, one that cannot be foretold, or counted. Successful subscription might indeed gesture toward the nightmare of a liberal public sphere, normatively disinterested and rational and yet always contaminated or scandalized by market (or private) interests.[16] Unsuccessful subscription, however, bespeaks multiple and various interests in production and at the same time, a reservation of judgment on and commitment to the product itself. And repeated unsuccessful subscription foregrounds the incommensurability between production and consumption as the defining circumstance in which discourse exists as a commodity and as a form of labor, a matter of time and energy endlessly reproducing itself, a continual process of loss and surplus. The subscription scenario suggests that we ought not to think of a public sphere in spatial terms but as a process and one that is simultaneously susceptible and resistant to efforts of control.

Taylor is most often invoked as a protojournalistic figure and as such might be said singularly to anticipate a public sphere identified with journalism proper. Both the sheer quantity and the range of Taylor's production also suggest that his writing might be provocatively juxtaposed to that of seventeenth-century polymaths who produced volumes of manuscript treatises on various topics. If, in both cases, the labor of production is apparently endless, the results of that labor are perceived in significantly different ways. The labor of polymaths is a gathering of knowledges, a process of accumulation, a formation of cultural capital. Though that cultural capital might be converted into economic capital by deploying it either privately (to secure elite forms of employment) or publicly (as a knowledge-factor of production) in the marketplace, its status as cultural capital depends on a continued accumulation apart from the market.

Taylor's endless production yields discourses that, in contrast, do not accumulate but are endlessly dispersed, a dispersal that, in turn, precipitates renewed production. The underlying logic is homologous with that of capital itself, which accumulates by means of continual dispersal.

If Taylor's pamphlet production, and specifically the subscription scenario, imply a public sphere conceived as a process, an endless production and dispersal of discourse, his enthusiastic apology for a developing capitalist economy also marks the historical entanglement of the public sphere with that emergent economy. But the classic liberal notion of a public sphere derives from the labor of the polymaths. Considered in spatial terms, the public sphere marks a privileged space of discourse, the sharing of accumulated cultural wealth and the shaping of choices about the deployment of that wealth, as if those choices could be made apart from not only state power but also the operations of capital. By focusing our attention on the structural homology between the operations of discourse and capital, Taylor's subscription scenario affords a means of rethinking the historical entanglement between the public sphere and a capitalist socioeconomic formation.

Notes

1. In 1642, John Taylor claimed to have written some 220 "books" in the previous thirty years. In his recent biography of Taylor, *The World of John Taylor, The Water-Poet, 1578–1653* (Oxford: Clarendon Press, 1994), Bernard Capp arrives at a lower figure of about 150 separate titles and half a million individual copies (66–67).

2. The evidence of subscription publication in the early seventeenth century is sparse, Taylor being the ubiquitous example and the only pamphleteer. See Marjorie Plant, *The English Book Trade* (London: George Allen and Unwin, 1965) and Phoebe Sheavyn, *The Literary Profession in the Elizabethan Age*, 2d ed., revised by J. W. Saunders (Manchester: Manchester University Press, 1967).

3. All the evidence for Taylor's subscription publication rests on claims Taylor makes in the published writing. Capp's biography does cite one piece of external evidence, a pledge of one pound toward Taylor's journey to Scotland (discussed below) recorded in Edward Alleyn's diary (64). Capp also compares what he calls Taylor's sponsored journeys with those undertaken by Gervase Markham, Thomas Coryate, and William Kemp. As I discuss below, money given in sponsorship of a journey or as a wager on the likelihood of the journey's success is not subscription per se.

4. *Pennilesse Pilgrimage* (STC 23784), discussed below, is entered to Gosson. It is possible that the entry was part of a deal between Taylor and Gosson, the pam-

phlet printed at Taylor's charges but distributed and sold by Gosson. Though Gosson did not reissue *Pennilesse Pilgrimage,* he did reissue a number of other pamphlets by Taylor and entered to Gosson. If Gosson indeed owned the copies of a number of Taylor pamphlets, he would, of course, have received a fee or some form of compensation when they were reprinted in the folio.

5. Karl Marx, *Grundrisse,* trans. Martin Nicolaus (Harmondsworth, England: Penguin Books, 1973), 91.

6. Printed by A. M[atthewes], entered to Henry Gosson. All citations of Taylor are from the Spenser Society reprints of his work in five volumes between 1869 and 1877. The folio is printed in its entirety in a single volume and the remaining pamphlets in four quarto editions. Only the folio reprint has editorially added continuous pagination. Citations from the folio refer to the page number of the Spenser Society reprint of the folio and take the form *Workes,* 00. Citations from the quarto collections refer to the pagination of individual pamphlets and take the form *Workes,* nth collection, 00.

7. *The Honorable, and Memorable Foundations . . . of divers Cities . . . Also a Relation of the Wine Taverns . . . .* (*Workes,* 4th collection, 6).

8. In *An Arrant Thief whom every man may trust . . . with a comparison between a thief and a book* (1622), life itself is figured as a continual loss. Good books/honest thieves transcend this condition of loss by "stealing the mind from vaine pretences," while "bad books through eyes and ears do breake and / take possession of the hearts fraile Center"(*Workes,* 286).

9. The examples he offers in support of his proposition encompass noneconomic and economic activities alike: "who ever is an Idolater . . . or lyer, or . . . usuerer . . . doth tempt God, adventure their soules, and upon returne, lose Heaven"; "a merchant doth adventure ships, and goods, . . . all for hope of profit, which often fayles"; "he or shee who are proud either of beauty, riches, wit, learning . . . does adventure to be accounted vainglorious" (*Workes,* 202).

10. In its second issue the pamphlet is called *The Scourge of Baseness.* It is the second issue that is reprinted in the folio.

11. In "Printing for the Author: From the Bowyer Printing Ledgers, 1710–1775," *The Library,* 5th ser., 27 [1972]: 302–9, Keith Maslen examines eighteenth-century evidence of publication at the author's charges using the ledger records to supply information lacking in imprints. He finds that imprints often do not indicate authorial investment in the economics of publication. To my knowledge no such records survive for printing or publishing houses in the late sixteenth or early seventeenth centuries.

12. In "The Peculiar Peregrinations of John Taylor the Water Poet: A Study in Seventeenth-Century British Travel Literature," *Prose Studies: History, Theory, Criticism* 6 (1983): 3–26, Warren Wooden suggests that Taylor initially set up "wagering journeys" with a "handicap" to excite interest and make the wager significant and then dropped the premise of a handicap. Wooden assumes that Taylor did indeed "develop [a] mass subscription system" (14), though he is primarily interested in the themes and modes of Taylor's travel narratives.

13. In his initial essay on Taylor, "John Taylor 'the Water-Poet,'" *History of European Ideas* 11 (1989): 537–44, Bernard Capp takes Taylor's assertions about

subscription, the number of subscribers, etc. at face value. The notion of sponsorship developed in the later biography offers the possibility of a more complex understanding, though Capp continues to assume subscription publication.

14. Capp, *The World of John Taylor*, 65.

15. *Grundrisse*, 92. Italics in original.

16. Jürgen Habermas, *The Structural Transformation of the Public Sphere* (Cambridge, Mass.: MIT Press, 1989) is the standard account. See also Bruce Robbins, ed., *The Phantom Public Sphere* (Minneapolis: University of Minnesota Press, 1993).

CHAPTER FOUR

Wither and Professional Work
Joseph Loewenstein

In his second publication, a collection of plaintive eclogues entitled *The Shepherd's Hunting* (1615), George Wither falls quite casually into an argument on behalf of the rights of literary labor:

> But, thou know'st, I am but yong,
> And the Pastorall I sung,
> Is by some suppos'd to be
> (By a straine) too high for me:
> So they kindly let me gaine,
> Not my labour for my paine.[1]

According to its title page, *The Shepherd's Hunting* was "written during the authors imprisonment in the Marshalsey," where he had been confined as a punishment for his first publication, *Abuses Stript and Whipt*.[2] Wither will not be constrained to mere complaint here or anywhere; again and again, *The Shepherd's Hunting* is enlivened by the way satire sharpens pastoral.[3] It's worth listening again to that snide "kindly" and to how faintly the ensuing "Trust me" curls the lip of Wither's speaker, Willy:

> So they kindly let me gaine,
> Not my labour for my paine.
> Trust me, I doe wonder why
> They should me my owne deny.

> Though I'me young, I scorne to flit
> On the wings of borrowed wit.[4]

It's interesting that Willy's argument should not come properly into focus until this last couplet: the language of "kindly" misappropriated labor so unexpected in pastoral, but appropriate enough to the actualities of rural labor, only serves, we finally gather, to counter the accusation that Willy, the pastoral figure for Wither's friend, William Browne, is a plagiarist.[5]

The Shepherd's Hunting was written in 1614, fairly early in Wither's career, but this passage in the fourth eclogue initiates a distinctive line of analysis, argument, and action that would carry right through his career. There is, of course, nothing particularly distinctive about rebutting a charge of plagiarism—such charges and such rebuttals had become staples of English literary culture during the previous two decades—but the emphasis on poesis as labor, on attribution as a wage, and on contested attribution as a misappropriation of labor power whereby the accusers "let me gaine / Not my labour for my paine," is pure George Wither, whether or not it is what Charles Lamb was thinking of when he wrote, in one of the few post-seventeenth-century appreciations of Wither, that "his poems are full . . . of a generous self-seeking."

Less than a decade after this firm, if rudimentary, assertion of the rights proper to poetic labor, Wither reissued *The Shepherd's Hunting* under the fastidious rubric of *Juvenilia*. The new rubric is gently dismissive, putting pastoral in a charming but trivial box. Despite a steady production of amatory verse in the intervening years, Wither had led a revival in the production of satiric poetry and had come more and more to take seriously his occasional stance as a poet-prophet. Thus in his 1614 *Satire to the King*, an unapologetic appeal for royal intercession during his imprisonment, Wither insists upon the moral and political responsibilities of the poet, and he sustains this insistence in the long poem of 1621, *Wither's Motto*, which also landed him in jail.[6] But during the same period that he so boldly asserted and assumed the poet's responsibilities to an elect nation, Wither had also been a self-seeking activist on behalf of the poet's rights: this decade of activism begins with the sketchy pastoral evocation of poetic labor and literary property in *The Shepherd's Hunting* and ends with a substantial elaboration of that sketch in *The Scholler's Purgatory*, the book with which I will be primarily concerned here.

This book and the events that surround it have not been much referred to in recent work on English authorship and the book trade, and my chief purpose is to make certain that they do not escape historicist attention. I want to restore Wither's place in the scholarly conversation, since he makes an appreciable contribution to that discourse of property—and in his case specifically, of intellectual property—that developed within the late Tudor and early Stuart struggle over monopolies.[7] Thanks to Lyman Ray Patterson, D. F. Foxon, and Mark Rose, students of the long eighteenth century can have a fairly clear sense of the commercial tensions and political arguments that gave rise to statutory copyright; it is common knowledge that authors themselves did little to advance the legislation and that, for a long time, they gained little by it.[8] But the myth has been perpetuated that authors before the Statute of Anne (1709), the statutory foundation of English authorial copyright, had little or no interest in the highly monopolistic structure of the book trade and that, insofar as authors exerted themselves to change the norms of publishing, theirs was a resistance, not to business as usual, but only to the various institutions of and explosions of censorship. The author of *Areopagitica* stands as the great mythographer of this conception of early modern authorship, although he makes passing dismissive remarks against "some old patentees and monopolizers in the trade of book-selling"; my mere purpose here is to present the author of *The Scholler's Purgatory* as the great historiographer of early modern authorship, or at least of that important aspect of authorship that was constituted specifically as a trade function.[9]

Wither addresses *The Scholler's Purgatory* to the Convocation of 1624, asking the bishops to take his part in a struggle that had erupted the previous year between himself and the Stationers' Company.[10] He had been walking a very thin line since at least 1621, when *Wither's Motto* was first printed. The wardens of the Stationers' Company, in their semiofficial status as press licensers, apparently refused to allow it; and when one of their company did print the book and then went on to print a second impression despite an explicit injunction not to do so, the printer was fined. Nor had the matter ended there. Because the book seemed to exult over the death of Northampton and to cast some aspersions on Buckingham, Wither and several of the stationers involved were called before a committee of the House of Lords in 1621, and Wither again landed in the Marshalsea where he endured a brief but apparently rigorous confinement. Jonson kept the matter alive by lampooning Wither in *Time Vindicated*, his masque for the 1622–23 Christmas season; this part of the story is particularly choice since it gives us Jonson attacking a writer for overearnestness, self-righteousness, and presumption to moral superiority. By this time

Wither's Motto had gone through several more or less surreptitious editions, and had won Wither an impressive popular audience: in *Fragmenta Prophetica* (1669) he claimed that the book sold 30,000 copies in the course of its early printings, and however exaggerated this may be, Jonson's attack in *Time Vindicated* also entails scorn for Wither's broad lower-class appeal. The attack backfired—nothing new for Jonson—but it backfired in a revealing way. John Chamberlain reported that "Ben Johnson . . . is like to heare of yt on both sides of the head for personating George Withers." Here is evidence that Wither was capable of more than popular appeal, that he had found himself at least some influential supporters—Pembroke certainly, but also, it seems, the king himself—and was not to suffer permanently for his pose as Chrono-mastix. Whatever one thinks of Wither as a poet, he had already occasionally shown a rich tactical instinct. Perhaps nearly anyone could have observed, as Wither had back in 1614, that "what care soe're we take, / Divers constructions of our Writings make," but few might, addressing the king, compare the polysemy of poetry to "your owne Lawes, which (as you do intend) / In plain'st and most effectuall words are penn'd" but which "cannot be fram'd so well to your intent, / But some there be will erre from what you meant." By means of this poem, the Satire to the King, Wither seems to have leveraged his position pretty adroitly. It had helped him gain his first release from the Marshalsea during his first time and its publication in 1622 advertised him as one who could speak plainly to his monarch. Jonson had chosen the wrong target.

For five weeks after the performance of Jonson's masque, on 17 February, James favored Wither with an extraordinary grant, a patent that conferred on Wither, his assigns, and heirs, what amounted to a fifty-one year copyright in Wither's *Hymns and Songs of the Church*.[11] Wither had demonstrated his interest in biblical poetry as early as 1619 when he published the *Preparation to the Psalter*, a long treatise in which Wither defends vernacular psalm translation, argues its tactics, and details the devotional uses to be made of an English Psalter.[12] In an attempt to create and shape an audience—what we might call a market—for his work, he had offered the work as a display of his own qualifications as a biblical translator and as a prospectus for the serial publication of fifteen "decades" of Englished psalms suitable for singing and thus presumably designed to compete with Sternhold and Hopkins.[13] The promised collections were slow in coming. The next year saw the publication of a volume of commentaries, verse and prose translations, meditations, and variations on the first psalm, but no "decades"; indeed, Wither's complete Psalter didn't appear until 1632. Still, Wither found another way to assume the mantle of biblical poesy by publishing *The Hymns and Songs of the Church,* which included translations of all the other lyrics in the canonical scriptures, including the Song of Songs, set to melodies by Orlando Gibbons. Vocational ambition partnered with commercial savvy, for the English audience had a deep, nearly physiological attachment to the Sternhold and Hopkins Psalter, which was not to be easily displaced, even by the most popular of contemporary poets. But the *Hymns* could make for an apt complement, and given Wither's popularity, its market would be large, so James's patent would have been a very substantial financial boon.

Although the royal grant of something like authorial copyright was highly unusual, it was not unprecedented. Timothy Bright had received a similar grant for his treatise on shorthand as early as 1589, though this looks less like an early determination of literary property than the protection of a new technology, which latter was quite a common object of protection by patent.[14] But a small number of authors secured patents in the sale of nontechnical works—John Norden for his *Speculum Brittaniae* in 1592; Arthur Golding, near the end of his life, for all his works; Thomas Middleton, for *The Peacemaker* in 1618, which patent he conferred on William Alley; Samuel Daniel for his *Historie of England,* also in 1618. Indeed, royal printing patents of one sort or another had been conferred since the second decade of the sixteenth century, though they had usually been conferred on members of the book trade. An old institution, the printing patent supervened upon the institution of guild copyright by which the Stationers regulated their own competitive practices: the novelty of these patents is that they gave authors a direct financial interest in the sale of their printed works. Still, the handful of authorial patents had not appreciably unsettled the normal structures of property and production in the book trade, but the grant to Wither was different, for it contained the unusual stipulation "that no English Psalme-Booke in Meeter, shall be bound up alone, or with any other Booke or Bookes, unlesse the said Hymnes and Songs of the Church be annexed thereunto."[15] The Stationers were outraged.[16]

The enormity of the grant is fairly easy to understand. The Psalter was one of the major texts of English devotional practice, perhaps the major text of private devotional practice; along with the Primer and the Catechism, it provided one of the crucial matrices of popular literacy and it was, therefore, a mainstay of the English book trade.[17] The Psalter was one of the first books protected by royal patent and was thus one of the primitive engines of accelerated capital formation within the Stationers' Company.[18] The patent had been frequently, almost steadily, infringed from 1560 forward, and by the mid-1570s it had become a focus of polarizing struggles within the book trade, an icon of monopolistic abuse.[19] During the eighties the holders of the most lucrative printing patents initiated a strategy of appeasement by selling an interest in their patents to a number of the leading malcontents within the company; out of these arrangements grew the English Stock, an immensely profitable joint-stock company within the stationers' guild. This mitigated but did not dispel discontent within the company, nor did it put an end to infringement of the patent in the Psalter. To secure this contested property, the leading figures of the company petitioned for renewal of the old patents within three days of Elizabeth's death. In the terms of James's grant, which no doubt reflects the language of their petition, we can detect all the cunning of the petitioners' bad faith: the patent was awarded to the Stationers' Company as a whole, which functioned as a general agent of the English Stock, but ostensibly "for the benefit of the poore of the same" company.[20] One does not need hindsight to perceive the bad faith. Wither details the imposture in *The Scholler's Purgatory* as he moves from a sly prayer that he might be the only man alive who sought his "owne glory, and inriching," to a well-informed and sharply focused debunking of the Stationers' own humbug: "And whereas they object I have compassed a priveledge to the publike greevance ... I did not, as some of the Stationers have done, in the name of many, and by pretending the reliefe of the poore (whome they may be prooved therby to oppresse) monopolize the principall bookes of Sale within this Realme (even those wherein the whole commonwealth have a i[u]st interest) which is really one of those Monopolies that our State abhores."[21] What the state abhorred, the Stationers cultivated sometimes at considerable cost: in 1614, when a William Alley challenged the sharers' rights to the Psalter, the company had had to petition for a new version of the patent grant, and the sharers had to settle with Alley for £600.[22]

Many booksellers kept a large stock of Psalters; but Wither's grant required that all previously bound copies be unstitched and rebound together with *The Hymns and Songs of the Church* so that binders would have to be paid a second time for all extant bound stock. The Psalter was carefully priced for a mass audience, but Wither's grant stipulated that the Psalter now be sold with a text that would yield a volume enlarged by 70 percent—perhaps too large now for a small-format book, which would decrease the kinds of choice that could be offered to consumers, and now inevitably more expensive and therefore presumably less attractive to at least some of those pious worshippers for whom the Psalter might be one of the few books, perhaps the only book, they might wish to purchase. Here was a book, a property, that had long been difficult to protect from the most unruly members of a stratified industry: but Wither's grant wrested this book from exclusive Company jurisdiction and seemed to constitute, or to sketch, a form of property that had hitherto been absent from commercial relations within the book trade.[23] After a fruitless attempt to make terms with Wither, the Stationers determined on a simple and ill-judged course of noncompliance, and in the tempest that ensued Wither took occasion to mount the first sustained defense of authorial property.[24]

This was not, however, the organizing tactic of *The Scholler's Purgatory*, which was overwhelmingly determined by parliamentary politics. Not only did the Stationers refuse to sell or even to print Wither's *Hymns* (so that he was forced to hire one of the book trade's most notorious renegade printers, George Wood, who was in and out of prison as frequently as Wither), but they also mounted a campaign for the withdrawal of Wither's grant. In November of 1623 they addressed a petition to James, and when he proved unresponsive, they turned to the Commons early in its session of 1624. Political historians know this session as the occasion of the second of the two great parliamentary assaults on economic monopolies. Elizabeth's last parliament had petitioned the Crown for restraint in the granting of royal patents, but not until 1621 did the lower house undertake a systematic campaign against monopolistic grants. The session of 1624 issued in yet another petition to the Crown, this time couched as an argument based on common law—a petition of right and not of grace and therefore an ominous challenge to the prerogative. This was complemented by the famous Act of Monopolies, which has been called "the first statutory invasion of the prerogative."[25] But the invasion was merely the culmination of the skirmishing that filled the days of both the sessions of 1621 and 1624, during which the Committee on Grievances, chaired by Coke, together with the Committee on Trade, functioned effectively as Courts of Commercial Law, with an established procedure and attorneys who specialized in pleadings before them. To the annoyance of the king and his officers, the investigating committees regularly impounded documents concerning royal grants, so it is hardly surprising that, in May, it was commanded that Wither's patent be brought in.[26] No action on the matter is recorded. Wither might have sought protection for his own patent under article ten of the Statute of Monopolies, the article protecting printing patents from challenge, but—at least according to Wither—the Stationers were assiduously lobbying Commons against his grant. Wither may have decided to finesse the parliamentary inquiry by presenting himself before the Privy Council a few weeks after his summons to Parliament; for its part, the council willingly endorsed the patent: the two sites of jurisdiction instance the epochal polarization of parliamentary rights and royal prerogative. But the support of the Privy Council only slightly alleviated Wither's difficulties in exploiting the patent, hence his strident supplementary appeal to Convocation in *The Scholler's Purgatory*.[27]

The larger political battle over monopolies crucially determines Wither's argument. From the outset he takes pains to counter the charge that his own patent amounts to a monopoly and to expose the monopolistic character of normal commercial practice within the book trade. This gesture of *tu quoque* turns out to be extremely incisive, since Wither not only indicates how frequently Stationers themselves have been the recipients of printing patents, but he also protests—and for the first time, to my knowledge, in the history of the English book trade—the whole system of registration whereby the members "of their Corporation ... can and do setle upon the particular members thereof, a p[e]rpetuall interest in such Bookes as are Registred by them at their Hall, in their severall Names: and are secured in taking the ful benefit of those books, better then any Author can be by vertue of the Kings Grant, notwithstanding their first Coppies were purloyned from the trueowner, or imprinted without his leave."[28] The analysis is both shrewd and prescient, since it registers the implicit competition between printing patent and stationer's copyright, and anticipates how that friction would lead to the formulation of an authorial copyright based on features of these its two ancestors.[29]

Modern historians of the book trade have made few important advances on Wither's general assessment of the structural tensions within early English publishing. Not only does he discern the potent stresses between the various forms of monopolistic competition in the book trade, but he is also alert to its increasing stratification.[30] He casts himself as a spokesperson for the disadvantaged among the Company: "And verily, if you had heard, as I have done, how many of the Printers, of the Bookebynders, and of the yonger Bookesellers among them, do complain against most of their Governors, and how many matters of great consequence they do probably object: You would thinke it were unsufferable"

(G7v). This is astute enough, yet Wither has his limits as a tactician: he attacks the more fully capitalized monopolists, the publishers, and seeks to ally himself with the binders against them, yet his patent was at least as detrimental to binders as to publishers. Small wonder, then, that the binders declined the proffered "alliance," as witness their broadside against Wither's patent.[31] In *The Scholler's Purgatory* (8r–v), Wither claims that they had been compelled to lobby against him in Parliament, yet he surely underestimated the willingness of groups within the book trade to rally in solidarity, when the company's general monopoly was publicly challenged. He may have overestimated how much support he might garner from within the trade, but his satiric instincts enabled him to expose what had been and would for the next century be the Stationers' persistent strategy, which was to evade an argument about property by means of an argument about values. In the first few sentences of the book he charges, pungently, that the Stationers have "vilified his Hymnes, rather as Censurers then sellers of Bookes" (sig. i2), and much of the book is devoted to ridiculing the Stationers' claims to ideological scruple.[32]

Wither's argument murmurs with an intriguing new vocabulary, a rhetoric of authorial labor, elaborated from the motifs of hard pastoral. I am not a monopolist, he tells us, the booksellers are; I am an author, and that is to say I am a worker. Or, to quote Wither precisely, "the Stationers have . . . usurped upon the labours of all writers, that . . . have consumed their youth and fortunes in perfiting some laborious worke."[33] This is one of Wither's legacies to Milton, who uses such rhetoric with far less resolution, for when Milton evokes the laboring author in *Areopagitica*, something very like embarrassment compels him to refigure authorial effort into something more heroic: "When a man hath bin labouring the hardest labour in the deep mines of knowledge, hath furnisht in all their equipage, drawn forth his reasons as it were a battell raunged, scatter'd and defeated all objections in his way, calls out his adversary into the plain, etc."[34] For Wither, the poet-prophet, poetry is a vocation and a job: "I did not leape on a suddaine, or irreverently into this employment; but haveing consumed almost the yeares of an Apprenticeshipp in studies of this kind, I entred therinto conscionably" (C2v); he then goes on to give a concise but powerful analysis of the specific technical difficulties of translating Hebrew verse into English—again with the goal of describing the translator's work as work.[35] The intrinsic claims of effort animate the defense of his patent against which "there can be no publike grievance truely named . . . except it bee a griefe to some fewe Idle drones, to behould the laborious lyving upon the sweate of their owne browes."[36] This rhetoric of labor receives an odd, but characteristic inflection, for as Wither goes on the offensive, his stance recalls that of his idiosyncratic pastoral persona. The Philarete of Wither's early works is not a lyric shepherd, but a satiric hunter; so too is the strenuous author of *The Scholler's Purgatory*: "The Booke-sellers do peremptorily challenge an interest in every mans labour of this kind [i.e., authorial labor]; and a worshipfull Lawyer was latelie pleased on their behalfe to say, that the benifit arising from the sale of bookes, was their ancient, and lawfull birthright. But ... unlesse he can prove, the Author hath sold them his birth-right (as often he doth, for lesse then a messe of pottage) he being the elder brother, the right first ... falleth unto him [and he goes on to instance other heirs—"the Printer, and Booke-binder"] that clayme just title before the booke-seller" (B6). Thus Esau speaks against the Jacobean printer.

For all the force of this libertarian language of property, Esau speaks on behalf of Jacobean prerogative, for he claims to seek nothing more than "repossession by the royall power" (B6). Wither's ideological location lies somewhere in this no man's land between authorial right and royal prerogative. He tells us that the booksellers have "cast upon me the unjust imputation of a base Monopolist: whereas I doubt not but I shalbe able to prove that his Majestie hath vouchsafed me nothing, but what was, IUS REGALE, and in his Lawfull power to confer" (G6v). No doubt this was good tactics. An author's common law property in his manuscript works had not been directly tested, although one can point to litigation loosely touching upon the question, whereas the king's prerogative was a talking point, a highly developed legal position.[37] Moreover, Wither knew quite well that the Stationers' own privileges rested on that prerogative and he wields this knowledge with fair exultance:

> If his Majesty hath not Authority to commaund the addition of a fewe leaves (for Gods glory, and the peoples edification) to such a booke, as hath allowance from the Prerogative Royall onely; Then, either the Stationers are very presumptious, in anexing the singing Psalmes and Robert Wisdomes Songs to the Bible and booke of Common prayer, at their owne pleasures, and for their owne profit: Or els their Prerogative is more absolute then the Kings.

This defense of the prerogative neutralizes the Stationers' charge of monopoly, but it does not exhaust Wither's argument. Under cover of this defense, Wither asserts a natural authorial property: "yf his Majestie hath not a legall power to confirme unto me that which is naturally myne owne, By what right then, doe they and others enjoy privileges for those books wherein every man hath as good property as they." This assertion of legal property constitutes a breakthrough in the history of authorship. Wither was no doubt aware of the fragile novelty of this line of argument: although the assertion of natural property is, by definition, absolute, it functions in *The Scholler's Purgatory* as a token of his relative merit, a device for bolstering his claim to be the preferable recipient of rights originating with the Crown.

The Scholler's Purgatory thus dances on the brink of authorial property. It tells us that Wither has no confidence in the self-evidence of his claims, which in turn explains why he takes such pains over dismantling the claims of the Stationers. Stationers' copyright, having developed as a means of regulating competition within the guild, rested on the traditional privileges of municipal companies, and, although those privileges had been buttressed by the Stationers' Charter, which had been confirmed by the Crown in the middle of the sixteenth century, they had developed into a substantial opposition to those special protections, the printing patents, which were confirmed by direct royal grant. Wither's project is to discredit Stationers' copyright and to defend a monopolistic competition founded immediately on the royal will, and quite secondarily on the natural claims of authors.[38]

The brink of authorial property would be traversed only very slowly. A decade later, another psalmodist, George Sandys, could more confidently petition King Charles for a patent in his own translations of the psalms and other biblical hymns: "whereas the Company of Stationers have an order, that no Printer shall print any booke but for one of their own Societie, thereby to ingrosse to themselves the whole profitt of other mens Labours."[39] By 1677, in the aftermath of yet another major inhibition of the granting of monopolies, a challenge to the almanac patent was rebuffed in *Stationers' Company v. Seymour*—one of a series of skirmishes between Seymour and the company over patented books—when the court held that the Crown had a right to grant this patent because "there is no particular author of an almanack".[40] The decision can only be loosely affiliated with Wither's protest: on the one hand, the author is here counterpoised to royal prerogative, not allied to it; on the other hand, the decision implicitly recognizes the legal priority and preeminence of authorial property, since in this case it is implied that only an intellectual "commons" like the almanac is available to Crown grant. Yet as had so often been the case, this crucial development in the legal history of authorial property unfolded by negation. Authorial property, indeed modern proprietary authorship, is a kind of improvisation in Seymour's case, almost inadvertently conjured as a confirming and delimiting boundary on the royal prerogative.[41] What is an author? Wither contends that an author is the most deserving recipient of patent protection; in Seymour's case, half a century later, an author is he or she whose writings could not properly be made the object of such protection.

Despite Wither's generally unarticulated, merely implied reference to the natural rights of authors, he does sketch one aspect of what would become the suite of modern intellectual property. Among the offenses of stationers, Wither refers to misattribution and to publication without the consent of authors. Of course, he operates here in a venerable tradition of complaint, for protests against unauthorized publication became a staple of prefatory epistles by the 1570s and protests against both misattribution and plagiarism come into vogue at the turn of the seventeenth century—and both, of course, have classical antecedents. As Willy's self-defense in *The Shepherd's Hunting* makes clear, even Wither's early pastorals had been hardened by plagiarism, real and imputed. *The Scholler's Purgatory* is as sensitive to such matters, and far more explicit. Towards its conclusion Wither imagines a typical stationer—"a mere Stationer," he calls him—going about his typically degraded business and he imagines that the mere stationer's response to *The Scholler's Purgatory* would be to deny its authenticity. This imagined slight provokes Wither to a strenuous insistence on the internal consistency of his oeuvre; the conceptual apparatus of Renaissance philology, with its flourishing science of attribution is here reflected back onto authorial self-consciousness, the author's authority confirmed by serial coherence. Even before writing *The Scholler's Purgatory*, Wither had sought an unusual degree and an even more unusual form of control over a printed volume. When John Marriott asked Wither for permission to publish *Faire-Virtue*, his last book of pastoral poetry, the poet refused; when Marriott was importunate, Wither agreed to the publication, but stipulated that Marriott report his reluctance in a prefatory epistle that is strange enough to deserve quoting here:

> And if you looked for a Prologue; thus much he wished me to tell you, in stead thereof: because (as he sayd) he himselfe had somewhat else to do. Yet, (to acknowledge the truth) I was so earnest with him, that, as busie as

he would seeme to be, I got him to write this Epistle for me: And have therunto set my Name. Which, he wished me to confesse. . . .

This peculiar authorial revenge on an industrial culture of misattribution is small, but epochal nonetheless, at least insofar as it insists upon the subordination of the stationer's to the author's name: as Wither would argue throughout *The Scholler's Purgatory,* "the reputation of Schollers, is as deare unto him [i.e., the ideal bookseller] as his owne: For, he acknowledgeth, that from them, his Mystery had both begining and meanes of continuance" (117).[42] Wither thus advocates what has become a modern orthodoxy: authorized publication and accurate attribution as a kind of trademark, a warrant of merchantability. Except in very unusual circumstances these "crimes of signature" are almost always described as offenses against honor and reputation. The novelty of Wither's protest—besides the novelty of sheer animus—is that he gives these crimes an unvarnished description as economic offenses, as stolen labor. *The Scholler's Purgatory,* therefore, comes close to enacting a rhetorical revolution, if not a conceptual one.

What Wither gives us here is the preeminent materialist defense of poesy, and so provokes a disciplinary reflection. It would be a useful contribution to literary history to insist on what has already been implied here, that *The Scholler's Purgatory* articulates social concerns already latent in Wither's earlier pastoral works, concerns that would be elaborated in the Levelling prophetic poems of Wither's latter career; it would be a useful contribution if only because literary historians have so often neglected the use of pastoral satire to protest secular abuses. Wither reminds us that it was the historical "mission" of early modern pastoral to provide an idiom in which an agrarian working-class would eventually come to know itself. Such a historiography of pastoral, in which Wither would figure significantly, might thereby "find a role and a dignity," in Franco Moretti's words, "in the context of a total history of society."[43] But far more sharply than does *The Shepherd's Hunting, The Scholler's Purgatory* indicates how a history of literature, in this case rewritten as a history of such cultural conventions as authorship, may find its role in the total history of society.

As C. B. MacPherson pointed out, modern political individualism is an essentially possessive individualism: during the Short Parliament, Harbottle Grimston would preempt a debate on how to assist the king in his war with the Scots by insisting, "Let therefore first our propertye be settled; and all woulde serve the Kinge for the preservation of the kingdome."[44]

The study of the unsettling of property and the consequent emergence of the proprietary subject must necessarily be dominated by the history of real property—by the so-called revolution on the land, the genesis of a land market after the dissolution of the monasteries, and the quickening of that market during the 1580s—for it was by means of these transformations that gentry, aristocracy, and Crown experienced the potential of capital for shearing off the feudal polity from the now more clearly determinant economy. But the political understanding of these transformations began to emerge within the late Elizabethan and Jacobean debate on monopolies, the occasion at which the liberty of the subject was first powerfully asserted and investigated.[45] It should be interesting for the intellectual historian to recall that many of the monopolies that fell under the most stringent scrutiny were patents in processes, technology, translations, *Hymns and Songs of the Church*, that is, in what now would be called intellectual property.[46] Since the antiregulatory sentiment of the gentry, the urban small producers, and the majority of England's commercial interests surfaced pungently in the sphere of literary production and dissemination, it requires no special pleading to assert this as an instance in which literary culture does not so much reflect revolutionary transformations in consciousness and practice as instigate them. To place the history of intellectual property within the larger history of economic monopolies is to discover that authorship is a leading case, a precedent in the development of possessive individualism and the object of direct analysis.[47]

Brilliant work has been done toward this historiographic end, which would certainly find a role and a dignity for literary history; I think first of all of Christopher Kendrick's study of the ideology of possessive individualism in Milton.[48] Literary scholars since Eliot and Leavis have had a tremendous investment in maintaining Milton's preeminence as the poet of the English Revolution, and as the historiography of that revolution becomes a less narrowly political one, Milton's place in that history has been made to adapt. Thus it has recently been asserted of *Areopagitica* that "it is a property argument based partly upon the limitation of monopoly to the author's ownership of his copy"—an exciting reading.[49] Nonetheless, the description seems far more appropriate to *The Scholler's Purgatory*. It will perhaps seem querulous to argue that Milton's relation to the unfolding history of intellectual property be recognized as relatively oblique and slightly tardy, at least when compared to that of Wither. But it is not my purpose to propose a poet of such uneven accomplishment as the patron saint of literary historicism; I have tried rather to unfold the logic of institutional development and capital formation that shaped his clash with the Stationers. Still, something must be said of the contribution of talent and temperament to the figure Wither must cut in a historiography of printed authorship. He could have had very little experience of the book trade when he composed the dedication to *Abuses Stript and Whipt:* it was, after all, his first printed book. But he anticipated his later relation to the book trade when he dedicated the book to himself. It seems an adolescent gesture (temperament), although this repudiation of patronage had a polemical purpose (talent), for it implies a criticism of royal favoritism and the general Jacobean inflation of honors. Of course, insofar as Wither became the beneficiary of what seemed extravagant royal benevolence, it would be easy to smirk over what looks like false consciousness. One of the piquant constants of the history of early modern authorship is that the frequent disruption of stationers' property by instances of royal patronage is one of the primary movers in the development towards statutory intellectual property: at the core of Wither's long campaign to secure independence or, rather, to secure the patronage of the market, is a recursion to royal patronage. That Wither was so alert to this and to other ironies in the predicament of authorship is what makes *The Scholler's Purgatory* so interesting. But Wither was an artist of predicament from the outset. Writing to James from the Marshalsea during his imprisonment for *Abuses Stript and Whipt* he begins a long and impassioned cadenza, "Oh save me now from Envies dangerous shelfe, / Or make me able, and I'le save my selfe" (444).

Notes

1. "The Fourth Eglogue"; I cite from the version reprinted from Wither's *Juvenilia* in *Publications of the Spenser Society* no. 10, 3 parts (1871), 2:540.

2. He may have been imprisoned for a first edition in 1611 of *Abuses Stript and Whipt;* he was certainly imprisoned for the fourth edition in 1613. According to Allan Pritchard ("*Abuses Stript and Whipt* and Wither's Imprisonment," *RES* 14 [1963]: 337–45), it was widely thought that several passages were aimed at Northampton; the antiparliamentary Northampton seems to have been instrumental in the imprisonment, which Pritchard notes endured from the time of the parliamentary elections (March), past Northampton's death in June, and through to the end of the parliamentary session at the end of July. Pembroke helped get him out, although Wither claimed that his satire written in prison and addressed to the king had contributed to his release.

3. There can be a psychological lilt, a gaiety to Wither's satire, even at its most cynical: "am I the only One guilty of studyinge myne owne profitt, in the course of my paynefull endevours for religious ende? I would to god I were, and that no

man living save I, were so wicked, as to make hi[s] owne glory, and inriching, the end and scope of hi[s] christian diligence. For doubtles, such an universall pietie, would be a powerfull meanes of drawing me to repentance" (*The Scholler's Purgatory*, B5).

4. Willy certainly stands for William Browne; Wither's persona, Philarete, exhorts Willy against despondency, but does not correct Willy's assessment of the place of poesy. The eclogue is a brilliant reworking of Spenser's October eclogue with much more emphasis on the dependence of prophetic/protest poetry on a sympathetic community, however small that community.

5. Browne's *The Shepherd's Pipe* appeared during Wither's imprisonment; its first eclogue was addressed to "Roget," plainly a figure for Wither.

6. The satire boldly reiterates (424) the attack on that "man-like Monster" described in the first epigram to the king affixed to *Abuses Stript and Whipt*. All he does by way of softening the sting of *Abuses* is to consider the possibility of having erred and to apologize if he has done so. But apology is always mitigated, as when he confutes those who allege that he "dare, or can, here taxe those Peeres / Whose Worths, their Honours, to my soule endeares": the line break, as much as the context, designates the firmly restrictive character of this second line.

7. Wither was not always so neglected. *The Scholler's Purgatory* served as an important piece of evidence, the merits of which had to be cautiously weighed in W. W. Greg's pained decision to side with Sidney Lee against A. W. Pollard in the question of the precise nature of how a stationer's copyright was established and what privileges it entailed. See *The Shakespeare First Folio: Its Bibliography and Textual History* (Oxford: Clarendon Press, 1955), 43–44 and 71–72.

8. Lyman Ray Patterson, *Copyright in Historical Perspective* (Nashville: Vanderbilt University Press, 1968); David Fairweather Foxon, *Pope and the Early Eighteenth-century Book Trade,* Lyell Lectures, 1975–76 (Oxford: Clarendon Press, 1991); Mark Rose, *Authors and Owners: The Invention of Copyright* (Cambridge, Mass.: Harvard University Press, 1993).

9. *The Complete Prose Works of John Milton,* ed. Don Wolfe et al., 8 vols. (New Haven: Yale University Press, 1953–82), 2: 570. In *The Scholler's Purgatory* Wither undertakes the tolerationist argument that Milton would later elaborate and, although Wither's case is admittedly self-serving, deploys his argument with an attractive (and uncharacteristic) sweetness. He impugns the piety of those who would militate against such varieties of worship as Wither has made possible by translating such biblical poetry as the Song of Songs: "And the same taxation are they worthy of, who in their pilgrimage to the spirituall Canaan dispise and seeke to abolish those generall furtherances, which their wiser Forefathers had provided, because they have in their own imagination [*sic;* imaginations?] found out some discipline fitter for their particuler inclinations. Let them use what Christian advantage they can in their private practice of pietie; but let them not measure the Church by their cubite.... Our holy Mother the Church, hath many Children of divers tempers and constitutions, and as the Maister of a great Feast provideth so, that every Guest may finde some what to agree with his appetite; so Gods Church hath established such discipline for her children, that every one may finde that which accordes with their capacities and inclinations" (E4v–5).

10. Though he appeals to Convocation, at one point (G1) he commends judg-

ment of his grievance to Parliament, which had in fact claimed as its proper jurisdiction the problem of regulating monopolies.

11. In *The Scholler's Purgatory* Wither implausibly claims to have applied for such a grant after his first imprisonment.

12. He cleverly cites verses of King James that argue the suasive power of verse (p. 9 in the Spenser Society reprint). It's worth noting here that Okes printed the *Preparation* without license and was fined a pound for the offense.

In *The Scholler's Purgatory* Wither claims that he applied for his patent in *Hymns and Songs of the Church* after the first imprisonment, though no documentary evidence supports this.

13. This had been followed in 1620 by the publication of Wither's *Exercises upon the First Psalm*.

14. Cf. Morley's Jacobean *ars memorandi*. Neville's very early privilege in Livy (1577) may have originated with the Stationers and not with the Crown; E. Arber, *A Transcript of the Registers of the Company of Stationers of London, 1554–1640*, 5 vols. (London and Birmingham, 1875–94), 2:312.

15. Cited (from State Papers Domestic, James I, vol. 187, art. 111A) in W. W. Greg, *Companion to Arber* (Oxford: Clarendon Press, 1967), 213.

16. But cf. John Speed's 1610 patent stipulating that his *Genealogies Recorded in the Sacred Scriptures* be bound in with all copies of the 1611 English Bible, an arrangement with which the Stationers seem to have happily complied; see Greg, *Companion to Arber*, 301.

17. The terms given in the abstract of the grant to Wither may be taken seriously: ". . . that the said Booke might be the more conveniently dispersed, for the instruction and private devotion of His Maiesties loving subjects" (Greg, *Companion to Arber*, 213). The Psalter is the state ideological apparatus par excellence.

18. John Day, City Printer, had received an Edwardian patent in the *A.B.C. with the Catechism*; with the accession of Elizabeth, he acquired the patent in the metrical Psalter, which he could job out for production at twopence half-penny a copy and then sell for sixpence. This patent overlapped that of his early partner, William Seres, who held patents in the *Primer With Psalter* and in the *A.B.C. with the Catechism*. By the mid-seventies they seem to have divided this huge monopolistic territory, with Seres publishing service books and Primers and Day publishing the *A.B.C. with the Catechism* and both printing Psalters—this is how the field seemed to have been divided to the anonymous author of a complaint dated 1577 (Arber, *Transcript of the Registers*, 1:177)—but it was not until the end of the decade that Seres and Day clarified the overlap by means of an agreement drafted in October 1578 and ratified before the Stationers Court of Assistants in January 1580. The agreement is transcribed in Cyprian Blagden, "The English Stock of the Stationers' Company: An Account of its Origins," *The Library*, ser. 5, vol. 10 (1955): 184.

19. See my discussion in "For a History of Intellectual Property: John Wolfe's Reformation," *English Literary Renaissance* 18 (autumn 1988): 389–412.

20. Cited Blagden, *The Stationers' Company* (Cambridge: Harvard University Press, 1960), 75.

21. Pp. 25–30 [consecutive; the original is misnumbered and, in this part of the book, missigned]. Wither continues, "But having composed a new Booke, which

no man could claime a share in, while it remayned myne owne, and in mine owne power to make public or no, & prposing the same to his Majestie ... I obtayned a free and gratious graunt ... such as the Stationers would have made of it without a priviledge if so be I had left it in their power."

22. It is hardly surprising that there may have been bad faith on both sides. Wither protests "how willfully they have misenformed the Kings Majestie & diverse honorable personages concerning my Grant (& my procedings) to procure my damage: How unjustly they gave out among their Customers, that my Grant was a Monopoly, & an exaction to the oppression of the people: How impudently & faulsly, they have verefied, that I had procured that no man might buy a Bible, Testament, or Communion-Booke which [sic] out my Hymnes" (95). But whether or not he had formulated the plan in 1624, that's exactly where he was headed. Wither finished his long-projected translation of a singing Psalter in 1633, though continuing hostilities with the Stationers obliged him to have it printed in Holland. He secured a new patent from Charles I stipulating that this Psalter be bound with all Bibles. This naturally led to a reprise of the original quarrel with the Stationers, who won support for their position from the House of Lords.

23. Fortunately for the Stationers, James's grant pegged both wholesale and retail prices for Wither's book to prevailing rates for the Psalter; Arber, *Transcript of the Registers,* 4:13–14.

More could be made of the jurisdictional issues. As was quite necessary, the patent granted Wither the right to enforce compliance: to search for and seize Psalters being sold without the Hymns. By the early thirties, Wither was plainly frustrated in his efforts to enforce his patent and it is easy to see why he decided to farm the patent to Robert Crosse and Toby Knowles who, as Messengers of His Majesty in Ordinary, stood a far better chance of success in dealing with noncompliant stationers. As it turned out, they too failed and in March 1634 petitioned the Privy Council "either to free them from their Contract, or for the better enabling them being so engaged, to confirm unto them, the enjoying of the aforesd royal Patent"; Greg, *Companion to Arber,* 217. It is hardly surprising, though worth noting nonetheless, that in a contemporaneous petition to Sir Francis Windebank, Crosse and Knowles report that several stationers had sought to purchase an interest in the grant.

24. William A. Jackson, *Records of the Court of the Stationers' Company, 1602 to 1640* (London: Bibliographical Society, 1957), 156, only a memorandum; unfortunately no further record of this meeting in March 1633 survives.

25. Charles Howard McIlwain, *Constitutionalism, Ancient and Modern* (Oxford, 1940), 138, emphasis added.

26. Wither claims that the Stationers secured a hearing by stationing "three or four of their Instruments, to clamor against me at the Parliament house dore." The London bookbinders issued a broadside attacking the patent (preserved at the Society of Antiquaries; Robert Lemon, *Catalogue of a Collection of Printed Broadsides in the Possession of the Society of Antiquaries* (London: Society of Antiquaries, 1866), no. 225), though Wither alleges that they were compelled to do so by the Company leadership. Had it been enforced, Wither's patent certainly would have benefited the bookbinders, at least in the short run, but apparently one of the

Stationers' principal means of evading its strictures was to ship the Psalter to the provinces in quires where they could be bound, more or less beyond the reach of official scrutiny, without Wither's *Hymns* included.

27. Because the book naturally had to be printed surreptitiously, without entrance or license, Wither entrusted it to the hapless George Wood: early in September, officials of the Stationers' Company duly raided Wood's shop and destroyed his equipment before the print run was complete. Both Wither and Wood were brought in for interrogation by the Court of High Commission, whereupon, to his discredit, Wither blamed Wood for the failure to secure license. The court seems to have approved the book for printing, and by December *The Scholler's Purgatory* had appeared, its latter sheets printed in a different font and probably at a different press. On Wither's moderate achievements in exploiting the patent during the late twenties, see Norman E. Carlson, "Wither and the Stationers," *Studies in Bibliography* 19 (1966): 210–15.

28. Both pagination and printed signing of this book are flawed; these pages are designated 28 and 29 and would correspond to B6v–7.

29. See p. 120: "If an Author out of meere necessity, do but procure meanes to make sale of his owne booke, or to pervent the combinations of such as he, by some Royall & lawfull priveledge: He presently cryes it downe for a Monopoly."

30. See, in particular, 108–9.

31. Lemon, *Catalogue of a Collection of Printed Broadsides*, no. 225.

32. Pp. 121–22. Wither takes great pleasure in recording this sort of hypocrisy. He reports that the company Wardens frequently collude in the printing of works that they knew could not secure official license and that on occasion they had confiscated certain books as "unlawful" and then sold them for their own profit.

33. To cite this at greater length: "For, by an unjust custome (as most of your Reverences well knowe) the Stationers have so usurped upon the labours of all writers, that when they have consumed their youth and fortunes in perfiting some laborious worke those cruell Bee-masters burne the poore Athenian bees for their hony, or else drive them from the best part therof" (A3). Compare the georgic figure of p. 120, where Wither argues that the Stationers' hostility to authorial monopoly "is just as reasonable a complaint, as if a Company of Haglers should preferr a bill against the Cuntry Farmers, for bringing their owne Corne & other provisions to the next markett. He will fawne upon Authors at his first acquintance, & ring [*sic*, but see "sounds" in the next phrase] them to his hive, by the promising sounds of some good entertainement; but assoone as they have prepared the hony to his hand, he drives the Bees to seek another Stall." To elaborate the idea of the author as worker, Wither has recourse to a durable rhetoric of capital as the effluvium of personal labor: "Many of our moderne booke-sellers, are but needelesse excrements, or rather vermine, who beeing ingendred by the sweat of schollers, Printers, and book-binders, doe (as wormes in timber, or like the generation of vipers) devour those that bred them. While they did like fleas, but sucke now and then a dropp of the writers blood from him, and skipp off when he found himselfe diseased, it was somwhat tollerable: but since they began to feed on him, like the third plague of AEGIPT without remooving, and to laye clayme to each Authors labours, as if they had beene purposely brought upp to

studye for their mayntenance" (10). Compare Richard Martin, in the 1601 Parliament, cited in Sacks, 98.

34. *Prose Works,* 2:562.

35. For an intensification of the rhetoric of work, see sig. C5: "If like an honest harted Gibeonit I have but a little extraordinarily laboured, to hewe wood and drawe water, for the spirituall Sacrifizes ... what blame worthy have I done?"; see also sig. C6.

36. B6; and see also A3.

37. As early as 1603, it was possible for Fuller openly to argue in *Darcy v. Allen*, the famous "Case of Monopolies," that "Arts, and skill of manual occupations rise not from the King, but from the labour and industry of men, and by the gifts of God to them" (Noy's Reports, King's Bench, 181).

38. Closely related to this project is Wither's attack on the practice, customary almost continuously since 1586, whereby the wardens of the Stationers' Company functioned as proxy licensers, referring only the hardest cases to the official licensers (34).

39. Document 76; Greg, *Companion to Arber*.

40. 3 Keble 792, 1 Mod. 256, 84 Eng. Rep. 1015; and see E. F. Bosanquet, "English 17th Century Almanacs," *The Library*, ser. 4, 10 (1929–30): 361–97.

41. The prerogative was further delimited in 1775, in *Stationers' Company v. Carnan*, when even almanacs were placed outside the circle of royal property. It was determined in Chancery that the Crown might still control the right to print statutes and proclamations, Bibles and prayerbooks, on the grounds that "codes of religion and of law ought to be under the inspection of the executive power, to stamp an authenticity upon them. Therefore Bibles, Common Prayer Books, and statutes are proper objects of exclusive patents. But almanacs are not of this kind" (96 Eng. Rep. 592). The patent here begins to merge with license.

42. As early as *The Shepherd's Hunting*, Wither had interested himself in establishing a professional hierarchy of naming. He draws on the venerable topos that describes an author as the parent of a book in order to distinguish himself from the stationer, "who bid himselfe God-Father" (Nn4v).

43. Franco Moretti, *Signs Taken for Wonders: Essays in the Sociology of Literary Forms*, trans. Susan Fischer, David Forgacs, and David Miller (London: Verso, 1983), 19.

44. Grimston is cited from J. P. Sommerville, *Politics and Ideology in England, 1603–1640* (London: Longman, 1986), 148. For a general introduction to the terms of debate on property, and for the relation between the rhetoric of property and the conceptualization of polity, see chapter one of Margaret Atwood Judson, *The Crisis of the Constitution: An Essay in Constitutional and Political Thought in England, 1603–1645*, 2d ed. (New Brunswick: Rutgers, 1988).

45. The development of opposition to monopoly protection has never been fully chronicled. The earliest precedent for a legal attack on the principle of monopoly may be found in the Case of Gloucester School (1410). Robert Bell raised a protest in Parliament in 1571, but no one joined his cause. It was not until the 1580s that opposition began to coalesce and to focus not only on a particular disruption of local economies, but on the principles implicit in such grants. The best available

account of the burgeoning protest movement may be found in chaps. 3 and 4 of Thirsk, *Economic Policy and Projects* (Oxford: Clarendon Press, 1978), 51–105. On the parliamentary history, the best narrative account is J. E. Neale, *Elizabeth and Her Parliaments, 1584–1601* (New York, St. Martins: 1958), 352–56 and 376–93. A richer analysis may be found in David Harris Sacks, "Parliament, Liberty, and the Commonweal," *Parliament and Liberty,* ed. J. H. Hexter (Stanford: Stanford University Press, 1992), 85–121. And see also Elizabeth Read Foster, "The Procedure of the House of Commons against Patents and Monopolies, 1621–24," *Conflict in Stuart England,* ed. William Appleton Aiken and Basil Duke Henning (London: Jonathan Cape, 1960).

46. Included in the patents under attack in 1601, for example, are not only the starch, tin, brimstone, and beer-transport patents, but also the patents for paper, for the printing of three-part songs, for the printing of schoolbooks, lawbooks, almanacs, translations of Tacitus, and the *Speculum Brittaniae* (*Journal of Sir Simonds D'Ewes from the First Recess of the Long Parliament to the Withdrawal of King Charles from London,* ed. Willson Havelock Coates [New Haven: Yale University Press, 1942], 650).

47. I make a more sustained effort to describe the preeminent contribution of literary practice and, specifically, of authorial self-consciousness, to the development of possessive individualism in my forthcoming *Authorial Impression: The Production of Intellectual Property in Early Modern England.*

48. Christopher Kendrick, *Milton: A Study in Ideology and Form* (London: Methuen, 1986), chaps. 2 and 3.

49. Nigel Smith, "Areopagitica: Voicing Contexts, 1643–5," *Politics, Poetics and Hermeneutics in Milton's Prose,* ed. David Loewenstein and James Grantham Turner (Cambridge: Cambridge University Press, 1990), 106.

Part Two

Manuscript and Print: Competition, Overlap, and Mutual Influence

CHAPTER FIVE

"The Merit of a Manuscript Poem": The Case for Bodleian MS Rawlinson Poet. 85

Randall Louis Anderson

> Many idle humorists, whose singularity allowes nothing good, that is common, in this frantik age, esteeme of verses vpon which the vulgar in a Stationers Shop, hath once breathed as a peece of infection, in whose fine fingers no papers are holesome, but such, as passe by priuate manuscription.
> —Richard Niccols, *The Furies* (1614)

> 'Tis ridiculous for a lord to print verses; 'tis well enough to make them to please himself, but to make them public is foolish.
> —John Selden, *Table-Talk* (1689)

> The merit of a MS. poem is uncertain; "print," as he excellently says, "settles it."
> —Oscar Wilde, "Pen Pencil and Poison"

While we can trace the first printed collections of English verse to the latter half of Henry VIII's reign, the compilation and publication of verse miscellanies did not become a regular activity of print shops until the end of the Tudor period. By making poetry from several hands available in a single volume, the printed miscellanies fed an eager market that saw verse as an indispensible medium of expression;[1] now those who had no fashionable literary connections could, for a sixpence, have access to the cloistered[2] world of "priuate manuscription." The printed Tudor miscellanies[3]—

foremost among them *Songes and Sonettes* (nine editions, and a total of ten printings, from 1557 to 1587), *The Paradise of Dainty Devices* (as many as ten editions from 1576 to 1606), *The Phœnix Nest* (1593), *England's Helicon* (editions in 1600 and 1614), and *A Poetical Rhapsody* (four editions from 1602 to 1621)—provide some of the best evidence of how an emergent vernacular verse first tries its legs, and stand as invaluable testimony to the evolution of literary taste. As such, they also leave traces of two different, but intimately related, processes that can best be characterized as "editorial." One is substantially influenced by economic pressures of the print trade: editorship by interception and selection of fugitive manuscript material and its publication in a printed miscellany. The other and more elusive editorial practice is necessarily antecedent to that of the publisher or printer: it is an individual's choice, from such circulating manuscript verse, of items to be copied into a commonplace book or manuscript miscellany.[4]

While the period between the first editions of *Songes and Sonettes* and *The Paradise of Dainty Devices* and those of *The Phœnix Nest, England's Helicon,* and *A Poetical Rhapsody* may seem "trifling"[5] in view of the *longue durée* of English literary history, we can see in the last quarter of the sixteenth century a shift in lyric sensibility comparable, in lasting impact, to the great vowel shift. This period (1578–91) between the early miscellanies (ending with *A Gorgeous Gallery of Gallant Inventions*) and the five collections that rapidly spilled from the presses between 1591 and 1602 (beginning with *Brittons Bowre of Delights*) provides a moment of hesitation and discovery to surpass the period between the first edition of *The Court of Venus*[6] and the first edition of *Songes and Sonettes*. We might say that this thirteen-year hiatus, through which only Tottel (two editions) and *The Paradise of Dainty Devices* (four editions) maintained any currency, marks the alchemical moment that exchanged, to use C. S. Lewis's famous distinctions, Drab verse for Golden lyrics:

> *Drab* is not used as a dyslogistic term. It marks a period in which, for good or ill, poetry has little richness either of sound or images. The good work is neat and temperate, the bad flat and dry. There is more bad than good.... The Golden Age is what we usually think of first when "the great Elizabethans" are mentioned: it is largely responsible, in England, for the emotional overtones of the word *Renaissance*. The epithet *golden* is not eulogistic. By *golden* poetry I mean not simply good poetry, but poetry which is, so to speak, innocent or ingenuous.... Only later, when the ingenuous taste has been satisfied, will it become necessary to seek for nov-

elty, to set oneself difficult tasks, to make beauty out of violence.... It is, of course, neither possible nor desirable that a Golden Age should last long. Honey cloys and men seek for drier and more piquant flavours. At the end of the century this is already beginning to happen.[7]

For Lewis *Songes and Sonettes* is the "greatest composite monument of the Drab Age" and, perhaps surprisingly, *The Phœnix Nest* is "predominantly a Drab anthology," while he finds *England's Helicon* a "genuinely Golden anthology."[8] Although he stops short of suggesting that Drab verse is inherently leaden, it is no small challenge to imagine how "neat and temperate"—if not wholly arid—verse naturally gives birth to "innocent" poetry. Douglas Bush was an early respondent to Lewis, and suggested that those Drab poets who display a "tougher ... sensibility and mode of utterance" often produce "a hotter fire, sometimes attended with dense smoke."[9] But it was Yvor Winters who eventually made the strongest case for the rehabilitation of much normally marginalized Tudor verse:

> Anyone who has read large amounts of the poetry of the sixteenth century will realize that most of it is poor, much of it astonishingly poor. For one thing, one can almost read the rhetoric books through the printed page, just as in the seventeenth century one can often read the devotional manuals. These poets were still going to school, and they were eager about it, and most of them were naïve. But ... some of the poetry is astonishingly good, and some of the best has been almost wholly neglected.[10]

While Winters is primarily concerned with the "native plain style" manifest in the early printed miscellanies, he suggests that the verse which "flourished mainly between Surrey and Sidney ... laid the groundwork for the greatest achievements in the short poem in English."[11] But it is one thing to urge a more generous assessment of inaccessible poetry; it is quite another to be able to identify the elements that, while difficult for us to appreciate, would have been embraced by Tudor audiences.

In the end the alchemical analogy suggested by Lewis, and echoed in the temptation to separate late Tudor verse from early, depends upon a view of the 1580s as a period of poetic stagnation or, perhaps, confusion over what to try next, or whom to follow—there was, after all, comparatively little new vernacular verse being printed across that decade. We tend, then, to look for some identifiable single moment that galvanized the poetic energies of Elizabethan England, but trends in poetry can sometimes be as glacial as they can be volcanic. While the printed residue of the 1580s may advertise a lyric ice age, we can occasionally find real sparks of fire in the manuscript verse of the same decade; not surprisingly, it can take some time for those fires to light the way to printers' stalls. The second group of miscellanies is clearly yoked to the Golden Age ushered in by Philip Sidney: the first of the five later miscellanies was published the same year as the first edition of *Astrophil and Stella* (1591), and the debt to Sidney is made all the more explicit by the elegies to him in *The Phœnix Nest, England's Helicon,* and *A Poetical Rhapsody* (seven, fourteen, and sixteen years after his death, respectively).[12] Remembering Yvor Winters's sensible claim that we have taken as "axiomatic" the belief that the end of the sixteenth century offers "the most characteristic movement of the century," with the late Elizabethan miscellanies in hand we might be able to argue that it is just as true that in the last quarter as well as "in the first three-quarters of the sixteenth century most of us look, perhaps not altogether consciously, for imperfect Sidneys."[13] It would seem valuable, indeed, to see how far Sidney's influence extended into the vast body of unpublished and forgotten poems of the manuscript miscellanies. The real test of Winters's axiom comes only when we place those poems preserved only in manuscript miscellanies alongside their printed counterparts.

 Ever since Bishop Percy scholars have shown particular appreciation for the light that manuscript transmission sheds on printed texts of poems, but in most cases such manuscripts have never really attained the status of equals.[14] Only recently have we seen significant reassessment of the value of manuscript materials both for process and product. Hilton Kelliher makes a thoroughly agreeable claim for the primacy of manuscript sources in any study of the early modern period: "While analysis of extant printed works offers us statistics about the market for creative literature, recovery of the precise contexts in which verse was read and copied will give us a far more detailed picture of contemporary taste."[15] And only very recently has anyone promoted the manuscript miscellanies *in spite* of the inaccuracies—and infelicities—they introduce. Arthur Marotti, Ernest Sullivan, and others have begun to suggest that we step away from our author-based predispositions, or biases, to recondition ourselves to accept "multiple, authoritative versions of texts."[16] Marotti has been the most vocal proponent of such revisionist textual criticism with his argument that "it is time to make that discipline less author-centered and to value as interesting elements of texts' socioliterary history some of those very 'corruptions' and 'errors' it has been the aim of traditional scholarship to purge."[17] It may well be time to retire the deerstalker—to be less the literary detective—

and to look at what we indisputably *know* about a poem that has been copied into a manuscript miscellany: we know what the compiler/copyist thought he was copying (whether a previously corrupt text, one that he corrupts on his own out of carelessness, or what he felt was an improved version of an "original"), and we often know whom the compiler/copyist thought he was copying (attributions in manuscripts are notoriously suspect, of course, but as proof of the copyist's ear such misattributed poems ought to bear some stylistic or tonal similarity to the nominated poet).[18]

We should also pursue the implications of what is evident about manuscript miscellanies through the *arrangement* of their contents:[19] what putative—or authentic—poet gets placed next to what other supposed poet. The company a poem or poet keeps in a manuscript miscellany—which therefore demands a larger view of the manuscript as a whole—is more important than the isolation of individual poems or poets. The proximity of one poem to another is made all the more compelling, too, when a block of Sidney's or Breton's or Ralegh's or Dyer's verse is interrupted by some scurrilous or bawdy lines, an occasional poem, or unintentionally doggerel verses by an acquaintance. One characteristic of the artifactual evidence many verse collections display is their *linear* nature: collections primarily devoted to poetry (or other *miscellanea*) grow by accretion, with each poem building upon its predecessors, and each new addition changing the tone and character of the whole.[20] We can assemble the growth (or stagnation) of a compiler's taste based on the shape of the collection.[21]

Author-based textual scholarship is still necessary, but all too often we forget about the larger artifact that yields up the these poems; in this respect the sum is indeed greater than the individual parts.[22] Arthur Marotti offers a sensible plea when he urges that

> either separately or as part of editions of whole manuscripts, we should give more editorial attention to the work of anonymous and non-canonical authors. This would broaden our sense of the literary and help us to see the social embeddedness of poetic texts in an historical period in which "literature" had not yet become segregated from the general social world as a supposedly autonomous institution.[23]

The Elizabethan manuscripts that contain at least noticeable traces of the printed miscellanies would seem the perfect point-of-entry to initiate a practical application of Marotti's recommendation. Steven May wisely outlines the full scope of such new inquiry: "the canon of the court must expand to consider not only a much wider range of authors than has yet been dreamt of in New Historicist methodology, but a range of anonymous texts including religious, elegiac, and satiric verse as well as love poetry."[24] Those poems unique to a given manuscript—particularly those arising from association with the compiler—are often the most revealing, even if they are unaccomplished; no modern Renaissance anthology can truly presume to be representative until it accounts for some of this vast body of miscellaneous verse that circulated alongside the more familiar poems to survive the late sixteenth century. While we cannot forget the significant achievements of careful Lachmannian textual scholars, the time has come to move away from diagramming stemmata—to move from a genealogy of *texts* to a genealogy of *tastes*.

By changing attitudes toward our received manuscript inheritance, we can also begin to explore the distinction between a *community* and a *society* of readers. Although Ferdinand Tönnies[25] originated the sociological distinction over a century ago, bibliographers like Roger Chartier have embraced the distinction as well:

> There are equally great differences between the norms and conventions of reading that define, for each community of readers, legitimate uses of the book, ways to read, and the instruments and methods of interpretations. Finally, there are differences between the expectations and interests that various groups of readers invest in the practice of reading. Such expectations and interests ... determine the way in which texts can be read and read differently by readers who do not have ... the same relationship with the written word.[26]

Harold Love refines Chartier's notion as he applies it specifically to manuscripts, explaining that

> there is an overwhelming tendency for the networks [of manuscript transmission] to coincide with social groupings of one kind or another—with families, with groups of individuals linked by common beliefs or interests, with institutions such as the court, the diocese or the college, and with geographical entities such as the county. Since an individual could well be a member of a number of these communities, the passage of a text might be a complex and also a very rapid one.[27]

He continues to describe the "societal functions" of scribal publication in terms particularly resonant of Tönnies:[28]

At a very simple level it was one of several means . . . to be chosen in preference to other media according to the audience addressed but also because this was usually privileged information, not meant to be available to all enquirers. . . .

[C]irculation might follow oblique or erratic paths arising out of shared enthusiasms. . . . An outbreak of oblique transmission might be an indication that long-accepted exclusions were under strain, pointing to stratigraphical stress within the system. . . .

[T]he printed text, being available as an article of commerce, had no easy way of excluding readers. Inherent in the choice of scribal publication . . . was the idea that the power to be gained from the text was dependent on possession of it being denied to others.[29]

Henry Woudhuysen's research arrives, then, at an expected conclusion: the early owners of Sidney's poems "do not appear to have wanted to share them with all and sundry, but to have kept them within tight communities."[30] How, then, could a manuscript compiler contaminate selections of highly coveted poems with long intervals of inferior verse? Given the high incidence of association poems in manuscripts, we need to be mindful that a manuscript may be more reflective of its compiler's taste in friends than his taste in poetry,[31] but which judgment should we invest with more authority: that of the printer who appeals to the "society of readers," or of the individual members of a "community of readers" who may have uneven, but self-assured, tastes?[32] The key to answering these questions of taste and cultural poetics is to work backward from the printed book to its sources, direct or collateral; any attempt to separate interior communities and exterior societies of readers must naturally identify the points of divergence between competing manuscript "sources" and the printed collections. Focusing on the evidence offered by manuscripts we can see how they can help us recover the plurality of tastes nurtured by the many communities of readers.

Within the vast and significant assortment of manuscripts added to Oxford's Bodleian Library in 1756 by Richard Rawlinson's bequest[33] is a late sixteenth-century miscellany that stands above its shelfmates for the often refined discernment of its unknown compiler (or compilers). Known today as Rawlinson poet. 85 (hereafter cited as RP 85), this manuscript of some 125 leaves and 145 poems[34] and fragments—and, regrettably, several lacunae[35]—is unsurpassed for its roll of "contributors": among others, Breton, Dyer, Oxford, Peele, Ralegh, Spenser,[36] and Surrey.[37] But the most frequently acknowledged contributor—with roughly two dozen poems to his credit—is Philip Sidney (who is represented by three of his songs—4, 8, and 10—from *Astrophil and Stella*, and an equal selection from *Certain Sonnets* and the *Old Arcadia*).[38] Although heavily relied upon by Hyder Rollins and, among others, the editors of Dyer (Sargent), Ralegh (Latham), and Sidney (Ringler), RP 85 particularly stands out from all of the other manuscript miscellanies for having the highest degree of congruence with the "Rollins group" of printed miscellanies—28 of its 145 poems are found in seven of the nine miscellanies, and several of them occur in more than one miscellany: 9 appear in *The Phœnix Nest*, 8 in *Brittons Bowre of Delights*, 7 in *England's Helicon*, and 5 in *The Arbor of Amorous Devices*.[39]

RP 85 is also significant for its interrelationship with a pair of important British Library manuscripts that are similarly notable for their overlap with the printed miscellanies: British Library Harley 7392 captures 21 of its 153 poems from the Rollins miscellanies, and Harley 6910 captures 20 of its 222 poems, which makes the congruencies among the tastes of these three mansucripts all the more intriguing—Harley 7392[40] and RP 85 share 45 poems in common, Harley 6910[41] and RP 85 share 20 poems in common, and there are 15 poems common to all three manuscripts. Had they shared an identical parent, it would be hard to imagine that three separate copyists would so radically rearrange that same parent—especially since these three manuscripts were produced *linearly*.[42] When you also consider the *accretive* nature of verse manuscripts, the compilers of RP 85, Harley 6910, and Harley 7392 would have then required the opportunity to revisit that growing parent, separately, at regular intervals for the most updated additions. It would seem fair to conclude that the congruencies between RP 85, Harley 6910, and Harley 7392—and to a slightly lesser extent Marsh's Library (Dublin) Z3.5.21,[43] Cambridge Dd.5.75,[44] and Folger V.a.89[45]—provide independent (rather than direct, genetically interrelated) evidence confirming the homogeneity of tastes.[46] Apart from the core of shared poems, of course, are the very interesting idiosyncratic selections that personalize each manuscript; what we really have are two coexistent "collections" that, for the compiler, must not have been as divisible as we view them today: the anthologist's golden verse, and the noncanonical residue that forms the bulk of the manuscript.

In addition to the high degree of congruence with the printed miscellanies, RP 85 is peculiarly interesting because it provides us not only with the compiler's tastes but also with a different, and perhaps slightly later, taste conveyed by an "editorial" notation (☞) that selects 68 of the 145 poems for special attention (and later discards two of these selections by striking through the finger).[47] Several poems that we might expect to be culled out for this special attention have been: "Callynge to mynde my eye longe went about,"[48] "In a groue most riche of shade,"[49] "Many desier but fewe or none deserue,"[50] and "My mynde to me a kingdom is."[51] But several other poems that are commonly anthologized[52] were omitted from the selection: "Onlye ioy now here you are,"[53] "As you went to Walsingham,"[54] "When werte thou borne desyre,"[55] "Like to a hermitt pore in place obscure,"[56] and "You goatherds godds."[57] The likelihood that the RP 85 manuscript was ever in the hands of a printer is extremely low, but there is an enticing coincidence: 19 of the 28 poems found in the printed miscellanies were marked with this index finger.

If we look at a wide range of anthologies produced over the last two centuries—antiquarian, belletristic, and academic—we see that the contents of RP 85 have been incorporated by these anthologists at a reasonably significant rate: roughly one quarter of its contents (35 of its 145 poems) have appeared in all but one of these twenty anthologies; less than half of these 35 poems (only 16) were made available in one of the printed Tudor miscellanies. The four modern anthologies most reliant upon RP 85— Hebel and Hudson's famous textbook (17 poems), Emrys Jones's significantly updated *New Oxford Book of Sixteenth-Century Verse* (16 poems), Norman Ault's manuscript-friendly anthology based on "original texts" (13 poems), and E. K. Chambers's original *Oxford Book of Sixteenth Century Verse* (13 poems)—clearly acknowledge their debts to the manuscript in their notes or, more prominently, in textual ascriptions that accompany the poems. If the significant attention paid to the manuscript by modern editors indicates its worthiness as a representative artifact of its own time, what will a wide-angle view of the contents tell us about its compiler or compilers? Or, more crucially, how can the study of such a representative manuscript's *full* contents be repaid? But RP 85 offers hardly a typical case of manuscript reception by the editorial community; few of the many surviving Elizabethan verse manuscripts win attention from modern anthologists, and even those manuscripts that are acknowledged favorites rarely yield up more than the obvious poems from established names.

A comprehensive view of RP 85 offers the kind of valuable insight we need to fill the gap in printed miscellanies. Besides the anticipated and almost dutiful inclusion of Sidney and some of his circle, there is a generic preoccupation with pastoral and epigram; a delight in coarse, bawdy, and often misogynistic humor;[58] an interest in reiterative verse technique, especially through anaphora, refrain, or apposition; an experimentation with quantitative verse and attempts at the composition of verse in Latin; and a clear topical connection to the St. John's College, Cambridge, of the mid-1580s. Aside from the expected ties to the Sidney circle (including several virtually obligatory elegies to Astrophil),[59] what can we make of these other characteristics? The manuscript's generic preoccupations share a common classical heritage; Sidney's presence is again felt in the many pastoral selections, while the epigrams take delight in compression of wit. But the sophs of St. John's growth fall short of Martial; their wit often takes the shape of coarse and misogynistic indulgences, among which are a strange *blason* that culminates with a complaint concerning inadequate feminine hygiene ("It was an oulde sayenge of S*ir* John Kettels"), and such feeble ballad stanzas as

> A sylence seldome seene
> That women counsayll keep
> The cause was this she wakde her witts
> And dullde her tongue a sleepe.
>   [fol. 91][60]

A few leaves later comes this attack on women's changeableness:

> When first of all dame nature wroughte
> Eche thinge in order for to knytt
> Full busilye and long she soughte
> To fetter faythe in womanns witt
>   Nay nay (quoth fayth) and the*n* she fledd
>   I will not byde in womans heade.
>   [fol. 105v][61]

There is also a formal interest in refrain and apposition—that is to say an interest more in scheme than in trope (thus perhaps an appreciation for the kind of rhetorical facility that a more sober commonplace book might cultivate)—which is borne out by such poems as "The ayre withe sweet my sences doth delyghte" (fol. 10),[62] "*Sweet* is the lyfe that is the *Sweet* of loue" (fol. 105),[63] "Those eyes that hould the hand of euery harte" (fol. 24v),[64] "Onlye ioy now here you are" (fol. 42),[65] "Fayne woulde I but I dare not" (fol. 43v),⁶⁶ and the single, backward-glancing acknowledgment of *Songes and Sonettes*, "The longer lyfe the more offence" (fol. 115v).⁶⁷ There are a number of plausible explanations for these recurrences: they are of course characteristic of songs, which, as part of one's cultural competence, could easily be set down from memory; they also fill out space or simplify movement from line to line, serving as convenient prototypes for fitful amateur poets; and they appeal to the mind and ear trained in rhetoric. There is also an ironic consciousness of decorum that is made more explicit than usual in the extremely curious (and long, at 312 lines) "Libell agaynst Bashe." This poem—solely confined to a life in manuscript⁶⁸—is particularly interesting for its 18-line address "to the Reader" that reveals both the anonymous poet's self-consciousness and assertiveness (and, notably, his familiarity with Chaucer):

> My masters you that reed my ryme
> I pray you count it for no cryme
> Although I vse some brauery
> In playne termes of knauerye
> For this surely haue I soughte
> To obserue decorum as I oughte
> My Master Chaucer taught me once
> A noblle lesson for the nonce
> That if a man would paynt a Pyke
> With asses eares it were vnlyke
> Wherefore if I wryte slouenly
> Bash is a slouen certaynlye
> If baudye wordes be my offence
> His baudye deedes be my defence.
>   [fol. 66]

But the poem is hardly as off-color as we may be led by this paratext to believe. See, for instance, what probably is the most libelous portion of the poem:

> He fell of consanguinetye
> And lynked in affinitye
> With baudes, brothells, whores and knaues
> Cutthroates, theeues, and bankrout slaues.
>   [fol. 67v]

This poem's *envoi* addresses itself not to the reader, but to the target of the libel:

> And now Mass Bashe I tell you trwe
> Me thynkes hyghe tyme to bydd adewe
> . . . .
> To tell what tourd myght please you beste
> A chyldes turd or a man*n*s tourde
> The deuyll turde or his dames turde
> Take euen which turde you lyst to chuse
> And se you do no turde refuse
> But vse it gentlye as your freende
> A tourde in your teth and ther an end.
> [fol. 72]

Not exactly rapier-like wit, nor really much of an excoriation that would make a point beyond its undergraduate audience.[69]

These explanations, taken together with the manuscript's generic and tonal tendencies, all reinforce its significant connection to St. John's College, Cambridge.[70] The evidence for this connection is abundant, from verses "Written vpon this occasion a certayne companye of youthes (schollers in Cambridge) rowinge downe the ryuer on daye in a boate for their plea=sure the boote chaunced by mischaunce to be torned ouer" (a poem as prosodic as its title, but which begins with great dramatic promise: "Neptune of whurlynge windes and huge waues terible Empror"), to the roughly two dozen poems by Robert Mills and James Reshoulde,[71] both of whom were graduated B.A. from St. John's in 1586–87. Many of the poems by Reshoulde have been crossed out; many of the poems by Mills were dedicated to his friend "I. F.," perhaps John Finet (1571–1641), who attended Cambridge during the mid-1580s but earned no bachelor's degree (and who is better remembered as Master of Ceremonies under Charles I). It is on the strength of the many poems dedicated to him, and his matriculation at St. John's, that Laurence Cummings is led to identify Finet as the compiler of RP 85. This conclusion would appear attractive because it explains away the chasm of poetic achievement that separates Mills's and Reshoulde's contributions to the manuscript from the poems that surround theirs. We readily disdain such old-fashioned, alliterative verses as Mills's "I passynge spyde a passinge ?owre to eye / Whose heauenlyke hew hayld me hir prime to plucke" (fol. 83), or the anonymous

> In vayne it is my carefull cares to weepe
> In vayne it is to moane my matchless myss
> In vayne it is to inuocate the deepe
> Vayne to behould the sky for any blyss
>   For teares nor moanes nor deepe nor sky can*n* saue
>   Whome starres bothe luckye and welknowne would haue.
>   [fol. 92]

While our ears may find this a tedious reminder of the alliterative revival (which *The Paradise of Dainty Devices* was unable to forget), *anaphora* was itself still praised by George Puttenham as late as 1589 as a figure that makes one word "lead the daunce to many verses in sute."[72] Puttenham provides, as one example of the "figure of *Report*," these "most excellent verses" of Ralegh's that perhaps provided the model for the stanza in RP 85:

> In vayne my eyes in vaine you waste your teares,
> In vayne my sighs the smokes of my despaires:
> In vayne you search th' earth and heauens aboue,
> In vayne ye seeke, for fortune keep my loue.

When we remove the weakest poems in imitation of more admirable models,[73] or written upon some occasion from one's undergraduate days, we are still left with an impressive remnant of verse from the penultimate decade of the sixteenth century.[74] But RP 85 is significant not only for the glories of Elizabethan verse that it preserves but also for the majority of its contents that have never been reproduced anywhere else. Laurence Cummings offers one explanation for John Finet's incongruous taste:

> Finet was brought up at court, which would account for the early sections of the manuscript containing the work of the courtly makers of a late 1570s and early 1580s vintage. He must have begun his collection at court in his middle teens. . . [which was probably by 1586 or 1587], . . . continued [it] at Cambridge and at court (or from courtly sources) in 1588 or 1589, and . . . completed [it] by 1590 or 1591. It has two distinctly Cambridge sections, but even these parts are peppered with originals or imitations of the writers who fill the non-academic sections—the courtly makers. . . . At the same time, the collegiate sections seem to have a distinct tone of their own, harkening back to older ways.[75]

Although Cummings also suggests that the lacuna coming two-thirds of the way through the manuscript is the result of Finet's embarrassment with his own poems and those of other associates—which argues "a man of growing discretion"[76]—the artifactual evidence does not bear this out: there are still over a dozen attributed, and numerous unattributed, poems from the undergraduate associates of his Cambridge period. In addition, several poems ascribed to "I. F." remain in RP 85. The example of *A Poetical Rhapsody*, apparently produced from Francis Davison's collection and containing, as it does, a substantial number of his own poems, suggests that it would not be unusual for a compiler to copy his own poems alongside those he has intercepted—but would a poet-compiler set his name to his own poems if the collection were for his private enjoyment? It would appear that this gesture of ownership accompanies a manuscript designed to be circulated; if John Finet *was* the sole compiler of RP 85—and this opinion is by no means universally accepted[77]—and he at one time was willing to share his own poems along with others written by his circle, what occasioned him to suppress his poems but not those of the others? And what made his preservation of the poems of Mills, Reshoulde, and other unknown authors unproblematic alongside those of Dyer, Ralegh, or Sidney?

Or can we forgive the compiler's apparent inconsistency of judgment due to a particular kind of self-interest—one that seeks to commemorate personal relationships? The opinion of Jean-François Lyotard—"as for taste, there is no need to be delicate when one . . . entertains oneself"[78]—would reinforce a view of RP 85 as an essentially sincere record of a young man who would include himself, for both the good taste and bad taste this group embodies, among a community of like-minded University Wits. The premium put on such association poems is abundant. Consider, for instance, the several poems by Robert Mills, such as "farwell to his freend. I. F.":

> Farwell good harte thoughe place vs parte
>   It is fortune forceth so
> Thoughe bodyes bothe be sondred lothe
>   Yet myndes together goe
> Sweet do not shrink, styll on me thynk
>   Tyll death deuyde our loue
> Than both to haue, God graunt, on graue
>   And both lyke place aboue.
>   [fol. 37]

The compiler was so taken with these lines that he forgot he had already copied them into his collection and repeats them on fol. 54v. On the verso one finds "R. M. ad amicum I. F.":

> Ad te saepe venit mea chartula (filtate Finnett).
>   Ad te saepe venit cor (peramice) meum.
> Hanc tu saepe vides, hanc et persaepe reuoluis:
>   Vidisti numquam cor (peramice) meum.
> Immo simul veniunt, tum cor, tuum chartula nostra
>   Inclusum charta cor latitare puta.
> Ambo videre potes, maculis mea charta notatis
>   Prouenit et purum cor tibi (chare) meum
> Tu quoque cum chartis cordis coniungito chordas
>   Cor duo sic vnum corpora rite regat.
>   [fol. 37v]

The last line sounds much like a posey of a ring—*cor unum una vita*. A few leaves later Mills reappears with verses described as having been "(written one the backsyde of the sheepheards Kalender) att his departure from Cambridge"—a revealing reference to the recreational reading of Cambridge undergraduates:

> Finnet, Amice, vale, fugit hinc tuus ecca (Robertus:)
>   Cor tamen hic tecum linquit, amice, suum:
> Corpus abest, cor, amice, manet; cor, amice, manebit:
>   Et maneat mecum cor, per: amice, tuum.
>   [fol. 41v]

Whatever his shortcomings as a poet (although he is able to engage in a little Latin wordplay, "*Corpus abest cor*"), we are compelled to believe that Mills's *heart* was in the right place where his Cambridge friends were concerned. Robert Mills was capable of attempts at longer verse, too, though he remained preoccupied by the theme of friendship. See, for instance, "To a feygned faythless and vngratefull frende":

> I passynge spyde a passinge flowre to eye
> Whose heauenlyke hew hayld me hir prime to plucke
> Butt ah when I her sweet perfumes should trye
> I stinged was, such was my peruerse lucke
>   A fayned freend lyke to a paynted flowre
>   Whose wordes are sweet whose workes are twyse as sowre
>
> One Christall yse (to syghte congealed stronge)
> As late I walke full nyce a harte could thynke
> They crakt I slypte me thought I had great wronge
> that wher I grownded trust there grownd should shrinke

> A fyckle freend is lyke to bryckle yse
> Once he keeps touche but fayles if trye him twyse
>
> A tender snake halfe dead Iwis for coulde
> I lately fownde and broughte her home to fyre
> Butt she reuyude, alas, waxte ouerboulde
> And by sharpe stinge repayde my courtyeous hyre
>   A fayned faythless and vngratefull freende
>   lyke flowre, yse, snake, are hurtfull in *the* ende.
>   [fol. 83]

While such alliteration tortures us today,[79] the central conceit of the poem is clever enough; the reanimated snake of broken faith slithers through the poem in brief flashes of sibilance, but equally noticeable are the harsh sounds of fracture that dominate the second stanza. Mills certainly has some idea of how sound makes an echo to the sense, but too much sound can also contaminate the air and distract attention.

While RP 85 preserves much more than these apparent weeds of the Renaissance literary garden, it is also important to establish how that garden is filled with variety—not variety of subject, theme, metaphor, or technique so much as a wide range of capacity. Much of the manuscript verse deemed forgettable by scholars is rejected because, while it can go mechanically through the steps of a poem, it goes dancing without the music. But even when an amateur poet's reach exceeds his grasp, his shortcomings often reveal where he stretched his hand: we can see what was considered most characteristic of, or imitable in, the poems canonized today. One such overlooked, but rather successful, anonymous poem (unique to RP 85) occurs near the end of a set of two dozen poems either unascribed or by St. John's poets. This speaker is preoccupied with learning how to mimic the cry of a dying swan, the favorite bird of this collection:[80]

> Singe gentll Swan*n* and lett me here thy sound
> Thy sounde wherein thou sweetly showest thy ende
> For in suche tunes my dayes remayne Ille spende
> Cursinge my lyfe w*hi*ch to all greefe is bounde
> The sad complayntes that other byrdes do sounde
> Alongst the groues w*hi*ch Diane dothe defende
> Do neuer please my eares althoughe thei tende
> Vnto the caus that causde my cursed end
> Singe then o Swan*n* whose songes I may admire
> And lerne by thee to laughe at fatall spyghte;

> The gastly shape of deathe in all his yre
> Affrightes the not nor dauntes thy pleasant sprig\<hte\>
> Then blessed swan*n* teche me by this thy songe
> To welcome deathe who can*n* reuenge my wrong.
>
> [fol. 91v]

In a sonnet[81] that concerns itself so much with a literal as well as figurative swan song, we would expect some impressive—and mournful—sound effects. The poet obviously feels the burden of his task, and does produce a sonnet full of buzzing (especially lines 3, 5–9, and 12) and sibilance (lines 1–6 and 8–13), but neither of these sounds is particularly mournful; if anything, the somnolence of the smooth sibilants is counterbalanced by the jarring buzz of *ears* and *cause* and *pleasant*. The many *s*'s do combine to make a striking impact, however—we can almost say that the text of the poem offers a kind of visual alliteration even when the same letter form generates different sounds. This poet does not entirely miss the mark, though; a dull, thudding threnody echoes from the last words of the first eight lines (which stand on a single rhyme), and is dotted about in earlier feet of most lines (2, 5–8, and 11–14). In this case the poem does make an echo to the sense: soun*d* en*d*s at *d*eath. In so doing, this overlooked poem's sensuousness easily competes with three of the most popular sonnets in RP 85: the Dyer-Sidney diptych "Prometheus when firste frome heaven hye" (fol. 8)[82] and "A Satyre once did runn awaye for dreade" (fol. 8v),[83] and Sidney's "Locke vp fayre lydds the treasure of mye harte" (fol. 9).[84]

Of the many sonnets in the manuscript, one of the most interesting has also been one of the most overlooked. Although it bears thematic similarities to poems from a number of sonnet sequences, "A secret murther hath bene done of late" appears in *The Phœnix Nest* but is not printed anywhere else, nor is it copied into any other Elizabethan manuscript. Although it appears unsigned in the *The Phœnix Nest*, it is attributed to one "Goss" in RP 85. Laurence Cummings reports the many inconclusive claims for and against this "Goss" as a truncation of "Stephen Gosson,"[85] but William Ringler's disdainful comment is most worth reporting: "the quality of the poem is low enough to be within Gosson's capacity."[86] Only Emrys Jones's recent *New Oxford Book of Sixteenth-Century Verse* offers this poem as an anthology piece:

> A secret murther hath bene done of late
> Vnkyndnes founde to be the blodye knyfe

And she that did the deed a dame of state
Fayre, gracious, wyse as any bearethe lyfe

To acquytt her self her awnswer did she make
Mistrust (quoth she) hath broughte him to his ende
Which makes the mann so muche himself mistake
To laye the guylte vnto his guyltless freende

Lady not so not feard I found my death
For no deserte thus murdred is my mynde
Butt yet befor I leaue this vitall breathe
I quytt the kyller thoughe I blame the kynd

You killer unkind I dy and yet am trewe
Att whose sweet syghte my wounde doth bleede anewe.
[fol. 108v]

The conceit that relies upon the unstoppable hemorrhage of the smitten lover is not novel, but it is not quite as overused as those figures that flood pages with tears, dry them out with long-smoldering sighs, and immolate them with ardent hearts' consumption of "fewell." At several turns this sonnet distances itself from what we have come to expect from the bleeding lover. The first stanza departs from the common notion of Cupid's arrows (*Astrophil and Stella* 2) or the "beamie darts" (*Astrophil and Stella* 48) shot from the lady's aspect; in this case the use of a "knyfe"—an edged weapon more suitable to "vnkyndnes" than to beauty or virtue (*Astrophil and Stella* 48)—cannot be exculpated so easily as the volley of arrows that can strike all beholders indiscriminately. If a stiletto, this knife would also be particularly suitable for a stealthy homicide. Herein lies an essential difference: this *is* a "secret murther," rather than the public offense that all beautiful women commit by showing their faces. Instead of elaborating any further on the cause of his smart, this speaker uses the middle quatrain to report the lady's excuse. In sonnet sequences we are not normally conditioned to expect direct citation of any contrary evidence from the woman in question; here the excuse appears not as paraphrase but, apparently, as unedited analysis of the lover's mistake. Crucially, her opinion is not shared face-to-face: the lover is referred to in the third, and not the second, person. Her explanation-*cum*-excuse culminates with an unusual twist; normally the lover reminds anyone who will listen that he is guiltless (consider, for instance, Spenser's *Amoretti* 20 and, especially, 38: "Chose rather to be praysd for dooing good / then to be blam'd for spilling guiltlesse blood"), but here the woman embraces that argument. The poem's problem comes in the last quatrain: the speaker is unable to convince us that the lady's astute assessment of the lover's fault—that he prizes himself too highly—is inaccurate. The neat couplet also plays with the equivocal sense of *die* that is such a favorite among Elizabethan poets.[87] It would not be impossible to transfer the more literal sense of life's blood that underpins the poem's conceit to the seminal fluid that is just as necessary to sustain life. This sonnet may be dissatisfying because, thanks to a rather meek, forgiving speaker, there is bound to be no change in his situation. There are no threats here, no recriminations—not even many frustrations.[88]

At the opposite end of the spectrum from unique poems such as "Singe gentll Swan*n*" and "A secret murther" is the single poem RP 85 shares with the most other manuscripts, "My mynde to me a kingdom is" (fol. 19r). Although attributed here to Edward Dyer, Steven May has made a persuasive case that the poem instead belongs to the Earl of Oxford;[89] whoever the author is, the confident assertion, "I seeke no more than maye suffyse . . . / Look what I lack my minde suppliese," is meant to be therapeutic:

> Some waygh theyre pleasure by theyre luste
> . . . .
> Theire treasure is theire onlye truste
> . . . .
> But all the pleasure that I fynde
> Is to mayntayne a quiet mynde.
>   [fol. 19v]

But serious, contemplative pieces do not predominate in RP 85. Another highly popular poem[90] could not be more removed from the tone or subject of "My mynde to me"; although its invention certainly reveals a mind well-stored with an imagination, it also reflects the motion of a distinctly *dis*quieted mind:

> Naye, phewe nay pishe? nay faythe and will ye, fye.
> A gentleman deale thus? in truthe ille crye.
> Gods bodye, what means this? nay fye for shame
> Nay, Nay, come, come, nay faythe yow are to blame.
> Harcke sombodye comes, leaue of I praye
> Ile pinche, ille spurne, Ile scratche, nay good awaye
> In faythe you stryue in vayne, you shall not speede.
> You mare my ruffs, you hurte my back, my nose will bleed

Looke, looke the doore is open some bodye sees,
What will they say? nay fye you hurt my knees
Your buttons scratche, o god what coyle is heere?
You make me sweate, in faythe here is goodly geare
Nay faythe let me intreat leue if you lyste
You marr the bedd, you teare my smock, but had I wist,
So muche before I woulde haue kepte you oute.
It is a very proper thinge indeed you goo aboute.
I did not thinke you woulde haue vsed me this.
But nowe I see to late I tooke my marke amysse
A lytle thinge woulde mak vs two not to be freends.
You vse me well, I hope yow will make amends.
Houlde still Ile wype your face: you sweat amayne
You have got a goodlye thinge with all this payne.
O god how hott I am come will you drincke
Ife we goe sweatinge downe what will they thinke
Remmember I praye howe you haue vsde me nowe
doubte not ere long I will be quite with you.
Ife any one but you shoulde vse me so
Woulde I put by this wronge? in faythe sir no
Nay goe not yet: staye supper here with me
Come goe to cardes I hope we shall agree.
                            [fol. 4]

This poem is headed with an epigram from Martial that would be particularly apt to several other portions of the manuscript—"*Lasciua est nobis pagina vita proba est.*" John Wardroper suggests that "Robert Browning would have admired the technique, if not the content," of these verses, and reveals the great staying power of the poem when he notes that this was "one of the great favourites of Charles I's time."[91] The dramatic situation presented by this piece is equaled, albeit from the opposite point of view, by Sidney's fourth song from *Astrophil and Stella*, "Onlye ioy now here you are." In Sidney's poem the argument to the reluctant mistress is built not out of elaborate rhetoric, but a kind of desperate logic; the urgency of the male speaker's condition makes him anticipate and swiftly dismiss every excuse why they ought not "take tyme whyle [they] may." By the fifth stanza the speaker probably wishes for a change of venue, but he presses ahead with the seduction of his nymph in her own house; by the eighth stanza he is forcing himself upon her.

While "Naye, phew nay pishe?" invents a personality for a female speaker, and Sidney suggests a personality of a woman we never hear speak in "Onlye ioy now here you are," we are perhaps more conditioned to encounter women as objects. The *blason*, of course, provides a template for the objectification of women. We find a somewhat nontraditional *blason* in these verses by Ferdinando, Lord Strange:

> My Mistress in hir brest dothe were
> Two apples bryghte that shyne
> And eke those apples strawberryes bere
> In bosome hers deuyne.
>
> Hir goddess brests for apples goe.
> Hir nypples be the berryes.
> The one doth shyne as whyte as snowe
> The other redd as cherryes.
>
> Loue came and suckte & I did see
> The bewty of hir brest;
> Yea happy I but happiest hee
> That founde suche place of rest:
>
> Butt yet vnhappy Mistress you
> Thatt suffered thus the blynde
> To sucke the sapp thats iustlye dwe
> For an vnspotted mynde.
>   [fol. 76v]

RP 85 is the only source for this poem, but it offers an instructive counterpoint to the standard *blason* of the sixteenth century. The speaker here is a bit of an accidental voyeur: rather than providing an inventory of the mistress's obvious features, and imaging those that modesty conceals, this speaker has apparently never disrobed his beloved in his mind. The chronology of the poem seems inverted: until the speaker sees Cupid suckle, his "vnspotted mynde" would not have conjured (his admission in line 10) the apples and strawberries he sees in his mistress's breast. At the same time his innocence gives way to his desire to take Cupid's place:

> Regarde sweet Mistress the*n* his faulte
> And loe in my behoue
> Some difference make betwyxtte a ma*n*
> And suche a chyllde as loue.
>   [fol. 77]

The decorous restraint of Lord Strange's verses, and their claim for what is "iustlye dwe" to the pure-minded lover, has its violation in an earlier poem in the manuscript (also unique to RP 85):

> It was an oulde sayenge of S*ir* John Kettels
> That a woman is made of fyue kynde of mettels[92]
> Hir lypps are of hony for they must be lyckte
> Hir Hypps are of porke for they must be pryckte
> Hir Belly is venyson for that must be prest
> Hir shoulders are mutton and so is her breste
> Hir buttocks are brawne euen downe to her thyghe
> By that same token*n* the mustard pott hanges bye.
> [fol. 50v]

Lasciva est pagina indeed![93]

Given the worldly observations of Sir John Kettel, we may be surprised to find that RP 85 also includes several poems attributed to women—not a common trait of the printed miscellanies—and not merely poems that assume a female persona. The very first poem in the manuscript is attributed to the most important woman in England, "Elysabetha regina":

> When I was fayre and younge and fauour graced me
>   Of many was I soughte their mystres for to be.
> But I did scorne them all and answerd the*m* therfore
>   Goe, Goe, Goe, seek som other wher,
>   Importune me no more.
>   [fol. 1][94]

The remaining three stanzas offer an interesting admission from the Virgin Queen: she acknowledges that she grew "prowder" with every heart she broke until Cupid repaid her for her coyness. He "plucke[s] [her] plumes," and she is afflicted with restless nights that leave her repentant. Another poem unattributed in RP 85 is acknowledged to belong to Anne Vavasour (who is named, in this manuscript, in the titles of several of Oxford's poems): "Though I seeme straunge sweete freende be thou not so" (fol. 17).[95] But one of the last poems in the manuscript, by an unidentified Mrs. M. R., supplies a most interesting woman's perspective. Here the commonplace notion of the woman's will and devotion to her honor as the sturdy fortress against all suitors[96] is adjusted by a view from inside the battlements:

> Howe can*n* the feeble forte butt yeelde att last
> Whom daylye force of sharp assaulte assayes
> . . . .
> Weake are the walls the batterye to abyde
> Of such as seek the spoyll of our renowne
> They lye in wayte the practyse and prouyde
> To stopp our streyghtes and beate our bullwarkes downe
> > To sacke our walles and in most cruel sorte
> > With can*n*on shott to roote our feeble forte
> > > [fol. 114r]

The walls that are seen as impregnable by the choir of sonneteers apparently are not so. If a woman is truly responsible for this poem, it might seem she degrades her sex for its weakness and feebleness. There is a tone of exasperation, to be sure, in the first two stanzas, but if we compare her last two stanzas to another of Sidney's poems in RP 85 from the *Old Arcadia* ("Reason tell me thy mynde if this be reason") we see how she has appropriated, and then inverted, the martial metaphors. Sidney is remarkable for his own revision of the blason, wherein hairs, breasts, and eyes are now missiles, pikes, and cannons:

> Her lose hears be the shot her brests the pykes be
> Skoute eche motione is, the handes the horsemen
> Hir lipps ar the riches the warrs to mayntayne
> Where well couched abydes a cofer of perlle
> Her legges the courage of all the swete campe
> Saye than reason I saye what is thy consaylle
>
> The cannons be her eyes, myne eyes the walls be
> Whiche at the fyrst volye gaue open entraunce
> No rampyre dothe abyde my brayne was vp blowne
> Vndermynde with a speche the percer of thoughte
> Thus weakned by my selfe no helpe remaynethe
> Say then reason I say what is thue counsaylle.
> > [fol. 24][97]

Mrs. M. R. picks up the martial metaphors, but gives them a much more erotic twist:

> Whatt should we do we pass the pykes w*i*th payne
> We catche the clapps and bere awaye the blowes

> With valor we retorne and rushe agayne
> The charged staues of our encountred foes
>> Wounded we parte and yet we neuer dye
>> & stryken downe we fall and neuer flye
>
> Thus seelye soules we stumble att the close
> Nought hauynge but the naked to defend
> Layde all along before our cruell foes
> We neuer yeeld butt fyghte it out to the ende
>> We stryue we thrust and nothyng yet the neer
>> Women poore soulles I see are borne to bear.
>>> [fol. 114v][98]

The phallic pikes now "pass . . . with payne," and leave women "wounded" in the exchange, lamenting that they are "borne to bear" the consequences of such an assault. The violence of the poem is barely moderated by the playful equivocation of the last two stanzas; Mrs. M. R. shows us a vulnerability that male voices do not seem to apprehend.

Given its importance as a bridge from the earliest to the latest of the Tudor miscellanies, it is fitting to look at the single poem RP 85 shares with Tottel's *Songes and Sonettes*.[99] Tied as the manuscript is to the last quarter of the sixteenth century, it is remarkable that a poem attributed to "E of Surr."[100] would surface in RP 85—and even more remarkable that the poem does not appear at the beginning of the collection, but near the end (it is the 139th of the 145 poems in the manuscript):

> The longer lyfe the more offence
>> The more offence the greater payne
> The greater payne the lesse defence
>> The lesse defence the lesser gayne
> The lesse of gayne longe ill doth try
> Wherfor come death and lett me dye.
>
> The shorter lyfe lesse connte I fynde
>> The lesse acconnte the soner made
> The count sone made the merier mynde
>> The meryer mynde doth though euade
> Short lyfe in truth this thinge doth try
> Wherfor come death and lett me dye.
>
> Come gentle death the ebbe of care
>> The ebbe of care the flode of lyfe

> The flods of lyfe the ioyfull fare
> 　The ioyfull fare the end of strife
> The end of strife the thinge wishe I:
> Wherefore come death & let me dye.
> 　　　　　　　　　[fol. 115v]

One is left wondering whether this poem was copied out of a later edition of *Songes and Sonettes,* or whether it was somehow still in manuscript circulation some half-century after Surrey's execution. Whatever the case, we see that the first important Tudor miscellany could still compete for space in the manuscript collections begun near the end of the century. It also becomes clear that the manuscript miscellanies were not completely replaced by print miscellanies; they continued to compete with printed counterparts, and deserve more generous attention as the equals that they are.

David Hume begins his essay "Of the Standard of Taste" with an observation that applies quite nicely to the nature of the Tudor verse miscellanies:

> Men of the most confined knowledge are able to remark a difference of taste in the narrow circle of their acquaintance, even when the persons have been educated under the same government, and have early imbibed the same prejudices. But those who can enlarge their view to contemplate distant nations and remote ages, are still more surprised at the great inconsistence and contrariety. We are apt to call barbarous whatever departs widely from our own taste and apprehension; but soon find the epithet of reproach retorted on us.[101]

Since we are removed by four hundred years or more from the tastes that were able to appreciate and consume poetry that for us sometimes seems wholly unpalatable, we need to recognize that the fault does not always arise from the apparent shortcomings we find in sixteenth-century poets and readers, but from our inability to reconstruct the preferences of ages past. Practical concerns intervene, and even the most serious and energetic student of the Tudor period cannot survey all of the poetry that was produced between *Songes and Sonettes* and *A Poetical Rhapsody*. We need a crutch, and so we turn to the anthologies that are designed to *represent* the Renaissance to us as efficiently as possible. The anthologist, then, wields tremendous power to limit, and thereby to shape, our vision of the most fertile period in English literary history. After glancing through important surviving sixteenth-century manuscripts, we notice that the poems that will appear typical of what was being read and circulated in the last half of the sixteenth century blur together: we soon lose count of how many poems set themselves in May, contain characters named Phillida or Corridon, describe the assault on the fortress of love, praise (or lament) Cupid's skills at archery, or lay fuel to smoky sighs. We are left looking for any shred of originality in these poems, and when we find it we attach ourselves to them. But how high was the premium on novelty in the Elizabethan period? Are we looking for something that did not preoccupy the audiences removed from us by four centuries? If so, can any modern anthology of Renaissance poetry *ever* presume to be representative of anything more than its *own* moment in literary history? These anthologies are indispensable, but are they responsibly produced? Ought we read only the "golden" verse of the sixteenth century? Or should we seek out an anthology such as David Norbrook's very catholic *Penguin Book of Renaissance Verse* in order to hear the marginal voices he has reclaimed? Although he admits into his Penguin anthology "a number of poems whose interest may be regarded as more historical than literary" in response "to the current movements to question the canon and reclaim alternative voices," Norbrook cautiously tempers these inclusions: "'Alternative' canons may have their own limitations, bringing the concerns of the present so heavily to bear on the past that they suppress differences; the challenge of difference can be as stimulating as the challenge of relevance."[102] Given his mission, I am surprised that Norbrook avoids so many texts from the miscellanies that would be suitable to a more generous, less author-conscious collection. Of all the recent anthologies, Emrys Jones's *New Oxford Book of Sixteenth-Century Verse* shows the greatest range in visiting the miscellanies and selecting poems that have not been reproduced by earlier anthologists.

Over a century ago William Hazlitt made the case that the printed "miscellanies serve, besides, as a weather glass for the changing literary tastes of the somewhat long period (1557–1602) over which these publications extended."[103] Douglas Bush leads a list of more recent critics who agree that, "apart from their varying intrinsic worth, the more general anthologies provide an index of changing taste."[104] But what was the taste that judged and preserved favorable variations and rejected others? What allowed a poem to survive—and in some cases change its format from manuscript to print (and, sometimes, back again)—and move from hand to hand? If RP 85 does not consistently offer us what we expect from the period of the most rapid and rich literary development in English literary history, it establishes—in the spirit of Yvor Winters—a strong case for a more generous and encompassing vision of that history by later readers. This is the same case made again and again by the activity of manuscript compilers, and which would seem to justify the modern anthologists' inclusion of lesser-known works based on the appeal they inarguably had to the eyes and ears of those breathing the same air that inspired the Tudor poets.

Appendix. Rawlinson Poet. 85

Print Miscellany	Ascription	Other MSS	Harl. 6910 MS	Harl. 7392 MS	Digit	Order	First Line
	the Queen	‡			☞	1	When I was fair and young and favor graced me
Helicon	Breton	[‡]	f. 140		☞	2	Fair in a morn, oh fair morn, was never morn so fair
		†				3	Scribere cur cessem misero de funere Greshem
Helicon	Breton				☞	4	In the merry month of May
						5	Pause a while my silly muse
						6	Nay, phew nay pish! nay faith and will ye, fie
					☞	7	In Libya land as stoies tell was bred and born
	Sidney					8	Phoebus farewell a fairer saint I serve
	Dyer	‡☞	f. 149	f. 23	☞	9	I would it were not as it is
	Dyer		f. 169	f. 34	☞	10	The man whose thoughts against him do conspire
Phœnix	Dyer	☞	f. 173	f. 23		11	As rare to hear as seldom to be seen
	Dyer	‡		f. 28	☞	12	O more than most fair full of the living fire
	Dyer	☞	f. 154	f. 25	☞	13	Prometheus when first from heaven high
Helicon	Sidney	☞		f. 25	☞	14	A Satyr once did run away for dread
Helicon	Sidney			f. 38		15	Lock up fair lids the treasure of my heart
	Sidney			f. 66		16	The dart, the beames, the string so strong I prove
Arbor	Sidney	‡		f. 39		17	The fire to see my wrongs for anger burneth
Bowre			f. 148	f. 38	☞	18	The air with sweet my senses doth delight
	Oxford/Vavasour	†		f. 63	☞	19	Sitting alone upon my thought in melancholy mood
		†		f. 38		20	If I could think how these my thoughts to leave
	Nowell					21	Finding these beames which I must ever love
						22	Fain would I kiss those lips
		†	f. 149	f. 70		23	Who hath his fancy pleased
	Peele			f. 69	☞	24	What thing is love for since love is a thing
				f. 68	☞	25	What thing is love? a vain conceit of mind
	Breton	‡	f. 146			26	Sitting late with sorrow sleeping

Paradise	Oxford	†		27	The lively lark stretched forth her wing
	Oxford			28	What is desire? Which doth approve to set on fire each gentle heart
Bowre	Oxford		f. 145	29	When wert thou born desire
Bowre	Oxford		f. 18	30	If women could be fair and yet not fond
	Oxford		f. 33	31	Who taught thee first to sigh alas my heart
		¶	f. 70	32	Though I seem strange sweet friend be thou not so
Phœnix		‡	f. 40	33	The gentle season of the year
			f. 63	34	My waning joys my still increasing grief
			f. 67	35	The dreary day when I must take my leave
	Dyer		f. 73	36	My mind to me a kingdom is
	Sidney			37	You goatherds gods that love the grassy mountains
		‡		38	Like those sick folk in whom strange humors flow
				39	When I behold the trees in the earth's fair livery clothed
				40	With two strange fires of equal heat possessed
	Sidney			41	Over those brooks trusting to ease mine eyes
				42	Reason tell me thy mind if this be reason
Bowre; Arbor; Phœnix				43	Those eyes that hold the hand of every heart
Bowre; Phœnix	Breton		f. 139	44	Fair fairer than the fairest
				45	Like to an hermit poor
	Sidney			46	At my heart there is a pain
	Breton			47	Deep lamenting loss of treasure
Bowre	Breton			48	Among the woes of those unhappy wights
Helicon	Sidney		f. 171	49	In a grove most rich of shade
	Mills			50	Farewell good heart though place us part [*sous rature*— see #77]
	Mills			51	*Ad te saepe venit mea chartula* (filtate Finnett)
	Mills			52	*Cum mea (mi Finnett) mors vitae tempora finit*
—	—			—	"*Oratio Illustrissimæ reginæ Elisabethæ apud Cantabrigiensis*"

continued

Appendix. Rawlinson Poet. 85 *(continued)*

Print Miscellany	Ascription	Other MSS	Harl. 6910 MS	Harl. 7392 MS	Digit	Order	First Line
—	—					—	"*Oratio sereniss: Reginæ Elisabethæ Acacæmiæ Oxonienssi habita*"
	Finet					53a	O mid mihi cum bellis servit <mea> cara puellis [*sous rature*]
	Finet					53b	Mars with thy wars [*sous rature*]
						54a	*Qui supra posse sursum tendit*
						54b	Who strives oft to be seated aloft in place where he should not
Phœnix	Dyer			f. 69		55	Divide my times and race my wretched hours
						56	*Fertur in convivius vinus, vina venirent*
	Mills					57	*Finnet, Amice, vale, fugit hinc tuus ecca*
Helicon	Sidney					58	Only joy now here you are
						59	Physic beginneth first with phy
						60	Late suppers and wine I did forbear
						61	*Serua mensuram: Habe curam*
	Ralegh		f. 154	f. 22	☞	62	Fain would I but I dare not
			f. 139		☞	63	The luck: the life: the love
					☞	64	Mine eyes leave off your weeping
				f. 67		65	I heard a noise and wished for a sight
Phœnix				f. 27	☞	66	Would I were changed into that golden shower
			f. 147			67	Many a maid have I gulled and many a wife have I kissed [*sous rature*]
						68	A thief condemned to die
				f. 76	☞	69	Some men will say there is a kind of muse
		¶		ff. 28/37	☞	70	Farewell false love, thou oracle of lies
				f. 52	☞	71	Wing'd with desire I seek to mount on high
Phœnix	Arll	†	f. 165	f. 28		72	Die die desire and bid delight adieu
	A. H.		f. 148	f. 50		73	Short is my rest whose toil is overlong
						74	It was an old saying of Sir John Kettel's
Helicon				f. 51		75	In peascod time when hound to horn

Reshoulde	[☞]	76	As a friend, friendlike to a friend far absent
Mills		77	Farewell good heart though place us part [see #50]
Thomas E.		78	As palm down press'd doth after kind spring aloft [*sous rature*]
Sidney		79	The scourge of life and death's extreme disgrace
Sidney		80	Woe woe to me on me return the smart
Sidney		81	Thou pain the only guest of loathed constancy
Sidney	☞	82	And have I heard her say (o cruel pain)?
		83	Dudleio simulac puer<um> de sanguine nas<ci>
Reshoulde	☞	84	An<n> parte florida caelo puriore
R. H.		85	A certain man upon a time
		86	Troianus paris et troianus origina Parry
		[87]	[My earthly mould doth melt in wat'ry tears] [frag]
		[88]	[Thus do I fall to rise thus] [frag]
E. Chapman		89	Ite procul tertreci perfricta fronte Catones
	‡	90	My masters you that read my rhyme
	†	91	And think you I have nought a load
		92	Cease fond desire to wish me better hap
Lord Strange		93	My mistress in her breast doth wear [*sous rature*]
Mills	☞	94	Bathed I have too long (sweet friend) my lady Thalia
Mills	☞	95	Neptune of whirling winds and huge waves' terrible emperor
Mills	[☞]	96	In prime of summer whenas all in a fiery fury
Mills	☞	97	In flowered meads as late I walked in May
Mills		98	I passing spied a passing flower to eye
	☞	99	Forsaken first and now forgotten quite [*sous rature*]
		100	Give not thy gifts to aged men
		101	A herd a swain a martial knight
Finet		102	[. . . Passions unfolded to say unfeignedly] [frag]
Finet		103	Are women so named
		104	Sweet Phyllis Venus' sweeting was, was none so sweet as she
Reshoulde	☞	105	What can I pray thee, tell me (sweet echo) learn me to love?

continued

Appendix. Rawlinson Poet. 85 (*continued*)

Print Miscellany	Ascription	Other MSS	Harl. 6910 MS	Harl. 7392 MS	Digit	Order	First Line
					☞	106	All in a sunshine day withouten cloud
					☞	107	With Spring of year began my prime of spite
						108	When course of years had weaned my wandering mind
						109	Distressed man what kind of thing is love?
						110	*Duret sacra ignis cui dat primordia <cae'um>*
						111	The trees surcharged all with leafy shade
						112	Mine eyes distressed with stormy winter's ire
						113	As silence seldom seen [*sous rature*]
						114	Sing gentle swan and let me hear thy sound
					☞	115	Fast ran the sun from fiery east to west
Rhapsody		¶		f. 26	☞	116	I said and swore that I would never love
	Dyer	†			☞	117	Perin agreed what new mischance betide
		†		f. 15	☞	118	Amarillis was full fair
Bowre						119	Near unto Wilton sweet huge heaps of stone are found
		††¶			☞	120	Conceit is quick, would so were sweet content [frag. of #137]
Phœnix		‡¶		f. 62	☞	121	The state of France as now it stands
Arbor	W. N.		f. 142	f. 36	☞	122	Calling to mind mine eye long went about
						123	Sweet is the life that is the sweet of love
						124	Three things in a morning look thou remember
			f. 158	f. 11		125	A heart I have a heart I crave
		†		f. 35	☞	126	When first of all dame nature wrought
		†				127	Whereas the heart at tennis play
	Mills				☞	128	When Phoebus Daphne long had wooed
	Breton				☞	129	O dear love when shall it be
Phœnix	Goss				☞	130	A secret murder hath been done of late

	Dyer	†‡	f. 158	f. 12		He that his mirth hath lost	131
					☞	At length comes oft too late	132
Bowre; Arbor					☞	Who takes a friend and trusts him not	133
	Mrs. M. R.				☞	Oh thou that dost my life alone sustain	134
				f. 71	☞	How can the feeble fort but yield at last	135
						Since thought hath leave to think at least	136
Bowre						A little fire doth make the faggot burn	137
Arbor						Knowledge doth much in care of most content	138
Tottel	Surrey				☞	The longer life the more offense	139
					☞	Many desire but few or none deserve	140
		¶		f. 33		Mine eye bewrays	141
				f. 33		Small rule in reasons want	142
	—					"There be fowre elements placed in the worlde"	—
	Ralegh					As you went to Walsingham	143
	R. T.					The fairest of beauty's band	144
						Change thy mind since she doth change	145
28			20	45	68	

Note: Numbers in last line are totals.

Harley 6910 = 20 in printed miscellanies.
Harley 7392 = 21 in printed miscellanies.
† = Marsh Z3.5.21 (Dublin); shares 13 poems with RP 85.
‡ = Dd.5.75 (Cambridge); shares 12 poems with RP 85.
¶ = Folger V.a.89; shares 10 poems with RP 85.

Notes

1. Steven May has identified some 35,000 different poems written in English just between 1558 and 1603; some 9,000 of these occur only in manuscript.

2. Michael Drayton is critical of those who are parsimonious with, if not falsely proud of, manuscript verse. In a versified companion to Francis Meres's *Palladis Tamia* (1598) [STC 17834] he appends to *The Battaile of Agincourt* (1627) [STC 7190], "Of Poets and Poesie," Drayton disdains those "rare" and "wonderous reliques" that "In priuate chambers . . . incloistered are, / And by transcription daintyly must goe" (sig. Dd2v).

3. Hyder E. Rollins edited the nine primary Tudor miscellanies: *Songes and Sonettes* (usually known as "Tottel's Miscellany"), *A Handful of Pleasant Delights, The Paradise of Dainty Devices, A Gorgeous Gallery of Gallant Inventions, Brittons Bowre of Delights, The Phœnix Nest, The Arbor of Amorous Devices, England's Helicon,* and *A Poetical Rhapsody.* Of the 1,110 individual poems available in print in these nine miscellanies, fewer than one-quarter survive in manuscripts in either the British Library or the Bodleian Library (which, together, house far more Tudor verse manuscripts than any other libraries—Steven May locates 270 Elizabethan MSS in the British Library and 87 in the Bodleian, with 56 in the Folger, 35 in the Huntington, 22 at Trinity College, Cambridge, and 18 each in the Cambridge University Library, and at Harvard, Yale, and Lambeth Palace).

4. Although these two labels have become more or less interchangeable, a *commonplace book* has traditionally described a special kind of manuscript collection. Despite the careful organization that typifies the format, even the most scrupulously maintained commonplace books devoted to the serious, if dull, activity of assembling a rhetorical arsenal often became contaminated with more vain pursuits; blank books often were home to a wide range of items—poems, anagrams, riddles, copies of letters and speeches, recipes, medicinal remedies, verses from the Bible, sermons, notes taken down from printed sources, and assorted bits of curiosa (such as "The Title of the Emporour of Russia" saved in Bodleian MS Ashmole 38). Peter Beal offers a good working definition of *miscellany:* "a manuscript consisting of works, or extracts from works, by various authors compiled for pleasure rather than as an aid to study" (*Index of English Literary Manuscripts . . . 1450–1625,* 2 vols. [London: Mansell, 1980], 1:ix). To show just how inconsistently these labels are applied to manuscript studies, compare Beal with Hilton Kelliher and Sally Brown: "a distinction should be made here between a commonplace collection, which includes examples of work by many writers, and a miscellany, which concentrates largely on a single author" (*English Literary Manuscripts* [London: The British Library, 1986], 20–21).

5. This is George Saintsbury's characterization of the interval between Tottel and "the glories of the later years of Elizabeth," in *The Earlier Renaissance,* Periods of English Literature, 12 vols. (London: William Blackwood, 1923), 5:277.

6. The earliest suggested date for the first edition of *The Court of Venus* is the late 1530s; see Russell A. Fraser, ed., *The Court of Venus* (Durham, N.C.: Duke University Press, 1955), 3–26, for a complete discussion of the three editions he dates to 1535–39, 1547–49, and 1561–65.

7. C. S. Lewis, *English Literature in the Sixteenth Century Excluding Drama* (Oxford: Clarendon Press, 1954), 64–65.

8. Ibid., 240, 467.

9. Douglas Bush, *English Literature in the Earlier Seventeenth Century: 1600–1660*, 2d ed., rev. (Oxford: Clarendon Press, 1962), 95.

10. Yvor Winters, *Forms of Discovery* ([Denver]: Alan Swallow, 1967), 1.

11. Ibid., 3. For a superb analysis of the sides taken by Lewis and Winters, see G. K. Hunter, "Drab and Golden Lyrics of the Renaissance," in *Forms of Lyric: Selected Papers from the English Institute*, ed. Reuben A. Brower (New York: Columbia University Press, 1970), 1–18. For other notable contributions to the debate, see Raymond Southall, *The Courtly Maker: An Essay on the Poetry of Wyatt and his Contemporaries* (Oxford: Basil Blackwell, 1964), and Douglas L. Peterson, *The English Lyric from Wyatt to Donne: A History of the Plain and Eloquent Styles* (Princeton: Princeton University Press, 1967).

12. Given Sidney's tremendous presence in circulating verse (see Beal SiP 1–219), and its explicit connection to him, it is odd that *The Phœnix Nest* contains none of Sidney's verse. It may be that the editorial process that produced *The Phœnix Nest* truly meant to render the collection a tribute to Sidney's influence and allowed the miscellany to reflect that influence without the direct competition from *il miglior fabbro*. The reader of *The Phœnix Nest* is thus challenged to make any connections to Sidney on a poem-by-poem basis. In some ways, then, the miscellany's title is particularly apt: the phœnix that emerges from its own ashes is the vehicle to describe the rebirth of Sidney's voice in the choir of his admirers and acolytes. The metaphoric funeral pyre that silences Sidney's pen simultaneously gives birth to countless nestling poets who echo, however infelicitously, their source.

13. Winters, *Forms of Discovery*, 1.

14. The most elaborate attempt to redress this imbalance is available in H. R. Woudhuysen's wide-ranging, immensely learned study *Sir Philip Sidney and the Circulation of Manuscripts 1558–1640* (Oxford: Clarendon Press, 1996).

15. Hilton Kelliher, "Unrecorded Extracts from Shakespeare, Sidney and Dyer," *English Manuscript Studies 1100–1700* 2 (1990): 183.

16. Ernest W. Sullivan II, "The Renaissance Manuscript Verse Miscellany: Private Party, Private Text," in *New Ways of Looking at Old Texts,* ed. W. Speed Hill (Binghamton, N.Y.: Renaissance English Text Society, 1993), 297.

17. Arthur F. Marotti, "Malleable and Fixed Texts: Manuscript and Printed Miscellanies and the Transmission of Lyric Poetry in the English Renaissance," in Hill, ed., *New Ways of Looking at Old Texts,* 160. For a more extensive treatment of his point, see the long chapter "Social Textuality in the Manuscript System" in Marotti's *Manuscript, Print, and the English Renaissance Lyric* (Ithaca: Cornell University Press, 1995), esp. 135–47. Mary Hobbs also argues for the refocusing of bibliography upon corrupt texts, though more for the clues they can provide to "evidence of authorship, of revision and of the nature and reliability of their particular line of textual transmission" ("Early Seventeenth-Century Verse Miscellanies and Their Value for Textual Editors," *English Manuscript Studies 1100–1700* 1 [1989]: 183).

18. Scholarly squabbles over matters of authorship lose some urgency when we

begin to look at sixteenth-century poetry as a process of dissemination and collection and not merely authorship. We confound ourselves by our need to know who wrote a particular poem so we can begin a sturdy study of a single author, but at the time of their births and earliest circulation, manuscript poems possessed much of their cultural capital due largely to unverifiable authorial ascription. It is, for some purposes, not so important that we correct faulty ascriptions but that we accept at face value the perceived source of the poem circulated from manuscript to manuscript and eventually frozen in print.

19. See Neil Fraistat, "The Place of the Book and the Book as Place" (3–17), and Earl Miner, "Some Issues for Study of Integrated Collections" (18–43), in *Poems in Their Place*, ed. Neil Fraistat (Chapel Hill: University of North Carolina Press, 1986).

20. This is, of course, more true of a ready-made blank book that awaits inscription (such as RP 85) than an assembly of loose leaves of various sizes that are later bound together (such as many of the Cotton manuscripts). The compiler of RP 85 assures the exact order of the manuscript's contents by installing catchwords on each page; it is unclear whether this was meant to allow the manuscript to be reassembled if disbound, or if the catchwords merely reflected the expected physical features of a printed book.

21. A commonplace book strictly confined to the arrangement of material under predetermined heads is, on the contrary, *episodic*, as befits a work of reference, and its individual parts are readily separable from the whole.

22. See, too, Harold Love, "The Feathery Scribe" (a review of Woudhuysen), *TLS*, 23 August 1996: "Most previous scholarship on [manuscript sources] has arisen from an editorial concern with particular authors; but editors have an unfortunate fondness for plucking texts from a mixed source without any serious consideration of what it signifies as a whole" (11). Although ostensibly tied to a single author, Woudhuysen's study is still skillfully able to suggest the wider impact that single voice had on the phenomenon of manuscript circulation: Sidney indeed "may have changed the private character of manuscript production, altering and reviving it while at the same time seeking to preserve its origins, which he saw as primarily literary" (8).

23. Marotti, "Manuscript, Print, and the English Renaissance Lyric," in Hill, ed., *New Ways of Looking at Old Texts*, 214–15.

24. Steven W. May, "Manuscript Circulation at the Elizabethan Court," in Hill, ed., *New Ways of Looking at Old Texts*, 279.

25. In his influential study *Gemeinschaft und Gesellschaft* (1887), Tönnies offers a distinction between human nature within community (*Gemeinschaft*) and society (*Gesellschaft*) that is particularly applicable to the literary transactions that circulated miscellaneous Renaissance verse in both manuscript and print formats. The affinities are striking when we transfer his concepts of *Gemeinschaft* and *Gesellschaft* to, respectively, the community of readers secure within the circles of coterie poetry and a society of readers whose individual members seek access to or exchange with that community. *Gemeinschaft* has its basis in close and instinctive family relationships, which we may extrapolate bibliographically to encompass consanguineous manuscript circles.

26. Roger Chartier, *The Order of Books,* ed. Lydia G. Cochrane (Stanford: Stanford University Press, 1994), 4.

27. Harold Love, *Scribal Publication in Seventeenth-Century England* (Oxford: Clarendon Press, 1993), 83. Marotti, *Manuscript,* 30–48, and Woudhuysen, *Sir Philip Sidney,* 163–73, offer concise surveys of manuscripts arising from a variety of such communities. See, too, Donald H. Reiman's Lyell Lectures for 1989, *The Study of Modern Manuscripts: Public, Confidential, and Private* (Baltimore: Johns Hopkins University Press, 1993), for an extended discussion of private, corporate, and public manuscript circles in the romantic period.

28. See Ferdinand Tönnies, *Gemeinschaft und Gesellschaft* (Leipzig, 1887), 46, 47, 50; *Community and Society,* ed. and trans. Charles P. Loomis (East Lansing: Michigan State University Press, 1957), 65, 68:

> Sondern hier ist ein Jeder für sich allein, und im Zustande der Spannung gegen alle Uebrigen. . . . [W]as Einer hat und geniesset, das hat und geniesst er mit Ausschliessung aller Uebrigen; es gibt kein Gemeinsam-Gutes in Wirklichkeit. Es kann solches geben, durch Fiction der Subjecte; welche aber nicht anders möglich ist, als indem zugleich ein gemeinsames Subject . . . fingirt oder gemacht wird, worauf dieser gemeinsame Werth bezogen werden muss. . . . Damit eine Sache überhaupt als gesellschaftlicher Werth gelte, dazu ist nur erforderlich, dass sie auf der einen Seite im Ausschluss gegen Andere gehabt, auf der anderen von irgend einem Exemplare der menschlichen Gattung begehrt werde.
>
> [Everybody is by himself and isolated, and there exists a condition of tension against all others. . . . (W)hat someone has and enjoys, he has and enjoys to the exclusion of all others. So, in reality, something that has a common value does not exist. Its existence may, however, be brought about through fiction on the part of the individuals, which means that they have to invent a common personality . . . to whom this common value has to bear reference. . . . For a thing to be of any value in the Gesellschaft, it is only neceessary that it be possessed by one party to the exclusion of another and that it be desired by one or another individual.]

29. Love, *Scribal Publication,* 177, 179, and 183. Marotti also lends his voice to the belief that, in a special way, manuscripts "serve as the medium of socioliterary intercourse within a restricted social group and the repository of texts generated within such an environment" and "give a better sense of the sociocultural functioning of such literary texts than printed editions do" (*Manuscript,* 39, xiii). See also Mary Hobbs, *Early Seventeenth Century Verse Miscellany Manuscripts* (Aldershot: Scolar Press, 1992), for her particular discussion of the post-Sidney scribal community of Christ Church, Oxford (79–82).

30. Woudhuysen, *Sir Philip Sidney,* 384; earlier (292–98) he describes the constitution of the tight Sidney community.

31. In his very thoughtful "Studies in Some Related Manuscript Poetic Miscellanies of the 1580s" (D.Phil. thesis, Oxford, 1970) L. G. Black puts its this way: "the

popular poems by leading writers of the time, and the private, usually occasional, poems written by or having some connection with the compilers of the miscellanies and their friends ... have thus a core and a fringe, a macrocosm and microcosm relationship" (2).

32. In his discussion of music manuscripts, Love asks a relevant question: to what extent were tastes in music "an outgrowth of the scribal culture to which [one] belonged rather than representing an autonomous aesthetic preference"? See *Scribal Publication*, 31.

33. For a fascinating profile of this eminent antiquary, see B. J. Enright, "'I Collect and I Preserve': Richard Rawlinson, 1690–1755, and Eighteenth-Century Book Collecting," *The Book Collector* 39 (1990): 27–54. Enright notes that Rawlinson's "bequest to the Bodleian was the largest collection it had ever received and one which took the Library over 150 years to catalogue" (27–28).

34. The manuscript is almost exclusively devoted to verse. The only exceptions are transcriptions of Latin orations delivered by Queen Elizabeth at Cambridge in 1564 and Oxford in 1566 (see Laurence Cummings, "John Finet's Miscellany," [Ph.D. diss., Washington University, 1960], 339–47), and a curious prose piece, "The conclusione of fowre dyuers quantityes, qualityes, propertyes and dygnityes," which parallels, both in theme and execution, an obscure volume by Nicholas Breton, *The Figvre of Fovre, or A Handfvll of sweet Flowers* (1631) [STC 3651].

35. Cummings ("John Finet's Miscellany," 48–58) identifies six crucial lacunae: original folios 1–13, 28, 55–60, 87–92, 134–36, and 170 are lost (these correspond to those portions of the surviving manuscript immediately preceding the renumbered leaves 1, 14, 37, 65, 84, and 118).

36. Only one of Spenser's poems, *Amoretti* 8, "O more than moste fayre full of the liuinge fyre" (fol. 7v), appears in RP 85—and there it is misattributed to Dyer. See also British Library Harley 7392 (fol. 28); Cambridge Dd.5.75 (fol. 37v); STC 23076. Beal SpE2-7. How this sonnet, which occurs so early in the manuscript, came to be misattributed will remain a mystery, but it is unusual to encounter individual poems from the *Amoretti*: Beal identifies only four sonnets from the *Amoretti* to occur in isolation in any literary manuscript—he also locates single instances of *Amoretti* 1 (SpE1), *Amoretti* 23 (SpE7.5), and *Amoretti* 64 (SpE7.8).

37. Enright notes the motto on Rawlinson's armorial bookplate, which is certainly confirmed by much of RP 85: *Sunt Antiquissima Quæque Optima*. For brief descriptions of the manuscript, see William Ringler, *The Poems of Sir Philip Sidney* (Oxford: Clarendon Press, 1962), 557–58; Black, "Manuscript Poetic Miscellanies," 41–42; Marotti, *Manuscript*, 63–65; and Woudhuysen, *Sir Philip Sidney*, 260–62. For a full description, see Cummings, "John Finet's Miscellany," 5–74.

38. Woudhuysen notes that RP 85 contains the second largest collection of Sidney's verse in any manuscript miscellany (*Sir Philip Sidney*, 261). There are only two poems considered misattributed to Sidney in RP 85: "The darte, the beames, the stringe so stronge I proue" (fol. 9) and "At my harte there is a payne" (fol. 25v).

39. RP 85 also contains one poem from each of the following: *Songes and Sonettes* (Surrey's "The longer lyfe the more offence," fol. 115v), *The Paradise of Dainty Devices* (Oxford's "The liuelye larcke stretcht forthe her winge," fol. 14v), and *A*

Poetical Rhapsody (the anonymous elegy on Sidney, "Perin agreed what new mischance betyde," fol. 93v).

40. For a brief discussion of this manuscript, see Ringler, *Poems of Philip Sidney,* 557. Harley 7392 has been variously attributed to a Gray's Inn man, St. Loe Kniveton (Ringler, and Hobbs, 19), and a Christ Church, Oxford man, Humphrey Coningsby (Marotti, *Manuscript,* 65–67, and Woudhuysen, *Sir Philip Sidney,* 278–86).

41. For brief discussions of this manuscript, see Ringler, *Poems of Philip Sidney,* 556, and Woudhuysen, *Sir Philip Sidney,* 262–63. See Katherine K. Gottschalk, "British Museum Manuscript Harley 6910: An Edition" (unpublished Ph.D. diss., University of Chicago, 1974), and her "Discoveries Concerning British Library MS Harley 6910," *Modern Philology* 77 (1979): 121–31. This manuscript is visually distinctive: it is clearly a scribally generated—almost calligraphic—substitute for many poems already available in print (especially Spenser's *Complaints,* which occupy the first 73 leaves of the manuscript). Gottschalk carefully catalogues the nearly two-thirds of the manuscript's contents that were copied from printed sources; of the remainder, only 17 poems are unique to Harley 6910 ("Discoveries," 122–24).

42. See my appendix for a sense of the reordering of the poems common to RP 85, Harley 6910, and Harley 7392.

43. For brief discussions of this manuscript, see Ringler, *Poems of Philip Sidney,* 559–60, and Woudhuysen, *Sir Philip Sidney,* 262. For a transcription of this manuscript see George Martin, "Marsh's Library MS Z3.5.21: An Edition of the English Poems" (master's thesis, University of Waterloo, 1971).

44. For a brief discussion of this manuscript, see Ringler, *Poems of Philip Sidney,* 554. For a transcription of this manuscript, see Steven W. May, *Henry Stanford's Anthology: An Edition of Cambridge University Library Manuscript Dd.5.75* (New York: Garland Publishing, 1988); May traces the compiler to Trinity College, Oxford.

45. For brief discussions of this manuscript, see Ringler, *Poems of Philip Sidney,* 560, and Woudhuysen, *Sir Philip Sidney,* 258–59.

46. The Marsh manuscript shares 13 poems in common with RP 85, the Cambridge manuscript shares 12 poems, and the Folger manuscript shares 10 poems. These six manuscripts, taken together, form the focus of L. G. Black's unpublished D.Phil. thesis, which primarily emphasizes the court poetry preserved in these manuscripts (he does, for instance, offer an anthology of miscellaneous manuscript verse by such poets as Breton, Dyer, Gorges, Ralegh, the Earl of Derby, and the Earl of Oxford). Black's thoughtful analysis of individual courtly authors offers a valuable contribution to manuscript studies, but his project was not intended to explore the noncourtly authors. Ideally, then, this essay's interest in the noncanonical pieces in RP 85 supplements the work done so admirably by Black.

47. The points of commonality between RP 85 and the two Harleian manuscripts are largely confirmed by the pointing finger as well: 31 of the 45 poems common to RP 85 and Harley 7392 are marked with the finger, and 15 of the 20 poems common to RP 85 and Harley 6910 are so marked. The pointing finger is

unusual, but not unique. See, for instance, John Lilliat's manuscript miscellany (Rawlinson poet. 148), edited by Edward Doughtie as *Liber Lilliati* (Newark: University of Delaware Press, 1985), which marks 33 passages or whole poems for attention. Roughly half of the poems in John Cruso's (Gonville and Caius) manuscript miscellany, St. John's (Cambridge) MS U.26, are also marked with a finger.

48. Harley 6910 (fol. 142v), Harley 7392 (fol. 36v); Cambridge Dd.5.75 (fol. 27); Folger V.a.89 (p. 19); National Library of Wales (Aberystwyth) 10905E (fol. 104v); STC 21516 (sig. K4v).

49. Harley 6910 (fol. 171); STC 3191 (sig. T2).

50. Occurs in no other manuscripts.

51. According to Steven May, this poem occurs in roughly three dozen manuscripts; for a full census of important manuscripts see his "The Authorship of 'My Mind to Me a Kingdom Is," *RES*, n. s., 26 (1975): 385–94. The poem occurs in only one of the other five manuscripts that overlap with RP 85: Harley 7392 (fol. 73v).

52. I have cross-indexed all nine of the miscellanies edited by Rollins, as well as RP 85, against the contents of twenty modern anthologies: M. H. Abrams et al., eds., *The Norton Anthology of English Literature*, 4th ed. (1979); Norman Ault, ed., *Elizabethan Lyrics from the Original Texts* (1925); William Stanley Braithwaite, ed., *The Book of Elizabethan Verse* (1906); E. K. Chambers, ed., *The Oxford Book of Sixteenth Century Verse* (1932); Paul Driver, ed., *Sixteenth-Century Poetry, Penguin Popular Poetry* (1996); George Ellis, ed., *Specimens of the Early English Poets* (1801); J. William Hebel and Hoyt H. Hudson, eds., *Poetry of the English Renaissance 1509–1660: Selected From Early Editions and Manuscripts* (1929); Geoffrey G. Hiller, ed., *Poems of the Elizabethan Age* (1977); John Hollander and Frank Kermode, eds., *The Literature of Renaissance England* (1973); Emrys Jones, ed., *The New Oxford Book of Sixteenth-Century Verse* (1991); Roy Lamson and Hallett Smith, eds., *Renaissance England* (1956); W. J. Linton, ed., *Rare Poems of the Sixteenth and Seventeenth Centuries: A Supplement to the Anthologies* (1882); Edward Lucie-Smith, ed., *The Penguin Book of Elizabethan Verse* (1965); Kenneth Muir, ed., *Elizabethan Lyrics* (1952); David Norbrook, ed., *The Penguin Book of Renaissance Verse 1509–1659* (1992); Francis Turner Palgrave, ed., *The Golden Treasury* (1861); Hyder E. Rollins and Herschel Baker, eds., *The Renaissance in England* (1954); Felix E. Schelling, ed., *A Book of Elizabethan Lyrics* (1895); Richard Sylvester, ed., *English Sixteenth-Century Verse* (1974); and John Williams, ed., *English Renaissance Poetry: A Collection of Shorter Poems from Skelton to Jonson* (1963).

53. STC 3191 (sig. B1). You can find the poem in Abrams, Ault, Braithwaite, Chambers, Ellis, Hebel and Hudson, Hiller, Jones, Lamson and Smith, Linton, Muir, Rollins and Baker, Sylvester, and Williams.

54. Occurs in no other manuscripts. You can find the poem in Abrams, Ault, Chambers, Hebel and Hudson, Jones, Lamson and Smith, Lucie-Smith, Muir, Norbrook, Rollins and Baker, and Sylvester.

55. Harley 3277 (fol. 13v), Harley 6910 (fol. 145), Harley 7392 (fol. 18v); Arundel-Harington MS (fol. 144); STC 3633–34 (sig. F2), STC 20519.5 (sig. Z4v). You can find the poem in Chambers, Ellis, Hebel and Hudson, Jones, Muir, Rollins and Baker, and Schelling.

56. Arundel-Harington MS (fol. 145v); STC 3633 (sig. B4v), STC 21516 (sig. K3).

You can find the poem in Chambers, Hebel and Hudson, Jones, Lamson and Smith, Muir, and Rollins and Baker.

57. Add. 38892 (fol. 160v), Add. 61821 (fol. 107v); St. John's College (Cambridge) 308/I.7 (fol. 184); Folger H.b.1 (fol. 167); Huntington HM 162 (fol. 147); STC 11338 (sig. D7v), STC 22539 (sig. N7v). This poem is a particular favorite among recent anthologists: see Abrams, Hiller, Hollander and Kermode, Jones, and Norbrook.

58. See Marotti, *Manuscript*, 56–57 and 76–82, for a survey of types of misogynistic and obscene verse often favored in manuscript.

59. "Deepe Lamentinge loss of tresure" (fol. 26v); see also Add. 34064 (fol. 10v) and National Library of Wales MS Peniarth 346A (p. 17). "Amonge the woes of those vnhappy wightes" (fol. 27); Add. 34064 (fol. 41); Chetham's Library (Manchester) MS 8012 (p. 143); STC 3633–34; Beal BrN 7–10. "Perin agreed what new mischance betyde" (fol. 93v); STC 6373. There is also an elegy on the death of Leicester's son, "Dudleio simulac puerum de sanguine nasci" (fol. 56v).

60. This poem is particularly hard to read—it, like a handful of others, has been crossed out. I defer to Laurence Cummings's readings of lines two and four. My transcriptions from RP 85 have been compared with Cummings's edition of the manuscript, "John Finet's Miscellany"; on a few occasions I have reconsidered my readings and (silently) adopted Cummings's versions, while on others I maintain my own.

61. Harley 6910 (fol. 158), Harley 7392 (fol. 11v); Marsh's Library (Dublin) Z3.5.21 (fol. 1v).

62. Harley 6910 (fol. 148v), Harley 7392 (fol. 68v), Add. 34064 (fol. 19v); STC 3633–34.

63. STC 3631.

64. Add. 34064 (fol. 7v); STC 3631, STC 3633–34, STC 21516.

65. Occurs in no other manuscripts. STC 3191.

66. Harley 6910 (fol. 154), Harley 7392 (fol. 22).

67. Cambridge Ff.5.14 (fol. 5v); STC 13863.5 (sig. G1). In *Tottel's Miscellany*, 2 vols. (Cambridge: Harvard University Press, 1928) Hyder Rollins also locates Add. 26737 (fol. 108) and Sloane 159 (fol. 23).

68. Add. 34064 (fol. 36); Cambridge Dd.5.75 (fol. 41); Arundel-Harington MS (fol. 137v).

69. See Marotti, *Manuscript*, 92–94, for a brief discussion of the subgenre of the libel poem. There is another libel immediately following in RP 85, "The Libell of Oxenforde" (fol. 72v), also in Rawl. poet. 172 (fol. 16) and Marsh Z3.5.21 (fol. 7).

70. See also Kelliher, "Unrecorded Extracts from Shakespeare, Sidney and Dyer," 163–87, for discussion of another manuscript arising from St. John's College, Cambridge, of the early to mid-1580s (Cambridge University Library Mm.3.29). This manuscript belonged to one Henry Colling, who went up to Cambridge in February 1582, but left in 1584 without taking his degree (see Woudhuysen, *Sir Philip Sidney*, 259 ff.); it contains only a few leaves of poetry, and no poems in common with RP 85—but it certainly establishes a link to "a particular circle of young men of literary interests" (179). Black identifies St. John's, especially the college of the 1580s, as a nursemaid of poets; to Black, old members such as Roger Ascham, William Webbe, Robert Greene, Abraham Fraunce, and Thomas Nashe

combine to form what he calls a "St John's movement" ("Manuscript Poetic Miscellanies," 338). It is worth remembering, too, that one of the fathers of Tudor verse, Sir Thomas Wyatt the elder, was also a member of St. John's several decades earlier.

71. Strong evidence exists to connect Marsh Z3.5.21 to this period at St. John's as well; Kelliher notes that it contains a section of Reshoulde's verses on fol. 20 ("Unrecorded Extracts," 181, 187 n.66). Kelliher also notes that the Marsh manuscript contains poems by another St. John's man of the early 1580s, Henry Constable. Woudhuysen suggests that the Marsh manuscript may instead be associated with Sidney's own college, Christ Church, Oxford (262). Whether Oxford or Cambridge, what *is* significant is our immediate association of the manuscript with a *university* community.

Given Constable's considerable presence in Marsh Z3.5.21 (he contributes 15 poems—three times as many as the next most common voice, Sidney), it is surprising that RP 85 contains none of his poems (although RP 85 does contain four of Sidney's sonnets, "made . . . when his Ladye hadd a payne the small poxe in her face" [fols. 55–56] that were printed in Constable's expanded *Diana* [1594] STC 5638). Constable would have been at St. John's slightly prior to Finet, Mills, and Reshoulde (he was graduated B. A. in 1580), but one might expect some of his juvenilia to have been in circulation after his departure; perhaps Constable's Catholic sympathies kept his poems out of RP 85.

72. George Puttenham, *The Arte of English Poesie* (1589) [STC 20519], Z1.

73. See, for instance, the explicit example by Reshoulde, "What can, I praye the, tell me (swete Echo) lerne me to loue?" (fol. 85), which is entitled "Eccho made in imitatione of S*i*r P: Sidneys echo goinge before, pag*in*a: 5." Page five of the manuscript is lost, but Cummings suggests it may have contained the echo poem from the *Arcadia*, "Fayre Rockes, goodly Rivers, sweete Woodes, when shall I see peace?" In most cases the amateur undergraduate poetry in RP 85—or, for that matter, a good deal of Elizabethan manuscript verse—reveals the creative tension between invention and imitation. The anxious observations of Astrophil at the outset of Sidney's sequence may indeed offer more truth than poetry on this point of conflict: "I sought fit words," Astrophil tells us, by "turning others leaves," but "Invention Natures child, fled step-dame Studies blowes" (*Astrophil and Stella* 1). Sidney explores this tension again in the oft-anthologized *Astrophil and Stella* 15 ("You that do search for everie purling spring"); there he addresses those poets who "wring" into their verse the inventions of others, and warns "You take wrong waies those far-fet helpes be such, / As do bewray a want of inward tuch: / And sure at length stolne goods do come to light."

74. As Cummings puts it, "while only some of the collegiate verse rises to mediocrity, what these versifiers try to do reveals what was thought worthy of emulation" ("John Finet's Miscellany," 33).

75. Ibid., 32, 45. See Woudhuysen, *Sir Philip Sidney*, 261, for a similar reconstruction of the compiler's activities.

76. Cummings, "John Finet's Miscellany," 43.

77. Woudhuysen defers to Cummings by using Finet's name interchangeably with "the compiler," but he carefully qualifies his acceptance—"if it is" (*Sir Philip*

Sidney, 261) Finet's handiwork—of Cummings's conclusion. The hand in RP 85 contains several peculiar letter forms that are employed with enough inconsistency to allow the possibility of multiple compilers, but Dr. Malcolm Parkes has looked at the manuscript with me and believes that the entire manuscript is the work of a single copyist. I have compared the hand in RP 85 with those later examples of Finet's hand on domestic state papers preserved in the Public Records Office (SP14/72:32, 92:104, 95:21, and 177:12; SP16/74:101, 143:29, and 185:48), and there is no correspondence between the two. The peculiarities of the juvenile hand, and the absence of them in the mature hand, might indeed be attributable to the differences between a student and an adult who had put his pen to several hundred more leaves of paper, but I am unconvinced. I have also compared RP 85 to the hands in the St. John's College admissions register (Arch.C3.1) and see no obvious similarities with any students who entered their names in the register in the 1580s. See Cummings, "John Finet's Miscellany," 46, 71–74.

78. Jean-François Lyotard, "Answering the Question: What is Postmodernism?" in *The Postmodern Condition,* trans. Régis Durand (Minneapolis: University of Minnesota Press, 1984), 76.

79. The alliteration in this manuscript can get even more oppressive; see, for instance, James Reshoulde's "Carmina Saphica" (a favorite stanzaic form in the later printed miscellany, *A Poetical Rhapsody*):

As a freende, freendlyke: to a freend fare absent
I thy frende, frendlyke, to the send a p*res*ente
That we frennds frendlyke, maye abyde I' freendshipp
Freendly together.
 [fol. 53v]

80. See also references to the swan's dying song in "With springe of yeere began*n* my pryme of spyghte" (fol. 88), and its plumage in "Woulde I wer changed into that goulden showre" (fol. 46) and "The fayrst of Bewtyes bande" (fol. 124v).

81. RP 85 reveals its compiler's precocious interest in the lyric form that would dominate in print in the 1590s: 19 of the 145 poems in RP 85 are sonnets (see my appendix, items 11–16, 21, 31, 34–35, 45, 79–82, 112, 114, 130, and 134). Only the *Arcadia/ Venus and Adonis* sexain can rival the sonnet for popularity in this manuscript.

82. Compare "Sing gentll Swann" with the alliterative description, here, of the Satyr's reaction to kissing fire: "Feelinge forthewithe the outwarde burninge powre / Wood withe the smarte with shoutes and shreekinge shrill" (lines 5–6). Harley 6910 (fol. 154v), Harley 7392 (fol. 25); National Library of Wales Ottley Papers (fol. 3); Folger H.b.1 (fol. 220), Folger V.a.89 (p. 21); STC 3191.

83. Harley 7392 (fol. 25); National Library of Wales Ottley Papers (fol. 3); Folger H.b.1 (fol. 220), Folger V.a.89 (p. 23); STC 3191. Beal SiP37–39.

84. Note line 3: "To her sweet sence, sweete sleepe? some ease inparte." Harley 7392 (fol. 38v), Add. 38892 (fol. 100), Add. 61821 (fol. 60v); Cambridge Dd.5.75 (fol. 26); St. John's College (Cambridge) MS 308/I.7 (fol. 109); Arundel-Harington MS (fol. 145); Folger H.b.1 (fol. 98v); Huntington HM 162 (fol. 93v); STC 11338. Beal SiP149–152.

85. See Cummings, "John Finet's Miscellany," 742. Agnes Latham places the poem in the "conjectural Ralegh group" from *The Phœnix Nest*.

86. William Ringler, *Stephen Gosson: A Biographical and Critical Study* (Princeton: Princeton University Press, 1942), 149. In the end, Cummings throws up his hands and suggests that "Gosson may be the person who Finet thought wrote it," but he does refer to the praise bestowed on Gosson by Francis Meres.

87. It took the *OED* some years to expand the definition of the verb *to die* to include the well-known sense "to experience sexual orgasm" (I.7.d), but these lexicographers only trace it back to 1599 and *Much Ado About Nothing*.

88. Cf. the fifth song of *Astrophil and Stella*—the particularly hostile, threatening lyric that William Ringler finds so out of place with the rest of the sequence that he argues for its place in the *Old Arcadia* instead (*Poems of Sir Philip Sidney*, 484). See, too, two of Michael Drayton's sonnets from *Idea*: "My heart was slaine, and none but you and I" (*Idea* 2) and "Plaine-path'd Experience, th' unlearned's guide" (*Idea* 46).

89. See May, "Authorship," 386. Another poem attributed to Dyer in RP 85, "As rare to heare as seldome to be seene" (fol. 7v) echoes the central point: "What discontente to liue in such desyre / To haue his will yet euer to requyre"; see, too, Harley 6910 (fol. 173), Harley 7392 (fol. 23), and Folger V.a.89 (fol. 17); STC 21516.

90. Cummings locates 16 manuscripts (but there are undoubtedly more): Rawlinson poet. 199 (p. 10); Add. 22582 (fol. 43v), Add. 22602 (fol. 19v), Add. 30982 (fol. 53), Egerton 923 (fol. 65), Egerton 2421 (fol. 21), Harley 6057 (fol. 48), Malone 19 (p. 75), Sloane 542 (fol. 36v), Sloane 1792 (fol. 125); Folger V.a.339 (fol. 182), Folger V.a.97 (fol. 52), Folger V.a.345 (fol. 7), Folger V.a.322 (fol. 43), Folger V.a.319 (fol. 50), Folger V.a.262 (fol. 74). Crum (N6) also traces it to Ashmole 38 (p. 150), CCC. 328 (fol. 87), Don. d. 58 (fol. 44v), and Eng. poet. e. 97 (p. 185). Steven May also notes the poem in ROS 1083/15 (p. 2v). See also Marotti, *Manuscript*, 77–78.

91. John Wardroper, *Love and Drollery* (London: Routledge and Kegan Paul, 1969), 289n.; see, too, Marotti, *Manuscript*, 77–78.

92. Cummings suggests "mettells" is confused for "victuals" ("John Finet's Miscellany," 441).

93. This particular commodification of the woman's body is a profane echo of the great comestible *blason* from the Song of Solomon 7:2–3, 6–9 (Bible [Geneva version] (1560) [STC 2093]):

> Thy nauel *is as* a rounde cuppe that wanteth not lickour: thy belly *is as* an heape of wheat compassed about with lilies.
> Thy two breastes *are* as two yong roe that are twinnes.
> . . . .
> How faire art thou, and how pleasant art thou, ô *my* loue, in pleasures!
> This thy stature is like a palme tree, and thy breastes like clusters.
> I said, I wil go vp into the palme tre, I wil take holde of her boughes: thy breastes shal now be like the clusters of the vine: and the sauour of thy nose like apple,

And the roufe of thy mouth like good wine,
which goeth straight to my welbeloued, & causeth
the lippes of the ancient to speake.

94. Harley 7392 (fol. 21v); Cambridge Dd.5.75 (fol. 38v); Folger V.a.89 (p. 12). See, too, Marotti, *Manuscript,* 83.

95. Harley 6910 (fol. 145), Harley 7392 (fol. 40); Folger V.a.89 (p. 8). See Marotti, *Manuscript,* 57–59, for the full text and a discussion of the poem.

96. See also Ralegh's poem in RP 85, "Many desier but fewe or none deserue / To foille the fort of thy most constant will" (fol. 116); see also Add. 22601 (fol. 71). See, too, another poem in the same vein from *Songes and Sonettes,* "When Cupide scaled first the fort" (sig. X2v).

97. Add. 38892 (fol. 83v), Add. 61821 (fol. 47v); St. John's College (Cambridge) 308/I.7 (fol. 87); National Library of Wales Ottley Papers (fol. 6); Folger H.b.1 (fol. 81); Huntington HM 162 (fol. 76); STC 11338.

98. Harley 7392 (fol. 71).

99. It is also worth noting that Harley 6910 ends (or, more accurately, leaves off) with a poem from *Songes and Sonettes* ("When Cupide scaled first the fort," fol. 175)—its only acknowledgment of Tottel's innovation, some four decades after the fact.

100. The poem appears in the "Vncertain auctours" section of *Songes and Sonettes;* Rollins suggests that Tottel's attribution cannot be taken seriously (2:68).

101. Hume, *Of the Standard of Taste and Other Essays,* ed. John W. Lenz (Indianapolis: Library of Liberal Arts, 1965), 3.

102. David Norbrook, ed., *The Penguin Book of Renaissance Verse 1509–1659,* 2d ed. (Harmondsworth: Penguin, 1993), xxxi–xxxii.

103. Thomas Warton, *History of English Poetry From the Twelfth to the Close of the Sixteenth Century,* ed. W. Carew Hazlitt et al., rev. ed., 4 vols. (London, 1871), 4:215.

104. Douglas Bush, *English Literature in the Earlier Seventeenth Century: 1600–1660,* 1st ed. (Oxford: Clarendon Press, 1945), 102.

CHAPTER SIX

Manuscript Transmission and the Catholic Martyrdom Account in Early Modern England

Arthur F. Marotti

In early modern England, especially during the times of harshest persecution, English Catholics relied for information and ideological support not only on printed books and pamphlets smuggled into England from the Continent and on some works printed by secret English presses but also on manuscript documents that circulated in the Catholic community. The manuscript system not only facilitated the distribution of censorable or politically dangerous texts but also served to unite a scattered and embattled minority, combating the English government's obvious strategy of cultural eradication. A wide variety of texts circulated in the manuscript medium: these included prose lives of Thomas More,[1] political libels like *Leicester's Commonwealth*,[2] the formulaic Catholic last will and testament discovered to belong to Shakespeare's father,[3] the politically explosive "Brag"[4] by Edmund Campion and "Treatise of Equivocation" by Henry Garnet,[5] the 1585 letter from Philip Howard, Earl of Arundel, to Queen Elizabeth explaining his (intended) flight from England for religious reasons,[6] Robert Persons's "A Memorial for the Reformation of Englande,"[7] Edmund Campion's *Two Books of the Histories of Ireland*,[8] and various literary works, including the poetry and prose of Robert Southwell, S. J., which continued to be copied in manuscript form despite its repeated printings.[9] In this essay, I focus upon one kind of circulating manuscript text, the martyrdom account. Normally in the form of either freestanding ballads, poems, or prose narratives or of reports in letters that may also contain other information, martyrdom accounts spoke to a persecuted Catholic community and, propagandistically, to a larger national and international audience.

Poems and ballads about the sufferings and martyrdoms of Catholic priests and laymen circulated at various times during the persecutions. They highlight the important dramatic moments of the imprisonment, trials, and executions, utilizing the conventions of the prose martyrdom accounts. For example, the Jesuit Laurence Anderton's ballad about the layman martyr John Thulis (executed in 1616) recounts the usual attempts by a Protestant minister to convert the imprisoned Catholic, the authorities' unsuccessful efforts to get him to swear the oath of allegiance, the martyr's declaration that he is innocent of treason, his charity to the poor on the way to his execution, the sympathy of the crowd of spectators (and even the reluctance of the hangman to quarter the body), people's seeking of his blood as relics, and the supernatural signs and wonders following the death (a light as bright as the sun pours from his mouth over his body, then disappears; in order to bury the pieces, ravens later pick the flesh from the quartered body set on the castle walls).[10]

In another ballad, the speaker welcomes the opportunity to suffer torture and martyrdom for the faith:

> Noe rope nor cruell tortour then
>   should cause my minde to faile;
> Nor lewde device of wicked men
>   should cause my corage quaile,
> On racke in *tower* let me be l[ai]d,
>   let Joynts at large be stretched;
> Let me abyde each cruell braid,
>   till blood frome vaines be fetched.
>   . . . .
> Let me be falslie condemned;
>   let Sherife on me take charge;
> With bo[w]es and billes let me be led,
>   least I escape at large;
> Let me from prison passe away
>   on hurdle hard to lye,
> To *Tyburne* drawne without delay
>   in torments there to dye.
>
> Let mee be hang'd and yet, for doubt
>   least I be dead too soone,

Let there some devillish spirit start out
   in hast to cut me downe;
Let bowells be burnt, let paunch be fryde
   in fier [e]r I be dead;
On *London* bridg, a poule provide,
   thereon to set my head.

O *London,* let my quarters stand
   upon thy gates to drye;
And let them beare the world in hand
   I did for treason dye;
Let cro[w]es and kytes my carkas eate;
   and ravens their portion hav[e],
Least afterwardes my frendes intreate
   to lay my corpses in grave.[11]

The poems appended to the surreptitiously printed Catholic *True Report* of the martyrdom of the Jesuit Edmund Campion were effective both within the Catholic community and in the larger social context—provoking at least one Protestant poetic refutation.[12]

Prose martyrdom accounts can be found in a number of different sorts of documents addressed to international and/or national readers. For example, a letter narrating the martyrdoms of four priests (George Haydock, Thomas Emerford, James Fenn, and Robert Nutter) was sent to Rome to Robert Southwell. It ends with the suggestion that it should be passed on to other readers: "What I have putt downe I hard myself, and therefore I may boldly speake it. If you please, you may show it to your friends, provyded alwaies you tell not my name."[13] Missives such as this were part of the international system of Catholic news reporting used by secular priests and Jesuits on the English mission: hence, for example, the annual reports sent by the Jesuit superior Henry Garnet contain narratives of particular martyrdoms,[14] letters to the well-networked Robert Persons, S. J., also have such material, and the Catholic news bureau managed in the Low Countries by Richard Verstegan regularly received and retransmitted such narratives. English exiles and other Catholic propagandists on the Continent ran a martyrology industry that from the early 1580s kept up a steady stream of manuscript and printed martyrologies aimed both at the general European market and at England. The letters that English Catholics and clerical leaders sent abroad, some of them containing eyewitness accounts of martyrdoms, were an essential source for these publications.[15]

When in 1626 Dr. Richard Smith, Bishop of Chalcedon (for England), called for local vicars to do an accounting of all the martyrs who had suffered in their areas, he was organizing this flow of information in a systematic way.[16] In effect, this involved sending to a center information and narratives circulating in the periphery—though there was always, of course, through reports of the martyrdoms to superiors and colleagues on the Continent, a centripetal force that facilitated the collection of martyrdom stories and their publication in Catholic martyrologies such as William Allen's *A Briefe Historie of the Glorious Martyrdom of XII. Reverend Priests* (1582), John Gibbon's *Concertatio Ecclesiae Anglicanae* (1583 and 1588),[17] Richard Verstegan's *Theatrum Crudelitatem Haereticorum nostri temporis* (1592), Thomas Worthington's *A Relation of Sixtene Martyrs: Glorified in England in Twelve Moneths* (Douay, 1601), and John Wilson's *English Martyrologe* (1608).[18] Such Catholic martyrologies gathered and, in some cases, illustrated with elaborate engravings the stories of those English laymen and priests who suffered and died for their Catholic beliefs. One of the most carefully crafted of these publications, *The Life and Death of Mr. Edmund Geninges, Priest* (St. Omers, 1614),[19] published twenty-three years after the martyr's death, contains beautifully crafted illustrations, including a depiction of the arrest of a large group of lay Catholics along with Gennings after hearing mass at Swithen Wells's house.[20]

One route of manuscript transmission of martyrdom accounts was through the Catholic family circles and networks within England. Thus the narrative of the martyrdom of James Duckett, a printer of Catholic texts, was penned by his son, who became a Carthusian priest (Pollen, *Acts*, 238). That of Thomas Sherwood, a middle-class hero whose father was a draper, was "A Relation written by his Brother for his Nephews."[21] The secular priest William Hart addressed a letter to his mother that also had considerable impact as a model of heroic resolve:

> ... perhaps you will say: I weepe not so much for your death, as I do for that yow are hanged, drawen, and quartered. My sweet mother it is the honourablest and happiest death that ever could have chanced to me. I dy not for knavery, but for vertue. I dy not for treason, but for religioun. I dy not for any ill demeanour or offence committed, but onely for my faith, for my conscience, for my Preisthood, for my blessed Saviour Jesus Christ.... How glad then may he bee to see mee a martyr, a Saint, a most glorious and bright starre in heaven.... I wish that I were neer to comfort you, but because that can not be I beseech you even for Christ Jesus sake

to comfort your self.... If I had lived I would have holpen yow in your age, as you have holpen mee in my youth. But now I must desire God to helpe yow and my brethren, for I can not. Good mother blesse mee. And now in your old daies serve God after the old Catholike manner.... one daie wee shall meet in heaven by Gods grace.[22]

We know from one martyrdom account that the mother of John Bodey "afterward hearing of her sonnes Martyrdome, made a great Feast to her neighbors, as her sonns marriage day, rejoycing of his martyrdom" (WDA 4:118).

A 1,785-page folio manuscript now in the Bodleian Library (MSS Eng.th.b.12) contains a rich compendium of Catholic documents, prepared apparently for a patron by Thomas Jollette, a musician who was a protégé of William Byrd: included are such items as a description of a 1585 meeting of Catholics at the house of Lord Vaux at which a service, sermon, and exorcism were held; lists of persecuted Catholics; speeches from 1559 and on by Catholic political figures; an account of a mass and sermon held in 1606 at the Spanish ambassador's house, after which the authorities arrested those who were leaving; some musical material connected with William Byrd; and accounts of the interrogations and executions of both the Jesuit Roger Filcock and Mrs. Anne Line,[23] both killed in 1601, and of Henry Garnet, executed in 1606.[24]

Beyond the family, however, martyrdom stories reached the Catholic community at large through the manuscript communication routes that Nancy Pollard Brown's interesting bibliographical detective work has uncovered: she has traced one route of manuscript dissemination of Catholic texts from Henry Garnet and the Countess of Arundel's house in the Catholic London neighborhood of Spitalfields to the country and its dispersed Catholic population.[25] The survival in manuscript of several versions of John Mush's life of Margaret Clitherow[26] (the only full texts of the story published before the nineteenth century, since the printed account was an abbreviated version)[27] testifies to the functioning of this network.

Preserved in the Westminster Diocesan Archives (WDA 4:121 ff.) is an eight-page sewn, professionally copied booklet containing accounts of Northern lay and clerical martyrs: it deals with Edward Watterson (executed at Newcastle in 1591), four priests executed at Durham on 27 May 1590, a shoemaker-martyr killed at York on 30 November 1586, Thomas Pallicer, Edward Osbaldson (16 November 1583), James Thomson (York, 1583), Peter Snow, Marmaduke Bowes ("condemned and executed, for giving a cupp of Beere at his dore to a Preist" [WDA 4:127]), Ralph Grimston, Robert Bikerdike, William Knight, and William Gibson. Such a collection was probably made in response to the Bishop of Chalcedon's 1626 request that each locality of England gather stories of martyrs, but it would seem that such texts were assembled both from Catholic oral folklore and from already-circulating manuscript accounts.[28]

Michael Williams has suggested that manuscript accounts of martyrdom, some surviving in multiple copies, were regularly used not only to edify and reinforce the faith of native English Catholics but also as a means of fund-raising for the Continental seminaries that were training the priests for the English mission.[29] And, of course, since Catholic *printed* texts could only reach English Catholics from secret English presses or by being smuggled into the country from abroad, manuscript communication was a crucial medium of communication for English Catholics and for the official church that wished to retain their allegiance.

Some of the features of the subgenre of the martyrdom account reveal the religio-political work intended or accomplished by the form in the two related contexts with which I am concerned: (1) that of the Catholic community meant to be affected by such stories and (2) that of the public relations struggle between Protestants and Catholics or, specifically, between the English government and the militant Catholic recusants. In terms of the first, martyrdom accounts celebrate an extreme form of religious heroism and deliberately include laymen as well as priests, women as well as men, and low-born as well as high-born victims of the persecution. In terms of the sectarian polemical and propaganda wars, martyrdom accounts argue for the superiority of the hardline Catholic position—in opposition both to Protestant adversaries and to less militant Catholics.[30]

Martyrdom narratives were especially meant to affect lukewarm or compromising English Catholics, particularly "Church Papists" who observed the requirements of outward conformity to the established church while maintaining private Catholic beliefs and devotional practices.[31] Catholic leaders knew that such accommodation to a program designed to erode Catholicism and to reduce the functioning Catholic community (combined with the enforcement of recusancy fines and of the laws against missionary priests and those who helped them) threatened the ultimate destruction of English Catholicism.[32] Especially after the failed invasion of 1588, when the likelihood of the military reestablishment of Catholicism in England was very small, patient suffering was idealized as the best way English Catholics could bear witness to their faith and create the best chance for its survival, while they hoped for either religious toleration, less harsh treatment by the queen and government authorities, or a reestablishment of Catholicism itself with the change of monarchs.[33] As one of the elegies published in the Catholic *True Report* of Edmund Campion's martyrdom had argued:

> God knowes it is not force nor might,
>   not warre nor warlike band,
> Not shield & spear, not dint of sword,
>   that must convert the land,
> It is the blood by martirs shed,
>   it is that noble traine,
> That fight with word & not with sword,
>   and Christ their capitaine.
> For sooner shall you want the handes
>   to shed sutch guitles blood,
> Then wise and vertuous still to come
>   to do their country good.[34]

Geoffrey Nuttall notes that, although the vast majority of Catholic martyrs in the long period from 1535 to 1680 were priests (219), there were also ninety-three lay martyrs. Of these only three were peers. Others included "seven . . . schoolmasters," an Oxford don, "a barrister . . . two printers, a weaver, a woolen draper, a tailor, a glover, a dyer's apprentice, a joiner, an ostler, a miller, a farmer, a husbandman, and five servants." They also included four women (three of whom have been canonized): Blessed Margaret Pole (Countess of Salisbury and mother of Cardinal Pole), St. Margaret Clitherow, St. Mary Ward, and St. Anne Line. There were, however, no women martyred between 1604 and 1680.[35]

The story of the lay martyr James Duckett, preserved in manuscript in near-complete form in the Westminster Diocesan Archives,[36] is a tale of conversion and heroism probably meant to inspire other lay Catholics. A younger brother from a relatively prosperous family, Duckett was apprenticed in London and raised as a Protestant (a "Puritan . . . so zealous that he would have heard 2. or 3. sermons on a day" [WDA 7:339]). After being given a book on "the foundation of the Catholicke religion" by a Catholic friend, which he read surreptitiously while he tended shop, he rejected Protestantism and was sent to Bridewell for nonattendance at church services, but was soon freed at the request of his master. After buying out his apprenticeship, he took formal Catholic religious instruction and was received into the church "by Mr. Weekes a venerable Priest, and a Prisener in the Gathowse" (WDA 7:340). After two or three years, he married a Catholic widow, taking up

> a poore taylers trade wherin his chiefe worke was to accomadat priests and those who laboured for the Conversion of sowles with garmentes fitt for their necessities; to make and mend up vestmentes to prepare church stuffe and all necessities for the alter. And that he yet farther might be an instrument to helpe and sett forward the common good he resolved to deale and trade in bookes wherewith he might furnish Catholickes as well for their owne comfort and devotion as for the satisfaction and instruction of others and therby both benefitt him selfe and them. (WDA 7:340)

When the authorities searched his house, they found "impression of our Ladie psalters with the picture of the Rosarie togeather with the presse" (WDA 7:341) and arrested both him and his printers. After two years in jail, he was freed, but arrested again after ten weeks, the stock of some devotional books having been found in his house. He was freed quickly, however, because his wife was in labor, but then was rearrested when more Latin and English books were discovered at his house. He was sent to "Limbos . . . [a] darke and dismall dungeon through which the Filth of the cittie ranne with no small stench" (WDA 7:342); when his wife visited him there, he "came up to her smiling with a merrie and full countenance while shee with a heavie heart stood weeping thinking shee should have seene in him the picture of a dead man farr from that chearfull countanance he brought with him from this place" (WDA 7:342). He was released after two months, but then betrayed to the authorities by a bookbinder hoping to escape his own punishment, the man revealing to Judge Popham that Duckett had republished Robert Southwell's *An Humble Supplication to the Queen*.[37] When the search of the house turned up other Catholic books, Duckett was sent to Newgate, tried, found guilty (after the notoriously harsh Judge Popham sent the jury, who had declared him not guilty, back to reconsider their verdict), condemned to death, and executed (but not before he had cheerfully forgiven Bullock for betraying him). Not only an example of conversion, Duckett is portrayed as the steadfast assister of priests and servant of the wider English Catholic community he affected through the Catholic books he printed or distributed. Repeated arrests and incarcerations did not deter him, and only execution brought to a halt his activities as a Catholic printer and priest-helper.

In his manuscript account of the trial and martyrdom of Edmund Gennings and his companions, James Young recounts the heroism of a servant who refused to buckle under the pressure from the authorities:

> Amongst these Catholics there was arraigned one Robert Sydney [Sydney Hodgson], sometime a serving-man, taken at Mass with Mr. Geninges; he, by the entreaty of the Judge, and of the Lord Anderson, asked pardon of the Queen for his fault, which being done the Judge told him that he had showed himself a good subject, and therefore should have favour at her Majesty's hands. Presently he was unpinnioned, every man thinking he should be dismissed; for he was not condemned with the others; but only was singled out as a poor simple man whom they thought would yield easily, and so every one said unto him, "Sydney, thou must go to my Lord of London [the Bishop], and he will instruct thee in the truth." To whom he answered, "My lord, I would not have you to think that I will deny my faith, although I have asked her Majesty's forgiveness. I will die twenty times first." (Pollen, *Unpub. Doc.*, 106)

Thereafter he is condemned to death with the other prisoners.

While lay martyrs like Duckett and Sydney exemplified patient suffering in the face of the judicial terrorism aimed at recusant Catholics, this was not always the response of strong-willed Catholic laymen. At his execution in Gray's Inn fields by his house, where the company of lay Catholics were arrested along with the priest who said mass there for them, Swithen Wells got into an argument with the Catholic-hunter Richard Topcliffe, a man whose relentless cruelty is a leitmotif of the Elizabethan martyrdom accounts. Topcliffe reproved Wells for asking for a blessing from Gennings and exclaimed, "'Dog-bold Papists! . . . you follow the Pope and his Bulls; believe me, I think some bulls begot you all.'" The narrator continues: "Herewith Mr. Wells was somewhat moved, and replied, 'If we have bulls to our fathers, thou hast a cow to thy mother'" (a Catholic misogynistic swipe at Queen Elizabeth in her role as "Supreme Governor" of the English Church). Wells immediately apologized, however, for his impatient outburst and said to Topcliffe, "'God pardon you and make you of a Saul a Paul, of a bloody persecutor one of the Catholic Church's children'" (Pollen, *Acts*, 108).[38]

In their battle with the Elizabethan establishment, Catholic martyrologists tried to capture the moral high ground, appropriating from the Protestant martyrological discourse represented in John Foxe's popular (and nationalistic) *Acts and Monuments* (or *Book of Martyrs*) the role of religious victimage; but of course the Catholic accounts differ narratologically and thematically from the Protestant ones in significant ways that reflect the changed method of execution (from burning at the stake to hanging and dismemberment) as well as the theological and devotional contrasts between Protestantism and Catholicism.[39] The Catholic martyrdom narratives include a number of regular features: the portrayal of the cruelty of the persecutors; the repeated references to the sympathy for Catholic victims of Protestant jailers, hangmen, and members of the crowd at executions—sometimes resulting in actual conversions (or "reconciliations"); the depiction of gallows humor and its power dynamics; the rehearsing of the final speeches, sermons, arguments, and prayers spoken at the places of execution; the sacralizing of these sites of suffering and execution by means of Catholic prayer, sacramentalism, and ceremonialism; the occurrence of supernatural signs and wonders; and the conversion of the bodies and body parts of the martyrs into saints' relics. While the first three might have their counterparts in Protestant martyrology, the last three certainly highlight specifically Catholic practices and beliefs.

Martyrdom accounts repeatedly emphasize the cruelty of jailors, interrogators, torturers, and hangmen/dismemberers. Catholics were sometimes put in the most pestilential prisons and dungeons, sometimes in a room called Little Ease, in which it was impossible to stand or lie down; they were tortured on the rack, but then, when racking in the Tower was something of a public embarrassment for the government, the torturing was moved to Bridewell and even, in some cases, to Richard Topcliffe's house, which contained a well-equipped chamber of horrors where the Jesuit Robert Southwell was tormented. Hanging victims on the walls for hours by the wrists, subjecting them to such tortures as thumbscrews and the iron glove called the "gauntlet," tormenters tried to extort "confessions" and information from them. The full gruesome treatment at the executions themselves, however, gets the most narrative attention. Typically, the victims were not allowed to hang until they were dead, but were cut down alive so that they would be conscious during the procedure in which they were castrated and eviscerated, their hearts cut out before their bodies were decapitated and quartered. A narration of martyrdoms sent to Robert Southwell at the English College, Rome, describes Thomas Hemerford's treatment: "He was cutt down halfe dead; when the tormentor did cutt off his membres, he did cry 'O! Ah!' I heard my self standing under the gibbet" (Pollen, *Unpub. Doc.*, 62). The martyrs' heroic suffering during their mutilation and disemboweling is often highlighted as a mark of their sanctity.

Martyrdom accounts often include evidence of the sympathy for the victims demonstrated by Protestant jailors, hangmen, sheriffs, and spectators, sometimes even pointing out actual conversions being occasioned by the behavior and words of the martyrs. Even the ex-Catholic John Donne remarked in one of his sermons: "We see at Executions, when men pretend to die cheerfully for the glory of God, half the company will call them Traitors, and half Martyrs."[40] Edmund Campion's keeper, who was sympathetic to him, was impressed by Ralph Sherwin's kissing the blood-stained hand of the executioner who had just finished with dismembering Campion (Pollen, *Acts*, 310). Ralph Miller, a husbandman from near Winchester, was allowed to come and go freely from prison by his keeper (Pollen, *Acts*, 85). At the 26 April 1642 execution of Edward Morgan, officers helped Catholics get relics: ". . . the officers calling for the people's handkerchiefs and gloves to wet in the blood, which they did, and delivered them again to the owners, and one got almost his whole heart out of the fire" (Pollen, *Acts*, 352). At the 12 October 1642 execution of the weak-voiced Benedictine Thomas Bullaker, a sympathetic sheriff tried to facilitate the martyr's scaffold speech despite the crowd noise and the constant interruptions of a zealous Protestant minister (Pollen, *Acts*, 356). One of the witnesses of Montford Scott's and George Beesley's executions was supposed to have said, "Is this treason? I cam to see traitors and have seen saints"—whereupon he was clapped in prison (Pollen, *Acts*, 303). At Edmund Gennings's execution, "the hangman taking him yet alive and speaking, he ripped his belly and showed his heart to the people crying, 'Thus God grant it may happen to all traitors! God save the Queen!' When scarce one voice was heard amongst all the people to say Amen, at which they much wondered who were the chief executors" (Pollen, *Acts*, 109). When the hangman at the executions of Thomas Somers and John Roberts held up the heart of one of them, saying, "'This is the heart of a traitor,'" expecting the crowd to answer, "'Long live the King,'" "not one person answered, but all remained silent as if struck dumb" (Pollen, *Acts*, 168). Thomas Reynolds, executed on 21 January 1642, was said to be "a man of singular meekness and most gentle manner, whereby he so far won the affection of the Protestants that many of them publicly declared with tears before his martyrdom that such a man ought not to be put to death" (Pollen, *Acts*, 340). Two criminals had last-second conversions on the scaffold when Thomas Reynolds and Bartholomew Roe were executed (Pollen, *Acts*, 342). At the execution of John Almond, 20 December 1612, "a Protestant beholding his undaunted courage and bold spirit, full of life and comfort, he concluded in himself that he only was happy for his religion. Thereupon he went from the gallows to the Gatehouse [prison], and desired to speak with a priest. They bringing him to Father Blackfan, he resolved to the best, and was reconciled within few days, for which my Lord of Canterbury clapt up close Mr. Blackfan" (Pollen, *Acts*, 193).[41] Henry Walpole, a young gentleman (later a Jesuit), was converted at Campion's execution after a drop of blood fell on him.[42]

In the immediate aftermath of the Essex revolt, the execution of the priest John Pribush, according to Henry Garnet, was handled and responded to in a revealing way: "though they [the authorities] held the execution so suddenly that not many people were able to be present, a public proclamation was made that all were to depart, for fear of revolt. And in fact all the people, already discontented by Essex's ill success, lamented and said: 'See! They have put to death a poor sick priest.'"[43] Even if we make allowances for Garnet's biases, it would still seem that the public-relations intention of executing Catholics did, on occasion, utterly fail its purpose.

The English government, of course, did its best to control the public's response to the executions, and it clearly tried to terrorize Catholics into religious conformity. The authorities sent a message to both Protestants and Catholics in local communities by sending people convicted in London back for execution in their places of residence or apprehension—and over half of those killed between 1570 and 1680 were executed outside of London.[44] The martyrdom accounts could also bring home to Catholics living outside the country's cultural and economic center the exemplary behavior of those who could be regarded as local heroes of the faith. Many were martyred in such Northern strongholds of Catholicism as Yorkshire, Lancashire, and Durham, with the city of York, for example, accounting for some fifty of the executions in this period.[45] As Geoffrey Nuttall points out, every English county, with the exception of Cambridgeshire, produced at least one martyr, and many of these were executed locally rather than in London. In 1588, a year in which there were thirty-four executions of Catholic priests and laymen, Sir John Puckering, later Lord Keeper, formulated plans for indictments and executions so as to produce a wide geographical distribution to send a message to Catholics in all parts of the country (Pollen, *Unpub. Doc.*, 152).[46]

Even within London, sometimes places other than Tyburn were carefully chosen to deliver a message. For example, the priest Thomas Pormort was executed in 1592 before the door of a haberdasher he had converted (Pollen, *Acts*, 120). The layman Nicholas Horner, condemned for making a jerkin for a priest, was executed before his own house in Smithfield (Pollen, *Acts*, 231). Swithen Wells was executed (along with the priest Edmund Gennings) in front of his house near Gray's Inn, which had been used for a Catholic mass.[47] Henry Garnet was executed between St. Paul's Cathedral and the bishop's mansion, the location used to celebrate the victory over the Spanish Armada.[48]

Many martyrs were portrayed as cheerfully and confidently facing their deaths, sometimes even indulging in gallows humor.[49] The night before his execution, the layman John Finch was visited by his friends and relatives in prison, who "came to comfort hyme in this last conflict and affliction; but they found hyme so merry in God and so joyfull of the next dayes banket (which he expected) that they were all mervelously comforted and edified by his rare fortitude" (Pollen, *Unpub. Doc.*, 87). On the hurdle, being dragged to the place of execution, Anthony Middleton was supposedly in such good spirits that "all the beholders, which were thousands, wondered at his gladsome countenance" (Pollen, *Unpub. Doc.*, 186). John Roberts, who was to be executed with Thomas Somers, "looking at the fire that was already burning to consume their bowels, said 'Here's a hot breakfast ready, despite the cold weather'" (Pollen, *Acts*, 166). Edward Morgan (executed 26 April 1642) supposedly had the following exchange with the hangman and the usual antagonistic Protestant minister:

> ... he with a merry countenance wished Gregory to do his office, and gave him a piece of money. Gregory going to dispose him in some posture, he said, "I pray thee, teach me, for I never was at the sport before."
>
> Whereupon the minister said, "Mr Morgan, this is not a time to sport, nor is it a jesting matter."
>
> "Sir," said Mr Morgan, "I know it is not jest, but good sober earnest; but you cannot deny but that God requireth a cheerful sacrifice...." (Pollen, *Acts*, 351)

Catholic victims even played to the crowd's sense of humor. Brian Lacey, in fact, succeeded in making the hated Richard Topcliffe laughable:

> Lacey, now having the rope about his neck, was willed by Topcliffe to confesse his treason. "For," saith he, "here are none but traitors who are of thy religion."

"Then," said Lacey, "answer me. You yourself in Queen Mary's days was a Papist, at least in show. Tell me, were you also a traitor?" At which the people laughed aloud. (Pollen, *Acts*, 110)

At Laurence Humphrey's execution, the martyr smiled at the unintended stupid rhyming of the hangman, who said: "Thou holdest with the Pope, but he has brought thee to the rope, and the hangman shall have thy coat" (Pollen, *Acts*, 237–38). The embarrassed man hit him in retaliation.

Because those who were about to die were allowed to speak their last words (in order to repent their supposed crimes and ask the forgiveness of God and of the monarch), priests and laymen about to be executed had the opportunity to bear witness to and argue the truth of their faith as well as to resist the power of the government and to argue with the Protestant ministers who were usually at hand to recruit them to the official Church of England. These occasions were, ironically, the only ones offered to Catholic priests to preach or dispute openly to a congregation that often numbered in the thousands. Henry Garnet's account of the sufferings and execution of Robert Southwell, S. J., depicts the martyr both making a formal speech from the cart before hanging and disputing one last time with a Protestant minister.[50] Another account reproduced a dialogue between Oliver Plasden and Sir Walter Ralegh occasioned by the former's praying for the queen from the cart before his execution: Ralegh was so moved by the man's loyalty and honesty that, even after Topcliffe intervened to ask a version of the "bloody questions" used to trap Catholics into a hypothetical choice between loyalty to country and loyalty to their religion, he ordered that Plasden be allowed to hang until dead instead of being cut down for vivisection (Pollen, *Acts*, 112–14). The relentlessly cruel Topcliffe "cryed out with a loud voyce" to Edmund Gennings when the latter was about to be executed:

> Geninges, Geninges, confess thy fault, thy Popish treason, and the Queene by submission (no doubt) will grant thee pardon. To which he mildly ansered; I know not M. Topliffe in what I have offended my deare annoynted Princesse, for if I had offended her, or any other in any thing, I would willingly ask her, and all the world forgivenesse. If shee bee offended with me without a cause, for professing my fayth and religion, because I am a Priest, or because I will not turne Minister agaynst my conscience, I shalbe I trust excused and innocent before God ... I must obey God rather then men, and must not in this cause acknowledge a fault where none is. If to

returne into England Priest, or to say Masse be Popish treason, I heere confesse I am a traytour: but I think not so.[51]

In reaction to these words, the angered Topcliffe "scarce giving him leave to say a Pater noster, bad the Hangman turne the ladder, which in an instant being done, presently he caused him to be cut downe" alive, his last words, on the dismembering table, being "'Oh it smartes.'"[52]

The secular priest Edward Morgan made the best of the opportunity given him by the sheriff to speak before his death, delivering an apologia/sermon to the crowd that "the doctor or minister-assistant" felt compelled to interrupt: "'Mr. Morgan, I would wish you to dispose yourself for death, and not to go about to seduce the King's people'"—after which they disputed with one another until Morgan pleaded:

> "Good sir ... trouble me no more," and returned to his discourse with great zeal, alacrity, and to the content of all the people; until at last the minister spake to him ... and wished him to put his trust in the merits of the Lord, and not in angels and saints. Whereunto Mr. Morgan replied, "Mistake not yourself, sir, for I put my whole trust and confidence in the infinite merits of my Lord and Saviour Jesus Christ, Who died for me."
> "That is well said," said the minister, and let him alone. (Pollen, *Acts*, 350–51)

Catholic priests and laymen, in effect, had the last word at their executions.[53]

Judicially and propagandistically, the English government tried to identify priests and those who helped them as political subversives and to execute them for treason—a characterization countered by Catholic claims that they were victims of conscience suffering for their religious, not for their political, activities.[54] It is not surprising, then, that those being executed should try to create a religious and devotional aura for the occasion. Often the priest-victims used gestures and words borrowed from Catholic religious ceremony and devotional practice to convert the place and paraphernalia of execution from the secular to the sacred, from the environment of punishment for felons and traitors to the holy space of martyrdom. Just as the celebrant kisses the stole he puts on as he dons the vestments for mass, many of the priest-victims who were about to be hanged made a point of kissing the rope before slipping it over their necks. Some of this ceremonial sacralizing of the material conditions of martyrdom was performed by laymen as well: in a manuscript account of John

Bodey's martyrdom (which was also put into print), he is reported to have said when he was laid on the hurdle on which he was to be dragged to the place of execution, "Oh, sweet bed, the happiest bed that ever man lay on! Thou art welcome to me." When the hangman was about to put the halter around his neck, he said, "Oh, blessed chain, the sweetest chain and richest that ever came about any man's neck!" and kissed it (Pollen, *Acts*, 62–63).[55] Futhermore, victims usually made a point of saying prayers in Latin, the language of Catholic liturgy and clerical devotion—an act that usually provoked anger on the part of the authorities. At his execution, the layman John Thomas was kicked by the hangman for insisting on praying in Latin (Pollen, *Acts*, 232–33). Even the treatment of the victims' bodies and blood after execution and dismemberment was quasi-sacramental: martyrs' relics were not just revered as ordinary saints' relics but took on, by association with Christ's sacrifice on the cross, a quasi-eucharistic character. Clearly, each time an execution of a Catholic priest or layperson occurred, the place of execution was contested ground between Catholicism and Protestantism, between the government and the Catholic minority, and between the religious and the secular.[56] The Protestant authorities' concern that Catholics might succeed in defining the executions as martyrdoms is reflected in the care they took to destroy the victims' innards in the fire, to keep Catholics from access to the blood and body parts, and to place the heads and quarters on the gates of the city of London (out of access for Catholics) for the birds to pick the flesh from the bones.

One of the important features of Catholic discourse in the period is the language of signs, wonders, visions, and miracles. This is a regular component of martyrdom accounts and the dissemination of stories with these elements was meant to keep alive the very elements of the "old religion" that Protestantism wished to eradicate. For example, an account of the experiences of the martyr Stephen Rowsam, a convert from Protestantism, notes:

> This Mr. Rowsam had divers strange visions, even being a schismatic, and many more after he was a Catholic and a priest.... Mr. Thompson, his fellow-prisoner ... got them of him, and let the writer have a copy, which he dispersed into many counties of England, but yet at the writing of this present had none with him, else he would have set them down at all. This only he doth perfectly remember, Mr. Rowsam being in [Oriel] college in Oxford, and running forth with many others one day to see strange meteors that then appeared in the sky, he beheld over his own head and very

near to him a crown very bright and splendent, which he showed to the fellows that stayed by him. God the Father and God the Son appeared sundry times to him when a priest; so did our lady with words as he would not utter. For the space of one night and day, or thereabout, being a prisoner, he lived in unspeakable joy, which he deemed a taste of Heaven. As he prayed once in the Tower of London, many singing birds came over his book and pictures which stood before him. (Pollen, *Acts*, 333–34)

Supposedly the very day that the priests Thomas Ford, John Shirt, and Robert Johnson were martyred (28 May 1582), "they appeared to Mr. Roswam in the Tower, and let him feel what pains their martyrdom had been to them, and with what joy they were rewarded" (Pollen, *Acts*, 334). Nicholas Horner, in prison "after his condemnation one night, as he was walking in his . . . close room alone, saying his prayers, happening to look aside, he did see about the head of his shadow against the wall, in proportion of a half circle, a far brighter light than that of a candle, even as bright as the light of the sun. . . . at last he began to think with himself, that it was a sign given him from God to signifiy a crown unto him. Therefore he immediately said, 'O Lord, thy will be my will,' or to that effect, and so within a while it vanished away" (Pollen, *Acts*, 230–31). The trope of the "crown of martyrdom" informs both accounts.

The story of John Bodey's martyrdom includes a prophetic dream:

[He] saw in a dream the night before his death, two bulls attacking him very furiously, but without at all hurting him, at which he was much astonished. The next day two hangmen came down from London to execute him, and as they walked on either side of him, he chanced to ask their names, and as they one after the other answered that they were called Bull, he at once remembering his dream, said: "Blessed be God; you are then those two bulls who gave me such trouble last night in my dream, and yet did me no harm." He then joyfully composed himself for death. (Pollen, *Acts*, 56)

One of the purposes of this account, and of so many others, was to persuade Catholics that the pain and terror of punishment and execution were endurable. The aged Nicholas Horner, a tailor arrested first for refusing to say he would defend the queen from foreign invasion, said that in prison he chased from him a devil who appeared first as a "bush of thorns" and then "in the likeness of a blackamoor." After his gangrenous leg was amputated, he was freed and then rearrested. In prison he reported to a female visitor that he experienced "a great light in his Chamber, and . . . an angel did come and comfort him" (Pollen, *Acts*, 311).

Regularly, martyrdom accounts state that the hearts of the executed martyrs leapt out of the fire into which they were thrown. The account of Everard Hanse's martyrdom in the Douay Diaries claims that "the concurrent testimony of several witnesses has come to us that when his hart was thrown in the fire, it leaped up out of the flames with great violence, and being again flung in and coverred with a faggot of wood, a second time it leaped up with such force as to lift the faggot out of its place and hold it for a time quivering in the smoke. 'As if,' adds the writer of his Acts, 'God would manifest the victorious constancy of His martyr by the miraculous impetuous movement of his heart.'"[57] A narrative of the execution of William Freeman, a priest killed on 13 August 1595, reports that "his hart trembled in the exequtioner's hand, & as some reported that saw yt, the same leaped thrice out of the fire: & his head chopt of, his mouth gasped twice" (Pollen, *Unpub. Doc.*, 359).

Signs and miracles demand witnesses other than the principals who experience dreams and visions. Hence sympathetic, neutral, and unsympathetic spectators are incorporated in martyrdom accounts to testify to such phenomena. One observer reports seeing Robert Sutton, a converted Protestant minister turned Catholic missionary, "enveloped in light" while praying in jail (Pollen, *Acts*, 325). A witness at the execution of Thomas Pilcher saw his "soul . . . carried by angels into Heaven," and "The keeper of the gaol fell presently sick, and said openly unto many standing by, that the devils did strive for him, and that they would presently carry him away; but that he saw Mr. Pilchard stand with a cross betwixt him and them" (Pollen, *Acts*, 321). Rev. Thomas Fitzherbert reported that "one of the Assessors to the cheefe Judge, found his hand spotted with bloud at the tyme of Fa[ther] Campions condemnation, and . . . he shewed yt to some with great admiration" (WDA 2:188).[58]

Some of the signs and wonders are associated with practices of relic collection and veneration. The story is told of the miraculous preservation from corruption of the thumb and forefinger of Robert Sutton, a minister-turned-priest converted by a brother who later became a Jesuit:

> After the lapse of a whole year [after his execution], the Catholics, wishing to have some relics from the holy body of the Martyr, carried off one night by a pious theft a shoulder and arm. All the flesh was consumed, torn, and eaten by the birds, except the thumb and forefinger, which were found

whole and uninjured and clothed with flesh; so that on these, which had been anointed with holy oil and sanctified by contact with the most holy Body of Christ, a special honour above the other fingers was conferred, even in this world, before the day of the Resurrection, when the whole body will shine like the sun in the sight of the Father.

The writer reports: "His brother, Mr. Abraham Sutton[,] ... showed me both these fingers thus wonderfully preserved, and gave me the forefinger. I have kept it deposited in a silver and glass reliquary with great reverence, with a paper on which the above account is briefly set down. Our Fathers in England have the reliquary with its sacred treasure, unless perchance, by the iniquity of these times, it have been made the spoil of the heretics" (Pollen, *Acts*, 325–26). The thumb of Edmund Campion, to which miracle cures were attributed, also had similar value because it was one of the fingers specially consecrated at the ordination ceremony.

Some of the accounts of relic hunting highlight the courage of recusant women. For example, a priest's narrative account of the martyrdoms of the priest Roger Dickenson and layman Ralph Milner notes that after Dickenson was killed and dismembered, "One of his quarters was taken away, shortly after they were hanged up on the gate, by a maid who was imprisoned for the Catholic faith, but yet made this adventure in the night, and returned to prison again with the quarter under her cloak; for the which afterward was made great search, but yet it could not be found" (Pollen, *Acts*, 96). Another woman yanked off a finger from one of the hands of the martyred Edmund Gennings as his quarters were being carried back to Newgate to be boiled: "taking the thumbe in her hand, by the instinct of almighty God, she gave it a little pull, onely to shew her love and desire of having it. The sequel was miraculous: for behold she not imagining any such matter would have followed, by the divine power, the thumbe was instantly loosed from his hand, and being separated she carried it away safely both flesh, skinne, and bone without sight of any, to her great joy and admiration."[59] The relic had value as a "holy and annoynted thumbe" that was "a part of his hand which so often had elevated the immaculate body of our B[lessed] Saviour Jesus Christ."[60] The woman allegedly later fled to the Continent, became an Augustinian nun, and mailed a portion of the thumb to Gennings's brother, who was a priest at Douay.[61]

To some extent, the circulation of martyrs' relics paralleled the circulation of the texts narrating their martyrdoms, though the destinations were frequently Continental ones, which presented the safest locations for preservation. For example, some of the relics of John Roberts (a Benedictine priest) and Thomas Somers (a secular priest) were, according to Bishop Challoner, kept in England, but others were sent to the Continent—some to Douay to a Benedictine convent, and one of Roberts's arms was sent to Spain to the Abbey of St. Martin at Compostella (Pollen, *Acts*, 169). Many of the relics at Douay were destroyed at the time of the French Revolution, but Douay manuscripts were preserved, ironically, by being returned to England (where many remain at the Westminster Diocesan Archives).

The behavior of Catholics at the religious executions, the folklore and devotional practices associated with the events and the remains of the victims, and the writing and circulation of martyrdom accounts all fostered the grassroots process of saint-making—the older method that the Counter-Reformation Church was trying to control through its institution of new, centralized, judicially elaborate procedures for canonization.[62] The Catholic Church was very slow to install the English martyrs in its official calendar of saints: for example, it took to 1970 for Philip Howard to be so recognized, along with thirty-nine other English and Welsh martyrs.[63] Although the Catholic Continental presses exploited the martyrdoms for polemical purposes in the propaganda war with English and European Protestantism, there are signs that martyrdom was being discouraged as a goal of English missionary priests and the Catholic faithful.

After the death of his colleague Edmund Campion on the first English Jesuit mission, the indefatigable Robert Persons not only used his pen to compose a steady stream of Catholic propaganda against the Elizabethan regime and its practices of persecuting Catholics but also undertook a biography of his beloved comrade.[64] Obviously much grieved by Campion's loss, Persons detailed his friend's personal and religious history, but he abandoned the project before he recorded the dramatic events of Campion's arrest, imprisonment and torture, debate with Protestant adversaries, and execution at Tyburn. The martyr's biography leaves off before the martyrdom. When Campion had entered England, he did so with no reluctance, as he said to the authorities, to "enjoy your Tyburn."[65] Like other militant Jesuits, he thought of himself as a martyr in the making—a not unreasonable expectation, given the government's murderous treatment of priests, especially Jesuit priests, in the 1580s and 1590s. The problem was, however, that most Catholics were (understandably) uncomfortable with such an idealization of the path of martyrdom. And Claudio Aquaviva, the Jesuit General, was disturbed by the attitude of his missioners, who seemed more eager to die for the faith than to survive and minister to Catholics or to "reconcile" the "schismatics" (Church Papists) to Catholicism. While all Catholics might have believed that "the blood of martyrs is the seed of the Church," it was also undoubtedly the case that the General preferred live missionaries to dead ones. Hence, there was good reason for Persons—the survivor of the persecution who escaped England and capture, for which his Protestant adversaries accused him of cowardice—to abandon, in effect, the composition of the life of the martyred Campion.[66] He was more interested in either overthrowing the English Protestant regime by foreign invasion or replacing it with a Catholic one by arguing succession claims of the Spanish Infanta than he was in propagating the message that the fate of English Catholics was to follow the example of those who suffered and died for their faith.

The 1604 peace treaty with Spain, King James I's irenic impulses, the fact that Charles I and Charles II had Catholic spouses, and the negative publicity from the religious executions forced the English government to back off somewhat from persecuting Catholics fully after the Elizabethan era—though, of course, especially after the failed Gunpowder Plot and at other times of crisis such as the 1641 Irish Rebellion and Titus Oates's concocted "Popish Plot," many Catholics were put to death. On the other hand, opposition within the Catholic Church to reckless pursuit of martyrdom caused a certain devaluation of martyrdom, and the martyrdom account was deemphasized as a literary subgenre. Although Catholics continued to be killed (the last Catholic religious execution at Tyburn occurred in the late eighteenth century), the martyrdom account diminished in cultural importance. Its power, of course, could still be tapped on particular occasions—for example, to John Milton's great annoyance, by conservative Protestants who wished, in *Eikon Basilike* (1649), to depict the suffering and execution of Charles I as a martyrdom.

Sometimes texts circulated within the Catholic community were not only reproduced in printed Catholic texts but also (recoded and) printed in new circumstances for other political purposes. Take, for example, the case of the famous speech from the scaffold by the priest John Southworth, killed during the Protectorate on 28 June 1654 in a well-attended execution by hanging.[67] From the cart he made a powerful speech, pointedly speaking a political rhetoric designed to embarrass a government sensitive to claims of freedom by religious dissenters. He made a sharp distinction between the religious and secular orders and made a strong claim for liberty of conscience:

Heretofore liberty of conscience was pretended as a cause of war; and it was held a reasonable proposition that all the natives shoud enjoy it, who should be forced to behave themselves as obedient and true subjects. This being so, why should then conscientious acting and governing themselves, according to the faith received from their ancestors, involve them more than the rest in an universal guilt? . . . It has pleased God to take the sword out of the King's hand and put it in the Protector's. Let him remember that he is to administer justice indifferently and without exception of persons. . . . If any Catholics work against the present govenment, let them suffer; but why should the rest who are guiltless (unless conscience be their guilt) be made partakers in a promiscuous punishment with the greatest malefactors?[68]

As Southworth's modern biographer points out, "there were at least five contemporary versions of the martyr's speech at the foot of the gallows. Copies were circulated among Catholics who, from the earliest days of the persecution, had treasured the final words of the martyrs. It was from one of these copies that a printed version was published by a non-Catholic in 1679, the year in which eighteen names were added to the Roll of Martyrs as a result of the machinations of Titus Oates."[69] Thus the printed pamphlet, *A popish priest at his execution at Tyburn June 28, 1654. Fully discovering the Papist's design to obtain Toleration and liberty of Conscience; and to that end the late Rebellion was begun and carried on. Printed from the true copy found among other papers at the Search of a Papist's house* (London, 1679). If Reynolds is right in stating that Roger L'Estrange published the book in order to counter the forces unleashed by Titus Oates, it is a good example of how an old text could have new life in new political circumstances. The martyrdom account could move from the context of communal oral communication, to manuscript transmission, to printed religious propaganda, to nonconfessional political discourse, its moral and sociopolitical force being utilized in various contexts for various purposes.

Notes

1. See Clark Hulse, "Dead Man's Treasure: The Cult of Thomas More," in *The Production of English Renaissance Culture,* ed. David Lee Miller, Sharon O'Dair, and Harold Weber (Ithaca: Cornell University Press, 1994), 217. See also H. R. Woudhuysen, *Sir Philip Sidney and the Circulation of Manuscripts, 1558–1640* (Oxford: Clarendon Press, 1996), 151.

2. William Shelley, a layman, was sentenced to death for owning a copy of this work; see John Hungerford Pollen, ed., *Acts of English Martyrs Hitherto Unpublished* (London: Burns and Oates, 1891), 307 (hereafter cited in the text as Pollen, *Acts*). See Woudhuysen, *Sir Philip Sidney*, 148, on its manuscript circulation.

3. Persons and Campion brought printed copies of this with them on the English mission in 1580, but there were also manuscript versions produced, such as the one for Shakespeare's father. See the discussion of this document in F. W. Brownlow, "John Shakespeare's Recusancy: New Light on an Old Document," *Shakespeare Quarterly* 48 (summer 1989): 186–91, and in Richard Wilson, "Shakespeare and the Jesuits," *TLS*, 19 December 1997, 11–13.

4. I discuss this in "Southwell's Remains: Catholicism and Anti-Catholicism in Early Modern England," in *Texts and Cultural Change in Early Modern England*, ed. Cedric C. Brown and Arthur F. Marotti (New York: St. Martin's Press, 1997), 39–41.

5. See Bodleian MS Laud. No. 968 (E.45), 282l.

6. See Woudhuysen, *Sir Philip Sidney*, 52–53, citing John Hungerford Pollen and William MacMahon, eds., *The Ven. Philip Howard Earl of Arundel 1557–1595, English Martyrs*, vol. 2 (London: Catholic Record Society, 1919), 99, 142–43, 281, 338. This much-copied text circulated very widely in the Catholic community.

7. Dennis Flynn, *John Donne and the Ancient Catholic Nobility* (Bloomington: Indiana University Press, 1996), 218 n. 10, notes that this circulated in manuscript after 1596.

8. Woudhuysen, *Sir Philip Sidney*, 124, notes that eight manuscripts of this work survive, that Holinshed used it for his *Chronicles* (1577), but that it did not get printed until 1631.

9. Southwell's poetry, despite its publication, continued to appear in manuscript collections in the seventeenth century. See, for example, Bod. MSS Eng. Poet. b.5 and e.113 and BL MS Harl. 6910. Robert Southwell's famous letter to his father was reproduced in many copies and circulated widely. Other literary texts circulated in manuscript include freshly copied versions of banned old mystery play cycles (Woudhuysen, *Sir Philip Sidney*, 145).

10. See Bod. MS Eng. Poet. e.122, fols. 31–36, and BL Add. 15225, fols. 25–27v, for copies of this poem: Hyder Rollins, ed., *Old English Ballads, 1553–1625* (Cambridge: Cambridge University Press, 1920), 88–94, transcribes the British Library version.

11. BL MS Add. 15225, fols. 2v-3, in Rollins, *Old English Ballads*, 149–51 (I emend in two places).

12. Thomas Alfield, *A True Reporte of the Death & Martyrdome of M. Campion Jesuit and Preiste, & M. Sherwin, & M. Bryan Preistes* . . . (1582), and Anthony Munday, *A breefe Aunswer made unto two seditious Pamphlets. . . . contayning a defence of Edmund Campion and his complices* . . . (1582). On Campion, see my essay, "Southwell's Remains," 37–65. In response to the execution of Everard Hanse, 31 July 1581, there was a libel published to counter the circulation in manuscript of accounts of his death, *A true report, of the Araignment and execution of the late Popish traitor, Everard Haunce, executed at Tyborne, with reformation of the errors of a former untrue booke published concerning the same* (1581). See the text published in *Miscellanea*, Catholic Record Society (London: John Whitehead and Son Ltd.,

1932)—noted in *Lives of the English Martyrs Declared Blessed by Pope Leo XIII. in 1886 and 1895*, written by the Fathers of the Oratory, of the Secular Clergy, and of the Society of Jesus, completed and edited by Dom Bede Camm, O.S.B., 2 vols. (London: Burns and Oates, Ltd., 1904–5), 1:261.

13. Rpt. from Grene's Collectanea M. pt. 2 (fols. 206–9) in John Hungerford Pollen, ed., *Unpublished Documents Relating to the English Martyrs, vol. 1, 1584–1603* (London: Catholic Record Society, 1908), 62; hereafter cited in the text as Pollen, *Unpub. Doc.*

14. See, in particular, Garnet's letters of 1594 (in Pollen, *Unpub. Doc.*, 227–33) and of March 1601–2 (Arch. S. J. Rom. Anglia 31, 172–83), which contain reports of many martyrs.

15. Pollen, *Unpub. Doc.*, 140–43, prints four letters written by Englishmen intended for Gibbons to use in revising his *Concertatio* for a second edition, but intercepted by the English authorities.

16. Pollen, *Unpub. Doc.*, 393, connects many of the notes found in WDA 4:1–14, 117–132, etc., with the responses to this call.

17. This, as Pollen points out, *Unpub. Doc.*, 144, was a translation of Allen's work, with Gibbons putting the lives in chronological order.

18. Pollen, *Unpub. Doc.*, 1–3, mentions, in addition to these works, the following other publications that contain accounts of martyrdoms or lists of martyrs: Nicholas Sander's *De origine et progressu Schismatis Anglicani Liber* (1585; 2d ed., 1586), *Relatione del presente stato d'Inghilterra* (Rome, 1590) (containing Dr. Richard Barrett's list of martyrs, also appearing in Tomaso Bozio's *De Signis Ecclesiae* [1591], Gregorio Nuñez Coronel's *De Vera Christi Ecclesia* [Rome, 1594], Juan Lopez Mancano's broadside sheet *Breve Catalogo de los Martyres que han side de los Collegios y Seminarios Ingleses* [Valladolid, 1590], and Pedro de Ribandeneira's *Historia ecclesiastica del cisma de Inglaterra* [1593]), Persons's *Elizabethae Angliae Reginae saevissimum edictum . . . cum responsione* (Lyons, 1592), which has a catalogue of laymen who died for the faith, and Fray Diego Yepes's *Historia particular de las persecucion de Inglaterra* (Madrid, 1599).

19. A manuscript version of this martyrdom account (by James Young) survives (Stonyhurst MSS Anglia vi.117). There is an interesting four-page folio pamphlet containing the story of Gennings's life and martyrdom and of a devout Catholic woman's seizure of one of his thumbs as a relic after his death: *Strange and Miraculous News from St. Omers: Being an Account of the Wonderful Life and Death of a Popish Saint and Martyr, names Mr. Edmund Gennings, Priest, who was Executed for Treason some Years since: with a Relation of the Miracles at, and after his Death. Wherein may be observed, what Lying Wonders the Credulous Papists are made to believe, both against Sense and Reason* (n.p., n.d.). The work has a short anti-Catholic introductory section, and a short, mocking paragraph of conclusion, but the body of the pamphlet is a Catholic account. The work may, therefore, have been posing as anti-Catholic propaganda to put into circulation a Catholic martyrological text.

20. As Woudhuysen and others note, often Catholic printed books and pamphlets from the Continent later returned to manuscript circulation when they were

given to copyists in England for reproduction and sale—see Woudhuysen, *Sir Philip Sidney*, 82, citing Leona Rostenberg, *The Minority Press and the English Crown* (Nieuwkoop, Netherlands: B. De Graaf, 1971), 81.

21. Stonyhurst MSS M. fol. 157, cited in Pollen, *Acts*, 2–8.

22. Letter dated 16 March 1583[4], Westminster Diocesan Archives [hereafter cited as WDA] 3:237–39.

23. D. Shanahan, "Petticoats on the Gallows," *Essex Recusant* 11 (Dec. 1968): 107. The text of this martyrdom account is reproduced on pp. 108–10.

24. See J. G. O'Leary, "A Recusant Manuscript of Great Importance," *Essex Recusant* 10 (1968): 17–20.

25. "Paperchase: The Dissemination of Catholic Texts in Elizabethan England," *English Manuscript Studies*, vol. 1 (Oxford: Basil Blackwell, 1989), 120–43. Brown traces a paper supply, with its distinctive watermark, to Henry Garnet, who distributed it to be used both for some printed works and for manuscript copying. Garnet, she guesses, probably took possession of the papers of Robert Southwell after the latter's arrest and saw to it that a number of his works were copied and printed.

26. There are four extant manuscripts of the life. One sixteenth-century version was used by John Morris for his nineteenth-century edition in *Troubles of Our Catholic Forefathers*, vol. 3 (London: Burns and Oates, 1877), 360–440; another is a copy of selected chapters dealing with the arrest, trial, and execution (St. Mary's College, Oscott—in Peter Mowle's collection); another sixteenth-century version of the selected chapters is York Minster Library Add. MS 151; and a seventeenth-century version is Vatican Library Barberini Latini, Codex 3555 (information provided in Katherine Longley, *Saint Margaret Clitherow* [Wheathampstead, Herts.: Anthony Clarke, 1986]).

27. *An Abstracte of the Life and Martirdome of Mistres Margaret Clitherowe* (Mackline, 1619). I discuss Clitherow in my essay, "Alienating Catholics in Early Modern England: Recusant Women, Jesuits, and Ideological Fantasies," in *Catholicism and Anti-Catholicism in Early Modern English Texts*, ed. Arthur F. Marotti (New York: St. Martin's Press, 1999), 1–34.

28. Cf. the eight-sheet quarto quire now in the Westminster Diocesan Archives containing "Of Mr Roger Cadwallader Pr. and martyr who suffered at Le[o]-m[in]ster, 27. Aug. 1610" plus some other items (WDA 9:211–26, the last two sheets of which are blank). There are two accounts of the 10 December martyrdoms of Roberts and Wilson in WDA 9:343 ff. An account of the martyrdom of John Lathom is preserved in manuscript in a small quarto booklet formerly among the Douay MSS (WDA 11:627 ff. [item #221]).

29. See Michael E. Williams, "Campion and the English Continental Seminaries," in *The Reckoned Expense: Edmund Campion and the Early English Jesuits*, ed. Thomas McCoog (Woodbridge, Suffolk; Rochester, N.Y.: Boydell Press, 1996), 295–96.

30. For an excellent discussion of the problematic and disputable meanings of these executions for contemporaries, see Peter Lake and Michael Questier, "Agency, Appropriation and Rhetoric under the Gallows: Puritans, Romanists and the State in Early Modern England," *Past and Present* 153 (November 1996): 64–107. Lake and Questier, 92–95, highlight the Jesuits' activism and ideological zealotry. Although

most of my essay was written before I read this study, I have learned much from it and am indebted to it.

31. See Alexandra Walsham, *Church Papists: Catholicism, Conformity and Confessional Polemic in Early Modern England* (Woodbridge, Suffolk: The Royal Historical Society and Boydell Press, 1993).

32. William Trimble, *The Catholic Laity in Elizabethan England 1558–1603* (Cambridge, Mass.: Belknap Press of Harvard University Press, 1964), 175, points out that, although the government distrusted time-serving Church Papists, "an occasional conformist was a lost Catholic, a fact increasingly true as Elizabeth's reign progressed."

33. In the late 1590s, Robert Persons's argument for the succession rights of the Spanish Infanta was the least persuasive means to restore Catholicism in England.

34. Louise I. Guiney, *Recusant Poets* (New York: Sheed and Ward, 1939), 181.

35. Geoffrey F. Nuttall, "The English Martyrs 1535–1680: A Statistical Review," *Journal of Ecclesiastical History* 22, no. 3 (July 1971): 193–94.

36. See WDA 7:339–42. This manuscript is the source for the (not always accurate) version in Pollen's *Acts* (238–48), which completes the story from the version of Bishop Challoner, who had the complete account.

37. A 1602 letter to Robert Persons by a Jesuit correspondent refers to the death of Duckett and to his having been used as an instrument by the (anti-Jesuit) Appellant party to print Southwell's work, which the (pro-Jesuit) "Archpriest" George Blackwell had not wished to be published at that time (Pollen, *Unpub. Doc.*, 390–91).

38. Lake and Questier, "Agency, Appropriation and Rhetoric," 81, also cite this example. Guiney, *Recusant Poets*, 174, prints from Peter Mowle's manuscripts a poem by Wells, "To Christ Crucified." See her discussion of Wells's life (171–73).

39. For a discussion of the Protestant technique of turning the body into a text and of some of the features of Protestant martyrdom accounts, see Catharine Randall Coats, *(Em)bodying the Word: Textual Resurrections in the Martyrological Narratives of Foxe, Crespin, de Bèze and d'Aubigné* (New York: Peter Lang, 1992). Coats argues that "Unlike Catholic hagiographical writing which may be characterized by a focus on the image, and the spatial rendering and localization of that image, Calvinist martyrologies are above all typified by an insistence on the word—be it of the martyr, of the author or of God" (2). For discussions of Protestant martyrdom, see also John Knott, *Discourses of Martyrdom in English Literature, 1563–1694* (Cambridge: Cambridge University Press, 1993) and Huston Diehl, *Staging Reform: Reforming the Stage: Protestantism and Popular Theater in Early Modern England* (Ithaca and London: Cornell University Press, 1997), 185–94 and passim.

40. *The Sermons of John Donne*, ed. George R. Potter and Evelyn Simpson, 10 vols. (Berkeley and Los Angeles: University of California Press, 1953–62), 5:382.

41. See the discussion of Almond's execution in Lake and Questier, "Agency, Appropriation and Rhetoric," 74.

42. See Richard Simpson, *Edmund Campion: A Biography* (London: John Hodges, 1896), 454–55. Pollen, *Unpub. Doc.*, 246–69, prints the later "confessions" of Walpole, who was repeatedly threatened and tortured by the authorities before his death.

43. Garnet, letter to Jesuit General, 11 March 1601 (Arch. S. J. Rom. Anglia 31, 172–83); translation in the English Jesuit Archives, London, kindly made available by Thomas McCoog, S.J.
44. Nuttall, "The English Martyrs 1535–1680," 195.
45. Ibid.
46. Lake and Questier point out that "Fourteen priests executed in 1588 in the closest the Elizabethan regime ever got to a 'terror' were sent off to 'sundry places neere London' to die" ("Agency, Appropriation and Rhetoric," 70).
47. *The Life and Death of Mr. Edmund Geninges*, 84.
48. Gary Wills, *Witches and Jesuits: Shakespeare's* Macbeth (New York: New York Public Library; Oxford: Oxford University Press, 1995), 101.
49. Thomas Laqueur, "Crowds, Carnival and the State in English Executions, 1604–1868," in *The First Modern Society*, ed. A. Beier, D. Cannadine, and J. Rosenheim (Cambridge: Cambridge University Press, 1989), 322, notes that the "*hilaritas* of the martyr . . . would have been . . . familiar to English audiences in Fox's *Book of Martyrs*."
50. See the text printed in Henry Foley, ed., *Records of the English Province of the Society of Jesus*, vol. 1 (London: Burns and Oates, 1877), 373–75.
51. *Life and Death of Mr. Edmund Geninges*, 84–85.
52. Ibid., 85–86.
53. Cf. the examples discussed by Lake and Questier, 73–75.
54. See, for example, the exchange between William Cecil, Lord Burghley, and William Cardinal Allen, in their two works: *The Execution of Justice in England* (1584) and *A True, Sincere, and Modest Defense of English Catholics* (1584).
55. Pollen is citing "R.B." (Robert Barnes?), the author of *Two Obstinate and Notorious Traitors, Slade and Body, their Execution and Confession* (1583?), a work that seems to use a veneer of hostility to disguise its sympathy for the martyrs. Cf. the account of their martyrdoms in WDA 2:341 ff.
56. Lake and Questier, "Agency, Appropriation and Rhetoric," argue that "the very ideological means by which the state sought to encode its own purposes in these proceedings opened up spaces in which those purposes could be challenged and subverted" (69) and "every time a Catholic priest was executed the issue of where legitimate royal authority ended and tyranny and persecution began was, through speech and gesture, reopened and thrust on to the public stage" (73).
57. Cited in Camm, *Lives*, 1:260–61.
58. In one of his letters to Cardinal Allen, William Barret reported three striking examples of divine punishment's being visited on the persecutors of Catholics: see *Letters of William Allen and Richard Barret 1572–1598*, ed. P. Renold (London: Catholic Record Society, 1967), 96–97.
59. *Life and Death of Mr. Edmund Geninges*, 96.
60. Ibid., 93.
61. Ibid., 94. Lake and Questier note that "in early modern England the hands of the hanged were thought to possess curative powers. In the events surrounding Gennings's death, élite religion, a Counter-Reformation sensibility obsessed with martyrs' relics, popular beliefs about the body of the hanged man, and garbled versions of humoral medical theory were all clustered together around the rites of

state violence in a fascinating, overlapping pattern of meaning and gesture" ("Agency, Appropriation and Rhetoric," 101).

62. See Peter Burke, "How to Be a Counter-Reformation Saint," in *The Historical Anthropology of Early Modern Italy* (Cambridge: Cambridge University Press, 1987), 48–62, 243.

63. Francis W. Steer, "St. Philip Howard, Arundel and the Howard Connexion in Sussex," in *Studies in Sussex Church History*, ed. M. J. Kitch (Falmer, East Sussex: Leopard's Head Press and The University of Sussex, 1981), 209–22, and *Archdiocese of Westminster. Cause of the Canonization of Blessed Martyrs John Houghton, Robert Lawrence, Augustine Webster, Richard Reynolds, John Stone, Cuthbert Mayne, John Paine, Edmund Campion, Alexander Briant, Ralph Sherwin, and Luke Kirby Put to Death in England in Defence of the Catholic Faith (1535–1582). Official Presentation of Documents on Martyrdom and Cult*, Sacred Congregation of Rites, Historical Section, 148 (Vatican: Vatican Polyglot Press, 1968). Cf. Stephen and Elizabeth Usherwood, *We Die for the Old Religion: The Story of the 85 Martyrs of England and Wales Beatified 22 November 1987* (London: Sheed and Ward, 1987).

64. This manuscript (Stonyhurst MS Collectanea P.76–148) was only published in the late nineteenth century: Robert Persons, *Of the Life and Martyrdom of Father Edmund Campian*, ed. Br. H. Foley, *Letters and Notices* (December 1877) (n.p.: Manresa Press, 1877), 219–42, 308–39, 1–68.

65. In his letter to the Privy Council ("Campion's Brag"), Campion wrote: "And touching our Society be it known to you that we have made a league—all the Jesuits of the world, whose succession and multitude must overreach all the practices of England—cheerfully to carry the cross you shall lay upon us and never to despair your recovery, while we have a man left to enjoy your Tyburn, or to be racked with your torments or consumed with your prisons" (text printed in Bernard Basset, *The English Jesuits: From Campion to Martindale* [New York: Herder and Herder, 1968], 456).

66. See John Bossy, "The Heart of Robert Persons," in McCoog, *The Reckoned Expense*, 146–47: "Acquaviva insisted that there was an obligation on Jesuits in England to be careful, which Campion had not been.... Persons ... abandoned the 'Life' for an account of the persecution of Catholics in England, and did not return to it for thirteen years. Then he produced a torso which was a good deal more conventional than what Acquaviva seems to have had in mind, and stopped before Campion's arrest. In practice Persons surely made it his business to din into departing missioners the message that they were being sent to do a job not, if they could help it, to get martyred."

67. E. F. Reynolds, *John Southworth: Priest, Martyr* (London: Burnes and Oates, 1962), 68, notes: "He was attended to the place of execution by two hundred coaches, and great many people on horseback, who all admired his constancy."

68. Ibid., 71.

69. Ibid., 72–73.

CHAPTER SEVEN

The Rapes of Lucina
Harold Love

The late classical story of the rape of the wife of Petronius Maximus by the Emperor Valentinian III inspired three striking treatments from seventeenth-century writers. The works concerned are the "Histoire d'Eudoxe, Valentinian, et Ursace" in the *Seconde partie* of Honoré Durfé's romance *Astrée* (1610), John Fletcher's tragedy *Valentinian,* written circa 1610–12, and Rochester's radical revision of *Valentinian* as *Lucina's Rape*, written circa 1675 and first performed in 1684. My examination of these treatments sets out to track the two that are best known to English readers in an unusual but not unique odyssey through the media, moving from print to the stage, then to manuscript circulation, then to print again, then back to manuscript, then to the stage again, and finally back to print. I will argue that significant aspects of the artistic handling are modified to meet the expectations of each new mode of transmission and its public.

The story has certain similarities with that of the rape of Lucretia. In a passage from Rochester's treatment the parallel is explicitly drawn:

>   I askt her
> After my many offers, walking with her
> And her many downe denyalls, How
> If the Emperour growne mad with love should force her:
> She pointed to a Lucrece that hung by,
> And with an angry looke that from her Eyes

> Shot Vestall Fire against mee, she departed.
> (2.2.87–93)[1]

Fletcher and Rochester thought it necessary for her to imitate Lucretia in expiating the crime against her by her own death; Durfé allowed her to pursue revenge. As in the better-known legend, whose many reworkings have been explored by Ian Donaldson, the crime against the woman precipitated the collapse of a royal line.[2] In history, for all practical purposes, the fall of the line was also that of Roman imperial authority; however, neither of the English treatments emphasizes this aspect, each concluding with a specious promise of political renewal. The principal difference between the republican and the imperial legend is that whereas Lucretia had been violated while living as a chaste wife in domestic seclusion, the predicament of Lucina (as Fletcher and Rochester call her) or Isidore (her name in *Astrée*) was that of a woman attempting to remain virtuous while involved in the public life of a lustful court.

The perpetrator of the crime, Valentinian III, was the emperor under whom Rome suffered its most catastrophic decline, losing Britain, Spain, most of transalpine Gaul, and parts of Africa. The rape had as a direct consequence Valentinian's misguided assassination of Flavius Aetius, conqueror of the Huns and Visigoths, and the one imperial general capable of holding back the invaders. The fullest account of the event (even then very brief and not giving us the name of the victim) is in book 3, sections 4–5 of Procopius's *History of the Wars*:

> This younger Maximus was married to a woman discreet in her ways and exceedingly famous for her beauty. For this reason a desire came over Valentinian to have her to wife. And since it was impossible, much as he wished it, to meet her, he plotted an unholy deed and carried it to fulfilment. For he summoned Maximus to the palace and sat down with him to a game of draughts, and a certain sum was set as a penalty for the loser; and the emperor won in this game, and receiving Maximus' ring as a pledge for the agreed amount, he sent it to his house, instructing the messenger to tell the wife of Maximus that her husband bade her come as quickly as possible to the palace to salute the queen Eudoxia. And she, judging by the ring that the message was from Maximus, entered her litter and was conveyed to the emperor's court. And she was received by those who had been assigned this service by the emperor, and led into a certain room far removed from the women's apartments, where Valentinian met her and forced her, much against her will. And she, after the outrage, went

to her husband's house weeping and feeling the deepest possible grief because of her misfortune, and she cast many curses upon Maximus as having provided the cause for what had been done. Maximus, accordingly, became exceedingly aggrieved at that which had come to pass, and straightway entered into a conspiracy against the emperor.[3]

In the continuation of the story, Maximus realized that in order for his plot to succeed he would need to dispose of the powerful and loyal Aetius, which he did by persuading Valentinian that the general was conspiring to usurp the diadem. After this, "Maximus slew the emperor with no trouble and secured the tyranny, and he married Eudoxia by force. For the wife to whom he had been wedded had died not long before" (45). Eudoxia then plotted against Maximus by persuading the Vandals under Gizeric to invade Italy. The Roman mob killed Maximus in an attempt to placate the Vandals.

This was the imaginative starting point for the versions of Durfé and Fletcher, each of whom then set off in very different directions. Fletcher is constantly said to have known Durfé's version, which may well be so, though it is hard to see much practical evidence. Both could well be independent developments of Procopius or of some intermediate common source derived from him. The "Histoire d'Eudoxe" is part of a prose romance famous for its length even among that long-winded genre (and judiciously shortened by its English translator), but as an embedded narrative with a separate heading and its own complex plot development.[4] In fact, it is simply one of a long series of discrete stories organized for purposes of convenience within a single overarching plot. Writing for recreational readers whose interests were sophisticated and court-oriented and whose lives seem to have been structured, like many of our own, around the daily consumption of interminable serial narratives, Durfé offers elegance of style, great refinement of sensibility, and a realistic assessment of the problems of combining Christian morality with participation in the great world. His work was a favorite with women readers and is in certain respects intended for them.

Durfé's Isidore is not Fletcher's and Rochester's Lucretia-like figure, but a "jeune fille des meilleures maisons de Grece" (813) who has come to Rome as the confidant of Valentinian's wife, the no less beautiful and sophisticated Eudoxe. (Eudoxe, naturally, has her own devoted but frustrated admirer in Ursace, who in this version is the eventual murderer of Maximus.) She is referred to repeatedly as "la sage Isidore" and is in every sense, apart from her refusal to succumb to the emperor, a woman of the world. Durfé's narrator regards it as rather bad form for her not to have accepted Valentinian's overtures when she was still single, but concedes her right to choose otherwise. Valentinian is persuaded by the eunuch, Heracle, to rape her. The device of the ring is handled much as in Procopius. Trapped by Valentinian and Heracle, Isidore resists their assault with spirit, striking Heracle with "un si grand coup, que le sang lui en sortit incontinent du nez" (856). Following that "Elle se mit bien à crier, et a faire toute la déffence que elle pust" (857). After the rape, Valentinian tells her that it would be in her best interest to keep it a secret from Maximus. Instead, as in Procopius, she goes straight to her husband and demands that he take vengeance on Valentinian. The revenge is performed more or less as narrated by Procopius but with the addition of an episode in which, after the murder of Valentinian, Isidore comes to the court to gloat over his headless body, washes her hands in his blood, and drops dead of overwhelming joy at the success of her revenge (887).

Fletcher's Lucina is Roman, not Greek, Greek women being unchaste by definition in *Valentinian* (see 1.1.23–31).[5] Here the exchange of media is demonstrably an influence on the artistic conception. While Durfé had the luxury of being able to develop his characters at his and his readers' leisure through the expansive medium of literary prose, Fletcher had to create his Lucina in under three acts (she dies in the course of 3.1) through the circumscribed theatrical skills of a boy actor. For one, Lucina is very young ("Not eighteene, not of age to know / Why she is honest" [1.1.21]). She is also immature and colorless when set beside her French counterpart: the life of her scenes comes from the animatedness of those around her—her two witty maidservants, and Valentinian's train of male and female bawds. Until the point at which she unleashes her scorn on the emperor in 3.1, her role in the drama is wholly reactive. Far from being "*sage*," she is ruled by a conception of marital fidelity as based on total female subservience. But Fletcher does give us an oppressive, and in its outcome horrifying, picture of innocence lured by evil into a trap from which the only escape can be death. This death is not, needless to say, from Isidore's excess of euphoria, but simple shame at having dishonored her husband through being herself dishonored.

> When first she enter'd
> Into her house, after a world of weeping,
> And blushing like the Sun-set, as we saw her;

> Dare I, said she, defile this house with whore,
> In which his noble family has flourished?
> At which she fel, and stirred no more; we rubd her—
> (3.1.363b–368)

Even her death is unassertive.

It is also the case that the story of Lucina gets rather lost in the narrative tangle of Fletcher's tragedy. In trying to cover the whole span of Procopius's narrative up to the death of Maximus, the play becomes overcrowded with incident. This too is media related. *Valentinian* is an ingenious but uneasy attempt to combine the conventions of the Roman play as perfected by Shakespeare and Jonson with those of Jacobean revenge drama. In the opening scenes, Maximus and Aecius (as his name is spelled in this version of the story) are presented as exemplary military leaders in the heroic Roman mold, linked in equally heroic friendship. That Maximus should turn against Aecius and become a Machiavellian intriguer gives rise to a strong sense of unmotivated dramatic contrivance. The theatrical centerpiece is the death of Valentinian rather than that of Lucina. But where Durfé has him almost perfunctorily slain while at dinner with Heracle, Fletcher introduces a complicated intrigue in which Maximus persuades another eunuch, Aretus, to administer a poison that produces unspeakable agony. While Valentinian in the early stages of his suffering sits surrounded by physicians and attendants, Aretus enters to announce that he has taken the same poison in order to demonstrate what Valentinian must expect to endure before he dies. The impetus to this confrontation is entirely theatrical. First, Aretus is required to describe and act out the torments produced by the venom, and next Valentinian is required to outdo him in the paroxysms of his own death. In effect two performers are primed to compete with each other in outrageous overacting—rather like jazz musicians trading virtuosity in alternating solos. Amid this frenzy the quiet death of Lucina is forgotten. In this and the closing scenes dealing with the revenge of Eudoxia, *Valentinian* is very much what the nineteenth century would have called a "sensation play." It was this imbalance in Fletcher's plot that Rochester set out to rectify. Anticipating the advice to be given by most of Fletcher's later editors, he lopped off the last act completely, ending the play with the death of Valentinian, and telescoped the action to focus attention on the sufferings of Lucina and the loyalty of Æcius (his spelling). He also reformed the character of Maximus by freeing him of any treachery to Æcius and making even his turning against the emperor thoroughly excusable.

But before we look further at these changes, it will be necessary to return to the media history of Fletcher's text. *Valentinian* was not published during Fletcher's own lifetime or for some time after, being carefully kept from the press by the King's Company according to their regular practice with their active repertoire, a practice that was also probably written into its contracts with its house dramatists, successively Shakespeare, Fletcher, Massinger, and Shirley.[6] Hardly anything is known of the play's performance history, but we may assume that it was similar to that of other works by the company's second most popular dramatist. The pattern seems to have been that plays would be kept in repertory while they continued to draw and then would be set aside for a while. In due course there would be a revival, for which it was customary for revisions to be undertaken by the current house dramatist.[7] The version eventually given to the world in print would usually include any such revisions. It is tempting to speculate that the idealization of Æcius as the upholder of Roman military honor, and the stress laid on the army's desire to engage in foreign war, followed from revisions made in response to the intense popular desire for Britain to engage on the Protestant side in the European religious wars that followed the loss of the Palatinate in 1620. Buckingham's 1628 expedition to the Isle of Rhé would also have made this aspect of the play very topical, though by this time Fletcher (who seems to have been the sole author) was dead.[8] It seems unlikely that such a lively and effective spectacle would have remained unrevived, though its attack on favorites and authoritarian kings may have led to some touchiness during the personal rule of Charles I. Scribal copies of some plays were available for unofficial sale at a high price, but none survives of *Valentinian*.

When the play did appear in print, it was as part of the monumental Beaumont and Fletcher folio of 1647.[9] This was issued after the closing of the theaters and drew for the most part on authoritative stage manuscripts. But it also marked a decisive shift in the reception history of the play, which from then on seems to have been available only as a reading text. Moreover, the context of reading was one that imposed two kinds of ideological tendentiousness from which it would have been hard to dissociate it. The first was political: the 1647 folio is a royalist document, embodying a deep nostalgia both for the now-silent theaters and the monarchist political order. Robert Markley notes that James Shirley, in his preface to the volume, "identifies Fletcher with an idyllic past of wit, courtly grace, youthful pleasures, and the joys of the theatre."[10] As an attack on corrupt courts and unprincipled rulers, *Valentinian* relates a little uneasily to this enterprise. Republicans could have read the play as confirming their worst suspicions about courts and kings. Royalist readers, on the other hand, were no doubt quick enough to reapply it to the autocracy of Cromwell, whom they insisted on seeing as a monster of lust as well as tyranny, while Maximus and Æcius might well have passed as crypto-cavaliers trapped in a misguided loyalty to a usurping ruler.[11]

The second kind of tendentiousness was literary. Quarto play texts, carelessly produced on cheap paper, were looked down on as reading matter even by those who admired the same works in performance, and seem to be have been read largely as a means of reviving memories of performance. D. F. McKenzie has written:

> It was of course self-evident that print was not the proper medium for plays; most reached the printinghouse in a fortuitous and often surreptitious manner; and because the London book trade lacked any kind of literary idealism that acknowledged the popular drama as commanding typographic respect, few plays showed any intelligent and sustained editing for press. As a result, the textual models we have adopted for the drama reflect only the commercial opportunism of printers in the early 17th century, a time when the theatre was alive and confident of its own distinctively oral and visual mode.[12]

The publishing of collections of plays in folio, pioneered by the Jonson *Works* of 1616 and the Shakespeare folio of 1623, was a plea for scripts to be read as literature, which, in the two cases mentioned, succeeded spectacularly in that aim. The Beaumont and Fletcher folio was an invitation to rank a third corpus of work (predominantly by Fletcher, as it happened, but with contributions by other assistants besides Beaumont) with these mighty predecessors. Like the two earlier folios, the plays were preceded by an advance guard of commendatory poems by leading writers of the time, which in this case were received as models of epideictic verse and are often found transcribed into personal miscellanies. One effect of this new context must have been to suppress the inclination to read the printed plays as records of the play as performed and to encourage reading practices more suitable for poems and romances.

Among these practices was the refined relishing of niceties of style:

indeed, we find that the case made for the literary importance of Fletcher's writing rested primarily on the grace and courtliness of his dialogue. Shirley's preface speaks of the volume as containing "the Authentick witt that made Blackfriers an Academy" and of Fletcher as the source of "all the felicity of witt and *words*." Commenting on these remarks, Markley points out that for both Shirley and the other contributors of commendatory material, "Fletcher is the great refiner of the English language, the dramatist who brought the 'conversation of gentlemen' to the stage."[13] As a representation of court life, written in a polished if at times overelliptical neo-Senecan manner, but with episodes (such as that of the waiting women and Chylax in 2.4 and the satirical interlude with Paulus, the court poet, in 5.5) of witty badinage, it demanded to be read for its language as much as for its somewhat equivocal substance.

The play is not known to have been revived after the Restoration; however, it was considered an important enough property to be specified in a list approved in January 1669 of plays to which the King's Company were to have exclusive rights.[14] Rochester's revision may well have been proposed to him by the Company. The three manuscript sources each contain a King's cast list of circa 1675, suggesting that it had at least come close to being performed. But another reason for Rochester's interest in the project—and the probable explanation for why a performance did not take place at that period—was the striking parallels the play now presented with the court of Charles II, of which Rochester himself had been an ornament. By the presumed period of the revision, he was moving into political opposition in the wake of his principal patron, George Villiers, second Duke of Buckingham. In what seems like an elaborate joke, but may be more than this, the parts of Valentinian's palace as described in the play have been made suggestive of the palace of Whitehall, with the actual scene of the rape placed, as far as can be seen, in Rochester's own apartment.[15] This device is one of a number of allusions that hint at a parallel between Charles II and Valentinian.[16] But it also suggests that Rochester was thinking of his revision as a work to be performed in the court theater to an audience of fellow courtiers rather than in the public theater to a town audience. This court theater was a fully equipped playhouse that charged for admission and had contracted out the right to sell oranges during performances: its only difference from the public theaters was the right to screen its clientele and the fact that performance was sporadic not continual. It was undoubtedly the best place to see plays in London in the 1670s.

Valentinian, then, was being rescued from its sojourn in the medium of print for oral performance in a particular, ideology-laden space. Despite its attack on courts, it was to be a popular play in that space, having at least three performances at Whitehall after Rochester's death. Reflecting this courtly emphasis, the action of the play acquires a certain enclosed, hothouse flavor in Rochester's rewriting. Its concern is very much with the behind-the-scenes conduct of court intrigues by bawds and the easily corrupted. Action that in Fletcher takes place in public galleries or in crowded rooms is more likely to be hived off by Rochester into secluded apartments. There is also some pointed acknowledgment of the court's fondness for creating its own theater forms. The play incorporates the rehearsal for one masque and the actual performance of another, as well as a rape that is to be disguised as a masque.[17] In addition, the writing of *Lucina's Rape* probably coincided with the most active months of the court theater's history, those that saw the interminable rehearsals for John Crowne's *Calisto,* another drama of attempted imperial rape, which was eventually performed in February 1675.[18] With theatrical creation happening all around him, it was natural for Rochester to wish to contribute to it.

In returning the play from print to the stage, Rochester was also releasing it into a very different kind of playhouse from Fletcher's, with a radically different balance between the auditory and the visual. Fletcher liked to keep his platform stage full and busy. Rochester, writing for a theater using artificial lighting to illuminate a performance in front of wing-and-shutter scenery, was better equipped to concentrate the attention of his audience on dialogues between two foregrounded individuals, and to extend these to much greater lengths than Fletcher was prepared to risk. The need for important scenes to be played in front of the proscenium directly beneath the single candelabrum limited the number of characters that could be involved in an exchange of any substance. In addition, the number and sequence of scenes had to be modified to suit by now well-established routines for the alternation of shutters, so that, for instance (as in Rochester's rearrangements of acts 2 and 3), the flats for an indoor scene could be drawn off to reveal a garden scene in deep perspective. All of this profoundly affected both the selection of material from Fletcher's text and the form of Rochester's additions to it.

There were also very obvious, media-related changes to the governing aesthetic of the tragedy. Onto Fletcher's not fully successful blend of a Roman play of the kind pioneered by Shakespeare and Jonson with a full-blooded Jacobean revenge tragedy, Rochester imposed the model of the

Restoration heroic play of Dryden and Lee, in which characters cease to be multifaceted and are reconstituted as quasi-allegorical embodiments of a particular vice, virtue, or "passion."[19] This is particularly noticeable in the presentation of Lucina, who in Rochester is allowed only two notes—those of outraged innocence and wifely fidelity. Fletcher, while not nearly so radical as Durfé, still allows us a richer figure—one who is capable in 2.4 of wisecracking with the bawds even after the realization that they have lured her into a trap. Arthur Colby Sprague praises Fletcher's delineation of her "forced show of gaiety to cover her growing concern" whereas in Rochester's revision she is "overlaid with sentiment and prudery."[20] Rochester has also drained the play of much of its everyday, unheroic detail. Sprague criticizes the expanded narrative of Lucina's death for its "mere conceitfulness," adding that "the one realistic touch in the original has been expunged."[21] He then cites Fletcher's line given above: "At which she fell, and stirr'd no more. *We rubb'd her*" (3.3.368). Instead, Rochester makes the death a kind of second rape conducted through metaphor:

> At this she fell Choakt with a thousand sighs;
> And now the pleas'd expiring Saint
> (Her dying Lookes where new borne beauty shines
> Or'e prest with Blushes) modestly declines,
> While death approacht with a Magestick grace,
> Proud to looke Lovely once in such a face.
> Her Armes spread to receive, her wellcome guest,
> With a glad sigh, she drew into her Breast.
> (4.4.345–52)

Writing of this kind is for the page much more than for the stage, and probably better appreciated by readers than viewers. Even in the playhouse its attraction would have been that of recited narrative rather than dramatic conflict. In a sense established by Parsons in a consideration of similar passages of reported action from Dryden, it is fundamentally untheatrical—an invasion of performance by print values.[22] In another potential fusing of the media, Rochester comes close to inventing the kind of political Roman play exemplified by Addison's *Cato* and Southerne's *The Fate of Capua* a quarter of a century later, which used Livy and Plutarch as a vehicle for party controversies of the kind more commonly conducted through prose pamphleteering. That he hints at a judgment on the royal management of England without quite taking the final step to an outright parallel may have been one reason that the planned King's Company production of the late 1670s never came to fruition. An audience inflamed by the disclosures of Titus Oates would have seen more in the behavior of Valentinian than was safe to be presented.

However, if we are looking for evidence of media crossover in Rochester's rewriting of Fletcher, the more profound influence was from scribal rather than print culture. After the failure of the production to eventuate, Rochester took no steps to print the play, preferring instead to circulate it in manuscript. Two copies survive of a scribal edition of *Lucina's Rape* together with Rochester's "Scæne" for Sir Robert Howard's *The Conquest of China*. A third manuscript, Yale University Library MS Osborn fb 334, includes the play without the "Scæne" in an anthology of Rochester's verse prepared after his death, probably for circulation within his extended family. A fourth, lost manuscript served as the ancestor of the 1685 printed text, and at least one more must have existed to account for the pattern of agreement between those that survive.[23] With this act the play once again crosses to a new medium with its own rules and expectations. Rochester's decision to restrict his play to scribal circulation is typical both of his general practice as a writer and that of many other poets of his century.[24] During his lifetime he only made a few, unwilling appearances in print: instead, his poems reached their (extensive) readership chiefly through copying, partly personal and partly the work of professional vendors of manuscript verse. It was only after his death in July 1680 that they could at last be made available, surreptitiously, in print, and not until 1691 that there was anything resembling an authorized edition. In being subject to this model of circulation they belonged with a huge corpus of libertine and state verse that did not, in many cases, make the transition to print until the following century, if at all.

Circulation of poems began for Rochester with copies made available to his small circle of intimates: the wits of the Buckingham circle and their hangers-on and clients. Further transmission, which in some cases has left us forty or fifty surviving contemporary manuscripts out of a far greater number that must once have existed, seems to have derived from copies they let slip in such hotbeds of transcription as the court, the Inns of Court, and the universities.[25] Other copies were likely to be sent down to the country through the newly expanded postal services, often accompanying newsletters. Still others were exchanged among the patrons of coffeehouses, which were also centers for the reading of both scribal and fugitive printed texts. The two manuscripts of *Lucina's Rape* in which the play appears together with the scene for Howard's tragedy probably come from a source very close to Rochester. One indication of this is that they nowhere mention his name, its appearance on the title page of the Folger manuscript being the work of a later corrector. Another is that the British Library manuscript, although in a scribal hand, shows a remarkable conformity to Rochester's own habits of spelling and punctuation. Osborn fb 334 belongs to a different genre of the manuscript book. Here the play is simply one part of a substantial anthology titled "Poem's By The Right Honourable John Earle of Rochester," with the naming of the author suggesting that it was intended for a wide readership and that it was written after his death. Seeing that the play is not accompanied in this case by the "Scæne," it is possible that it derives from a separate copy prepared by Rochester for transmission to the King's Company, though this can only be speculation, as is the possibility that the copy used by the United Company as the basis of their stage version came to them from the King's Company with the union of 1682.

The scribally circulated text appealed to readers by promising certain freedoms in what could be said. Being free from the stringent censorship that controlled print, scribally circulated satire was frequently subversive, seditious, and indecent, characterized by furious personal attacks on political leaders and town ladies. It could be specific where print had to be circumspect, outspoken where print had to be ironic. Needless to say, it was also nearly always anonymous, and those ascriptions that do appear are rarely to be trusted. Its most characteristic form is the lampoon, a no-holds-barred form of satire compiled from malicious gossip and written with the declared aim of shattering reputations. *Lucina's Rape* is a play for the censored public medium of the stage by a writer who was one of the stars of the uncontrolled private medium of scribal publication, and who was unwilling entirely to sacrifice those freedoms. The play's constant suggestion of veiled satire on the English court is part of its alliance with the lampoon culture. Indeed, if we knew more about such characters as Mall Howard, Mary Knight, William Chiffinch, Bab May, and Catharine Crofts, the bawds and procuresses of the play might be found to have been aligned in revision with originals from Whitehall. The character of Proculus, for whom Rochester wrote more new dialogue than in the other cases of this kind, certainly reads as if a personal model existed. His scene with Æcius in 5.1 is a gem of satirical portraiture. It is also in the spirit of manuscript satire that the play should break the taboo against the open discussion and onstage representation of homosexuality. In 2.2.178–88, Chilax the bawd argues in a soliloquy that male catamites, because they endure pain in order to give pleasure, should be regarded as morally superior to women, who in his view merely exchange pleasure for pleasure, probably making a profit in the process. At the beginning of 5.5, Valentinian and the eunuch Lycias are "discover'd on a Couch" exchanging "moist kisses." These two passages, which have no counterpart in the performed Restoration drama, were sufficiently unsettling even in the scribal medium for a reader of the British Library manuscript to have ruled through both so as to make them illegible. In the transference to the stage, the episodes were apparently left, but ingeniously disarmed by having the eunuch played by a woman, the suitably plump Susannah Mountfort.[26] But their being retained in the posthumous 1685 printing made them a matter of scandal. An early nineteenth-century editor of Fletcher declared that Rochester's version contained passages (the above no doubt among them) "so disgusting, that they ought to condemn the altered play to entire oblivion."[27] Different media directed at radically different readerships had to be careful about what was transferred and in what form.

In Rochester's version, *Valentinian* had a stage history that lasted well into the eighteenth century, but it has not been revived since that time. Editions prior to my own give only the broadest of guidance as to which sections of the play are by Rochester and which by Fletcher and are no help in trying to unravel the detail of the adaptation. It has been my own experience that casual readers of these editions routinely overestimate the extent of Rochester's contribution, and that it comes as something of a shock for them to discover that most of its strongest scenes are still fairly pure Fletcher. Yet the task of comparison is a necessary one if we are to understand the mutations undergone by the story of the rape of Lucina as it was told in French prose and in two influential works for the English stage and promulgated in performed, handwritten, and printed form. This wider narrative—that of the mutations—is in turn exemplary for any consideration of the influence of media on the operations of art.

Notes

1. Text from *The Works of John Wilmot Earl of Rochester*, ed. Harold Love (Oxford: Oxford University Press, 1999).

2. Ian Donaldson, *The Rapes of Lucretia: A Myth and Its Transformations* (Oxford: Oxford University Press, 1982).

3. Procopius, *History of the Wars,* trans. H. B. Dewing (Cambridge, Mass.: Harvard University Press, 1916), 2:39, 41.

4. Quotations are from *L'Astrée de Messire Honoré D'Urfé, Seconde partie* (Paris, 1614). See also *Astrea: A Romance, written in French by Messire Honoré D'Urfe; and Translated by a Person of Quality* [John Davies of Kidwelly] (London, 1657).

5. The edition cited is that of Robert K. Turner Jr., in *The Dramatic Works in the Beaumont and Fletcher Canon,* gen. ed. Fredson Bowers, vol. 4 (Cambridge: Cambridge University Press, 1979), 261–414.

6. The fullest presentation of the evidence for this rule is in Gerald E. Bentley, *The Profession of Dramatist in Shakespeare's Time, 1590–1642* (Princeton: Princeton University Press, 1971), 264–92. The provision is explicit in Richard Brome's surviving contract with Queen Henrietta's Company.

7. See Bentley, *Profession of Dramatist,* 235–63.

8. The case against revision by another hand is made on the basis of spelling tests in Cyrus Hoy, "The Shares of Fletcher and His Collaborators in the Beaumont and Fletcher Canon (I)," *SB* 8 (1956): 129–46.

9. *Comedies and Tragedies Written by Francis Beavmont and Iohn Fletcher* (London, 1647).

10. Robert Markley, *Two-Edg'd Weapons: Style and Ideology in the Comedies of Etherege, Wycherley and Congreve* (Oxford: Oxford University Press, 1988), 578.

11. This is the theme of such retrospective Cavalier apologetics as Orrery's *The General* (1662). For the wider field of Cavalier strong misreadings, see Lois Potter, *Secret Rites and Secret Writing: Royalist Literature 1641–1660* (Cambridge: Cambridge University Press, 1989).

12. D. F. McKenzie, "Typography and Meaning: The Case of William Congreve," in *Buch- und Buchhandel in Europa im achzehnten Jahrhundert,* ed. Giles Barber and Bernhard Fabian (Hamburg: Hauswedell, 1981), 83.

13. Markley, *Two-Edg'd Weapons,* 578.

14. Judith Milhous and Robert D. Hume, *A Register of English Theatrical Documents 1660–1737,* 2 vols. (Carbondale: Southern Illinois University Press, 1991), vol. 1, no. 479.

15. These identifications are explored in Harold Love, "Was Lucina Betrayed at Whitehall?," in *That Second Bottle: Essays on Rochester,* ed. Nicholas Fisher (Manchester: Manchester University Press, forthcoming).

16. Two passages of the play are quite explicit in their political reference. That at 1.1.97–100 describing the emperor's mildness towards malefactors could hardly not have been seen as a reflection on Charles's behavior in cases such as Blood's attempted theft of the Crown jewels. Likewise the emperor's speech at 5.5.82–90 (beginning "Ah what a Lamentable Wretch is he") on the folly of princes who allow themselves to be dominated by a favorite, would have pointed just as surely for contemporary hearers to Charles's capitulation to Danby and the Anglican antitolerationists. Both Rochester's verse and his voting in the Lords ally him with Danby's opponents of the "antichurch" party, though he may not have followed Buckingham in his active wooing of the Dissenters. For the political background to this, see Mark Goldie, "Danby, the Bishops and the Whigs," in *The Politics of*

Religion in Restoration England, ed. Tim Harris, Paul Seaward, and Mark Goldie (Oxford: Blackwells, 1990), 75–105.

17. Cf. 4.2.191–96:

> *Emp:* About it straight, 'twill serve to draw away
> Those listning Fooles who trace it in the Gallery;
> And if (by chance) odd noises shoud bee heard,
> As womens shrieks or soe, say tis a play
> Is practicing within.
> *Lycini:* The Rape of Lucrece
> Or some such merry pranck it shall bee done Sir.

18. Lucina's speech on her awakening from her dream in Rochester's 3.2 and the dance of satyrs that has preceded it both have counterparts in Crowne's act 3 and may well be derived from it.

19. I follow here Philip Parsons's interpretation of the aesthetic of the heroic play presented in his "Restoration Tragedy as Total Theatre," in *Restoration Literature: Critical Approaches,* ed. Harold Love (London: Methuen, 1972), 27–68.

20. Arthur Colby Sprague, *Beaumont and Fletcher on the Restoration Stage* (Cambridge, Mass.: Harvard University Press, 1954), 69–70.

21. Ibid., 170.

22. Parsons, "Restoration Tragedy," 31–36. Parsons is still for me the only writer to have understood how these plays were meant to work in the theater.

23. The lost exclusive common ancestor of Osborn fb 334 and the 1685 edition. Evidence for its existence is presented in Rochester, *Works,* 626–29.

24. The broad phenomenon of the "reserved" publication of texts through manuscript is discussed in my *Scribal Publication in Seventeenth-Century England* (Oxford: Oxford University Press, 1993). Three major discussions of the circulation of literary texts by this means are Arthur F. Marotti, *Manuscript, Print and the English Renaissance Lyric* (Ithaca: Cornell University Press, 1995), H. R. Woudhuysen, *Sir Philip Sidney and the Circulation of Manuscripts 1558–1640* (Oxford: Oxford University Press, 1996), and Peter Beal, *In Praise of Scribes: Manuscripts and their Makers in Seventeenth-century England* (Oxford: Oxford University Press, 1998).

25. For an invaluable descriptive listing of surviving copies, see Peter Beal, *Index of English Literary Manuscripts,* vol. 2, *1625–1700* (London: Mansell, 1993), 2:225–87.

26. I assume they were played from their presence in the printed edition, which includes five inadvertently included prompter's cues, indicating it was set from the promptbook.

27. *The Works of Beaumont and Fletcher,* ed. Henry Weber (Edinburgh, 1812), 4:365.

CHAPTER EIGHT

Ann Halkett's Morning Devotions: Posthumous Publication and the Culture of Writing in Late Seventeenth-Century Britain

Margaret J. M. Ezell

Perhaps it is time for us to consider posthumous publication. Not for ourselves, of course, although there are times when that seems a simpler solution than tenure and promotion procedures, but rather in regards to what the term and its application by literary historians reveal about both past and present practices. The term is suggestive not only of the nature of early modern authorship but also of how specific generations of historians and critics imagined the experience of being an author in earlier times.

"Posthumous publication" is another of those oddly named phenomena, along with the "piracy" of manuscripts, that are associated with being an author in early modern England before the advent of copyright law. I think we tend to accept without much comment or scrutiny that our literary forebears chose such odd ways of getting into print because literary historians traditionally have presented authorship in the later part of the seventeenth century as being either a commercial, profit-oriented production or a strictly amateur, dilettante pastime. In particular, coterie and "closet" writing is depicted as amateur in its financial nature, but also— and perhaps even especially so when we discuss early modern women writers—amateur in its relationship to technology. The curious case of Anne Halkett's literary career and of the resulting texts may suggest to us that the presence of a posthumous edition of a late seventeenth-century writer may not signal a maidenly avoidance of technology but a literary life engaged with print culture in interesting and complicated ways. We will also be reminded that other variables than the author's personality must be at play before an author can fully utilize a new technology of production.

Readers today know about Anne, Lady Halkett from a posthumous edition. We know her as having been a passionate Royalist, actively involved in preserving Charles I's family in the early days of the English Civil War and later as a memoirist of some merit. Her life spanned much of the seventeenth century, from 1623 to 1699, and she was present during some of the most dramatic moments in English history. Her memoirs in their manuscript form, which cover her life from childhood through 1656, were the basis of a short biography published in Edinburgh in 1701, and this printed text was in turn summarized in George Ballard's mid-eighteenth-century entry on her in his *Memoirs of Eminent Ladies*. Halkett's memoirs themselves were printed first in 1875 by John Nichols for the Camden Society, and then redone in an excellent edition for Oxford University Press by John Loftis in 1979. Most recently, they have been excerpted for the sixth edition of the *Norton Anthology of English Literature*.[1]

Her critical standing, in short, finds Lady Halkett and her one primary text praised for her novelistic abilities by Loftis and for her courageous partisanship in the Royalist cause by the Norton editors; she stands in our literary consciousness as one of those intriguing, perhaps eccentric, seventeenth-century figures who were caught up in the key events of a period and who had the grace to record for succeeding generations the essence of their singular, extraordinary historical moment. Furthermore, because her text was not printed until nearly two centuries after its composition, she also appears to be a classic example of an early modern author who rejected, perhaps for gender reasons, the emerging world of print culture in favor of the older model of the social author and the manuscript text.

What our focus on Halkett as a memoirist of the Civil War does not reveal to us, however, is the literary context in which she wrote that text, and her own thoughts on what she was doing as a writer. The memoirs published by Nichols and Loftis are actually only a fragment, with missing pages at the start and missing pages from the middle, and which ends abruptly in midsentence. That particular manuscript is held at the British Library, donated to it in 1884;[2] in the National Library of Scotland manuscript collection, however, we discover an additional body of her manuscript writing that suggests a completely different profile of Anne Halkett as a writer. Instead of being a single, fragmentary text, the Civil War memoirs in fact are a small part of a lifelong literary career; her extensive manuscript volumes are artifacts of a culture of reading and writing that raises questions for us about the material conditions that affected the practices of reading, writing, and authorship during this period, in particular as they relate to print culture versus a script one.

Fifty years of work and practice at the art of writing resulted in her leaving behind on her death an astonishing twenty-one folio and quarto manuscript volumes composed between 1644 and the late 1690s, along with, as her contemporary biographer assures us, "about thirty stitched Books, some in Folio, some in 4to. most of them of 10 or 12 sheets, all containing occasional Meditations."[3] Halkett herself observed in one of the volumes begun in 1676, approximately half-way through her long literary life, that "It is naturall for all persons to please themselves in pursuing what is most suitable to there inclination. & to aime att an eminency in what ever profession there Genius lead them to, from wch many have arived to Great Knowledge in Severall Arts and Sciences."[4] What pleased Ann Halkett during her long adult life was the exercise of authorship.

Because they so clearly register the impact of reading print texts and of absorbing their conventions, Halkett's manuscript texts shed light on important developments in early modern literary culture and on the history of reading and writing in the period. She does not conform to our expectations of a social, manuscript author in many regards and, indeed, her work raises questions about our sense of the clear and distinct division between notions of "public" and "private" writings that characterize some theories of print versus manuscript practice. Halkett's manuscripts are not examples of what Harold Love has called "scribal publication," where script text is reproduced in order to compete with print,[5] nor are they part of what I have analyzed as circulated manuscript texts, or of Arthur Marotti's field of interactive coterie writing.[6] While there is no indication that Halkett showed her texts to others until shortly before her death, she is nevertheless not following the same authorial model as another Scottish memoirist, Sir John Clerk, who opened the manuscript memoirs of his life from 1676 to 1755 with the blunt statement, "I absolutely prohibit and discharge any of my Posterity from lending them or dispersing them abroad. They are to remain in the House of Pennicuik"—a condition of reading he felt so strongly about that he also placed it on the title page of the manuscript.[7] Instead, Halkett's manuscript volumes show an author closely engaged with the world of print texts, its conventions and readership; the manuscripts show numerous indications that she was consciously shaping her own manuscript writings for a print readership rather than a manuscript one.

Devoted Halkettites, of which I must admit there are extremely few, are aware that in addition to her biography by "S.C." published in 1701, three other texts by her were also printed in 1701 by the same printer, Andrew Sympson, namely *Instructions for Youth. For the Use of those young Noblemen and Gentlemen, whose Education was Committed to Her Care*, *Meditations on the Twentieth and fifth Psalm*, and *Meditations and Prayers Upon the First Week*. All of these texts are derived from the same sizeable body of manuscript writings left behind at her death. What can this group of texts rather than an isolated autobiographical printed fragment tell us about the culture of writing and the impact of print technology? It is significant, too, that when discussing Halkett, one cannot simply classify her work as "English," for although Anne Halkett was born in London and spent most of her early days there, during the period in which she was mainly writing these texts, from the late 1650s on, she resided principally in Scotland—and this, as will become apparent, had a material impact on her practices of authorship.

Roger Chartier, in his call for a history of reading in "Laborers and Voyagers: From the Text to the Reader," speaks of establishing what he refers to as "protocols of reading or sites of memory," delineating as the challenge to the historian the reconstruction of the "variations that differentiate the 'readable space' (the texts, in their material and discursive forms) and those which govern the circumstances of their 'actualization' (the readings seen as concrete practices and interpretive procedures)."[8] For this new type of history of reading, Chartier wishes to unite three generally separate areas of literary and historical study: first, that of traditional literary history, which is concerned with

> either canonical or ordinary texts, deciphered in their structures, themes and aims; second the history of books and more, generally, of all the objects and forms that carry out the circulation of writing; and finally, the study of practices which in various ways take hold of these objects or forms and produce usages and differentiated meanings. (50)

What Chartier urges for the history of reading—a study of the material practices and the circumstances that affected them, drawing together the skills of the literary historian, the bibliographer, and the social historian—still needs to be done, in my opinion, for the history of early modern British authorship, or more particularly for the interests of this collection, for the history of authorship and its relationship with technology in England,

Scotland, Ireland, Wales, and the American colonies. The large body of writing left behind by this seventeenth-century woman offers us a splendid opportunity to investigate some of the "protocols of authorship," as they were affected by the writer's response to print technology as well as issues involving gender and geographical region and their impact on an author's relationship with print technology.

First, by looking at the range of Halkett's manuscript texts rather than the single autobiographical fragment, it becomes clear that writing or, rather more accurately, composition was a central activity in Halkett's adult life and that it was part of her daily devotional practice. Her texts are not casual jottings or notes but a series of short compositions or meditations on various topics. Loftis notes in his introduction to the memoirs that the manuscript showed evidence of author's revisions, "in the form of interlineations over canceled words, reveal[ing] lady Halkett's concern for precision and grace of prose style."[9] In commentaries found on the end pages lining the volume covers and on the first and last leaves opening and concluding the volumes, Anne Halkett gives her own thoughts on her activities, the subject matter included, her own sense of the nature of her authorship, and, for what I shall focus on for the rest of this piece, the relationship of her texts to print and print culture and the material circumstances surrounding her habits of reading and writing that affected her relationship with print technology and print writers.

There are several interesting features in Halkett's presentation of her materials that suggest her conscious inclusion of elements of print culture into the preparation of her manuscript materials. It was Halkett's practice, for example, to include a "Table of Contents" for her volumes, a practice that made her contemporary biographer's task of listing her writings much easier. Her decision to do so, however, also suggests that she already viewed her writings as texts, requiring those assistances to the reader found in printed volumes. This is quite different, for example, from her contemporary Elizabeth Burnet's memoirs and meditations, which show no such extra-organizational apparatus, or, to offer a better-known text, Samuel Pepys's multivolume diary with its systematic, well-composed shorthand entries but with no index or other notations of the author's thematic organization. The presence of such reader's aids also suggests her belief that these manuscript texts would be read at some distance from the original circumstances of their composition, either when her own memory might not be sufficient or when they might be read by another. The practical necessity for this textual apparatus is clear when one considers that the volumes are quite frequently over three hundred pages in length. What is intriguing here is that there is no indication that she went back at a later time and rewrote or reframed her materials to make them "books" rather than notes. It appears that her practice of authorship from the first was in conformity with what we typically expect to find in a printed text rather than a so-called "private" script one. It is also of note that when the texts were published two years after her death, the publisher found little need to emend her original manuscript texts. It is easy to become confused by S.C.'s references to her manuscripts as "books," but it does indicate the closeness of her manuscript compositions to the conventions of print texts. The publisher, who clearly had access to the complete body of her writings, was able to select individual pieces and transfer them directly into print ("the words and expressions are very little varied," asserts the publisher in his preface), as though she had prepared them for that purpose.

This ease of transforming her manuscripts into print suggests a possibility that I believe is supported by her own comments in her texts about the whole issue of "public" and "private" texts. We are accustomed to think of works from the point of view of readers whose primary reading experience is printed texts, where print is the norm, and manuscript the exception that must be explained. Furthermore, we see texts as being either "in print" or "not in print," as though those two conditions are mutually exclusive. Halkett's texts remind us that a writer can shape his or her writings so that they conform to the expectations of print (tables of contents, titles, page numbers, marginal glosses) while still remaining in manuscript.

In addition to tables of contents indicating the subjects, many of the volumes are also given specific titles, such as the one she called "The Art of Divine Chemistry," written in 1676, or "The Widow's Mite," with a subtitle, "relating partly to the King," composed in 1674. Very often these titles are in two parts, with a short title indicating the genre of the composition—meditations on a specific holiday, or the mother's legacy to her unborn child—followed by a descriptive subtitle. It becomes clear in the process of reading the texts that she was aware of the different demands of these genres and that in some instances she had printed models in mind, or conversely that she is pleased to note that her composition is without printed precedent (which, of course, suggests she views her own work in a print context). She notes, for example, in a postscript at the end of the volume composed in London between 1660 and 1663 that "since I ended the Meditations upon the festivalls of the church I have seene another booke upon the same subject whc yett I have nott had time to Looke over."[10] In

1684, she likewise notes that "I now designe to place my thoughts upon . . . the Prophesy of the Prophet Jonah wch I have never read any upon."[11]

From the subtitles it also becomes clear that while some of pieces in the volumes, as would be expected, are derived from personal circumstances—such as the early "Meditations and Vowes upon Psalm 56," written on some remaining leaves of one book, upon her "deliverance from the danger of Child-Birth, June 13, 1658"—many others offer her response to public events. For example, we find one written in May 1660, "Occasional Meditations . . . upon several publick and privat Occurences; whereof the two last are upon the late Change of Publick Affairs, and upon the Return of the King." As I shall discuss at the end of this piece, public politics and personal events are merged in the contents of these volumes and, in my opinion, in the writer's perception of the task of authorship and the nature of her texts.

In addition to the presence of reader's aids, which suggests that Halkett was familiar with the protocols of printed texts and anticipated a further readership for her writings, she occasionally comments directly on the nature of her activity. For Halkett, composition was both part of her religious devotions and part of her desire to understand the times in which she lived. On the first page of the volume begun on Monday, 21 May 1688, she states, "Having so often mentioned the advantage I have found by fixing my morning thoughts upon some pious Meditation I need not insist further upon that [practice], only [to] reflect upon the reason I had to make this day the date for beginning this booke."[12] Her biographer S. C. explained that she regularly set aside five hours a day for devotion, "from 5 to 7 in the Morning, from one in the afternoon to two, from 6 to 7, and from 9 to 10, together with nine [hours] for Business," and "ten for necessary refreshment" (55). During her devotional hours, she read and also produced the twenty-one volumes of commentary and composition that are housed in the Library of Scotland, and perhaps others that were lost through the years in her travels or after her death.

She herself clearly viewed her devotions as "books" as well. While explaining, presumably to an imagined reader, how she determined the subject matter for one of her last volumes, composed between 1 December 1697 and 26 November 1698, she observes on the first page that "having by the mercyfull goodness of God and the assistance of his holy spirit Lived to Write above 17 bookes and lately ended on F. 373 page and having Looked over the Content of them all Wherein nothing particular of the Apostles Creed," she determined that this omission must be rectified, and she then investigates the topic for the next 341 pages.[13] She is not without the conscious thought that her writings are comparable with printed texts, which she refers to as "public" meditations, and, as we have seen, her own compositions are structured and presented with print texts as their pattern.

Her representation of the nature of her writings, however, is always qualified. Referring to another print text on a similar topic to her meditation, she comments in 1660, "Those Meditations are publicke whc I never intend these; but if any unexpected occasion should ever bring these to light, all I desire is, that as every good notion or desire comes from God, so hee may nott been dishounored by any reflection upon my incapacity of performing what those of great parts thought worthy theire imployment."[14] In another volume begun in 1679, she observes in the opening comments that tackling the trials of Joseph as a subject is a major undertaking and that "Should any know what I have writt, or what I now designe to insert in this Booke, . . . at least they would beleeve me vaine or impertinent: As if I though my selfe fitt for what may imploy the highest capacities and that I might rather Satisfy me selfe with reading what is writt by them, then add to what too many hath done allready," for, she observed (foreshadowing the MLA book exhibition), "of [the] making many bookes, there is no end."[15] Nevertheless, she continues,

> . . . never intending while I live to lett any see the morning refreshments [I write] . . . and if the Lord think fitt to manifest them when I am Dead, I hope (whose ever hands they fall in) that ye blessed spirit of God will so influence what himselfe hath wrought in mee, that it shall make them studious to perform . . . what make harmony & Concord with the Glorified spirits, for they & we have but one object.[16]

Thus, while Halkett declares at various times throughout the years that she is not writing *directly* for publication, she nevertheless clearly had anticipated the possibility of an unknown reader perusing her books.

It is clear from her contemporary biographer that while Halkett entrusted the manifestation of her writings to God, she also took the practical step of communicating the existence of her texts to earthly agents in the hopes that they would be preserved and perhaps even printed. In the late 1690s, her biographer informs us, Halkett took this step. "But a few Years before her Death, . . . she made known, to some, in whom she reposed great confidence, that she had written such Books; being moved to make the discovery by hearing of several Persons, who died suddenly" (58). S. C. suggests in the dedication to the dowager Lady Pitfirrane that her family possessed Halkett's papers after her death and that S. C. had access to them through the dowager; it is suggested that it was perhaps a shared desire to publish "this short account of her *exemplary life,* and some of these Religious Exercises, which were a great part of the Imployment & Comfort of her life" (A3v). Clearly these individuals were responsible for the printed versions of her compositions that appeared in 1701, but it was Halkett's own lifelong habits of writing for her unknown reader that had already prepared the materials for print, whether she stated such as her intention or not. Her desire that her texts, unlike those of unfortunate authors who died unexpectedly, should not perish with her suggests her openness to the world of print readership and the demands of its technology on her as an author.

At this point, I can only speculate on why she so clearly prepared her materials to enter the world of print only after her death. There is the obvious argument based on the theory of gender, that as a woman she would have felt intimidated from venturing into a print world, a theory given some support by her self-consciousness that she is writing on topics on which those with the "highest capacities" had directed their scholarly training. Her contemporary biographer describes her revealing the existence of her "books" "with bashfullnes, and reluctancy, occassioned by her Modesty and great Humility" (58). Given the lack of conventionality in the events that shaped her life, however—her relationship with Colonel Bampfield, her facing down of the English troops at Fyvie who accused her of being "the *English* Whore, that came to meet the King" (23)—and especially in her involvement with matters of the public political sphere at the highest level, the argument that feminine modesty prevented her seeking a publisher is less convincing with Halkett perhaps than with some of her contemporaries. At the very least, it seems an overly simple explanation for what was clearly a complicated relationship between the author, her texts, and the printed word.

In addition to her situation as a widowed female living in the shadow of her husband's relatives, it should also be recalled that her involvement with Royalist politics of the Civil War left her with a public persona, and as her devotions clearly reveal, she never lost her keen interest in national events. The evidence suggests that she compiled the manuscript that has been printed as her memoirs in 1677–78; in 1679, of course, the Exclusion Crisis began. The 1680s, therefore, would not seem like a promising time to secure the publication of the memoirs and meditations of a person, male or female, who had aided the escape of the future King James II in the war years. Halkett had already experienced how her political reputation could be used against her: in the 1650s, she believed that her suit to recover money from the Earl of Kinnoul was hampered by the English judges who viewed her as "a great Malignant" (27). Thirty years later, another political alliance led her again into being publicly denounced: "it put her in great consternation," her biographer wrote when she heard "the Chancellor declaring himself Popish ... she her self was also attacqued by several Letters" (45–46).

Indeed, Halkett still had ties to James II during the 1680s. In 1685, Halkett was awarded a pension by him, in spite of the fact that she herself had little sympathy with James's Catholicism. In her devotions, she expressed "the greatest abhorrence to the mischievous designs of the Rom[an] Ch[urch] whose pernicious Counsells and violent methods had threatened the totall subversion of Religion and Liberties, and had actually Sacrificed the King and Three Kingdoms, to promote their Interest" (*Life of Lady Halkett*, 48). Nevertheless, she still had sympathy for James, feeling that he had been misled by treacherous advisors. On hearing in 1688 of "the King's departing to France, she bewailed his misfortune with abundance of Tears; and earnestly prayed that God would Sanctifie the Severity of that dispensation to him; and the wonderful Success to the Prince [of Orange]" (47). If her own involvement with the fortunes of James II and his government were not enough, her only son Robert served as a captain under James II in Ireland and was taken prisoner in London in 1690, not being released until 1692.

Anne Halkett never censored her thoughts concerning the politics of the day when writing her meditations; even in this sensitive political climate, her meditations on religious topics and events in the Bible are intertwined with her continuing investment in contemporary political matters. As her biographer recorded, "there was nothing of moment either in publick affairs, or in mere private occurences, which came to her notice, which she did not make the subject of a serious meditation or reflection: shewing herself a diligent observer of the works of God, Zealously concerned for the publick" (38–39). One should note, too, that the posthumous publications that appeared in 1701 of her meditations do not include any of her thoughts on public events, although her biographer makes lavish use of those in constructing her biography.

In addition to her political involvements that might have made publication difficult, Lady Halkett was in severe financial distress in the 1670s until just before her death. After her husband's death in 1670, the debts incurred during the war years and the loss of her property weighed heavily on her thoughts. During the years of the Exclusion Crisis and the ascension of William and Mary, Halkett was residing at Dunfermline, the estate of her late husband's son by his first marriage, Sir Charles Halkett, caring for the children of various aristocratic friends and relations, including the son of Sir George MacKenzie, to supply an income. To escape her debts, in 1697, she assigned to "a Friend & Kinsman" half of her jointure "but also her whole Houshold Plensishing and Furniture . . . laying them aside under Seal, for his use" (52), through which means she was able to satisfy her creditors. Presumably, her books would be included under the listing of "Houshold Plensishing and Furniture." This too might have made seeking a publisher more difficult, since securing a printer for her texts probably would have involved a financial commitment on Halkett's part, if only in traveling to Edinburgh to secure a printer. Although Dunfermline is geographically not more than a day's travel from Edinburgh across the Firth of Forth, such travel away from Dunfermline was sufficiently rare that her biographer records only two visits to Edinburgh, one in 1672 and one in 1676.[17]

These reasons—her gender, her political ties, and her financial situation—are all explanations that focus on the situation of the individual author. Halkett, to borrow from John Guillory's recasting of Bourdieu's concept of "cultural capital," was not well situated to gain access to the "distribution of cultural capital, or more specifically . . . to the means of literary production and consumption."[18] If one shifts away from the personal pyschology of the author, away from the individual, as being the sole explanation for her not publishing her texts during her lifetime, there are additional reasons why posthumous publication was a practical response to conditions of printing in Scotland during this period. During the period when Halkett was composing her final volumes of meditations, the institution of printing and the practical considerations governing what was printed and where offer still more compelling reasons for Halkett's texts to remain in manuscript until after her death. In addition to her gender, her political ties, and her financial difficulties, it would be well to remember that she resided in Scotland for most of the last forty years of her life. From 1671 until roughly 1680, printing in Scotland was controlled by monopolistic patent to the King's printer.[19] Supposing for a moment that Ann Halkett—in spite of political instability, her son's imprisonment, her precarious financial situation, and of course, her alleged feminine modesty—had indeed desired to have her texts printed during her lifetime, what would have been her options?

In 1671, the Royal Patent for printing in Scotland was given to Andrew Anderson; it was held by him and his heirs for forty-one years.[20] "By this Gift the Art of PRINTING in this Kingdom got a dead Stroke; for by it no Printer could print any thing from a Bible to a Ballad without Mr. Anderson's Licence," wrote James Watson in 1713; after Anderson's death, his widow Agnes aggressively defended the Royal Patent, extending it to cover not only Bibles but all printed documents.[21]

> Mrs. Anderson, considering that her Gift was now entirely in her own Person . . . and that it was the most extensive that ever was heard of . . . resolv'd to make the Privleges of the Gift entire to herself: She persecuted all the Printers in *Scotland; Robert Sanders* (who succeeded *Andrew Anderson* in *Glasgow* about the year 1668) was fin'd and imprison'd. *John Reid* (who set up with *Patrick Ramsey,* about the Year 1680) was also imprison'd, and had his Doors shutup. And *John Forbes* in *Aberdeen* (who set up about 1660) was process'd, and put to vast Charges. (12–13)

Although the Anderson family was not entirely successful in closing down all other printers even before James granted further printing privileges to Watson's father in 1685, clearly the publishing environment in Scotland, where Halkett was residing, was a contentious one and also, until the late 1690s, an extremely limited one in terms of the availability of a printer to produce one's texts.

Assuming a printer could have been secured, what would have been the literary context in which Halkett's meditations would have appeared if she had pursued print during her lifetime? What types of texts were being printed in Scotland? Between 1680 and 1699, approximately 1,738 items were printed in Scotland, according to Aldis's catalogue.[22] Of these printed texts, many were "Advertisements" or announcements ("Advertisement. These are to give notice . . . [that students of Edin. Univ. will burn the pope's effigy, on Dec. 25]" published in 1680 by "Heir of A. Anderson"), Acts of Parliament, Proclamations by the Privy Council, almanacs, or accounts of public events of interest such as the "Grand juries address to the mayor of Bristol" (1681) or the "True and exact relation of the . . . seige of Vienna" (1683). During the War of the English Succession, the printers were engaged with issuing Acts of the Privy Council concerning "Punishment of those who refuse to serve in the foot-militia"(25 October 1688) and "Against the spreading of false news" (10 November 1688); texts printed in 1689 were concerned with the coronation and William III's proclamations, and those produced in 1690–92 were overwhelmingly dominated by accounts of the defeats of the Jacobites and the fighting in Ireland and the continent.

Before and after these crisis years, during the early 1680s and the late 1690s, one does find similar types of texts as Halkett's being printed in Edinburgh. Francis Quarles's *Enchiridion* was printed in 1680, along with the *Psalms of David in metre. Newly translated.* There were also prose texts such as James Canaries's *A discourse. . . . manifestation of the will of God* and William Gild's *Moses unveiled,* produced by "the Heir of A. Anderson" in 1684, which would have been similar in nature to Halkett's texts. Perhaps most interesting to consider as part of our speculations about Halkett's attitude toward print is the repeated reprinting in Edinburgh of Elizabeth Melville, Lady Culross's *A Godly Dream* (1603), which reappears in 1680 and was reprinted in two more editions in 1698, one in Edinburgh and one in Glasgow.[23]

Thus, Lady Halkett, as the references in her writing show, would have been aware that texts such as her own had been printed, even texts by women writers that used their names. However, not only her personal circumstances—poor finances, access to Edinburgh, political connections to James II—but also the conditions of publishing in Scotland during that period would have very much limited her options. In short, there appear to have existed more personal and institutional reasons not to pursue print culture than to embrace it. Nevertheless, Halkett appears to have left her texts ready for the publisher.

The men who produced the texts after her death, Mr. Andrew Sympson and Mr. Henry Knox, are interesting examples of the rigors of attempting to work in the print culture during this period. Watson notes that "in 1700, Mr. *Matthias Simpson,* A student in Divinity, set up a small House; but he, designing to prosecute his Studies, left the House to his Father Mr. *Andrew,* one of the Suffering Clergy, who kept up the House till about a year ago, that he died" (Watson, 18). Plomer tells us that Sympson was located "in the Cowgate, near the Foot of the Horse-Wynd, 1699–1706"; he did not produce many texts in the seven years he operated the press, but in addition to publishing Halkett's pieces, he also produced the second edition of Sir George Mackenzie's *Laws of Scotland* (1699).[24] In 1705, he published his own work, *Tripatriarchicon; or, the lives of . . . Abraham, Isaac and Jacob,* a title that suggests why Halkett's texts might have appealed to this particular printer. Likewise, although the son of a bookbinder, Henry Knox had been a minister in the 1680s until caught up in crisis over the oath of allegiance in 1689; and like Andrew Sympson, Knox appears to have been a Nonjuror who, on the loss of his flock, changed professions. Plomer describes him as operating as a bookseller in Edinburgh between 1696 and 1716, but he had been the minister of Dunscore and later Bowden around 1681 until he was ejected by the Privy Council in 1689 (Plomer, 182).

These were obviously precarious times to be a publisher of texts, even though the earlier problems with the Anderson family had passed. Not only did Sympson face competition from larger printing houses, as Aldis's catalogue of titles makes clear, but print was still the medium of government announcements more than a vehicle for individual authors. Although religious meditations clearly were desirable titles from the point of view of the bookseller, from the point of view of the author, given the intertwined nature of politics and religion, to print one's meditations could be to declare one's political allegiances. Nevertheless, Halkett preserved her library of "books" that she had compiled since living in London during the Civil War years; she took steps to ensure that her bulky manuscript library would have a chance at a continuing life after her death, all the while stating her lack of interest in creating texts specifically for print.

As a "posthumous" author, Anne Halkett might well seem to represent a class of writer who shunned the world of print culture and held fast to that of the tradition of "private" writing. She would appear to exemplify, as her contemporary biographer described her, the truly humble and pious woman maintaining the social boundaries between public and private, masculine and feminine authorship. However, the body of manuscript texts she left behind does not fit well within our models of manuscript, social authors—she did not write for friends and only rarely for her children. She did not intellectually interact with another group of writers with interdependent texts, nor does she mention any readers of her texts whose comments encouraged or hindered her activities. Instead, her literary "community" was made up of printed authors, not friends, of references to other printed texts and to the Bible as they intersected with the circumstances of her own life.

While focusing on Halkett's projected psychology as a seventeenth-century female writer presents us with what seems the perfect example of the private or "closet" writer, looking closely at the content and presentation of her manuscript texts and her construction of them argues that she anticipated future readers. Unlike some of her contemporaries, she did not create a secret, personal text in cipher, as did Robert Hook for example, which would have discourged the outside reader. Perhaps even more significant, she did not leave instructions for the destruction of her manuscripts, but instead communicated their existence to friends specifically so that they would not die with her. The fact that Lady Halkett left behind for us, for an imagined future generation of print readers, such perfectly prepared texts to enter that print world suggests that the impact of that technology on the practice of authorship during this period was dissolving the seemingly clear boundaries between private and public, print and manuscript, activities.

The texts of Anne Halkett taken as a whole rather than as consisting only of her fragmentary memoirs offer a valuable opportunity to study the different factors that might affect the practices of authorship in a changing literary culture apart from merely concentrating on the author's mental condition. In Halkett's situation, a widow living in a small Scottish town, securing a printer would have been difficult and expensive, regardless of her own personal feelings about print, "publick" texts, and being a woman writer. These geographical and economic factors, however, did not prevent her from consciously shaping her lifelong practice of writing in conformity with the conventions of the print texts she also was reading. Nor did they prevent her from situating her texts so that they could at some future time be produced in print for future readers. In the case of posthumous publication, ironically, we have a situation still to be explored where the death of the author is *required* to bring about the life of the printed book, but one that also suggests that we should look further into the relationship between the author and existing forms of literary transmission and at the larger material circumstances surrounding the creation and distribution of texts themselves.

Notes

1. For editions of her writings, see Ann Halkett, *Autobiography,* ed. John Gough Nichols (London, 1875); *The Memoirs of Anne, Lady Halkett and Ann, Lady Fanshawe,* ed. John Loftis (Oxford: Clarendon Press, 1979); and "Lady Anne Halkett," in *The Norton Anthology of English Literature,* ed. M. H. Abrams et al., 6th ed. (New York: W. W. Norton and Co., 1993), 1732–35. For biographical and critical accounts of Halkett and her memoirs, see S. C., *The Life of the Lady Halket* (Edinburgh, 1701); George Ballard, *Memoirs of Several Ladies of Great Britain* (1752), ed. Ruth

Perry (Detroit: Wayne State University Press, 1985); Margaret Bottrall, *Every Man a Phoenix: Studies in Seventeenth-Century Autobiography* (London: Murray, 1958); Mary Beth Rose, *Women in the Middle Ages and Renaissance: Literary and Historical Perspectives* (Syracuse, N.Y.: Syracuse University Press, 1986); and "Anne Halkett," in *A Dictionary of British and American Women Writers 1660–1800*, ed. Janet Todd (London: Methuen, 1987), 146–47.

2. British Library [hereafter BL] Add. MS 32376.
3. S. C., *Life of the Lady Halket*, 64.
4. National Library of Scotland, MS 6494, fol. 1.
5. Harold Love, *Scribal Publication in Seventeenth-Century England* (London: Oxford University Press, 1993).
6. See Ezell, *The Patriarch's Wife: Literary Evidence and the History of the Family* (Chapel Hill, N.C.: University of North Carolina Press, 1987), chap. 3; Arthur F. Marotti, *John Donne, Coterie Poet* (Madison: University of Wisconsin Press, 1986), and more recently his *Manuscript, Print, and the English Renaissance Lyric* (Ithaca, N.Y.: Cornell University Press, 1995).
7. *Memoirs of the Life of Sir John Clerk of Penicuik, Baronet . . . 1676–1755* (Edinburgh, 1892), 10.
8. Roger Chartier, "Laborers and Voyagers: From the Text to the Reader," *Diacritics* 22, no. 2 (1992): 55, 50.
9. Loftis, *Memoirs of Anne, Lady Halkett*, 4.
10. National Library of Scotland [hereafter NLS], MS 6491, fol. 326.
11. NLS, MS 6496, fol. ii.
12. NLS, MS 6498, fol. I.
13. NLS, MS 6502, fol. 1.
14. NLS, MS 6491, fol. 326.
15. NLS, MS 6495, inside cover.
16. NLS, MS 6495, fol. ii.
17. Thanks to Peter Davidson and Hilary Gaskin for information concerning Dunfermline and seventeenth-century travel in Scotland.
18. John Guillory, *Cultural Capital: The Problem of Canon Formation* (Chicago: University of Chicago Press, 1993), ix.
19. M. Pollard, *Dublin's Trade in Books 1550–1800* (Oxford: Clarendon Press, 1989), 8.
20. For a contemporary account of the state of Scottish printing during the 1680s and 1690s, see James Watson, *The History of the Art of Printing, Containing an Account of its Invention and Progress in Europe* (Edinburgh, 1713); written by the son of one of their rivals, this text offers a bleak view of Anderson and his widow Agnes Campbell Anderson's control of Scottish printing. For more recent accounts, see the brief entries on Anderson and his heirs in Harry G. Aldis, *A List of Books Printed in Scotland Before 1700*, rpt. ed. (New York: Burt Franklin, 1970), 107–8, and Paula Backscheider, *Daniel Defoe: His Life* (Baltimore: Johns Hopkins University Press, 1989), 305–8.
21. Watson, *History of the Art of Printing*, 12.
22. Aldis, *A List of Books*, 59–83.
23. See the headnote to Melville's entry in *Kissing the Rod: An Anthology of 17th*

Century Women's Verse, ed. Germaine Greer, Jeslyn Medoof, Melinda Sansone, and Susan Hastings (London: Virago Press, 1988), 32–33; thanks go to Isobel Grundy, Georgianna Ziegler, and Fran Teague for their assistance in unraveling aspects of the publication history of Melville's text.

24. Henry R. Plomer, *A Dictionary of the Printers and Booksellers Who Were at Work in England, Scotland and Ireland from 1668 to 1725* (Oxford, 1922), 283–84.

Part Three

Spectacle, Theater, and the Culture of Print

CHAPTER NINE

Reforming Resistance: Class, Gender, and Legitimacy in Foxe's Book of Martyrs

Steven Mullaney

On 28 May 1556, Perotine Massey of Guernsey was arrested along with her mother and older sister on suspicion of harboring stolen property. An investigation cleared them of the original criminal charges but also discovered, in its course, that the three women had not been attending mass; that is to say, they had been behaving suspiciously like Protestants. On the 1st of July they were reimprisoned, examined in their religious beliefs, found guilty of heresy, and ordered "to be burned, until they be consumed to ashes, in the place accustomed, with the confiscation of all their goods, movables, and heritages."[1] By this point in Mary Tudor's reign the sentence was typical, but Perotine Massey's death itself was not. What follows is an excerpt from John Foxe's account in his *Acts and Monuments,* popularly known as *The Book of Martyrs:*

> The time being come, when these three good servants and holy saints of God, the innocent mother with her two daughters, should suffer, in the place where they should consummate their martyrdom were three stakes set up. At the middle post was the mother, the eldest daughter on the right hand, the youngest [Perotine] on the other. They were first strangled, but the rope brake before they were dead, and so the poor women fell in the fire. Perotine, who was then great with child, did fall on her side, where happened a rueful sight, not only to the eyes of all that there stood, but also to the ears of all true-hearted Christians that shall read this history.

235

> For as the belly of the woman burst asunder by the vehemency of the flame, the infant, being a fair man-child, fell into the fire, and eftsoons being taken out by one W. House, was laid upon the grass. Then was the child had to the provost, and from him to the bailiff, who gave censure that it should be carried back again, and cast into the fire, where it was burnt with the silly mother, grandmother, and aunt, very pitifully to behold. And so the infant baptized in his own blood, to fill up the number of God's innocent saints, was both born and died a martyr, leaving behind to the world, which it never saw, a spectacle wherein the whole world may see the Herodian cruelty of this graceless generation of catholic tormentors, ad perpetuam rei infamiam. (8:229–30)

Perotine's mute death itself could not rival the explicit and articulate Protestant message of someone like Hugh Latimer, who as the fire licked at his feet declared, "We shall this day light such a candle, by God's grace, in England, as I trust shall never be put out" (7:550). I suspect, however, that even those of us who have read extensively in *The Book of Martyrs* would agree with Foxe himself, that the story of Perotine Massey's child, born, baptized, and martyred in the flames (see figure)[2], constitutes at least one of the most "Tragical, Lamentable, and Pitiful" histories in his entire and massive chronicle.

Our horror, however, is different from that which Foxe seeks to elicit, nor was it shared by all of his contemporaneous readers. In his unremarked (and hence all the more remarkable) synaesthesia, Foxe characterizes the event as a "rueful sight . . . to the ears of all true-hearted Christians that shall read this history." The rhetorical and ideological maneuver here is an aggressive one in its full historical context, and no matter what our own religious persuasion, we are excluded by it. Whatever our religious faith or lack thereof, we are not and could never be what Foxe means by "true-hearted Christians." If we *were* sixteenth-century English men or women— that is, the audience Foxe seeks not so much to address as to bring into being—our affective response would have a significant ideological register. Insofar as our ears viewed this account as a rueful sight, we would be accepting, adopting, embracing, being interpellated as, "true-hearted Christians." But if, as sixteenth-century English men or women, we differed with Foxe's definition of a "true-hearted Christian"—in contemporary parlance, if we did not subscribe to the emergent Protestant hegemony—we would be, let us say, conflicted. Our conflict would be lodged where ideology and affect intersect, which seems to me to be a terrain of immense and

From John Foxe, *Actes and Monuments* ... (London, 1563). Photo courtesy of the Ohio State University Libraries.

productive interest, and precisely the cultural site that Foxe's work seeks to map out, occupy, and colonize.[3]

Although I am primarily concerned here with a rather particular aspect of Foxe's work—the ways in which women do or do not fit within the confines of the imagined community[4] he is endeavoring to realize—I begin with the story of Perotine Massey and her child because it was one of the most well known and fiercely debated passages in the sixteenth century, prompting a series of extensive and fierce attacks that sought, in effect, to deny the affective import of the account: to deny, that is to say, that it was either tragical, lamentable, or pitiful. The most rabid and overdetermined attack was lodged in 1567 by Thomas Harding, a churchman who had been a zealous Protestant divine under Edward VI but became an even more zealous Catholic under Mary Tudor and continued as such under Elizabeth. According to Harding, the story was first of all an entire fiction, a fable. Second, even if it did happen, Harding points out that Foxe's narrative mentions no husband, and takes this silence to mean that Massey was unmarried, hence guilty of whoredom, hence deserving of her fate (here

Harding forgets that it was radical Protestants, not Catholics, who were lobbying to make fornication a capital crime, although even they did not prescribe burning as the means of execution). Third, Massey made no mention of her pregnancy to the authorities, whom Harding assures us would have delayed her execution until after the child was born, had they known; Harding ascribes her failure to do so to her guilt and shame over her whoredom, and asserts that her silence makes her and not the authorities guilty of the murder of her child.[5]

Foxe dealt extensively with Harding's charges in the 1570 edition of the *Acts and Monuments,* providing the name of Perotine's husband and castigating Harding at length for his "uncharitable railing and brawling . . . against the dead" and his effort "to accuse of murder the parties that were murdered" (8:241).[6] Both the debate and the exfoliating expansion of Foxe's work serve to remind us that the Reformation in England was hardly a tidy or linear or even a singular affair, as Christopher Haigh's aptly titled *English Reformations* details at some length.[7] Both serve to clarify as well the complex nature of Foxe's project, his massive textual monument to what had been an underground and outlawed resistance movement—English Protestantism in the mid-sixteenth century under the Catholic reign of Mary Tudor. Foxe's text was not, however, an agent or participant in that underground movement. Mary Tudor died, after all, in 1558; the first, Latin edition of *Acts and Monuments* was published in 1559, in a single folio volume printed in Basel after the accession of Elizabeth, whom Foxe himself hailed as the "defendour of the faith . . . next under the Lorde" (1:vi). For English Protestants, in other words, the fire at the stake was out, but this did not deter Foxe—just the opposite. The second edition, published in English and at three times the length of its predecessor, appeared in 1563, and the work continued to grow in the editions of 1570, 1576, and 1583, with new material and cases added to each. Nor did the work grow more encyclopedic only in scope. As Mark Breitenberg has pointed out, it also grew more encyclopedic in the genres it included: government records, articles of religion, royal proclamations, sermons, transcriptions of interrogations, letters, diaries and other first-person accounts, all interwoven with Foxe's own narratives. "The effect," Breitenberg suggests, ". . . is to fashion a Protestant community by including a vast number of texts, authors, events and individuals . . . to construct a larger boundary that serves to identify (and give identity to) the membership of a new state church . . . . [and] to amass an entire Protestant 'state' of texts in his book."[8] The "actual" Protestant state, itself involved in its own fraught process of expansion and consolidation, recognized the ideological value of its textual double. Although it was not, as historians asserted well into this century, ordered to be "chained side by side with the Bible"[9] in every parish church in England, the work was required to be placed in all cathedral churches and to be owned by all archbishops, bishops, deans, archdeacons, and "everie chief Residentarie, whom they call the dignities of the Church."[10] It was, as John Knott has said, an "inescapable text."[11] Written and exhaustively rewritten neither to bring Mary down nor to produce an end to the persecution of English Protestants (God, in Foxe's terms, had accomplished that), invested with the mantle of officially sanctioned "truth," it was one of the most widely disseminated texts of the sixteenth century, not so much the product as the ongoing *production* of the English Reformation. Foxe's project, in other words, was not to record or commemorate recent history but to interpellate the affective and ideological parameters of an emergent historical formation. What this means is that, despite its vast historical range, the *Acts and Monuments* is not a retrospective but a proleptic work: less a mass of documentary evidence than a series of sites for the apprehension, affective investment, and reconfiguration of the ideological and political subjects who read it. It is a continuation of the work begun by the resistance of those who died, a corporate, collaborative project that might be described as a vast cultural translation: one we might frame, in simple but clarifying terms, as the translation or transvaluation of "heresy" and the official rituals surrounding it—translated first into martyrdom, and then (or such is the hope) into stable religious orthodoxy.

The interrogation, torture, sentencing, and execution of a pronounced heretic was a complex official ritual, with elaborately prescribed codes and what were meant to be carefully orchestrated effects. Burning was probably *not* the most painful way to be executed in the period, an assertion I make with cavalier assurance and, I am glad to say, absolutely no empirical evidence; other forms of execution were at least more protracted.[12] My point is that the degree of pain inflicted was not the point being made by such executions. Immolation was culturally encoded as the most shameful way to be put to death; reserved for heretics and for those found guilty of petty treason, particularly women convicted of murdering their husbands or masters and thus of violating the divinely sanctioned "natural" social, political, and gender hierarchy,[13] it was indiscriminate both in its treatment of the body, leaving nothing recognizable behind, and in its application to the status of the victim. For secular crimes, high- and low-born were executed by different means, with beheading coded as the more privileged way to go; hanging was reserved for the lower classes and in rare instances for those of higher birth whose transgressions were so extreme as to warrant the debasement of their rank in the process of their death. Once convicted of heresy, however, you were removed from this rigidly prescribed social hierarchy and subjected to a ravaging form of democracy whatever your rank or status or lineage. Immolation for heresy was thus an act of ritual humiliation, aimed (in a symbolic but also nearly literal sense) at the total annihilation of the physical body, an erasure of it from existence and memory. Ritual immolation registered the spiritual shame and indeed the annihilation of spiritual being that the heretic had, from the church's viewpoint, already performed on him or herself, by removing that self from both the community of proper believers and from the divine. Recantation, although strenuously "encouraged," did not necessarily save one from death if the heresy were grave and manifest enough; from the church's point of view, immolation was more a ritual observance of what the heretic had already done than an act of retributive punishment, a fact that helps to explain why Mary occasionally ordered Protestants exhumed from the grave for a posthumous immolation.[14]

One of the effects of the official public ritual was supposed to be the solidification of the audience as a Christian community, fashioned into a stronger corporate body by their vicarious and oftentimes festive participation in the ritual shaming and annihilation of the heretic. The psychosocial dynamics involved here are also characteristic of the many less-deadly juridical rituals common to early modern society and centered upon the isolation and public humiliation of a member of the community, the latter accomplished by means of devices such as stocks, pillories, bridles, or cucking stools. Early modern England was neither a "shame" nor a "guilt" culture, but it was very much a "shaming" culture; ecclesiastical courts regularly ordered scolds to be bridled or dunked in a cucking stool, and adulterers to be stocked, not only as punishment for the offending party but also as a juridical means of inducing an internalization of social and sexual mores in those looking on, of fostering a "theater of conscience" in the community at large. Such practices, however, are designed to purge or cleanse both the community and the person thus exiled from it; once the social taint is removed through public humiliation, the figure in the stocks returns to the fold. In the case of heresy, the community can be cleansed only through a shaming that is conceived on a cosmic and eternal scale, produced by absolute and full annihilation. In order to have its intended effect, however, the execution of a heretic had to be an extraordinary and special event—precisely because the heretic, in order to be viewed properly, had to be produced, by and within the ritual, as an extraordinary, isolated individual. Mary Tudor, for one, seemed oblivious to this aspect of the cultural logic behind the official ritual, and as a consequence aided the Protestant cause by making heresy seem almost an everyday matter rather than an extraordinary one.

Heretics were almost more dangerous to punish than to let be; they had a nasty tendency not to resist their fate but to embrace it, to use the forum designed to humiliate and annihilate them as a stage to act out and demonstrate the power of their own faith. Recognizing the dangers inherent in allowing heresy such a forum, French authorities were at least initially more circumspect in the use of public execution by immolation, and also sought to assure (as Mary did not) that official records of interrogations and trials could not be used to immortalize those put to death. All such records were to be burned along with the condemned, effecting a textual as well as corporal annihilation that at least seriously complicated the compilation of a French *Book of Martyrs*.[15] Amply documented by official and unofficial records of rich variety and diverse venues, Foxe's Marian martyrs live (and die) through subsequent editions and consequent rereadings, displaying over and over again what is sometimes an appalling resolve, even when they lack the eloquence of a Latimer and are entirely silent. Among many disturbing examples is that of Richard Bayfield, who not only went "manfully and joyfully" to the pyre but also silently prayed there for three quarters of an hour while the inadequately built fire consumed him. "And when the left arm was on fire and burned," Foxe writes, "he rubbed it with his right hand, and it fell from his body, and he continued in prayer to the end without moving" (4:688).

Resisting death, registering fear or pain, could only highlight the efficacy of the shame visited upon the prescribed heretic; but this same shame could be appropriated, the official forum for punishment and ritual shaming transvaluated into a stage of valor and honor, turning exemplary punishment into a theater of resistance and the heretic into a martyr—etymologically a witness, one who testifies, here to the power of his or her faith to transform ritual immolation into "the basis for a symbolics of power."[16] Foxe's text bears witness as well, in a manner that makes it not merely a recording but a textual enhancement and even sequel to such moments of cultural transvaluation. In remote Guernsey, only a handful of people witnessed the death of Perotine, her family and child; Foxe restages that "rueful sight, not only to the eyes of all that there stood, but also to the ears of all true-hearted Christians that shall read this history," almost as though he imagines a truly animated text, one that not only incorporates an entire Protestant community through their documentary traces but is also inspired by it, speaking with its communal voice. The "spectacle," as Foxe describes it, that the child left behind for "the whole world" to see was not his actual death but its incorporation into the *Acts and Monuments*. Foxe's work thus seeks something closer to homology than analogy with, or mere transcription of, the deaths it details: a further act of "testimony" on an encyclopedic scale, it displaces the authority of the (Catholic) church not with a resolved Protestant death but with a resolved Protestant book. As Stephen Greenblatt has remarked on the "investment of power in the book" during the Reformation, "[Protestant] identity is achieved at the intersection of an absolute authority and a demonic other, but the authority has shifted from the visible church to the book."[17] The identity Foxe is attempting to achieve by publishing and republishing *his* book, *after* Mary's death, is that of a national Protestant community, one brought into being by reforming resistance into stable orthodoxy,[18] defending against a resurgence of Catholicism but also—and here the project becomes more complex—defending against any continuation of resistance itself. He needs to produce or at least to help catalyze a corporate national and Protestant body that is as inclusive as possible, not merely composed of learned or high-born but also of the lower orders whose deaths he chronicles along with the Latimers and others, but he also needs to guard against encouraging further resistance to established authority—especially among those lower orders, many of whom belonged to more radical sects than the Elizabethan compromise, the Anglican church, envisioned as legitimate. It is here that his treatment of women of differing classes becomes significant.

Perotine Massey is referred to throughout as a "silly woman" or, as in the passage I began with, a "silly mother." Although this has troubled some recent commentators, Foxe appears to have no pejorative connotation in mind. In the sixteenth century, the term meant unlearned, unschooled, or innocent; if Massey did indeed fail to notify the authorities of her condition, Foxe asserts, she was not to blame, for her failure stemmed from her ignorance of the law, her "mere simplicity" (8:237). Throughout the *Acts and Monuments*, Foxe tends to describe lower-class women as "silly" in this sense, but their lack of education and elocution does not detract from their martyrdom. It does, however, make them typically silent witnesses to the faith. "Silly" is also a term intended to evoke pity of an undeniably patronizing and paternalistic variety, as the case of the five women martyred at Canterbury illustrates. The Canterbury martyrs too are "silly poor women, whose imbecility the more strength it lacketh by natural imperfection, the more it ought to be helped, or at least pitied" (8:326). Such women do not violate the period's insistence, visited with particular strength upon the general populace and lower classes, that women be chaste, silent, and obedient; they are resolved in their deaths but neither remonstrative nor overly demonstrative, less individual agents of resistance than vessels taken over by "the Lord Omnipotent" who has chosen to possess them, "to animate their womanyshe and wyvishe hartes, into a bolde and manlye stomach."[19] Their strength is not their own: it is virile but, visited as it is upon them by God, their "manlye stomache[s]" cannot be perceived as a transgression of social or religious or gender codes. Despite or even, in Foxe's terms, because of their "silly" natures, such women fit fully into the Protestant community being fashioned by the *Acts and Monuments*.

Nor are Foxe's lower-class women all restricted to the category of mute and stoic emblems of faith. Joan Dangerfield is another lower-class mother, imprisoned along with her child a scant fourteen days after giving birth; denied a fire in her cell (the conditions of which will eventually cause the death of both mother and child), she is reduced to warming her baby's clothes in her bosom. Her husband was also imprisoned but in a separate cell, where he was separately questioned and falsely informed that his wife—the presumed weaker vessel—had already recanted. Although the strategy succeeded in producing the husband's recantation, Joan was adamant in her faith and remonstrated with her husband for breaking his "first vow made to Christ in baptism." Foxe not only admires Joan for her resolve (and her animated rebuke to her husband) but also invokes an extraordinary biblical context for her story in his description of the deceit practiced on her husband: "In the mean season while they lay thus enclosed in several prisons, the husband and the wife, the bishop beginneth to practise not the woman first, as the serpent did with Eve, but with the man, craftily deceiving his simplicity with fair glozing words, falsely persuading him that his wife has recanted" (8:253). Joan is the new, reformed Eve, a recovery and restoration of the original mother; not only is she spared the ignominy of being the weaker vessel, the serpent's preferred entry, but she also refuses to play the role of Adam and does not go along with her helpmate's fall.

Foxe is also quite comfortable with high-born female martyrs, who are characteristically given more extended treatment but also more license in their behavior. Katharine Parr, Henry VIII's queen, is presented as an exemplary figure even though she persuades her spouse and king to spare her life—not through recantation but through an adroit and intelligent display of female submissiveness. As Carole Levin remarks, "she survives by posing as a 'silly poor woman.'"[20] But with the high-born, at any rate, Foxe is by no means receptive to or inspired by only those women who adhere to prescribed models of feminine etiquette and behavior. He invests the case of Anne Askew—"born of such stock and kindred that she might have lived in great wealth and prosperity" (5:550)—with all of his considerable narrative skills, devoting a full and extended treatment to her interrogation, torture, and death, highlighting rather than downplaying the brash, witty, and quite impertinent eloquence that she visited upon her tormentors. When her citations of Scripture led the bishop's chancellor to accuse her of violating Paul's strictures against women "to talk of the word of God," she corrected him by citing from memory 1 Corinthians 14.34, "that a woman ought not to speak in the congregation by the way of teaching"; she then asked him how many women he had seen preaching from the pulpit, and admonished him "to find no fault in poor woman, except they had offended the law" (5:538). Even her refusal to address certain questions could be pointed and eloquent. Asked "whether a mouse, eating the host, received God or no?" she made no answer, but smiled. Directed to explain how she interpreted passages from the Bible that she had thrown back at her interrogators, she refused to share her reading with them, saying, "I would not throw pearls amongst swine, for acorns were good enough." Hard nuts to crack, acorns are, and the same would prove true of Anne Askew. Although normally chary with details of the lives of female as opposed to male martyrs, Foxe details Askew's life as well as her death, going so far as to assert that she died "as a blessed sacrifice unto God ... leaving behind her a singular example of christian constancy for all *men* to follow" (5:551; my italics).

The case of a woman named Elizabeth Young is quite different, however, and as my final example will suggest that, despite Foxe's massive efforts to fashion a genuinely all-inclusive Protestant community, certain intersections of gender and class fall outside the bounds of that community. In 1558, Young was arrested for selling Protestant books she had obtained on the Continent. Although of unknown origins—she refuses to say where she was born, or who her father and mother were—she is clearly of low birth, and no less clearly literate, even though she seems to have had no formal education. She is no "silly woman": forthright, articulate, sharp-witted, and well-informed about her faith, she stands up to so many repeated interrogations that she goes through a remarkable number of examiners, each new one of a higher rank, office, and degree of learning, progressing from one Master Hussey through a cleric named Martin to the bishop of London and eventually the Dean of St. Paul's. She seems to be at least in part the product of an underground Protestant conventicle—possibly an Anabaptist, given her repeated refusals to swear an oath of any sort. In her questioning, however, it is the combination of her low birth and her gender that her questioners find impossible to align with her powers of articulation and her knowledge of the Bible. A woman such as she, it seems, is not supposed to be. The chancellor to the bishop of London concludes that she must be a priest's concubine: "What priest hast thou lien withal, that thou hast so much Scripture? Thou art some priest's woman, I think" (8:544). She not only couldn't have learned on her own (despite the evidence to the contrary, such as her verbal acuity and her evident literacy), the ideas in her head can't really be hers—they are some reprobate priest's, who poured them in the porches of her ear, so to speak. When her articulate and well-informed resolve frustrates Sir Roger Cholmley (whose command of the language is decidedly inferior to hers), he hits upon a more extreme solution for the quandary she presents:

> Then said the bishop, "Why wilt thou not swear before a judge? . . .
> Elizabeth: "My Lord, I will not swear that this hand is mine."
> "No!" said the bishop, "and why?"
> Elizabeth: "My Lord, Christ saith, that whatsoever is more than yea, yea, or nay, nay, it cometh of evil. And moreover, I know not what an oath is; and therefore I will take no such thing upon me."
> Then Cholmley said, "Twenty pounds, it is a man in a woman's clothes! twenty pounds, it is a man!"
> [Bishop] Bonner: "Think you so, my lord?"
> Cholmley: "Yea, my lord," etc.
> Elizabeth: "My lord, I am a woman."
> Bishop: "Swear her upon a book, seeing it is but a question asked."
> Then said Cholmley, "I will lay twenty pounds, it is a man."
> Then Dr. Cooke brought her a book, commanding her to lay thereon her hand.
> Elizabeth: "No, my lord, I will not swear; for I know not what an oath is. But I will say that I am a woman, and have children."
> Bishop: "That know not we: wherefore swear."

> Cholmley: "Thou ill-favored whore, lay thy hand upon the book; I will lay on mine:" and so he laid his hand upon the book.
> Elizabeth: "So will not I mine." (8:539–40)

A man in woman's clothes *and* an ill-favored whore,[21] virtually in the same breath: as stated before, a woman such as she is not supposed to be. For Cholmley, but also for far subtler members of his gender in this period, if she is not a man in woman's dress then her tongue makes her something even worse, an unnatural creature whose articulate intelligence, low birth, and gender combine to make her an ideological conundrum, a kind of linguistic hermaphrodite.

I must confess to a particular fondness for Sir Roger; in addition to his other demonstrable attractions, he is a marvelous Catholic anticipation of Jonson's rabid Puritan, Zeal-of-the-Land Busy, in *Bartholomew Fair*. When at the end of that play Busy encounters the puppet show, he assumes, like Sir Roger, that what looks like a woman is really a man in woman's dress, and thus a hermaphroditical "abomination." The "nothing" that Busy discovers beneath the puppets' skirts differs, of course, from the kind of "absence" (or so Freud would later construct it) that Sir Roger Cholmley would have found if he had succeeded in disrobing Elizabeth Young; however, the accusations of both register gender anxieties of the sort often evoked by the transvestite playing practices of early modern English dramatic companies. Young makes her first appearance in *The Book of Martyrs* in the edition of 1570, at a time when those companies had begun to seek out new ground for dramatic performance, to refashion their theatrical enterprise as a professional, quasi-institutionalized cultural phenomenon. It was in 1567, after all, that John Brayne went east of Aldgate to Stepney, where he erected a theater called the Red Lion, the first permanent building expressly designed for dramatic performances to be constructed in Europe since late antiquity. Young makes her second appearance in the edition of 1576,[22] the very year when The Theatre was erected in the liberty of Shoreditch, outside the city wall of London proper. Although the coincidence of dates is mere accident, there is a more substantive connection to be made between Foxe's work and the popular stage. Foxe's readers were among the large segment of the population that would regularly attend this and other playhouses in the years to come, where they would indeed see what Sir Roger presumed to confront in Elizabeth Young: lower-class men taking on women's clothing, to the often spluttering outrage of figures of authority.

Treating recent and even current historical figures with the same weight and import as classical and biblical martyrs, Foxe's text helped to establish the affective power of the contemporaneous and particular over the classical or general or typological. As Michael McKeon has suggested, Foxe's historical particularity would have significant consequence for the emergence of the novel as a genre,[23] but such affective power was first explored and experimented with on the popular stages of Elizabethan England. One of the unintended effects of Foxe's effort to imagine and bring into being a Protestant community was to help the popular stage think its way beyond the morality tradition of earlier indigenous drama, with its abstract personification of states of being, and toward the particular, discursive, and theatrical embodiment of affective characters.[24] The shift away from this deeply ingrained way of imagining the relationship between theater and affect was neither automatic nor inevitable, nor was the phenomenal success of the emergent mode of dramatic representation guaranteed. As I have argued elsewhere, the new modes of drama emerging precisely at this moment succeeded only insofar as they successfully reconstituted their audiences, reconfigured their affective thresholds by demanding and producing new powers of identification, projection, and apprehension, altering the threshold not only of dramatic representation but also of self-representation, not only of the fictional construction of character but also of the social construction of the self.[25] That the popular theater did indeed exercise such power on its audiences—but in ways that did not always accord with the desires of the Protestant hegemony—is amply testified to by Foxe's more rabid heirs, in their attacks upon, and their eventual dismantling of, that theater.

But to return to the case of Elizabeth Young, and a brief conclusion. Neither a silly poor woman nor of the high birth that might explain her learning and skills, Young drives her interrogators to distraction because she is, in a very real sense, a living contradiction to the class and gender systems of the age—even if we don't agree with Sir Cholmley's more homely way of saying something similar. Her interrogators' incapacity to deal with her, however, is mirrored in Foxe's own apparent incapacity. I have been quoting from the *transcripts* of her various examinations, as reproduced verbatim in Foxe's text. Foxe provides only the briefest introduction to Elizabeth Young's remarkable demonstration of faith, otherwise supplying simply the bare transcripts of the dialogues as recorded by her interrogators. Although the *Acts and Monuments* is an encyclopedic *copia* of documentary genres, such authorial reticence is highly unusual, to say the least. In the case of the Canterbury martyrs, Foxe himself attributes their courage to their "manlye stomaches," but their courage was also manifested in silence, as befitted their station, and this virile resolve was also endowed, after all, by God. Properly attributed to the ultimate patriarch, their manly resolve can receive full and ample narration from Foxe, as Elizabeth Young does not. Perhaps Young is too much of a social paradox and conundrum, rather than a religious one, for Foxe as well as for her interrogators. Perhaps he, like Cholmley, cannot triangulate among her gender, class, and tongue to perceive a woman capable of being imagined more concretely, or being fully represented. An articulate contradiction of the class/gender systems of the period, she also occupies and thus articulates an ideological blindspot in Foxe's narrative representation, a contradiction outside the limits of at least his narration—included in the community of the book but only as an undigested text and not as a figure brought to life by Foxe's storytelling powers. If she is brought to life it is not on the page, through Foxe's narrative skills, but in the apprehension of the reader who invests her dialogue with imaginary voice and affect, much in the way he or she might do with a character in a play text, written for the public stage.

Elizabeth Young herself proved to need neither Foxe's narrative nor our own quasi-theatrical resuscitation. Her story is one of the few accounts in the *Book of Martyrs* that no one, then or now, for whatever reason, would find tragical, lamentable, or pitiful. For she so puzzled her captors that they delayed sentencing her and continued interrogating her, again and again and again—until Mary conveniently died, and they had no choice but to release her. All we know of her after that is that she went home, and resumed the care of her children.

Notes

1. *The Acts and Monuments of John Foxe*, ed. Josiah Pratt (London: Religious Tract Society, 1877), 8:229. Further page references to this (the fourth) edition will be included in the text; references to sixteenth-century editions will be by notes, below.

2. It is not unusual that the woodcut does not so strictly illustrate the narrative account, but is designed to highlight certain aspects of it. There is no sign of the ropes used for the unsuccessful effort to strangulate the women prior to immolation, nor have they fallen into the flames; their posture and their nakedness (they were not executed without clothing) thus serve not as illustration of the moment but to foreground the opening of Perotine's womb and the emergence of her child.

A later, seventeenth-century reproduction of this woodcut, with the crowd cropped out but in full color, appeared as the dust-jacket illustration for a recent book by Robin Briggs, *Witches and Neighbours: The Social and Cultural Contexts of European Witchcraft* (London: HarperCollins, 1996). However, the illustration was therein described as a depiction of the execution of witches in Guernsey, an error presumably prompted by the (unidentified) seventeenth-century source, which I have not yet located. After a review of Briggs's book in *The Times Literary Supplement*, a letter from Patrick Collinson corrected the misapprehension (see *TLS*, no. 4862 [1996]: 17).

3. Although traditional discussions of ideology effectively ignore emotion and other forms of affect, more recent approaches have clarified the degree to which ideology necessarily works upon, shapes and reshapes, and even constructs new forms of affect. The work of Raymond Williams has played a significant role in such developments, especially notable in British cultural studies; see his discussion of hegemony and "structures of feeling" in *Marxism and Literature* (Oxford: Oxford University Press, 1978), esp. 128–35. For a very different approach that combines Lacanian theories of desire with a dynamic understanding of ideology, see Slavoj Zizek, *The Sublime Object of Ideology* (London: Verso, 1989), esp. 87–129.

4. For an excellent and influential discussion of imagined communities and the origins of nationalism, see Benedict Anderson, *Imagined Communities: Reflections on the Origin and Spread of Nationalism* (London and New York: Verso, 1991).

5. For Harding's charges, see his *A reioinder to M. Iewels replie...* (1567).

6. Foxe's historiography here has been upheld by modern scholars; Perotine Massey was married to a Protestant minister, David Jores. For a examination of this and other issues relating to the Reformation in Guernsey, see D. M. Ogier, *Reformation and Society in Guernsey* (Woodbridge, Suffolk: Boydell Press, 1996).

7. See Christopher Haigh, *English Reformations: Religion, Politics, and Society under the Tudors* (Oxford and New York: Oxford University Press, 1993).

8. Mark Breitenberg, "The Flesh Made Word: Foxe's *Acts and Monuments*," *Renaissance and Reformation* 13, no. 4 (1989): 388, 392.

9. J. M. Stone, quoted by Leslie M. Oliver, "The Seventh Edition of John Foxe's *Acts and Monuments*," *Papers of the Bibliographic Society of America* 37 (1943): 246.

10. *A Booke of certaine Canons ... of the Churche of England ...* (London: John Day, 1571); quoted by Oliver, "The Seventh Edition," 246.

11. John R. Knott, *Discourses of Martyrdom in English Literature, 1563–1694* (Cambridge: Cambridge University Press, 1993), 2.

12. I do not mean to underplay the excruciating torment caused by immolation, especially when the fire was not well built—a common enough occurrence that did indeed inflict a level of prolonged and severe pain that is difficult to imagine. But such pain was not integral to the ritual. To cast the purpose of ritual immolation as such—as an effort to inflict maximal pain—is thus to misunderstand the theological symbolics of the ritual, and I feel that Janel Mueller does so in an otherwise illuminating essay, "Pain, Persecution, and the Construction of Selfhood in Foxe's *Acts and Monuments*," in *Religion and Culture in Renaissance England*, ed. Claire McEachern and Debora Shuger (Cambridge: Cambridge University Press, 1997), 161–87. Seeking to correct the universalized understanding of the body that characterizes Elaine Scarry's influential study, *The Body in Pain: The Making and*

Unmaking of the World (Oxford: Oxford University Press, 1985), Mueller provides extraordinary insight into the culture-specific ways in which the Protestant body is constructed, in pain and martyrdom, in Foxe's work; however, she uncritically adopts Scarry's overgeneralized notion of torture, defining ritual immolation as a form of torture. Since "torture" has a quite rigorous history—one that is explicitly codified, and was officially sanctioned in the early modern period—it is a term to be used less figuratively than either Scarry or Mueller have done.

13. On the burning of female traitors, see J. H. Baker, "Criminal Courts and Procedure at Common Law 1550–1800," in *Crime in England 1550–1800*, ed. J. S. Cockburn (London: Methuen, 1977), 15–48, esp. 42–43. For more recent discussions of petty treason in the context of literary representations, see Frances E. Dolan, "The Subordinate('s) Plot: Petty Treason and the Forms of Domestic Rebellion," *Shakespeare Quarterly* 43 (1992): 317–40, and her book *Dangerous Familiars: Representations of Domestic Crime in England, 1550–1700* (Ithaca: Cornell University Press, 1994). I am also indebted to Ruth Perry and Cynthia Herrup for their comments on this issue.

14. Thus were the bodies of Martin Bucer and Paul Fagius first exhumed and then tried and burned posthumously. Catherine Martyr, the wife of Peter Martyr, who had been buried near the bones of St. Frideswide at Oxford, was also exhumed for similar treatment, but the authorities found they had insufficient evidence for a trial; as a former nun, however, she was found guilty of violating her vow of celibacy and as fitting punishment was reburied in a nearby dunghill.

When Elizabeth assumed the throne, Catherine's remains were recovered in order to be interred in a more dignified resting place; to assure that a subsequent regime would not repeat the desecration, however, her bones were commingled with those of St. Frideswide. As Carole Levin has remarked, the commingling "demonstrates the fragility of the Anglican settlement and fears about the future of Protestantism in England." I derive this information and quotation from her unpublished essay, "St. Frideswide and St. Uncumber: Changing Images of Female Saints in Renaissance England."

15. On this and other points of contrast between English and French practices, see David Nicholls, "The Theatre of Martyrdom in the French Reformation," *Past and Present* 121 (1988): 49–73, esp. 50–51.

16. Breitenberg, "The Flesh Made Word," 402.

17. Stephen Greenblatt, *Renaissance Self-Fashioning: From More to Shakespeare* (Chicago and London: University of Chicago Press, 1980), 76.

18. I do not mean to suggest here that such stability was already an accomplished fact, or that Foxe embraced the Elizabethan compromise wholeheartedly or without significant reservations and disagreements. For a discussion of his differences with the emerging Anglican establishment, see Jane Facey, "John Foxe and the Defence of the English Church," in *Protestantism and the National Church in Sixteenth-Century England*, ed. Peter Lake and Maria Dowling (London: Croom Helm, 1987), 162–92, as well as Knott's excellent discussion of such issues in *Discourses of Martyrdom*, esp. 84–150.

19. *Actes and Monuments...* (London, 1563), 1571.

20. Carole Levin, "Women in *The Book of Martyrs* as Models of Behavior in

Tudor England," *International Journal of Women's Studies* 4, no. 2 (1981): 199. Levin's article was one of the first to focus critical attention on the representation of women in Foxe, and I am indebted to it throughout.

21. Although *whore* is not entirely gender-specific in the period and could be applied to men as well as women, Cholmley's accusations make "sense" in context only if one assumes that his "logic" is indeed contradictory and overdetermined.

22. For an excellent recent examination of the 1576 edition, see Jesse Lander, "Foxe's *Book of Martyrs*: Printing and Popularizing the *Acts and Monuments*," in *Religion and Culture in Renaissance England*, ed. McEachern and Shuger, 69–92, esp. 89.

23. See Michael McKeon, *The Origins of the English Novel, 1600–1740* (Baltimore: Johns Hopkins University Press, 1987), esp. 92–93. John R. Knott has also examined the ways in which Foxe's text gains much of its power by eschewing the conventional language of martyrology in favor of concrete and individualizing detail. "It is the deviations from the unwritten script of martyrdom, the unpredictable things like soot on the hands or a fire that will not burn right, that make Foxe's Protestant saints seem vividly human and their heroic suffering within the reach of ordinary members of a holy community" ("John Foxe and the Joy of Suffering," *Sixteenth Century Journal* 27 [1996]: 733).

24. I should note here that I am not suggesting that morality plays are aesthetically inferior to later Elizabethan drama, but that the tradition was informed by very different assumptions about the affective power of general versus concrete modes of representation, and that the assumption that only general or typological figures could command a broad affective response from an audience was still very influential.

An example would be in order here. In 1580, Nicholas Woodes published a play called *The Conflict of Conscience*. The play was based on the story of the persecution, recantation, and eventual death—perhaps in despair over his recantation, perhaps after a return to his true beliefs—of an Italian Lutheran named Francesco Spiera. It was a story that had been discussed throughout Europe by Protestant dissenters, retold and debated in print so extensively that Spiera had became, by the time of Woodes's play, one of the most well known individual cases of Protestant persecution. Woodes, however, announces in his preface that the "vices of one particular man" cannot touch a large and diverse audience (despite the fact that the life and death of Spiera had already done so), and so abstracts the historical figure into a personification of learning named Philologus. For a full examination of the European investment in Spiera's case, see Michael McDonald, "*The Fearefull Estate of Francis Spira*: Narrative, Identity, and Emotion in Early Modern England," *Journal of British Studies* 31 (1992): 32–61.

25. See Steven Mullaney, *The Place of the Stage: License, Play, and Power in Renaissance England* (1988; rpt., Ann Arbor: University of Michigan Press, 1995), 88–115, and "Mourning and Misogyny: *Hamlet, The Revenger's Tragedy*, and the Final Progress of Elizabeth I, 1600–1607," *Shakespeare Quarterly* 45, no. 2 (1994): 139–62, esp. 142–45.

CHAPTER TEN

Staging the News

F. J. Levy

On Christmas Eve, 1620, James I's Privy Council sent forth a proclamation "against excesse of Lavish and Licentious Speech of matters of State." In it, his Majesty prided himself on the fact that "in Our owne Nature, and Judgement, Wee doe well allow of convenient freedome of speech," but noted nevertheless that "a more licentious passage of lavish discourse, and bold Censure in matters of State" had grown too common, more so indeed than was tolerable in any well-run kingdom. The nub of the matter was foreign policy and—though the King did not say so—most especially the Spanish marriage proposed for Prince Charles. It was this contentious business that generated "a greater opennesse, and libertie of discourse, even concerning matters of State, (which are no Theames, or subjects fit for vulgar persons, or common meetings)" than had in former times been permitted; and it was discussion of the marriage that the King wished to suppress. The proclamation then went on to command all the English, "from the highest to the lowest," to cease meddling, either by pen or by speech, in such "causes of State, and secrets of Empire," which were indeed far above their "reach and calling." But, while its tone was sharp, the proclamation specified no penalties; its author, Lord Chancellor Bacon, wanted no more than a warning. And no wonder, for the proclamation itself gave the game away, by stating baldly that "the multitude and generalitie of Offenders in this kinde" might not be cited in mitigation.[1]

A little more than half a year later, it was all to be done again. A new proclamation rehearsed the terms of its predecessor, and lamented that "Wee are given to understand, that notwithstanding the strictnesse of Our commandement, the inordinate libertie of unreverent speech, touching matters of high nature, unfit for vulgar discourse, doth dayly more and more increase."[2] But what did all this mean? John Chamberlain, the insatiable collector and vendor of news, reported that the common people had no idea of how to understand it, nor did they comprehend "how far matter of state may stretch or extend," with the predictable result that "they continue to take no notice of yt."[3] Indeed, as Chamberlain himself noted a few months later, the principal effect of the proclamation was to puzzle and annoy the members of the newly arrived House of Commons, who wondered whether it might be applied even to their discussions.[4] In the end, of course, the members did enter into forbidden territory, asking such impertinent questions as whether "*Great Britain* was become less than little *England*"? As that rather malicious chronicler Arthur Wilson pointed out, "*So dangerous it is for Princes by a flegmatick remissenesse, to slacken the ligaments of the peoples tongues, for such an overflux of bad Humor may bring their obedience to a Paralytick!*"[5]

But James had not, in fact, been all that remiss: the two proclamations were merely shots fired in a campaign begun earlier in 1620 by the presentations, running to nine or more, of Ben Jonson's masque, *News from the New World Discovered in the Moon*.[6] Jonson's cast assembles the usual villains: a pair of heralds who bring back news from the lunar sphere, together with a Printer, a Factor, and a Chronicler who process that news, each according to his métier. The Chronicler need not concern us: his main interest is in filling out his swollen tomes with trifles, unimportant at the best of times, and probably untrue as well. The Printer deals with the same events, though in a fresher state: "I'll give anything for a good copy now, be't true or false, so't be news."[7] The Factor, however, good businessman that he is, claims a kind of superiority. The news he distributes is English; his role is that of a middleman, a clearinghouse, exchanging news between "mine own ministers in town and my friends of correspondence in the country;" his vehicle is the letter, written by hand, but in multiple copies.[8] The Factor and the Printer, though, are sworn enemies, for the former hates the very thought of a press: "it is the printing I am offended at. I would have no news printed; for when they are printed they leave to be news. While they are written, though they be false, they remain news still."[9] News, like rumor, is malleable, adaptable to circumstances, as long as its circulation is in the indefinite form of manuscript—newsletters were not uncommonly tailored to suit the recipient. The Printer's customers, on the other hand, believe only what's in print: it's the printing that makes it news. The social distinction is clear: for the well-to-do, the "surreptitious" form of scribal publication itself acts as a guarantee; for the lower orders, the opposite is the case: "I love a ballad in print, o' life, for then we are sure they are true."[10]

Jonson's effort to distinguish print culture from scribal culture is of particular interest nowadays, and it is one to which we shall return. Nevertheless, his point here is that these two apparently opposite cultures have one crucial element in common: the absence of truth. However they prefer to distribute their end product, the Printer, Factor, and Chronicler all put their faith—literally—in a lunatic cloud-cuckoo-land; all three lack the means to descry the truth. It is the king, to whom all turn, who "alone is able to resolve," who alone is the guarantor of truth, and whose virtues will rather be trumpeted forth by bright Fame than by the mundane trio of newsmongers.[11]

The world Jonson conjures up is stable, traditional, perhaps a little old-fashioned. It is a world where speech and writing are restricted, both by the workings of the royal prerogative and through the operations of the social system itself. Yet precisely at the moment that Jonson mounted his first defense of the royal position, the picture began to alter. Under the pressure generated by the beginnings of the Thirty Years' War, personified in England by the dispossession of King James's daughter, Elizabeth, and her husband from the Palatinate, the king and his ministers themselves began to find it expedient to allow a wider scope to the dissemination of news. James's efforts to find a Spanish bride for his heir—in the hope of using the match to regain the Palatinate for his daughter's family—intensified discussion.[12] In the five years between *News from the New World Discovered in the Moon* and *The Staple of News*, the Crown and its ministers changed the rules of the game. Thus the last years of James's reign saw a gradual shift in the ways by which regal power was exercised, a shift that played itself out at court, in Parliament, and in the interrelationships between court and country. News, newspapers, and topical drama, all closely linked, supplied one arena in which the shift of power might be examined.[13] Jonson's two dramatic productions—plus *Sir John Van Olden Barnavelt* and *A Game at Chess*—not only commented on the transformation but, by keeping it in the forefront of conversation, helped effectuate it.

During Queen Elizabeth's reign, and much of King James's, a few topics—foreign policy and the marriage of royal children among them—were seen as being in the royal domain, a point both monarchs found it necessary to repeat to their recalcitrant Parliaments. There was more to this than a defense of *arcana imperii*. Open speech or print, for or against a particular policy, might well spur the London ambassador of a friendly power to turn hostile. As the Privy Council put it, when ordering the suppression of one of William Elderton's patriotic broadsides, such language might tend "to the descreditt of some prences with whom the Queene's Ma[jes]tie standeth presently in terms of amytie."[14] More directly, the Tuscan ambassador's complaint about the depiction of his master in Robert Dallington's *A Survey of the Great Dukes State of Tuscany* led to the book's being burned by the public hangman.[15] The old queen had also tried, rather less successfully, to keep entire control of religion, to the discouragement of those of her subjects, in Parliament and out, who felt that the remnants of Catholicism were not being removed fast enough. When religion and foreign policy overlapped, as they often did, the level of danger increased: Sir Philip Sidney's "private" protest against the Alençon marriage led to his rustication, John Stubbes's open appeal to the public at large to the loss of his right hand.[16]

In addition, however, to defending their prerogative, Elizabeth and James also wished to restrict public comment on matters of state and religion for the sake of preserving national unity. The king instructed his delegate to the Synod of Dort to advise the Dutch churches "that the ministers do not deliver in the pulpit to the people these things for ordinary doctrines which are the highest points of schools and not fit for vulgar capacity but disputable on both sides."[17] James was happy to give the same advice to his own theologians: a matter such as predestination should not be susceptible to public argument even by the ordained clergy, let alone the laity, lest respect for religion (and hence public order) suffer. The same concern for public order, it may be added, also led to the suppression of rancorous secular debate, for example, the overheated literary quarrel between Nashe and Harvey, or the long-running feud between Sir Edward Dymock and the Earl of Lincoln, which ended when Dymock was heavily fined "for contriving and acting a stage play . . . containing scurrilous and slanderous matter against the Earl by name."[18]

Such caution might, in times of emergency, come very close to national paranoia. Henry VIII had been immoderately troubled about the effects of uncontrolled prognostications and political riddles and—as so often with

Henry—his worries brought men to the scaffold.[19] His successors shared his concerns, if not always with the same dire results. Nor was such concern without cause. A few months after the hubbub created by the king's narrowly escaping the Gunpowder Plot, the country was again rocked by rumors that James had been murdered, stabbed with a poisoned knife. The news threw London into turmoil: the gates of the palace were locked, the Tower prepared, the guards readied. Such rumors spread quickly. The Earl of Kent at Wrest Park had to wait several days before a friend on the Privy Council informed him the news was false; elsewhere in the country, the people trembled until the hastily prepared official proclamation finally caught up. Even in Devonshire, and weeks later, Walter Yonge felt constrained to write in his diary, "There was a sudden speech all about London, and also over all England about this time, that the King was slain."[20] Still, in the aftermath of Guy Fawkes, the universal rejoicing over the king's safety probably did more good than harm. But that was not always the case. In the 1590s, for example, an Elizabethan government faced with the combination of large-scale famine and a major war clamped down on all forms of communication. The Lord Keeper hectored the audience at Star Chamber against spreading rumors; proclamations bolstered the same point. Yet there was a general air of nervousness, which even the great and near-great could not altogether avoid. Rowland Whyte, Sir Robert Sydney's factor at court, insisted on the necessity of secrecy in writing and speech: "Burn my letters, else shall I be afraid to write. Be careful what you write here, or what you say where you are. Now are letters intercepted and stayed."[21] The same fear was echoed by John Donne, backed into a corner by a politic courtier, when he "felt my selfe then / Becomming Traytor, and mee thought I saw / One of our Giant Statutes ope his jaw / To sucke me in."[22]

Even without the real pressures of the 1590s, fear of prosecution continued as an undercurrent. Perhaps a dozen years later, Ben Jonson's poem, *The New Cry*, echoes and updates Donne; now the overripe statesmen "carry in their pockets Tacitus, / And the gazetti, or *Gallo-Belgicus:* / And talk reserved, locked up, and full of fear."[23] Though equipped with the latest foreign intelligences, they remained dangerous malcontents still. Such talk was not limited to the overheated imaginings of poets. Even in 1617— a most quiet year—that sober gentleman Sir John Holles could remind Lord Norris how, despite "these times being safer for ignorance then knowledg," he had treated his friend as "a cabinett, wherin I have trusted what I hould deerest, even that which else wher had been dangerous to have known."[24] Nor was the Suffolk clergyman-diarist, John Rous, writing in 1627, able to rid himself of the fear that public disagreement over policy was the first step toward insurrection.[25]

Behind all this lay the ancient notion of decorum, the expression in action of the even older idea of degree. The rigid hierarchies of which society was composed should, it was believed, be visible in small things as in large. Sumptuary legislation provides a perfect example. Excess in apparel—with the poor leading the way—was a symbol of the national moral collapse, leading "to the disorder and confusion of the degrees of all estates ... and finally to the subversion of all good order."[26] The same point, however, might equally be made about the reading of Scripture. A first move in the direction of general permission for all to read the Bible was quickly followed by a retreat. An act of 1543 ("for the advancement of true religion") restricted the laity, allowing only noblemen, gentlemen, and merchant householders to read Scripture aloud (if in the privacy of their own homes), permitting noblewomen and gentlewomen to read it to themselves, and forbidding all of lower rank to read it either privately or openly.[27] The pressures of social mobility ultimately made sumptuary legislation moot. In the same way, the force of Protestant evangelizing soon lifted the restrictions on Bible reading: by 1559, all were encouraged to study the Scripture, though without contention. The parallel limitation, restricting the knowledge of news and, by extension, any discussion of the meaning of that news to members of the political nation, was by the early seventeenth century also becoming strained.

One source of such pressure came from within the government itself. Fletcher and Massinger's "news play," *Sir John Van Olden Barnavelt,* provides an instructive example. To understand precisely what was going on, we must glance at the political situation. Barnavelt—as the play consistently refers to him—had for long been one of the leading figures in the revolt of the Dutch provinces against the Spanish; as the chief politician in Holland, the largest and wealthiest of the Dutch provinces, he had supplied the money and forged the alliances that bolstered independence. His pride in "the labourinthes of pollicie, I haue trod / to find the clew of saffetie for my Cuntrie"[28] was by no means unjustified. Nevertheless, over the years Barnavelt had come into increasing conflict with the United Provinces' chief military commander, Maurice, Prince of Orange, a conflict now exacerbated by Barnavelt's support of the liberal, "free will" Arminian faction of the Dutch Protestant Church as a counterweight to Maurice's backing of the much more rigorously Calvinist Remonstrants. When Barnavelt tried to oust his rival by setting up his own army, Maurice accused the old man of conspiracy, and had him tried and executed. That execution took place on 3 May 1619, and the English ambassador, Sir Dudley Carleton, wrote of the event to King James on the same day. On 8 May, Carleton's London correspondent, John Chamberlain, wrote "We heard here on Thursday"—that is, on 6 May—"of Barnevelts defeat by some that were eye-witnesses, but there were few or no letters come of any particulers."[29] The first of the newsbook publications on the subject—largely translations of Dutch documents—was registered on 17 May; a vitriolic broadside ballad, undated and unregistered, must have appeared at the same time. Less than three months later, Thomas Locke informed Carleton, "The Players heere were bringing of Barnevelt vpon the stage, & had bestowed a great deale of mony to prepare all things for the purpose," and then added that "at th'instant were prohibited by my Lo: of London," that is, by Bishop John King. Two weeks thereafter, the Bishop's objections had been overcome, and the "players haue fownd the meanes to goe through wth the play of Barnevelt & it hath had many spectators."[30]

While the story appears to be relatively straightforward, there are nevertheless a number of oddities. One is a matter of good fortune: while there is no contemporary printed version, *Sir John Van Olden Barnavelt* is one of the few plays for which the manuscript survives, with the markings of the censor, Sir George Buc, intact. Those markings—by no means all deletions—permit us to hazard some guesses about the play's purposes. Fletcher and Massinger's text had depicted a Barnavelt who, despite possessing the realities of power and wealth, nevertheless also sought glory and applause. To gain followers for his ambition, he was prepared to turn Arminian, not as a true believer, but for expediency; he was also prepared to plot against his country, stirring up religious revolt at home, treating with the enemy abroad. Buc left that picture essentially unaltered, though he did cut some of Barnavelt's self-justification and—perhaps more tellingly—excised a passage in which he compared himself to Cato and Prince Maurice to Augustus in language too close for comfort to the oppositionist rhetoric of the 1590s. Buc did, however, reshape Maurice, changing him from a man hovering on the edge of tyranny to a merciful prince, almost too ready to forgive past injuries, until driven to resist by his enemy's unceasing machinations. No one, it appears, was more responsible for Barnavelt's execution than Barnavelt himself.

Buc's alterations were well in line with James's policy toward the Low Countries. The king did not approve of their form of government, and would have preferred to welcome Maurice into the club of monarchs. In addition, he heartily disliked Barnavelt, not so much because of his so-called Arminianism but because he had earlier opposed James's persecution of the heterodox Dutch scholar Conrad Vorstius. Moreover, the English ambassador in those years, Sir Ralph Winwood, kept up a steady barrage of attacks on Barnavelt for his opposition to the Calvinist Remonstrants and hence to their chief supporter, Prince Maurice.[31] James, at least, was unlikely to lament Barnavelt for long. Nevertheless, as John Chamberlain reported, "I will not dissemble that divers of goode judgement thincke he had hard measure, considering that no cleere matter of conspiracie with the enemies of the state appeares, or can be proved, so that yt seemes to be meere matter of faction and opposition rather then infidelitie or treacherie."[32] Chamberlain hinted that he had, for a time, himself shared that view, but had changed his mind because he had read the sentence against Barnavelt—that is, the tract printing a translation of the Dutch court judgment, one of the many such newsbooks issued in London in the wake of the execution. It is worth noting that printing pamphlets of this sort required the censor's permission, and that in other cases the government had had no inhibitions about preventing such publication, and had done so in the aftermath of Henry IV's assassination.[33] If Chamberlain is the ideal reader at whom the barrage of news was aimed, then the pamphlets had done their work well. And I would argue that it is no mere coincidence that the play, in a scene that is almost intrusively long, rehearses in detail all the charges against Barnavelt.

As a staged newsbook, *Sir John Van Olden Barnavelt* is unusual in the long history of Elizabethan and early Stuart drama. Other examples, such as the lost *Battle of Turnholt*, were records of English victories, intended no doubt to set the groundlings cheering, but no danger to the conduct of England's Continental affairs. That had, of course, been the trouble with previous "news" plays. Marlowe's *Massacre at Paris* clearly seems to have generated some official response, probably a protest from the French ambassador that the English found convenient to ignore. In any case, the story was certainly remembered and flung in the face of the English ambassador when, almost a decade later, he found himself complaining about a derogatory play enacted in Paris by a troupe of visiting Italians.[34] Marlowe's story, which consisted in the main of long descriptions of the Machiavellian perfidy of the French, praise of the constancy of the English, together with some very delicate questions about the new king, was perhaps only slightly provocative at its first appearance in 1593.[35] Revived for a very long run in

1594, in the immediate aftermath of Henri de Navarre's decision that Paris was indeed worth a mass, it must now have seemed extremely convenient. The case with Chapman's *Biron* is rather more complicated, not least because of its none-too-oblique parallels to the death of the earl of Essex. What is certain is that the French ambassador lodged a protest, and the resultant furor led to a temporary closure of the theaters and a large fine for the players, as well as to Chapman's having to seek refuge and protection in the house of the duke of Lennox, the king's cousin. Additionally, the players were forced to agree "no longer to perform any modern histories nor speak of contemporary affairs on pain of death."[36]

Fletcher and Massinger's *Barnavelt* clearly flouted this last prohibition. So, too, did the King's Men in putting it on; moreover, as we have already noted, they added to their risk by bestowing a great deal of money on the production. In addition, as Trevor Howard-Hill has pointed out, the whole operation was conducted with remarkable speed: three months, he argues, is about as rapidly as it could have been done.[37] That the company would rush into such a risky and expensive production leads me to conclude that the authors and players had been promised protection if not outright encouragement by someone in a position of considerable authority, most likely by a member of the Privy Council. The play still had to make its way through Buc's censorship but, as we have seen, that served mainly to make it hew more closely to the official line. The only puzzle is Bishop King's interference. I am inclined to agree with Richard Dutton's suggestion that the bishop, no great admirer of the Remonstrants or their English Calvinist supporters, wished to make sure that a play intended to allay political controversies did not arouse religious ones.[38] Once he was satisfied, performances began. My point here is simply that an obtrusive system of censorship would not have found it difficult to suppress the play altogether. It did not choose to do so. Moreover, the very fact of the bishop's intervention, and its temporary nature, lends credence to my argument that the whole business was officially inspired, for Bishop King was a member of the Privy Council and can hardly have helped being aware of what was going on.

The events surrounding the playing of *Sir John Van Olden Barnavelt* may well be seen as yet another illustration of the point made by so many historians of the early seventeenth century, that much of what we see as "division" or "opposition" is no more than a reflection of debates within the Privy Council itself.[39] The same point has, of course, been made about the events surrounding the performances, in August 1624, of Middleton's

A Game at Chess. Thanks to a spate of recent publications, the story has become familiar, and I need not spend a great deal of time on it.[40] Nevertheless, it is important to remember that the occasion was, so far as we know, unique. Oblique references to contemporary politics had become commonplace, and even the censors had become accustomed to them. Direct references to foreign princes were, as we have seen, relatively unusual, though not altogether unknown. But *A Game at Chess* came in the wake of the failure of the hated Spanish marriage negotiations and, under a light veil of allegory, depicted events of great contemporary interest involving England, involving countries with whom the English had only recently been in negotiation, involving even portraits of nobles and monarchs at home and abroad, and did so for an unprecedented run of ten consecutive days (with time out for the Sabbath). For all that time, the house was full; indeed, Sir John Holles, who did manage to get in, claimed that tickets were almost unprocurable. It is not impossible that nearly 10 percent of the total population of London saw the play; certainly contemporary sources, with great if pardonable exaggeration, claimed the playhouse took in £1500. Holles pointed out the moral of the play, "that the Jesuits mark is to bring all the christain world under Rome for the spirituality, and under Spayn for the temporalty," then went on to describe the stage as a chess board, with England as the white house, Spain as the black. The character of Gondomar explained at length "how many Jesuites and priests he loosed out of prison, and putt agayn into their necessary work of seducing, how he sett the Kings [of England] affayrs as a clock, backward, and forward." In the last scene, the white prince, "making a full discovery of all their knaveries," put all the black pieces into the bag—on stage, a hell's mouth— and so it ended.[41] The Spanish ambassador, whose predecessor and whose king had been pilloried so mercilessly, protested as soon as he got word but, with King James out of town, no one seemed eager to move quickly. James, indeed, complained that his own Council altogether neglected to inform him of what was going on, and that only the Spanish protest alerted him. Sorting out all the details, at this late date, is nearly impossible. What is clear, however, is that all London rejoiced at this unparalleled opportunity to see Spanish perfidy unveiled. As the Spanish ambassador reported, "there was such merriment, hubbub and applause that even if I had been many leagues away it would not have been possible for me not to have taken notice of it."[42]

King James was understandably furious. He remembered well "there was a commaundment and restraint giuen against the representinge of anie modern Christian kings in those Stage-plays, and wonders much both at the boldnes nowe taken by that companie, and alsoe that it hath ben permitted to bee so acted."[43] No wonder. The Florentine ambassador wrote home that it was impossible thus to expose Gondomar's way of dealing "without depicting him as a man of influence . . . , and consequently without reflecting the weak judgment of those who had believed in him and had daily dealings with him."[44] The Venetian ambassador—no friend to Spain—also considered that the king's reputation was hurt much more deeply than Gondomar's. Such responses go far toward justifying James's personal distaste for having discussions of foreign policy brought into the open; they also present presumptive evidence that King James, at least, was not behind the production.

No commentator from that day to this has been able to resist the temptation to speculate on the identity of those responsible. Certainly one cannot help but agree with Sir John Holles's guess that "thes gamsters must have a good retrayte, else dared thei not to charge thus Princes actions, & ministers, nay their intents."[45] Whether the councillor involved was the consistently anti-Spanish earl of Pembroke, or Pembroke's former opponent and new ally, the duke of Buckingham, or both together, there can be little doubt that this production was backed by an anti-Spanish cabal within the government itself in order to stir up popular support for their policies. If it took three months to write the play and bring it onto the stage, then Middleton began it early in May 1624, when the Parliament was still in session, and while Prince Charles and the duke of Buckingham, the heroes of the hour, were still running into some difficulty in converting King James to their newfound anti-Spanish war policy. That same summer saw a liberalization of the royal policy that normally kept the more virulent anti-Catholic pamphlets off the bookstalls, or even out of the country. Indeed, one of the strongest such attacks, Thomas Scott's *Second Part of Vox Populi*, became a source for Middleton, a fact already noted in a contemporary letter. The connection between the bellicose pamphlets of Scott and his friends and Middleton's play has occasioned Thomas Cogswell to remark that "the King's Men very kindly acted out for them [the masses] all the main themes of these tracts."[46] All this suggests that the play was one component of a plan of propaganda, in which the cheering crowds played no small part.

The King's Men spent a great deal of money and energy in assembling the props and costumes, which included—according to a rumor picked up by the ever-vigilant John Chamberlain—a cast-off suit of Gondomar's clothes acquired for the purpose, and so it was no wonder that the theater was "followed with extraordinarie concourse, and frequented by all sorts of people old and younge, rich and poore, masters and servants, papists and puritans," nor was it a surprise that even ripe statesmen thronged the benches. Sir Henry Wotton was there, and Sir Albertus Morton, both former ambassadors, Sir Benjamin Rudyerd and Sir Thomas Lake, "and a world besides." The uniqueness of the occasion, the sheer spectacle, no doubt had much to do with it. But it is also true that this was a society accustomed to getting its news in small doses, and its analyses in smaller doses yet, and here was feast enough to surfeit on.

Even the fact that the news came in the form of drama did not put people off. This was a society accustomed to treating the theater and the world of politics as somehow interchangeable. Sir John Holles, who admitted he had not been in a playhouse for ten years, nevertheless saw the world around him in theatrical terms. While instructing his son in the arts of politics, Holles insisted "all is but a play, yet for us of these tyms more instruction is to be had at the starr-chamber, then at the globe." All the advantages the theorists had attributed to the stage were more true still of the political arena: "uppon this stage see what yow ar to avoyd, what to follow, and by others errors, learn to play your owne part better, when your turn cums: or by others harms grow so wys, as yow may still conserve your self a spectator, and a philosopher."[47] But young John Holles was in London only occasionally, and his father less often still, and what would replace those educational moments spent in that theatrical showplace called Star Chamber? An occasional letter from a friend might alleviate the tedium, but did little to give a self-rusticated politician any sense of what was going on—and for Holles, who had been active in his time, and whose son Denzel was later to be imprisoned for his part in preventing the Speaker of the House from rising to end the ill-fated 1629 session of Parliament, such ignorance was acutely frustrating. "The cuntry hath news as well as the citty," he wrote disgustedly, and "yeelds more tastfull conversation; for there is nothing so barreyn that affoards not a comment." Then turning to his correspondent, he added, "Your Lordship by this praeludium may guess, I have little more to say . . . : and it is trew, for where the court is, there shynes the sunn only, all we heer sitt in darknes."[48]

The means by which men like Holles kept informed had been the letter of news, sporadic, from a friend or relative who chanced to be in a position to acquire matter of interest—and I should like here to make a distinction between that traditional form, quintessentially private and occasional, and the "newsletter," which was both more public and more predictably regular. Examples of the first sort are not hard to find: a glance at, say, the late sixteenth-century Gawdy papers reveals letter after letter mingling news of friends and relatives, replies to requests for paper and pins, and tidbits of information about national (and even international) politics. At a time when accurate intelligence was scarce and valuable, any family member who happened to be in London on business was duty-bound to send what news he could home to Norfolk.[49] What the Gawdys did almost by reflex, Sir John Holles did more conscientiously and at greater length—twenty years on, the demand for news had increased. Nevertheless, Sir John kept his amateur standing. Other cases are not so clear-cut. Rowland Whyte, a minor gentleman with court contacts, kept the absent Sir Robert Sidney informed of the ever-changing political alignments of Queen Elizabeth's last decade; but Whyte was a Sidney retainer, and sending news served his purposes as well as those of his master. And the better-known John Chamberlain, who seems to have had a private income sufficient for his needs, made of news a lifetime avocation: keeping well-informed was both his delight and his passion, and he did so by trading information the way a modern hobbyist might trade postage stamps.[50]

Still, even as Chamberlain was keeping Dudley Carleton and others of his circle apprised of events in London, professional writers of newsletters began to appear. Peter Proby, in the 1590s, sent budgets of news to a number of noblemen temporarily absent from the court and the city.[51] By the 1620s, newsletter writing had become a profitable business.[52] John Pory, Edmund Rossingham, and their fellows offered "subscriptions" for the steep sum of £20 a year, and they did not lack for customers. At that price, they could afford to tailor their letters to the tastes of their subscribers; and they would, at need, send along appropriate newsbooks as well. Moreover, both Pory and Rossingham had sufficient social standing to allow them to get hold of "official" documents: their claims to be including news from letters recently received at court appear justified, and the fact that this sort of claim could be made regularly suggests that by the late 1620s or early 1630s the "newsletter business" had come to be accepted as commonplace.[53]

The activities of Rev. Joseph Mead at Cambridge during the 1620s illustrate how the system worked. Mead collected news on his own account, and to forward to his friend Sir Martin Stuteville, deeper in the country. The correspondence makes clear that Cambridge offered an active market for news: after the post had come from London, the recipients of newsletters rushed to each other's residences, compared notes, traded information (or, occasionally, whole letters) and—so far as I can determine—gossiped interminably. Printed corantos, that is, collections of snippets of recent news from abroad, also formed part of the exchange, and Mead regularly passed these on to Stuteville. So too did topical pamphlets. On one unusual occasion, when a friend passing through Cambridge showed Mead a particularly rare tract, he cut in it pieces and set three of his students to transcribe it in enough copies to satisfy all his curious correspondents. On another occasion, Mead informed Stuteville, "I saw a letter of December 19, from Sir Isaac Wake's secretary at Turin in Savoy, wherein is this passage...."[54] Mead himself was writing on 13 January: three and a half weeks was a remarkably short time for an official letter to go from Italy to London and then filter through to the provinces. More prosaically (but also of more importance), Mead and his friends received regular, detailed reports of doings in the 1626 Parliament—yet another indication that the secrecy enjoined on the members of Parliament was by this time more often breached than observed. Nor was the situation at Cambridge unique. The minor Cheshire gentry family of Moreton was also heavily involved, and had the advantage of a son with connections in the "diplomatic service." Yet even young Peter Moreton—despite knowing that his father used news to swagger in the neighborhood—had to confess that his father's other sources for parliamentary speeches were often more efficient than he could be. Nevertheless, aware that his letters were being shown around the county (and perhaps read aloud), Peter's style gradually changed until, by the early 1630s, it too resembled that of the professional newswriters.[55]

Two points emerge from all this. In the first place, despite the complaints of men like Holles that they were altogether cut off from news at the center of events, the networks for distributing news throughout the country were in place by the 1620s, if not before. That is a matter to which I shall return in a moment. In the second, it would appear that the various ways in which news might be packaged mattered relatively little. Mead and his friends depended on printed corantos and news pamphlets as much as they did on manuscript newsletters and handwritten copies of parliamentary speeches. At the production end, John Pory not only included printed materials with his newsletters but offered his subscribers copies of a variety of discourses, foreign and domestic, as well as parliamentary speeches, trial reports, and the like; and Pory made no bones about giving as his address the shop of Nicholas Bourne and Nathaniel Butter, publishers of the weekly corantos.[56]

Despite the complete absence of domestic news, the coranto's sudden irruption onto the English scene did nevertheless mark a substantial change.[57] The outbreak of the Thirty Years' War in 1618, the deposing of King James's son-in-law first as King of Bohemia, then as Elector-Palatine, was seen by many Englishmen as yet another shot in the long-running war between Catholic Spain and the Protestant states that should have been led by England. Foreign policy increasingly became a subject of national interest, to the extent that even newssheets in Dutch circulated in England—indeed the English ambassador, Sir Dudley Carleton, sent them to his friend, John Chamberlain.[58] Thus the Dutchmen who in 1620 first translated their own newssheets and then sent them across the Channel simply reacted to indications of the potential existence of a very lively market. There is evidence that an enterprising English printer then pirated the Anglo-Dutch newssheets. King James immediately sent to the Netherlands to have the export of corantos prohibited; the orders were issued, but the corantos continued to flow.[59] The first English corantor, Thomas Archer, was jailed, ostensibly for adding to his texts: I must assume, in the absence of surviving copies, that he intermingled English news with foreign. By the end of 1621, the government abandoned its efforts to suppress the trade, and permitted others to market translations from the Dutch. These, however, were now registered by the Stationers' Company after passing the censor—that is, they were subject to all the usual controls exercised by the Crown over materials printed in England, and so were preferable to unconstrained imports. Thereafter, for the next decade, corantos appeared with both increasing regularity and more sophisticated format.

At first glance it is hard to take the corantos seriously. Shaaber, for example, quotes from a 1622 newsbook that opens its report from Rome by stating baldly, "The King of *Spaine* hath bestowed vpon the Cardinall *Spinola* 30000 crownes, besides his yearely provision and revenue. And the Duke of *Braciano* is to receiue every yeare 6000 crownes in the kingdome of *Naples*. Hee hath likewise giuen charge to the Duke of *Saragola* to leauie a Regiment of foot, and to conduct them in *Veltolina*." Nor is the news from Venice or Vienna much fuller. But we should remember that the vast majority of Englishmen had never had access to detailed foreign news, and were accustomed to snippets of this sort as being the ordinary contents of family letters from London—when those were available. Moreover, we must remember that even the snippets were intended to be cumulative. The brief stories from various parts of Germany contained in a single issue might be combined to give a kaleidoscopic view of the conduct of the

Thirty Years' War; but in addition the reader was expected to keep the story in memory, and add to it week by week. At the center of the corantos was a quite consistent coverage of events in which Englishmen had suddenly developed a great interest. While few were enraptured by the fact that "To morrow is the Prince of *Lichtenstein* to receiue the Goulden Fleece," a great many might take seriously the news from Brabant, just across the Channel, that the Spanish general "Spinola makes him ready to muster his souldiors / and to march into the Fields," and the additional news that only Spinola had the money to pay his troops may well have generated some alarm.[60]

Nor is there any reason to doubt the accuracy of the reporting. I do not wish to argue that everything reported in a coranto was necessarily true, merely that the level of accuracy was no lower than might be found in any group of letters reporting news from abroad. Then as now, the reports were no better than their sources, admittedly variegated; yet we know the Dutch publishers of corantos established their networks with some care. The editors of the various English corantos, which were largely translated from the Dutch, thus had some cause to complain about their readers, who rushed into the shops "and aske every day for new Newes; not out of curiosity or wantonness, but pretending a necessity either to please themselves or satisfie their Customers," then turned and argued that the news was untrue. "I can assure you," the printer replied,

> there is not a line printed nor proposed to your view, but carries the credit of other Originalls, and justifies itself from honest and understanding authority; so that if they should faile there in true and exact discoveries, be not you too malignant against the Printer here, that is so far from any invention of his owne, that when he meets with improbability or absurdity, hee leaves it quite out rather than he will startle your patience, or draw you into suspition of the verity of the whole, because some one passage may be untrue.[61]

Moreover, during the years that the editor was Captain Gainsford, exsoldier and literary jack-of-all-trades, the news was even digested into organized sections, making the reader's task considerably easier.[62] Despite all this, the satirists continued their mockery. Richard Brathwaite insisted that the news gatherer acquired his stock in the fashion of his predecessors: "*Paules* is his Walke in Winter; *Moorfields* in Sommer. Where the whole discipline, designes, projects, and exploits of the *States, Netherlands,*

Poland... and all, are within the Compasse of one *Quadrangle walke* most judiciously and punctually discovered."[63] That would have been unkind even applied to so notorious a Paul's-walker as Chamberlain. But Brathwaite also tells us something of the customers, who rushed into the shops of a Monday morning, shouting "*Stationer have you any newes.* Which they no sooner purchase than peruse; and early by next morning (lest their Countrey friend should bee depriued of the benefit of so rich a prize) they freely vent the substance of it." And that appears to be a fair summary of the situation: the well-to-do complained about the corantos and laughed at their occasional inaccuracies, but read them all the same: as we have seen, John Pory had no compunctions about sending them to his customers, nor did Joseph Mead and his friends object to their weekly chore of reading and comparing their various sources of news. In the provinces, such bounty was a novelty still.[64]

Nor is Brathwaite's characterization of the country customers altogether wrong. They did pant for news, for relatively few had the resources to "subscribe" to corantos, or even to buy more than an occasional newsbook; newsletters were out of reach of all but the very wealthy. Walter Yonge, a barrister and justice of the peace in Devonshire, far from the center of events though with London contacts, whose diary begins just after the accession of James I and thus well before the news boom of the 1620s, had to labor mightily to get news and authenticate it.[65] The diary indeed is a wonderful source on the spread of rumor: "2 Dec. 1614. It is said that the King of France hath proclaimed himself supreme head of things ecclesiastical as well as in temporal things in France."[66] How or from whom Yonge heard this is unclear. But some while after writing the rumor in his diary, he returned to the entry and marked it "*False.*" In other cases, he marked as "true" entries that at first glance must have seemed improbable. One example is the news that Prince Charles and Buckingham had gone into Spain; but if that were true, then there was at least a likelihood that various prominent English lords *were* taking up commands in the Spanish army, or that the earl of Rutland had forbidden evening prayers or the singing of psalms on board the fleet he commanded. In the end, Yonge marked those last two tales "false," but the diary does give a vivid picture of the rumors swirling around the countryside in 1623.[67] Yonge is not only avid for news, but careful in accepting and recording it. The diary bears marks of retrospective editing: besides marking entries "true" or "false," Yonge also completed stories as he received more information. In addition, he does sometimes tell us what his source was: news of a House of Commons bill against pluralities came "as Mr. Drake's letter imported, which he received from Mr. Wm. Pole, which letter he read to me."[68] Sometimes the letters came to Yonge directly. As the diary entered the 1620s, the quantity of information (foreign and domestic) recorded in it rose markedly, a reflection, one supposes, of both interest and availability. By that date, though Yonge continued to write "false" beside an occasional entry, he ceased to note what his sources were, and one can only speculate whether they were print or manuscript.

John Rous's diary shows signs of the same care. A clergyman living in rural Suffolk, Rous had fewer opportunities to collect news than Yonge. Even royal proclamations were something out of the ordinary: Rous only saw them posted in neighboring villages larger than his own Downham. Rumor spread in Suffolk, too, and Rous noted stories he had heard confirmed or denied by friends who attended the Cambridge commencement. Printed material occasionally came to his hand: "Newes came in October of count Mansfeld, that he had given diverse overthrowes to the emperor's parte, and slaine the duke of Friedland in the field. Newes is newes. Many corantoes confirmed an overthrowe given to the duke of Friedland."[69] Buckingham's expedition to the Isle of Rhé fascinated Rous, and a visit to the nearest large city added to his stock of information: "October 29 [1628], I had a coranto at Norwich, wherein was a liste of the names of fifty-two shippes, Rochelers and English, that joyned with our navy at Plimmouth; where I was also tould, that a former coranto had a liste of the navy from Portsmouth."[70] After 1632, when the weekly corantos were suppressed, Rous somehow acquired the semiannual newsbooks that replaced them, and notes the dates of their appearance.

All this goes far to counter the argument that those living in the country had access to little news, and that often false. The news available was sporadic and unpredictable, but interest in news was intense, and many people made at least some effort to be well informed. Yonge and Rous checked whatever came to them as best they could. So too did William Calley, who noted the rumors circulating in Wiltshire and regularly sent them to a friend in London for confirmation. And the same is true as well of Lady Joan Barrington, the center of a large family circle all of whose members appear to have been under orders to send news home to Essex. As her correspondence makes clear, she too checked out the floating rumors, and her relatives had the latest corantos sent her: "Dear grandmother," wrote Joan St. John at the end of 1631, "here is litle nuss [news] stiring but what the booke relats which my husband sent you last week; as soun as any more coms out you shal have it."[71] Her son, Sir Thomas, shared her skepticism, passing on what he heard in London with appropriate doses of salt. And when he was home, Sir Thomas continued the family tradition of news gathering and distribution: his surviving book bills testify to his passion for works of religious controversy, piety, and news—some bought in multiple copies to pass on to his friends.[72]

By the 1630s news in its various printed and manuscript forms had become established as a customary part of life in London and even in the provinces. By comparison to the situation even fifteen years earlier, this was, I would argue, a major change. Jonson's *News from the New World Discovered in the Moon* of 1620, written to be performed within the confines of the court, came at the very beginning of the shift; by 1625, events had moved far enough for Jonson to take his case to so much of the wider public as was represented in the audience of the commercial theater. *The Staple of News* of 1625 comments trenchantly on changes already well under way. Jonson's main point here appears to be that news had become commodified, an object (much like an old, stinking fish) to be bought and sold after gaudy packaging.[73] The news itself had changed not a whit: it was, as it had always been, neither truthful nor relevant, "a weekly cheat to draw money."[74] We first hear of the staple of news from Tom Barber—and, appropriately enough, that traditional source of gossip becomes, for a time, a clerk in the news office. As for the staple itself, it is no more than an adaptation of the Merchant Adventurers' usual way of doing business in broadcloths. Master Cymbal, the projector, sends forth emissaries,

> Men employed outward, that are sent abroad
> To fetch in the commodity. From all regions
> Where the best news are made—Or vented forth—
> By way of exchange or trade.[75]

Then the results are brought to the news office,

> And there be examined, and then registered,
> And so be issued under the seal of the Office,
> As Staple News, no other news be current.[76]

The News Office seal authenticates the news just as the Adventurers' leaden seal guarantees the exported cloth; the seal is also the mark of monopoly power. Cymbal's news business will thrive because all others will have been made illegal. Monopoly, plus an infusion of cash, will permit Cymbal to extend his operation, to gain more country correspondents, gather more news; and the office staff will file it away, subdivide it, recombine it, seal it, and issue it to whoever is willing to pay—say, the old countrywoman who wants a tidbit as a gift for her vicar.

But it is rumor that constitutes the advertising, the loss leader bringing in the customers:

> 'Tis the house of fame, sir,
> Where both the curious and the negligent,
> The scrupulous and careless, wild and staid,
> The idle and laborious: all do meet
> To taste the *cornucopiae* of her rumours,
> Which she, the mother of sport, pleaseth to scatter
> Among the vulgar. Baits, sir, for the people!
> And they will bite like fishes.[77]

And flock they do, clamoring for news. Like the newsletter writers, Cymbal's company prepares news suited to the taste of each customer. Each gets what each can afford. And all are happy, except the four old women who play the chorus, Gossip Mirth, Gossip Tattle, Gossip Expectation, and Gossip Censure, who complain the news is "monstrous! Scurvy and stale! And too exotic; ill cooked, and ill dished!"—in other words, still too serious, and not enough like the ballad of the monstrous fish or the devil's visit.[78]

The news office Jonson mocked already hovered on the verge of existence; indeed, a generation later, the Restoration government sponsored one for its own purposes.[79] Still, this is mockery by association. The Staple of News is a manufactory of newsletters, a form of news only the rich could afford, but the customers Jonson describes come from an altogether lower segment of society. Like so many satirists, Jonson would inflict death by snob appeal: the constant clamor for ever more fresh news deplored by Brathwaite and his ilk is a trait of precisely those people who could not be trusted to analyze the news when once they found it. As so often, Jonson plays the role of the moralist. He has created

> this ridiculous Office of the Staple, wherein the age may see her own folly, or hunger and thirst after published pamphlets of news, set out every Saturday but made all at home, and no syllable of truth in them; than which there cannot be a greater disease in nature, or a fouler scorn put upon the times.[80]

Ultimately, it is the "disease in nature" that troubles Jonson most. In his ideal society—the society adumbrated in *News from the New World*—the ruler serves as guarantor of truth, in news as in much else. And it is the poet's role to act the part of royal advisor: truth—that is, the truth of the higher ideal rather than the low fact—is the poet's stock in trade. Jonson had made the point a quarter century before in *Poetaster* by concluding his play with a dignified Augustus, Virgil by his side, judging those lesser mortals immured in quotidian affairs. He continued to take the same view in his *Epistle Answering to One That Asked to Be Sealed of the Tribe of Ben*. Those who merely vent their libels, who spew out "their deal / Of news they get, to strew out the long meal," such are excluded from Jonson's ideal community.

> What is't to me whether the French design
> Be, or be not, to get the Valtelline?...
> Whether the dispensation yet be sent,
> Or that the match from Spain was ever meant?
> I wish all well, and pray high heaven conspire
> My prince's safety, and my king's desire,
> But if for honour, we must draw the sword,
> And force back that, which will not be restored,
> I have a body, yet, that spirit draws
> To live, or fall, a carcass in the cause.[81]

That was to keep control of news within the court, to limit the decision-making power to the king and his chosen councillors, and to allow the subject no role other than obedience—a position so conservative, even in 1625, as to leave Jonson looking rather like King Canute.

In the five years between Jonson's masque and his play, the government's own position changed. I do not know who made the decision, or even if it was consciously made. I suspect that the failure, first to suppress, then to control the early corantos may well have had a good deal to do with it. So too did the insistence of the House of Commons on discussing foreign relations, along with the Crown's capitulation on that point. By 1624, when Prince Charles and the duke of Buckingham were trying to drum up popular enthusiasm against Spain, the ban on discussing "causes of State, and secrets of Empire" made little sense, and efforts to reimpose it later proved futile. Instead, the "government" took pains to shape the news that was available, by censorship if necessary, by issuing its own version of events when possible. This was not, of course, a novelty. Still, the discerning might have detected some first signs of change when the King's Printer began his official account of the execution of Sir Walter Ralegh with the rather portentous statement:

> Although Kings be not bound to giue Account of their Actions to any but God alone; yet such are his Maiesties proceedings, as hee hath always been willing to bring them before Sunne and Moone, and carefull to satisfie all his good people with his Intentions and courses. . . . [82]

Proclamations could be used to the same purpose. Certainly by 1635, when William Davenant wrote his imitative *News from Plymouth,* his newsmonger-general, Sir Solemn Trifle, accepts with complete equanimity the notion that the state might manipulate news for its own purposes: "grant it [news] should be false, / It will give satisfaction to the State, / How the people stand affected."[83] The year 1635 was one of the half-dozen years when, in a desperate effort to stem the tide of bad news, Charles's government prohibited the weekly corantos. But by then, forbidding one form of news distribution was no longer sufficient to suppress the news. The newsletters continued to circulate. Rumor continued to blow his trumpet. And the commodification of news, without royal authorization, so much deplored by Jonson, became the order of the day.

Notes

1. *Stuart Royal Proclamations,* vol. 1 [James I], ed. James F. Larkin and Paul L. Hughes (Oxford: Clarendon Press, 1973), 495–96. For Bacon's role, see James Spedding, *The Letters and the Life of Francis Bacon,* 7 vols. (London: Longman, Green, Longman, and Roberts, 1861–74), 7:152–57.

2. *Stuart Royal Proclamations,* 1:519–21 [26 July 1621].

3. *The Letters of John Chamberlain,* ed. Norman Egbert McClure, 2 vols. (Philadelphia: American Philosophical Society, 1939), 2:396 [London, 4 August 1621].

4. Ibid., 2:411 [London, 24 Nov. 1621]. On parliamentary reaction, see Robert Zaller, *The Parliament of 1621* (Berkeley and Los Angeles: University of California Press, 1971), 28, 38, 40.

5. Arthur Wilson, *The History of Great Britain* (London: printed for Richard Lownds, 1653), 190.

6. Paul Sellin, "The Performances of Ben Jonson's *Newes from the New World Discover'd in the Moone,*" *English Studies* 61 (1980): 491–97.

7. Ben Jonson, *News from the New World Discovered in the Moon*, in *Ben Jonson: The Complete Masques*, ed. Stephen Orgel (New Haven and London: Yale University Press, 1969), 293.

8. Jonson, *News*, 293.

9. Ibid., 294.

10. *The Winter's Tale*, 4.4.2082.

11. Jonson, *News*, 303.

12. On this see Thomas Cogswell, "England and the Spanish Match," in *Conflict in Early Stuart England*, ed. Richard Cust and Ann Hughes (London and New York: Longman, 1989), 107–33; Cogswell, *The Blessed Revolution* (Cambridge: Cambridge University Press, 1989), 20–35; and Richard Cust, "News and Politics in Early Seventeenth-Century England," *Past and Present* 112 (1986): 60–90.

13. I have placed these matters in a broader context in "How Information Spread among the Gentry, 1550–1640," *Journal of British Studies* 21 (1982): 11–34.

14. *A Transcript of the Register of the Company of Stationers of London*, ed. Edward Arber, 5 vols. (London and Birmingham, 1875–1894), 5:lxxvi.

15. *Calendar of State Papers and Manuscripts... Existing in... Venice*, ed. Horatio Brown, vol. 10 [1603–1607] (London: Her Majesty's Stationery Office, 1900), 240, 245; Anna Maria Crinò, *Fatti e Figure del Seicento Anglo-Toscano* (Florence: L. Olschki, 1957), 41–48.

16. See John Stubbs, *Gaping Gulf*, ed. Lloyd E. Berry (Charlottesville: University Press of Virginia, 1968), xxxiii ff.

17. John Platt, "Eirenical Anglicans at the Synod of Dort," in *Reform and Reformation: England and the Continent c. 1500-c. 1750*, ed. Derek Baker (Oxford: Basil Blackwell for Ecclesiastical History Society, 1979), 223.

18. Richard Dutton, *Mastering the Revels* (Iowa City: University of Iowa Press, 1991), 186.

19. Sharon L. Jansen, *Political Protest and Prophecy under Henry VIII* (Woodbridge: Boydell Press, 1991), 20–61.

20. *Diary of Walter Yonge, Esq.*, ed. George Roberts, Camden Society, o. s., 41 (London, 1848), 5; Edmund Lodge, ed., *Illustrations of British History*, 3 vols. (London: G. Nichol, 1791), 3:305–6 [The Earl of Kent to the Earl of Shrewsbury, Wrest, 23 March 1606]; John Stow, *Annales* (London: Thomas Adams, 1615), 881–82; Wilson, *History of Great Britain*, 32.

21. Historical Manuscripts Commission, *Report on the MSS. of the Lord De L'Isle & Dudley*, ed. C. L. Kingsford, vol. 2 [Sidney Papers] (London: His Majesty's Stationery Office, 1934), 397 [Rowland Whyte to Sir Robert Sydney, 30 Sept. 1599].

22. John Donne, *The Satires, Epigrams and Verse Letters*, ed. W. Milgate (Oxford: Clarendon Press, 1967), 18.

23. Ben Jonson, *The Complete Poems*, ed. George Parfitt (New Haven and London: Yale University Press, 1975), 65.

24. *Letters of John Holles 1587–1637*, 3 vols., ed. P. R. Seddon, Thoroton Society, Record Series, vols. 31, 35, 36 (Nottingham: Derry and Sons, 1975–86), 2:175–76 [18 July 1617].

25. *Diary of John Rous*, ed. M. A. E. Green, Camden Society, o. s., 66 (London, 1856), 12.

26. *Tudor Royal Proclamations,* ed. Paul L. Hughes and James F. Larkin, 3 vols. (New Haven: Yale University Press, 1964–69), 2:278–79.

27. J. R. Tanner, *Tudor Constitutional Documents* (1922; rpt., Cambridge: Cambridge University Press, 1951), 94.

28. John Fletcher and Philip Massinger, *Sir John Van Olden Barnavelt,* ed. T. H. Trevor-Hill, Malone Society Reprints, 1979 (London: Malone Society, 1980), 2.

29. *Letters of John Chamberlain,* 2:236 [Chamberlain to Carleton, London, 8 May 1619].

30. T. H. Howard-Hill, "Buc and the Censorship of *Sir John Van Olden Barnavelt* in 1619," *Review of English Studies,* n. s., 39 (1988): 39–63, esp. 42.

31. Frederick Shriver, "Orthodoxy and Diplomacy: James I and the Vorstius Affair," *English Historical Review* 85 (1970): 449–74, and more generally, C. Grayson, "James I and the Religious Crisis in the United Provinces 1613–19," in Baker, ed., *Reform and Reformation,* 195–219.

32. *Letters of John Chamberlain,* 2:239 [Chamberlain to Carleton, London, 31 May 1619].

33. Janet Clare, *"Art Made Tongue-Tied by Authority"* (Manchester: Manchester University Press, 1990), 153.

34. Edmund Sawyer, ed., *Memorials of Affairs of State* [Winwood Papers], 3 vols. (London: W. B. for T. Ward, 1725), 2:425 [Ralph Winwood to Mr. Secretary Cecil. Paris, 7 July 1602, o.s.].

35. See Christopher Marlowe, *Dido Queen of Carthage* and *The Massacre at Paris,* ed. H. J. Oliver, The Revels Plays (Cambridge, Mass.: Harvard University Press, 1968), xlix ff., for the stage history. Oliver mentions Henry's conversion and its possible effects on an English theater audience on lxiii.

36. Dutton, *Mastering the Revels,* 183; see also A. R. Braunmuller, ed., *A Seventeenth-Century Letter-Book* (Newark: University of Delaware Press, 1983), 435–37.

37. T. H. Howard-Hill, "Crane's 'Promptbook' of *Barnavelt* and Theatrical Processes," *Modern Philology* 86 (1988–89): 146–70.

38. Dutton, *Mastering the Revels,* 207, 217.

39. That would be the "revisionist" position: for a summary and criticism, see Richard Cust and Ann Hughes, "Introduction: after Revisionism," in *Conflict in Early Stuart England,* 1–46.

40. Jerzy Limon, *Dangerous Matter: English Drama and Politics in 1623/24* (Cambridge: Cambridge University Press, 1986); T. H. Howard-Hill, "Political Interpretations of Middleton's *A Game at Chesse* (1624)," *Yearbook of English Studies* 21 (1991): 274–85; Thomas Cogswell, "Thomas Middleton and the Court, 1624: *A Game at Chess* in Context," *Huntington Library Quarterly* 47 (1984): 273–88; T. H. Howard-Hill, "The Unique Eye-Witness Report of Middleton's *A Game at Chess,*" *Review of English Studies* 42 (1991): 168–78; A. R. Braunmuller, "'To the Globe I Rowed': John Holles Sees *A Game at Chess,*" *English Literary Renaissance* 20 (1990): 340–56; and T. H. Howard-Hill's Revels edition of the play (Manchester and New York: Manchester University Press, 1993).

41. *Letters of John Holles,* 2:289 [John Holles to the Earl of Somerset, 11 August 1624].

42. Sara Jayne Steen, ed., *Ambrosia in an Earthern Vessel: Three Centuries of Audience and Reader Response to the Works of Thomas Middleton* (New York: AMS Press, 1993), 40.
43. Ibid., 44.
44. Ibid., 45.
45. Ibid., 43.
46. Cogswell, *Blessed Revolution*, 302.
47. *Letters of John Holles*, 2:222 [John Holles to his son, John Holles, 26 Jan. 1619].
48. *Letters of John Holles*, 2:297 [John Holles to Lord Wallingford, 6 February 1625].
49. *Letters of Philip Gawdy*, ed. I. H. Jeayes, Roxburghe Club (London, 1906); British Library [hereafter BL], Egerton MS 2713.
50. On Chamberlain, see Wallace Notestein, *Four Worthies* (New Haven: Yale University Press, 1957), 29–119.
51. Lawrence Stone, *The Crisis of the Aristocracy 1558–1641* (Oxford: Clarendon Press, 1965), 388.
52. Cust, "News and Politics in Early Seventeenth-Century England"; see also Harold Love, *Scribal Publication in Seventeenth-Century England* (Oxford: Clarendon Press, 1993), 9–22.
53. On Pory, see William S. Powell, *John Pory* (Chapel Hill: University of North Carolina Press, 1977); a few of Rossingham's newsletters appear in *Documents Relating to the Proceedings against William Prynne in 1634 and 1637*, ed. Samuel Rawson Gardiner, Camden Society, n. s., 18 (Westminster, 1877), 70–95; others are calendared in John Bruce et al., eds., *Calendar of State Papers, Domestic Series, of the Reign of Charles I*, 20 vols. (London: Longman, Brown, Green, Longmans & Roberts, 1858–97), vols. 11–16 (1637–1640).
54. Thomas Birch, ed., *The Court and Times of Charles the First*, 2 vols. (London: H. Colburn, 1848), 2:50. Mead's correspondence is included in these volumes and in Thomas Birch, ed., *The Court and Times of James the First*, 2 vols. (London: H. Colburn, 1848). This paragraph draws on both sets.
55. BL Add. MS 33935, fol. 52v, fol. 308, fol. 317.
56. Powell, *John Pory*, 56.
57. There is a substantial literature on early English newspapers; unfortunately, more attention has been paid to the considerable bibliographical problems involved than to the actual contents. See Folke Dahl, "Amsterdam—Cradle of English Newspapers," *The Library*, 5th ser., 4 (1949): 166–78; Folke Dahl, *A Bibliography of English Corantos and Periodical Newsbooks 1620–1642* (London: Bibliographical Society, 1952); Joseph Frank, *The Beginnings of the English Newspaper* (Cambridge, Mass.: Harvard University Press, 1961); Michael Frearson, "The Distribution and Readership of London Corantos in the 1620s," in *Serials and Their Readers 1620–1914*, ed. Robin Myers and Michael Harris (New Castle, Del.: Oak Knoll Press, 1993), 1–25; Laurence Hanson, "English Newsbooks, 1620–1641," *The Library*, 4th ser., 18 (1938): 355–84; Stanley Morison, "The Origins of the Newspaper," in *Selected Essays*, ed. David McKitterick, 2 vols. (Cambridge: Cambridge Uni-

versity Press, 1980), 2:325–57; Leona Rostenberg, "Nathaniel Butter and Nicholas Bourne, First 'Masters of the Staple,'" *The Library*, 5th ser., 12 (1957): 23–33; Matthias A. Shaaber, "The History of the First English Newspaper," *Studies in Philology* 29 (1932): 551–87.

58. *Dudley Carleton to John Chamberlain 1603–1624*, ed. Maurice Lee Jr. (New Brunswick: Rutgers University Press, 1972), e.g., 246, 261, 275, 278, 282, 286, 291.

59. F. S. Siebert, *Freedom of the Press in England 1476–1776* (Urbana: University of Illinois Press, 1965), 150.

60. Shaaber, "History of the First English Newspaper," 551–87, esp. 572; *Courant Newes out of Italy, Germany, Bohemia, Poland, &c.* (Amsterdam: George Veseler, 1621), verso [Dahl, #11].

61. Stanley Morison, *The English Newspaper* (Cambridge: Cambridge University Press, 1932), 9–11.

62. Mark Eccles, "Thomas Gainsford, 'Captain Pamphlet,'" *Huntington Library Quarterly* 45 (1982): 259–70; see also Joseph Frank, *Beginnings of the English Newspaper*, 9–11, and S. L. Adams, "Captain Thomas Gainsford, the 'Vox Spiritus' and the *Vox Populi*," *Bulletin of the Institute of Historical Research* 49 (1976): 141–44.

63. Richard Brathwaite, *Whimzies: Or, A New Cast of Characters* (London: Felix Kingston for Ambrose Rithirdon, 1631), 17.

64. Frearson, "Distribution and Readership of London Corantos," argues that readership was widespread throughout the country.

65. On Rous's and Yonge's diaries, see Cust, "News and Politics," 79–87.

66. Walter Yonge's diary, 24.

67. Ibid., 67.

68. Ibid., 20.

69. John Rous's diary, 7.

70. Ibid., 31.

71. *Barrington Family Letters 1628–1632*, ed. Arthur Searle, Camden 4th Series, 28 (London: Royal Historical Society, 1983), 222.

72. Mary Elizabeth Bohannon, "A London Bookseller's Bill: 1635–1639," *The Library*, 4th ser., 18 (1938): 417–46.

73. My reading of the play owes most to the work of Donald McKenzie: "'The Staple of News' and the Late Plays," in *A Celebration of Ben Jonson*, ed. William Blissett, Julian Patrick and R. W. van Fossen (Toronto: University of Toronto Press, 1973), 83–128, and *The London Book Trade in the Later Seventeenth Century*, Sandars Lectures, 1976 (Typescript deposited in the British Library), especially Lecture 1, "Poetry, Politics and Press." Also useful are Richard Levin, "*The Staple of News*, the Society of Jeerers, and Canters' College," *Philological Quarterly*, 44 (1965): 445–53, and Mark Z. Muggli, "Ben Jonson and the Business of News," *Studies in English Literature* 32 (1992): 323–40.

74. Ben Jonson, *The Staple of News*, ed. Anthony Parr, The Revels Plays (Manchester: Manchester University Press, 1988), 152.

75. *The Staple of News*, ed. Anthony Parr, 80.

76. Ibid., 79.

77. Ibid., 165–66.

78. Ibid., 187.

79. James Sutherland, *The Restoration Newspaper and Its Development* (Cambridge: Cambridge University Press, 1986), 6–8.

80. *The Staple of News,* ed. Anthony Parr, 152–3.

81. Jonson, *Complete Poems,* ed. Parfitt, 192.

82. Quoted in Sandra Clark, *The Elizabethan Pamphleteers* (London: Athlone Press, 1983), 86.

83. *The Dramatic Works of Sir William D'Avenant,* ed. James Maidment and W. H. Logan, 5 vols. (Edinburgh: William Paterson; London: Sotheran & Co., 1872–74), 4: 171

CHAPTER ELEVEN

Shamelessness in Arden: Early Modern Theater and the Obsolescence of Popular Theatricality

Michael D. Bristol

Rosalind, Celia, and Touchstone, liminary exiles from the fratricidal violence of Duke Frederick's court, have reached the goal of their perilous journey. "Well, this is the Forest of Arden."[1] Rosalind declares that the characters have arrived at their destination after a long journey. Her words call for an ostensive gesture, showing the audience an imaginary woodland on the bare stage of the playhouse. The primary intonation then has the force of simple observation, along the lines of "Here we are! I've heard about this place and now I can see it for myself" or, more simply, "So this is what the Forest of Arden is like." But this "showing" is something more than the barren miming of nonexistent trees. Rosalind's words are also a performative gesture that have the strong sense of *fiat sylvius,* or, let this bare stage be the Forest of Arden.[2] The primary intonation depends on a secondary intonation with the stronger force of a declaration, inviting members of the audience to agree to the stipulation that they are now "in" a forest, or at least situated in such a way that they can watch what is happening "there." To the extent that the audience gets what's going on then, Rosalind's utterance establishes a consensual agreement binding within the delimited space of the theater for the duration of a performance of *As You Like It.* Her speech demonstrates the authority of theater to act in social space.[3]

It has long been recognized that the characteristic forms of popular festivity and folk ritual find a permanent home in the urban theaters of early modern London.[4] Indeed, as Robert Weimann has so conclusively demonstrated, the new public theaters of Elizabethan London derive their very considerable vitality from a rich tradition of misrule and "impertinency" in early modern plebeian culture.[5] The institution of theater exhibits a complex dialectic of "bi-fold" social authority between an official order and diverse forms of popular resistance.[6] More concretely, the dramatic works composed for the early modern playhouse were administered by two competing jurisdictions: the Revels Office, which supervised the actual performances, and the Stationers' Company, which licensed the printing of plays.[7] This state of affairs corresponds to an additional dialectical tension between the authority of the public stage and the authority of the printed book. Although the guild cycles of medieval drama were based on written scripts, most of the traditional forms of mummery, skimmington, and other popular festive forms only made their way into written records when somebody got into trouble with the law. Works such as *As You Like It*, by contrast, were performed by professional actors whose most basic qualification was their ability to read scripts written by professional writers. Early modern public theaters are institutions created within a rapidly expanding culture of the printed book that fundamentally transformed the aims of social authority as well as the mechanisms of social discipline and control.

Because they emerge in a society characterized by rapidly expanding literacy and the widespread availability of cheap printed books, the new theaters take on a new and fundamentally different social character that separates them from the familiar immediacy of the old popular forms. Theaters like the Globe and the Curtain were elements in a larger technological infrastructure devised for the rapid circulation of cultural goods and services. The enjoyment of a performance was now made available for purchase to a diverse audience of anonymous consumers; it no longer required any of the time-consuming effort that had been necessary for putting on the traditional shows and popular festive observances. Theater had become a commodity, in the sense of something available for purchase.[8] But it was also a commodity in Albert Borgmann's sense of "the device paradigm" in making rich cultural experiences accessible and "commodious" for any consumer who could afford the price of admission.[9] Of course the commodious and disburdening effect of technical innovation comes at the cost of diminished social identification with friends and neighbors. But this "existential loss" may in fact be the very aspect of the professional theater that best accounts for its long term success.

As You Like It is a very interesting work to consider in this context, since it quite openly asserts the theater's right to exist as an institution that derives its legitimacy not from the *longue durée* of the traditional community, but from the regime of commodity exchange. Rosalind's evocation of the Forest of Arden foregrounds the displacement of social immediacy in the theater to the virtual space of theatrical make-believe. But part of the joke here is in the characters' resistance to any reactionary nostalgia for the "lost" face-to-face immediacy of the traditional community. *As You Like It* is addressed to the differentiated social and demographic space created by the circulation of printed books.[10] Plays are "performed books" that transcend the parochial interests of the traditional community, in part because playwrights and their audiences have become accustomed to the complex discursive ambiguities made possible by printing.[11] At the same time, *As You Like It* opens up possibilities for a new way of being-together-in-the world that no longer depends on ancestral technologies of shame and intimidation that characterized the forms of popular festivity.

The volumes in the *Records of Early English Drama* provide a wealth of research material on the relationship between early modern popular culture and the commercial theaters that were emerging in London toward the end of the sixteenth century. The recent publication of the records from Somerset, focusing as they do on court proceedings and other evidence of social conflict, make it possible to carry out detailed analysis of popular cultural forms as a medium for social and political action.[12] This essay looks at a number of examples of improvised social dramas that exploded out of the popular tradition in various towns and villages in Somerset in the early years of the seventeenth century. Each of these events emerges out of well-established local customs like Christmas mummery and skimmington. Each of these events also has political valences, though these are often difficult to sort out from the expression of personal animosity and private grievance. The episodes reported from Somerset have a conservative or "time-binding" character.[13] In each case the transgressive performance event staged in a local community is an attempt to defend customary license or privilege or to reassert traditional standards of social conduct.

Ass's Ears

In the town of Bathampton, sometime during the twelve days of Christmas in 1602 or very early in the New Year of 1603, a disturbing incident took place at the home of a certain Thomas Powle or Poale (the spelling varies) when he was visited by a company of holiday mummers. Exactly what happened to upset Thomas Powle and his wife is unclear, but it certainly must have caused a bit of a stir in the neighborhood because it led to the taking of depositions in the Bishops' Court on 10, 11, and 12 January in 1603. The story begins with testimony about the stealing of cob loaves from houses in and around Bathampton.

> *Deposition of Eleanor Crouche, aged 25*
>
> Ther was a man arrayed in a sarplar, whearwith he being disguised did goe about to diuerse houses of the neighbourhoode at Bathampton, to steale Cobb loves, according as hath byn don in ancyent tymes and this examinate did see a man in such a disguised habit at the house of ffather ffissher in Bathampton , [and] but this examinate doth not certanlye knowe the man so disguised . . .
>
> the partye disguised as aforesaide was termed by the name of Iames, but whether it weare Iohn Skryne the younger this Respondent knoweth not, nor what was meant by naming the disguised person Iames.[14]

The theft of cob loaves was not, in all likelihood, what led the neighbors involved before the episcopal court. Eleanor Crouche, one of the deponents, describes stealing cob loaves as a custom sanctioned by antiquity and carried out according to local tradition in the neighborhood of Bathampton. Stokes notes additional references to similar customs and suggests that stealing cob loaves was a kind of game connected with Christmas hospitality and celebration (2:879). The "theft" of small loaves of bread prepared specifically in anticipation of the mummers' visit would have been a playful variation on the traditional forms of Christmas hospitality and gift exchange. The cob loaves are clearly intended as a kind of symbolic gift or sharing between householders and their guests. The pretended theft or appropriation might express a sense of entitlement on the part of the mummers as well as an admonition to the host that surplus wealth should be distributed to those in need. A more urgent question here for the parties involved lay not in the taking of cob loaves but in determining just who the man disguised in a "sarplar" really was and why, if it was really John Skryne, he had adopted the name of James in this mummery.

John, a.k.a. James, evidently had his head covered, perhaps with a winnowing sheet arranged in the form of a cowl, but self-concealment would have been a socially acceptable element in the "ancient" custom of mummery. The wearing of a priest's surplice may have been a more serious offense, but the thief, whoever he was, evidently did not offend Father Fisher when he appeared in this disguise at the priest's home. The real offense was of a rather different kind. When the "man in a sarplar" appeared at the home of Thomas Powle he had apparently added something new and ominous to his masquerade.

Deposition of Elizabeth Skryne, aged 20

this deponent well knoweth that there was a man [clad &] arayed in a Surplar that went about the parishe of Bathampton articulate, [to] in the twelff dayes last to steale Cobloves, and saieth that man went amongest other houses to Thomas Powles house and there he was, & the companie with him quietlye lett in, and stoale a Cob loaf there the wiffe of the saide Poale beinge well pleased therat & verie merrie and saieth that the saide man did behaue him self at that house as at other houses, and that the saide man had [of the sarplar] the form of a paire of asses eares, made uppon his head in the saide Sarplar & no otherwise as she believeth. And saieth that she believeth it was [Iohn Skryne] a brother of hers that played that part Et aliter nescit. (1:29)

A third element has been added to the stealing of cob loaves and the wearing of a priest's surplice. The offender, whoever he was, has added "a paire of asses eares" to his mummer's outfit.

Ass's ears are a widely known and traditional symbol of foolishness. King Midas acquired ass's ears as a consequence of his senseless and uncontrolled greed. The floppy appendages on a fool's cap are a pretty good, though rough, approximation of ass's ears, and indeed this is how Folly describes her own headgear at the beginning of her oration.[15] But the ass has additional symbolic valences in the context of Christmas holiday observances. Mary arrives in Bethlehem riding on an ass. The ass is present at the Nativity, and appears again carrying Jesus to safety on the flight into Egypt. And of course Jesus is traditionally depicted riding an ass as he enters Jerusalem on Palm Sunday. As the "bearer" of the burden that is Jesus, the ass figures as a symbol of humility and patient endurance. In the closing passages of *The Praise of Folly*, Erasmus celebrates the asinine foolishness of Christian faith.[16] The feast of the ass is a traditional variant of the feast of fools occasionally celebrated by junior clergy as a boisterous and grotesque parody of traditional Christmas liturgy.[17] This is a traditional carnivalesque uncrowning of hierarchy and established authority prompted by the scriptural text in which it is prophesied that "He shall bring down the mighty from their seats."

The "man in a sarplar" certainly had a general warrant to play the fool at Christmastime. His irreverent disguise and transgressive behavior would have been recognized as the expression of festive conviviality and the affirmation of holiday exhilaration. The celebration of Christmas as a Feast of Fools captures aspects of meaning that are simply not available either in the canonical liturgy or in other secular forms of observance. So there was nothing particularly remarkable or out of the ordinary about the disguised man's performance, at least not until the mummers paid their visit to the Powle household. Two points in particular were at issue in the ecclesiastical hearings. First, who was the man in the ass's ears? Second, did he or did he not commit some kind of social or even criminal offense in the home of Thomas Powle? One thing that ought to be kept in mind here is that Christmas mummers may be intent on "keeping mum" about their identity. The importance of an opaque or impenetrable disguise is connected with what is now known as "deniability," because mummery may be something more than a jolly Christmas pastime or neighborly conviviality. In this case the mummers may have had a score to settle with Thomas Powle.

According to Elizabeth Skryne, who appears to have been a witness to whatever happened at the Powles', the man in the ass's ears did nothing different from what he had done in other houses in the neighborhood. The company was let in quietly and Mrs. Powle at least seemed to enjoy the merriment that transpired. But Elizabeth may have been trying to protect her younger brother John from accusations of wrongdoing. More ambiguous and troubling testimony comes from Agnes Jeffries.

Deposition of Agnes Jefferie, aged 25

There was a man arayed upp in a Surplice and that uppon his head there weare two thinges, which weare called Asses eares, and that he was called by the name of mr. Iames, And that this man went from house to house this Christmas last, in Bathampton to steale Cob loaues. And yat amongest other houses he went to Thomas Powles house, & that there he did thrust his head at Thomas Powles wiffe as if he had hornes to bush her, But whooe that man was she knoweth not, but as she hath hard, it was young Iohn Skryne. (1:30)

The specific provocation that seems to have upset Thomas Powle and his wife was not the stealing of cob loaves, not the wearing of a sarplar, not even perhaps the ass's ears, at least not all by themselves. What really got things going was the head-butting gesture of the ass's ears in the direction of Mrs. Powle. This gesture suddenly transforms irreverent but essentially harmless ass's ears into something more like horns, specifically cuckold's horns. And this would then explain "what was meant by naming the disguised person James." James would have been James Charnberne or Chamberne, whose wife, Sarah, was suspected of having an adulterous affair with Thomas Powle. According to James Stokes, horns had been hung over the Chamberne home (2:880). John Skryne's head-butting impersonation of the cuckolded husband would have been an unmistakable threat of retaliation against Thomas Powle on behalf of James. And the aggressive form of the gesture might even have suggested the possibility that Charnberne intended to rape Mrs. Powle.

John Skryne kept mum. In a deposition taken on 12 January, he admits to being the man in the sarplar but denies that anything offensive occurred during the mummers' visit to the Powles' home.

> *Deposition of John Skryne the younger, aged 17*
>
> this respondent is the man that was arayed in a Sarplar or winno sheete as is in thease Interrogatories specified, & had two things upon his heade, formed as it weare two [ye] eares And sayeth that he went soe arayed to most houses in the parishe of Bathampton in that strange attyre to steale Cobloves And saieth that he & the companie with him went unto the saide Poles house, & theare this Respondent did as he did in other houses, and did not use himself in anye sorte otherwise then he had donne in such other houses, and as well the saide Powle as his wiffe seemed to be in noe sorte displeased therwith a pretty while, until Iames Charnberne came in And saieth that this Iurat in the saide disguised habit was called by another name vzt. Iames. (1:30)

Skryne freely acknowledges the sarplar, the ass's ears, the stealing of cob loaves, as well as adopting the name of James "in the saide disguised habitt." He did pay a visit to the Powles, but by way of extenuation he points out that he and his company performed their mummery in most of the houses in Bathampton. What displeased the Powles, according to John Skryne's own sworn testimony, was not any menacing gesture or threatening impersonation on his part, but the appearance of James Charnberne *in propria persona*.

It seems reasonable to infer that some sort of animosity already existed between neighbor Powle and neighbor Charnberne, and that this animosity was exacerbated on the occasion of a Christmas mummery. But one can scarcely guess from the fragmentary testimony preserved in these depositions whether James Charnberne deliberately planned to get even with Thomas Powle, or what role, if any, John Skryne actually played in the conflict between his neighbors. Like any juicy bit of neighborhood gossip, the incident arouses all kinds of salacious interest. Did Thomas Powle really have an affair with Sarah Charnberne? And if not, then why did someone put horns on top of the Charnberne house? Did John Skryne take an active role in threatening Thomas Powle, or was he just unwittingly caught up in the dispute as he claimed? A more sober historian would like to know more about the relative wealth and status of the men involved. Was this just a relatively straightforward and banal instance of sexual rivalry or were there also issues of class difference involved? What is clear is that Mr. and Mrs. Powle decided to seek redress for the disruption of their domestic tranquility in civil court.

The incident at Bathampton is evidence of a shared habit of active engagement in the day-to-day political and social life of the local community. Christmas mummery is a complex technique for the affirmation of shared values of conviviality and the just allocation of limited social goods.[18] It is also a way to enforce a collective social discipline through the practice of mutual surveillance. This disciplinary function does not take the form of an ideology imposed on "subjects" by a dominant culture that has its social being somewhere outside the community.[19] The people who took part in the events at Bathampton were not clearly separated into specialized producers of ideology [performers] and passive consumers [spectators]; mummery is an "ancient custom" based on well-understood forms of interactive participation. Mummery is also a form of coercive intimidation, designed to admonish or humiliate community members who deviate from the familiar norms of everyday life. But these are not the standardized procedural norms typical of contemporary liberal society. They are simply customary ways of doing things, a shared background of being together in the world in which persons are deeply and unreflectively embedded.[20] But, as the Christmas mummery at Bathampton suggests, the idea of an "organic" community in the sense of a harmonious and supportive *Gemeinschaft* is very misleading. The incident is prompted as much by vindictive animosity between neighbors as it is by any notion of shared social values. In this particular case the strains and tensions of social life break out of the relatively placid flow of social time into the mise-en-scène of eventful history. The performance that took place at the home of Thomas Powle initiates a three-part movement from the customary forms of folk ritual to improvised social drama and finally to a judicial restaging of events before a local magistrate. A similar shift in the staging of popular theatricality is evident in many of the episodes documented in the Somerset records.

A Dogg in a Coate of Blacke

In the village of East Brent in 1620, the local curate Thomas Hill was summoned by the consistory court in Wells Cathedral to testify against Richard Dodd for christening a dog. Bishop Arthur Lake heard the case, which was followed by additional hearings at the Ilchester Quarter Sessions in the spring of 1621. These "parallel proceedings" suggest that profanation of the sacraments was viewed as an extremely serious matter by both secular and ecclesiastical authority (2:901). Hill's testimony describes Richard Dodd as the ringleader of a group of hard-drinking ruffians who refused to go to church. Dodd and his friends apparently spent a lot of time hanging out at the Red Lyon, carousing and playing at fives. The incident with the dog, which took place on Saturday, 20 May, was apparently provoked by an earlier dispute on the previous Wednesday. Hill testifies that while he was at breakfast at the Red Lyon, William Thomas, one of Dodd's drinking companions, took some leather thongs out of his pocket and whipped the curate about the legs. When Hill demanded to know why Thomas attacked him, he was told, "I will use all priestes so yat will come unto oure company and will not pay . . . (1:107).

It's not clear exactly why William Thomas and Richard Dodd had it in for Curate Hill. They may have had a bad opinion of priests generally. Alternatively, they may have felt a particular resentment against Hill for bringing a gloomy, Malvolio-like demeanor into the tavern and refusing to join in its spirit of conviviality. The strait-laced Hill certainly disapproved of the Red Lyon crowd, and his appearance at breakfast on this particular Wednesday might well have been interpreted by Dodd and his friends as priestly meddling. But William Thomas's comments about "priestes . . . who will not pay" brings out another aspect of this affair. The incident at the Red Lyon is a territorial dispute between the social regimes of "church" and "tavern." Dodd's gang is incensed over the arrogance of Curate Hill, who has invaded their space and breached its standards of social behavior. In effect the troublemakers at the Red Lyon are asserting the traditional privilege of the tavern as a social space exempt from priestly surveillance. A priest who refuses to pay shows contempt for customary forms of social authority that mandate the public house as a space of recreation, conviviality and the sharing of resources. The whipping of Curate Hill is a form of social protest against a radically innovative and intrusive standard of social discipline.

The attack on Thomas Hill's person was certainly an aggressive challenge to his authority, though it might have been nothing more than the expression of hostility to an officious priest who thinks that because he is virtuous there shall be no more cakes and ale. But Dodd and his friends were clearly not satisfied with the warning they had given Hill, and a few days later they staged a much bolder act of defiance that took the matter well beyond the clash of individual personalities.

> ... on satturday morninge the xxth of May nowe laste paste or thereabouts the aboue named Richard dodde, Emanuel Crosseman, William dinghurste and Iohn dinghurste of Eastbrente aforesaid (as this examinate hath heard comonlie & generalie reported amonge the honest & substantial parishioners theare) being in companie togethears with other persons in the said Inn called the redd lyon, they hade a dogge with them unto whome they gaue twoe cannes of ale or beere and that after the said dogge had Drunke the said drinke, they putt a tabacco pype in the dogges mowth, and that hee helde the pype faste in his mowthe and tha the said Iohn dinghurste being hyred by the said Richard dodde, do make a blacke coate of stuffe with a hoale over his heade for the sayde dogg, and putt it uppon him, with a girdle about the midle, & turned him loose about the streate and called him by the name of cutt glasyer, saying yat they would make a younge priest of him. And that the said Emanuel Crosseman toulde this respondent that they weare like to have sent for the prieste to christen the said dogg.... (2:106–7)

Well, it's one thing to get into a rumble with the local priest because he disapproves of your drinking habits. It's another matter altogether to take on the entire institution of the priesthood, and by extension the Church of England itself. Despite the obvious risks, however, Dodd went out of his way to make a mockery of ecclesiastical authority, bespeaking a priest's coat to be fitted for a dog with John Dinghurst, the local tailor.

There is no evidence that John Dinghurst was present when Thomas Hill was attacked on Wednesday, 16 May. However, he was certainly present on Saturday night when the hapless dog, ludicrously got up like a priest, was made drunk and possibly "christened" by the Red Lyon crowd.

Examination of John Dinghurst, tailor

> He confesseth that about midnight the time abouesaid Richard Dodd abouesaid and Emanuell Crosman came to this examinate he dwelling next house to the red lyon and called him upp to make a cote for a dogg, and promised him 5 s. for to doe it whereof he payed but 6d.
>
> He told him it should be made like mr Hills cote and the colour should be black or nothing. After the cote was made and sowed about the dogg, they carried this examinate with them to the taverne, and wher they found satt down to drink at the table, on which they putt the dogg, and putt cannes of beare about him, and made the dogg drunk, Dodd holding open his mouth and pouring in the drink, and they sayed that they would change his name from Cutte-glasier to Cutte-Hill and therypon powring some of the drinke before them yppon the dogg head made the signe of the crosse ouer him: and saied that Robert Glasier and Emanuell Crosseman should be his godfathers. but he denythed that he vsed any other wordes when he powed the drink on the dogg, but Cutte-Hill.
>
> He further sayth that Dodd did threaten him if euer he did confesse anything, saying it should be the worse for him with other great wordes. (1:109)

It's apparent that Dinghurst wants to put the best possible face on his own involvement in this elaborate farce when he implies that he was "carryed" to the tavern by Dodd and Crosseman. At the same time he admits that he followed Dodd's very specific instructions to make a coat like Mr. Hill's, so he can hardly claim to be an innocent bystander. Maybe if Dodd hadn't stiffed him for the price of the dog's coat, Dinghurst would have been less willing to turn in his friends. Dodd and Crosseman were eventually fined and sent to jail for this prank. The fate of the dog is unrecorded.

The staging of a mock baptism by Richard Dodd and Emanuel Crosseman was clearly an act of open and premeditated defiance of religious authority. Since the priesthood was also in effect an administrative cadre for the Jacobean monarchy, Dodd and Crosseman were also guilty of sedition or even *lèse majesté* as well as blasphemy in their doggy travesty of priestly dignity. In a somewhat similar case of dog christening recorded from Crewkerne, the local bell-ringers got drunk one night and dunked a dog in the baptismal font. Since there was no evidence of deliberate premeditation, the case was not pursued (2:901). The Red Lyon gang might well have been drunk when William Thomas whipped Curate Hill, but the impersonation of a priest by a dog was clearly planned when Dodd and Crosseman were cold sober. The elaborate dog baptism staged at East Brent is clearly something more than a drunken impulse that one immediately regrets in the cold light of the morning after. The incident of 20 May was pretty obviously an act of social protest. What remains opaque here, however, is the exact nature of the protestors' motives.

Emanuel Crosseman had been in trouble with the ecclesiastical authorities long before Richard Dodd conceived his plan to convert a stray dog into a priest. In 1612 he was cited in the consistory of Wells Cathedral for open defiance of the episcopal court itself.

> Officium domini contra Emanuelem Crosseman
>
> ffor that uppon the sonday nexte after the Annunciacion of the virgin marie last past, hee togeather with Edward wates of Sowthbrent & Iohn Hooper of East Brent aforresaid being in the howse of dinghows widowe of the said parishe of Eastbrent, deriding, & skoffing att ecclesiastical aucthoritie, and especially against the consistorie coort of the lord bishopp of Bathe and Welles, kept (as they called it) a coort, and called one Iohn Boyce (then and theare present), bastard and would have had one Thomas Matue of Limpsham to have borne an office among them, but hee refused to bee partaker of theire follye. And the nexte morning they did the like, and called one by the name of doctor Iames, annother mr Methwin, annother mr Huishe and annother mr Maicock, and annother Chipper. (1:105)

"Dr. Iames" was Francis James, L.L.D., the vicar general; Mr. Huishe was the notary public and registrar at Wells Cathedral; Chipper was the summoner. Emanuel Crosseman obviously had some kind of grievance against the church administration in Somerset, but it's not clear what, if any, larger principles were involved in this earlier protest. He certainly did not agree with the way the ecclesiastical courts were being run. And he might well have taken issue with the program of administrative and liturgical reforms instituted under James I. But episodes like the mock court and the dog baptism might also represent a more parochial and diffuse tradition of carnivalesque uncrowning of pompous and self-important government officials. Whatever the motives of the Red Lyon gang may have been, however, the court records show that an active defense of local customs and of popular institutions like the tavern now carried significant penalties as the authority of the administrative state extended the scope of its discipline into small communities like East Brent.

The dog baptism performed by Richard Dodd and Emanuel Crosseman seems to have been organized in the framework of a larger, explicitly political agenda, unlike the mummery at Bathampton, which was apparently about a personal grudge between two men. What was at stake in the mock sacrament at East Brent was not the regulation of domestic conduct but rather the allocation of institutional authority. Dodd and Crosseman didn't want to go to church, they wanted to hang out at the Red Lyon, and they didn't see why Curate Hill should make it his business to interfere. This was unquestionably a political position, and a pretty bold one at that in a society where the official church was an extension of the coercive apparatus of state power. At the same time, however, the East Brent episode has much in common with the Bathampton mummery. For one thing, those in the Red Lyon gang were clearly interested in getting even with someone they didn't like. The politics of dog baptism are very difficult to separate here from the strictly personal hostility Dodd and his friends felt toward Curate Hill. Additionally, the technique of farcical mockery obviously depends on the efficacy of shame and derision as an instrument of social regulation. Thomas Hill was not indifferent to this kind of sanction. But he had access to a more powerful and efficient system of social regulation.

A Mopp Made Like a Man

In 1637 Oliver Chiver, a parson in Brislington, filed a complaint with Archbishop Laud against Samuel Moggs, along with several other officials of the local congregation. According to Chiver, his churchwardens were guilty of "wilfull contemptes" of their duties and were openly defiant of his authority. Chiver's grievances are listed in a bill of particulars annexed to his petition. Among the many specific contempts noted here is an item claiming that Moggs, along with one Cowling, "inhibited the young people their lawfull sport after evening prayer ... and ... sett the musitians by the heeles" (1:61). This "inhibiting" took place on Whitsunday, when music and dance were permitted after the evening service. But Chiver complains that Moggs himself permitted "unlawfull gaming & tipling almost euery Sunday." In his notes for this incident, James Stokes suggests that the offenses recorded in Chiver's bill of complaints were part of a simmering conflict between subordinate church officials with Puritan leanings and a parson loyal to the High Church ideas of Archbishop Laud. The preliminary disposition of the case is recorded in a note in Laud's own hand, directing Sir John Lamb and Dr. Duck to "giue me an Accompt what is fittest to be done for the Iustice of the Cause and the Peticioners reliefe."

Samuel Moggs may have had Puritan sympathies, but he does not seem to have been a model of puritanical virtue. He may in fact have been something of a neighborhood bully and a general troublemaker in the parish of Brislington, just as Chiver suggested. Like Richard Dodd in East Brent, Moggs turned his dispute with the local curate into a public spectacle. In "proceeding of the court held in the consistory before Thomas Wesly, MA, and William Hunt, clerics, surrogate judges, in the presence of James Huishe, notary public," Moggs is accused of organizing a skimmington that eventually concluded in a violent "uprore."[21]

> Contra Samuelem Mogg.
>
> Denunciatur domino Iudic ... that vppon Saint [Mathias] last 1636 hee procured one to ride Skimmington in theire parish, att the time of divine service both forenoone, & after noon, by meanes wherof manie of that parish, & other neighbour parishes weare absent from church, and hyred one of Bristoll to beate a drumbe att that time. (1:62)

Moggs was accused basically of disturbing the peace, but he might have been responsible for a more serious offense. A marginal note records that "Att this vprore there was a child killed by throwing a stone" (1:62).

It's clear that just as in the mummery at Bathampton, the judicial proceedings in Brislington issued from a conventional popular festive observance that simply got out of hand. And again, as at Bathampton, the events were provoked by a deviation from conventional standards of domestic and sexual order. This is evident in a specific indictment recorded against Reginald Moggs.

> Contra Reginaldum famulum dicti Mogg
>
> Pro eodem delicto, & for being attyred in womans apparell did ride behinde a Mopp made like a man, & beateing him with a basting ladle. (1:62)

This text, though brief, is nevertheless wonderfully evocative of the form as well as the spirit of skimmington or charivari. On a Sunday afternoon, when people were supposed to be in church, the Moggses organized a noisy procession clearly intended for the public humiliation of a local married couple. The central figures were a domineering wife, impersonated here by Reginald Moggs, and a submissive husband, represented by a mop. The symbolic elements, notably female impersonation, the comical misuse of kitchen utensils, and the display of an "apron fastned to a long staffe" and displayed as the "ensinge" of the proceedings all unmistakably express resentment and fear of insubordinate women.[22] But the mockery was not directed exclusively against the cross-dressed "wife" and her basting ladle. An equally important target of the abusive mimicry was the mop "made like a man," significantly referred to in the text as "him" rather than "it."

A skimmington ride was often performed to chastise and humiliate community members whose marital behavior was irregular, especially men who were "beaten" by their wives. An incident of this kind is recorded at Cameley in 1616. John Hall, a blacksmith, had a falling out with his wife, Mary, and her mother, Joan Sage. Evidently Mary "would not sett a Henn a broode ... and thereupon she stroke him uppon the back with a frying pann." The injury prevented Hall from meeting an engagement with "one Mr. William Hobbes of the same parish" (1:69).

> Wherevpon afterwardes the same being knowne abroad in the parishe some men there upon a worken day usually used for makeing merry as theire Revill day there to mak some sport, had one to Ryde upon mens shoulders by the name of Skymerton without any hurt don or misdemeanors otherwise at all. (1:69)

The Cameley incident appears to have been mostly unplanned. It does reflect a kind of community "surveillance" of marital behavior, if only because the "ryde upon mens shoulders by the name of Skymerton" occurred in a context of local gossip and scandal over the beating of John Hall by his wife. But the brief court records suggest that the ride was arranged on the spur of the moment, mostly for the enjoyment of the participants. James Maggs and the other riders must have intended to ridicule and abuse Hall for his failure to control his wife's aggression, but they did not take the trouble either to stage anything much by way of a spectacle or to make provision for an audience. If the events at Cameley were intended as the admonition of a weak husband and the correction of a disobedient wife, they had little apparent effect. Mary Hall was not intimidated; after a subsequent quarrel, she threatened to cripple her husband "if she were able." The whole affair seems too hastily improvised to be taken seriously as an instance of popular justice and the policing of domestic behavior. Whatever they may have intended to accomplish by their "sport," the skimmington riders were bound over to answer for their disorderly conduct by the justice of the peace. Regulation of social behavior and the enforcement of community standards were staged by official justice at the Quarter Sessions in September of 1616.

A skimmington was usually more elaborate and theatrically colorful than the improvised horseplay at Cameley. The point, after all, was to make a public spectacle of someone whose conduct was offensive to his or her neighbors. The working men at Cameley clearly had a specific target in mind for their "skymerton ride," but there's no indication they intended to put on much of a show. Samuel Moggs, by contrast, had arranged a proper full-dress skimmington, complete with mops, basting ladles, a long staff with an apron for an ensign, a man (or boy) in female dress, and perhaps a horse or donkey for the boy to ride. He also went to considerable expense to hire a professional drummer, and one from Bristol at that. Was this skimmington organized to chastise someone's wife for actually beating her husband, or was the farcical assault on the mop with the basting ladle intended to represent a more general pattern of female disobedience? Unlike the spontaneous ride at Cameley, the uproar at Brislington does not identify a specific target for its ritual abuse. The "mopp made like a man" seems more a generic figure of cringing and flabby ineptitude than any specific hen-pecked husband.

Samuel Moggs was something of a troublemaker in Brislington. It may be that the thrashing of the mop was not an ordinary skimmington organized to shame a particularly feckless member of the parish. The elaborate preparations suggest that the events at Brislington were some kind of more generalized social protest, perhaps connected with Moggs's open contempt and defiance of Parson Chiver in the previous year. The "mopp made like a man" might have represented Chiver, who certainly had a disobedient congregation if not a disobedient wife, or even Archbishop Laud himself. And this would account for the presence of spectators from "neighbor parishes," who would not be likely to be on hand for something like the improvised horseplay at Cameley. It would also help to explain why such a vivid and derisory spectacle might provoke an even more violent uproar and lead to the inadvertent killing of one of the children in the crowd.

The disturbance at Brislington seems to be a manifestation of intractable conflict over church governance, liturgy, and the control of the local culture (1:477) rather than a specific admonition directed toward one of the local families. Moggs and his associates adopted the vocabulary of skimmington to heap shame and abuse on their local opponents. This metaphorical displacement of topsy-turvy gender relations into the more public domain of religious controversy does not, of course, weaken or diminish the misogynist tenor of the skimmington. The thrashing of the "mopp made like a man" only makes sense against a social background in which opposing partisan factions share a common opinion that the spectacle of a man physically dominated by a woman is shameful. Even so, although the incident at Brislington clearly depends on a popular festive vocabulary derived from a patriarchal social order, the skimmington is only incidentally about gender and sexuality. The specific matter in dispute here concerns a rather narrow matter of church governance.

In his bill of complaint to Archbishop Laud, Chiver argues that the churchwardens in the parish at Brislington had been sworn, under oath, to administer certain articles related to a new program of episcopal visitations. Specifically the churchwardens were required to report any and all offenses against the new regulations.

> oath was administred & charge given unto all Churchwardens and Sidemen to present all faults and crymes without partiality and according to the booke of Articles then delivered unto them. And to that end the Churchwardens and sidemen of Brislington in the County of Sommerset had at least 6. weekes if not two months respite given them to bring in their presentments. yet notwithstanding one Henry Dicke, Samuell Moggs the new intrusive Churchwardens Bartholomew Sheward, Anthony Sanders the true Churchwardens, Nicholas Cowling and Tobias Pope Sidemen or Assistants unto them, did contrary to their oath make many frivolous and false presentments against your poore peticioner & voluntarily neglected to present the notorious Crimes herunto annexed. (1:60)

Among other things, the local churchwardens had refused to show their accounts to Chiver, suggesting that he was but a "hireling" who had no business with church administration other than to read prayers. Here the political cast of the popular resistance is unmistakable. The local community defended its authority by staging a farcical and derisory uncrowning of a newly centralized church administration. The efficacy of this protest was, however, limited by the technical resources available to Moggs and the parochial organization of authority he alleged to represent. As in the previous episodes discussed here, the protestors were here more preoccupied with embarrassing Parson Chiver than they were with the tedious work of political and ideological mobilization. The sanctions of shame and derision are certainly powerful, but only at the scale of a small community wherein politics is practiced in direct, face-to-face interactions. These sanctions are ineffective as social distance is increased.

Virtual Space and Performative Gesture in *As You Like It*

Shakespeare's *As You Like It* has ass's ears, horns, mock sacraments, and cross-dressing. Orlando is not exactly a mop dressed like a man, though he is moppish at times. Documents of the kind James Stokes has collected from Somerset can all be used to gloss the text of this play. The records of the early English drama show how gender is constructed, and by what means the subordination of women was maintained. They also help to identify important features of the social and ethical lifeworld in which people organized their daily lives. And these documents are also helpful in showing how the conventions of dramatic performance were understood. But despite the many formal and thematic continuities with the tradition of popular theatricality, a play like *As You Like It* can only exist in an institutional setting radically different from the typical mise-en-scène of plebeian culture. Christmas mummery, the stealing of cob loaves, skimmington, dog baptisms are ephemeral events that happen in actual locations: Thomas Powle's home, the church grounds at Brislington, the Red Lyon Inn. A Shakespeare play is, by contrast, a stable form that doesn't really "happen" anywhere at all, except in the virtual space known as "the" theater.

Arden is an ambiguous place. Geographically it is the Ardennes Forest, in France, which is where the story of the play is set. But it is also the less remote and more familiar Arden Forest, near Stratford, Shakespeare's hometown. More important, Arden is the literary space of pastoral. One thing Shakespeare does with pastoral in this play is to satirize the genre by taking its conventions literally. Instead of idealized literary shepherds who spend a lot of their time composing poetry, this play presents country bumpkins and tries to show how absurd it is to imagine them doing the things that are done in the literary pastoral. But there are, as always in Shakespeare, more complicated things going on. In a way the pastoral is a kind of forerunner of the contemporary genre of science fiction.[23] Pastoral and science fiction are literary thought-experiments that represent the underlying structure of existing social relations and also project alternative social possibilities. In *As You Like It*, the audience is taken to the world of

Robin Hood, where people live at the level of basic subsistence and where goods are held in common.

Shakespeare's depiction of the forest pastoral allows for an affirmation as well as a satire on the traditional myth of a golden age or state of nature characterized by primitive communism. The absence of social pretension, hierarchy, and invidious distinction creates favorable conditions for true self-knowledge.

> *Duke Senior.* . . . Are not these woods
> More free from peril than the envious court?
> Here feel we not the penalty of Adam;
> The seasons difference, as the icy fang
> And churlish chiding of the winter's wind,
> Which, when it bites and blows upon my body
> Even till I shrink with cold, I smile and say
> "This is no flattery: these are counsellors
> That feelingly persuade me what I am."
> (2.1.3–11)

Arden is a privative or minimalist Utopia. For the Duke it is not a place of exile but a place of refuge from the fratricidal violence of the court. In the Forest of Arden minimal conditions necessary for an ordered social life can be met. People can thrive and cooperate in Arden because the "chiding" of the winter's wind forces a recognition of what it is to be an embodied human self. And this is what makes it possible then to recognize and to care for other human selves. The false and deceptive civilization of the court fails to guarantee the minimum conditions of trust and security necessary for any kind of truly social existence.

The *démarche* from the murderous reality of the court to the social harmonies of Arden can only happen in the imaginary space of the literary pastoral. Duke Senior's commitment to a stoic philosophy represents something more like wishful thinking rather than a reliable description of the forest as a social environment. Touchstone has a more sober and disenchanted view: "Ay, now am I in Arden, the more fool I. When I was at home I was in a better place; but travellers must be content" (2.4.14–16). Touchstone's lines are most often read as an invidious comparison between the austerities of country life and the amenities of the court. But his comment can also be an expression of the actor's preference for the warm comforts of his own home over the chilly atmosphere of a London theater. It is clear what the dramatic character wants to imply: his home at Duke Frederick's court was a lot nicer than anything the impoverished pastoral simplicity of Arden has to offer. This is a court jester's knowing satire of the sentimental foolishness of the literary idyll. And part of the wit here is that even a fool can see that he's better off as a servant in a great household than he would be "enjoying" the independence or the natural immediacy of country living.

Touchstone's speech also plays as a direct reply to Rosalind's performative gesture establishing the virtual space of the playhouse: "Well, this is the Forest of Arden." But if the point of her speech is to situate everyone in the Forest of Arden, why does Touchstone immediately nullify this stipulation and say that when he was at home he was in a better place? The secondary intonation of these lines declares that the actor's home is a better place for him to be than in the theater where he is performing *As You Like It:* Whatever this place is, I would be better off at home. If the play was being performed in a public playhouse like the Globe, the lines might well be a reference to the physical exposure of players and their audience to the discomforts of the weather. At home at least I could have a warm fire and a roof over my head, but here we're all exposed to the elements. Interestingly, *As You Like It* can be performed as a bad-weather play, with the characters in Arden stoically enduring the rigors of winter. But Touchstone's dismissive assessment of the felicities of Arden has additional significance as a way to reinforce rather than to contradict Rosalind's self-conscious gesture toward the reality of theatrical space.

In the interior space of a private theater, bad weather would not be an immediate problem for the actor or his audience. Here the irony of Touchstone's lines is perhaps more self-deprecating, suggesting that the performer is not really at home in a space reserved for a privileged and courtly audience. But his resigned acceptance of travel and his wistful preference for being at home also speaks powerfully to the instability and pathos of the actor's condition: vulnerability to the ingratitude of an audience and exposure to its hostile judgment. This pathos is made dramatically explicit in *A Midsummer Night's Dream* and *Love's Labor's Lost*, where the lower-class performers are subjected to ridicule and contempt by their aristocratic audience. And many other plays of the period are supplied with prologues or epilogues that seek to appease the audience or to ward off their displeasure. On this account then, "when I was at home I was in a better place" identifies the theater as a place of shame and abjection. And perhaps this is the real meaning of the "bad weather" in *As You Like It;* when Touchstone wishes he were at home, he is not so much afraid of the wind and the rain as he is of the risk of a chilly reception by the members of his audience.

There is, finally, an additional sense to Touchstone's lines that resonates with deep and persistent currents of suspicion and fear of the theater itself. When I was at home I was in a better place because the theater is a shameful place for anyone to be in. The public playhouses of London were in a bad part of town, as Steven Mullaney has shown.[24] Touchstone's gesture picks out the petty thieves and prostitutes working the crowd, if indeed such low-life types were present at theatrical performances as has often been alleged. But the shamefulness of the theater is not just an incidental feature of its location or its unsavory clientele. There is a veiled and ironic reference here to beliefs about the fundamental wickedness of theater itself, captured in the theological valences of "being in a better place." Touchstone's ironic response to finding himself in the virtual mise-en-scène of Arden echoes Mephistopheles' "Why this is Hell, nor am I out of it."

Arden is a virtual space that exists in the actual space of the playhouse. Duke Senior and his entourage are not local parishioners performing a story of Robin Hood and his merry men; they are professional actors in the urban setting of the commercial theater. Yet Duke Senior's description of a "wide and universal theater" in act 2 refers to the commonplace medieval and renaissance figure of *theatrum mundi,* theater of the world: "This wide and universal theater / Presents more woeful pageants than the scene / Wherein we play in" (2.7.137–39). The temporal lives of the audience are no more real than scenes from a play, especially when considered from the perspective of eternity. Awareness of the "theatricality of everyday life" calls into question the truth and permanence of social identity. But the "wide and universal theater" is also just the immediate environment of early modern London, and the Duke's lines have a rather more concrete sense: There are eight million stories in the Naked City.

The metaphorical links between the imaginary space of the forest pastoral and the contingent reality of the London neighborhoods from which the audience is watching is given specific expression in Jaques' speech about the wounded deer. Interestingly, we never see Jaques actually utter these words. Another character reports his words to the Duke as an instance of Jaques' interminable moralizing. At the same time the actor playing the minor role of First Lord has an opportunity to mimic his own colleagues' performance in the larger role of Jaques.

[*First Lord.*] "Poor Deer," quoth he,
"thou mak'st a testament

As worldings do, giving thy sum of more
To that which had too much." Then being there alone,
Left and abandoned of his velvet friend,
"'Tis right," quoth he, "thus misery doth part
The flux of company." Anon a careless herd
Full of the pasture jumps along by him
And never stays to greet him. "Ay," quoth Jaques,
"Sweep on, you fat and greasy citizens,
'Tis just the fashion: wherefore do you look
Upon that poor and broken bankrupt there?"
(2.1.47–57)

Jaques' foolish moralizing, if that's what this is, is a fable about ideas of social obligation. Are we called upon to help those who have suffered some kind of personal catastrophe? How and in what way are we responsible for each other? This is nonsensical if it is literally applied to the behavior of animals in the forest. But it has undeniable cogency as a reflection on the social attitudes of the actual citizens of early modern London who were present at the early public performances of *As You Like It*. Jaques' parable of the deer points to the callous indifference of the complacent and self-interested city dweller—the bourgeois—to human suffering. The regime of the commercial bourgeoisie, in this view, is characterized by competitiveness, alienation, and the disintegration of the traditional community.

Jaques' wounded deer is one of the "woeful pageants" in the Duke's "wide and universal theater." The importance of this metaphor lies in its ability to link the virtual space of Arden with the accelerated exchange of commodities in the urban economy of early modern London. The "fat and greasy citizens" move too fast to help the "poor and broken bankrupt." Jean-Christophe Agnew, in *Worlds Apart*, describes the early modern development of rationalized commodity exchange as a "placeless market" in which "artificial persons" can interact.[25] In this view, the panic expressed in the antitheatrical literature masks a deeper and more diffuse anxiety about the market. Traditional forms of social identity, status, and position dissolve into a universal mummery. But it's not just the collapse of valued forms of identity that makes people worry about the deceptive "theatricality" of market relations. In the placeless market, the traditional forms of reciprocity and mutual concern give way to the calculation of strategic advantage and the fervent pursuit of imaginary desires.[26] The market is literally "shameless," just like the theater, but this is not just because the customary rules and boundaries of class or gender are transgressed. The sanction of shame depends on immediacy, proximity, and familiarity in the social life of a small community. Shame comes from being seen by people who know who you are.[27] The wide and universal theater of urban London creates conditions of anonymity and social distance in which the feeling of shame no longer matters all that much.

When Touchstone says that when he was at home he was in a better place he might well mean that a real home in a traditional community is a better place than the virtual space of theater or the placeless market. But despite his skepticism about Arden, Touchstone soon discovers, in his wooing of Audrey, that there are interesting possibilities in the shameless regime of theatrical space. Since he is among strangers, he can pursue his desire for Audrey without worrying about what the neighbors will think. More specifically, he doesn't have to worry about the possibility of cuckold's horns even if Audrey ends up in some other man's bed.

> *Touchstone.* . . . A man may, if he were of a fearful heart, stagger in this attempt; for here we have no temple but the wood, no assembly but horn-beasts. But what though? Courage! As horns are odious, they are necessary. It is said, "Many a man knows no end of his goods." Right! Many a man has good horns and knows no end of them. Well, that is the dowry of his wife; 'tis none of his own getting. Horns! Even so, poor men alone. No, no; the noblest deer hath them as huge as the rascal. Is the single man therefore blessed? No; as a walled town is more worthier than a village, so is the forehead of a married man more honorable than the bare brow of a bachelor; and by how much defense is better than no skill, by so much is a horn more precious than to want. (3.3.48–63)

This is obviously Touchstone's ironic acceptance of the risks of marriage as an institution. But it is even more interesting in its interpellation of the men gathered in the early modern audience as an "assembly of horn-beasts." No one can tell whose wife is unfaithful in the group of strangers and passing acquaintances gathered "here" in Arden. The risk of horns is a destiny common to the noblest deer and the rascal. Arden, wherever it is, makes possible a public and mutual acknowledgment of this shared fate free from the derisory rituals of abjection. Social distance and disengagement make it possible to accept the sluttishness of human sexuality with genuine courage. Touchstone's discourse on horns suggests a fundamental reversal of the nostalgic sense that home is a better place. Arden is the rustic, parochial, archaic world of the traditional community. All things considered, it's better to be at home in the anonymity of the city.

Rosalind's shamelessness equals or exceeds Touchstone's. To begin with, Rosalind is a young woman who not only wears a man's clothing but also adopts a man's demeanor and social role. Her insouciant mannishness is exactly what provokes some of the strongest antitheatrical vituperation. But the entity known as Rosalind only comes into being in the early modern theater through the ambiguous practice of "boying" of a woman's identity.[28] The real scandal enacted by Rosalind goes beyond these forms of surface transgression. As Susanne Wofford points out, Rosalind claims a right to utter performative speech. Rosalind is the uncanny voice of the theater itself, confounding dramatic performance with performative utterance and gesture.[29] When J. L. Austin formulated his theory of performative utterance, the last thing he had in mind was the sort of meretricious fakery that goes on in theaters. For Austin the performative is a special type of speech act endowed with the power to cause real effects when uttered within a particular social ontology.[30] Performative does not have the sense of pretending to do something, as when an actor performs a role, but rather the sense of just doing something, as when a priest performs a ritual or a military officer performs his duty. The performative is not a self-conscious and self-ironic performance intended to disclose the socially constructed and purely relative character of someone's gender or social status. Instead, performative speech acts are those that reflect the executive capacity of language.[31]

Performatives are magic words, but the magic of the words depends on the social conditions of their utterance. The words themselves have no effect unless they are pronounced by the right person, which usually means someone who occupies a particular office. Touchstone will not be properly married to Audrey if Sir Oliver Martext performs the ceremony.

> *Jaques.* And will you, being a man of your breeding, be married under a bush like a beggar? Get you to church, and have a good priest tell you what marriage is. This fellow will but join you together as they join wainscot; then one of you will prove a shrunk panel, and like green timber warp, warp. (3.3.83–89)

A real priest is needed to perform a real marriage. This is not because priests have some kind of mysterious, arbitrary, and ultimately unjustified power, but rather because a priest is someone who can "tell you what marriage is." The point here is that the words of the marriage ceremony are not what really matter. The social effects of the performative issue not only from a clear articulation of social norms but also, and more crucially, from the prior acceptance of those norms by the members of the society. The social effect of performatives depends on who executes them. But it's not enough just to occupy a particular office; performatives imply conditions of reciprocity and consent. Even a priest or justice of the peace cannot just go around pronouncing people man and wife.

The traditional marriage ceremony generally invokes the presence of "God and these witnesses." Even more important, before the priest can pronounce the couple man and wife, they must first declare publicly their mutual and reciprocal consent to being joined in matrimony.

> *Orlando.* Pray thee marry us.
> *Celia.* I cannot say the words.
> *Rosalind.* You must begin, "Will you Orlando—"
> *Celia.* Go to. Will you Orlando, have to wife this Rosalind?
> *Orlando.* I will.
> *Rosalind.* Ay, but when?
> *Orlando.* Why now, as fast as she can marry us.
> *Rosalind.* Why then you must say, "I take thee Rosalind, for wife."
> *Orlando.* I take thee, Rosalind, for wife.
> *Rosalind.* I might ask thee for commission; but I do take thee, Orlando, for my husband. There's a girl goes before the priest, and certainly a woman's thought runs before her actions.
> (4.1.127–41)

Thematically, *As You Like It* experiments with a social world where the idea of mutual consent is really taken seriously. At the end of the play, an archaic fratricidal order has simply withered away, to be replaced by radically new forms of social desire. Rosalind's utterance of the performative in this scene asserts the values of autonomy and self-determination over and against the tradition of patriarchal authority. In the meantime Orlando has agreed to marry someone who is both a man and a woman. But there's no reason to worry about how we can tell the boys from the girls in the new agential space of the early modern theaters. Rosalind, whoever or whatever she is, represents the new social reality of the market, where desire is a polymorphous commodity requiring only mutual consent between parties to the exchange of sexual goods.

As You Like It captures a sense of the larger possibilities of the early modern professional theater. When the boy actor who plays at being Rosalind steps out to pronounce the epilogue, he articulates the new social conditions the theater helps bring into being.

> I charge you, O women, for the love you bear to men, to like as much of this play as please you. And I charge you, O men, for the love you bear to women—as I perceive by your simpering that none of you hates them—that between you and the women the play may please. If I were a woman I would kiss as many of you as had beards that pleased me, complexions that like me, and breaths that I defied not. And I am sure, as many as have good beards, or good faces, or sweet breath, will for my kind offer, when I make curtsy, bid me farewell. (epilogue, 12–23)

Here theatricality decisively rejects the social functions of shame, intimidation, and derisory spectacle in favor of mutual forbearance and urbane tolerance. Day-to-day political concerns may be expressed here, but they are in an important sense bracketed in ways not available in the ancestral popular forms, or in the judicial stagings where popular expression is made to answer for its disturbances of social peace and its derangement of civility. Because it is a freestanding institution based on a consensual undertaking between players and their audiences, the early modern theater represents a new kind of social interaction based on disengagement, social distance, and the acknowledgment of difference.

Notes

1. All references to *As You Like It* are from *The Riverside Shakespeare*, ed. G. Blakemore Evans (Boston: Houghton Mifflin Co., 1974). Additional citations are given in the text.

2. Susanne L. Wofford, "'To You I Give Myself, For I Am Yours': Erotic Performance and Theatrical Performatives in *As You Like It*," in *Shakespeare Reread*, ed. Russ McDonald (Ithaca: Cornell University Press, 1994).

3. Louis Montrose, "'The Place of a Brother' in *As You Like It:* Social Process and Comic Form," *Shakespeare Quarterly* 32 (1981): 28–54.

4. S. L. Bethell, *Shakespeare and the Popular Dramatic Tradition* (London: P. S. King and Staples, 1944); Michael Bristol, *Carnival and Theater: Plebeian Culture and the Structure of Authority in Renaissance England* (London: Methuen, 1986); E. K. Chambers, *The English Folk Play* (Oxford: Clarendon Press, 1933); Michael Hattaway, *Elizabethan Popular Theatre* (London: Routledge and Kegan Paul, 1982); François Laroque, *Shakespeare's Festive World: Elizabethan Seasonal Entertainment and the Professional Stage*, trans. Janet Lloyd (Cambridge: Cambridge University Press, 1991).

5. Robert Weimann, *Shakespeare and the Popular Tradition in the Theater* (Baltimore: Johns Hopkins University Press, 1981).

6. Robert Weimann, "Bifold Authority in Shakespeare's Theatre," *Shakespeare Quarterly* 43 (1991): 401–17. On the various aspects of popular resistance see, for example, Mario DiGangi, *The Homoerotics of Early Modern Drama* (Cambridge: Cambridge University Press, 1997); Jean E. Howard, *The Stage and Social Struggle in Early Modern England* (London: Routledge, 1994); Louis Montrose, *The Purpose of Playing: Shakespeare and the Cultural Politics of the Elizabethan Theatre* (Chicago: University of Chicago Press, 1996); Stephen Orgel, *Impersonations: The Performance of Gender in Shakespeare's England* (Cambridge: Cambridge University Press, 1996); Annabel Patterson, *Shakespeare and the Popular Voice* (Oxford: Basil Blackwell, 1990).

7. Richard Dutton, *Mastering the Revels: The Regulation and Censorship of English Renaissance Drama* (Iowa City: University of Iowa Press, 1991); Michael Bristol, *Big-Time Shakespeare* (London: Routledge, 1996), 41–58.

8. Jean Christophe Agnew, *Worlds Apart: The Market and the Theater in Anglo-American Thought, 1550–1750* (Cambridge: Cambridge University Press, 1986); Douglas Bruster, *Drama and the Market in the Age of Shakespeare* (Cambridge: Cambridge University Press, 1992); Lars Engle, *Shakespearean Pragmatism: Market of His Time* (Chicago: University of Chicago Press, 1993); William Ingram, *The Business of Playing: The Beginnings of the Adult Professional Theater in Elizabethan London* (Ithaca: Cornell University Press, 1992); Kathleen McLuskie and Felicity Dunsworth, "Patronage and the Economics of Theatre," in *A New History of Early English Drama*, ed. John D. Cox and David Scott Kastan (New York: Columbia University Press, 1997).

9. Albert Borgmann, *Technology and the Character of Contemporary Life: A Philosophical Inquiry* (Chicago: University of Chicago Press, 1984), 9.

10. Ann Jennalie Cook, *The Privileged Playgoers of Shakespeare's London: 1576–1642* (Princeton: Princeton University Press, 1981); Andrew Gurr, *Playgoing in Shakespeare's London*, 2d ed. (Cambridge: Cambridge University Press, 1997); Eve Sanders, *Gender and Literacy on Stage in Early Modern England* (Cambridge: Cambridge University Press, 1998).

11. Robert Weimann, "Towards a Literary Theory of Ideology: Mimesis, Representation, Authority," in *Shakespeare Reproduced: The Text in History and Ideology*, ed. Jean E. Howard and Marion F. O'Connor (London: Methuen, 1987), 265–73; Paul Yachnin, *Stage-Wrights: Shakespeare, Jonson, Middleton, and the Making of Theatrical Value* (Philadelphia: University of Pennsylvania Press, 1997).

12. James Stokes, ed., *Records of Early English Drama: Somerset*, 2 vols. (Toronto: University of Toronto Press, 1996).

13. Harold A. Innis, *The Bias of Communication* (Toronto: University of Toronto Press, 1991), 92–131.

14. Stokes, ed., *Records of Early English Drama*, 1:29. Additional citations are given in the text.

15. Desiderius Erasmus, *The Praise of Folly*, trans. John Wilson (Ann Arbor: University of Michigan Press, 1967), 3.

16. Ibid., 141.

17. Mikhail Bakhtin, *Rabelais and His World*, trans. Hélène Iswolsky (Cambridge: MIT Press, 1967), 78.

18. On the social meaning of mummery see Laroque, *Shakespeare's Festive World*, 48–60 ff.

19. Weimann, "Towards a Literary History of Ideology," 265–73.

20. Charles Taylor, *Sources of the Self* (Cambridge, Mass.: Harvard University Press, 1992), 44 ff.

21. On skimmington and related folk rituals see Violet Alfort, "Rough Music or Charivari," *Folklore* 70 (1959): 505–18; E. P. Thompson, "Rough Music: Le Charivaria Anglais," *Annales: Economies, Sociétés, Civilisations* 27 (1972): 285–312; Natalie Z. Davis, "The Reasons of Misrule: Youth Groups and Charivari in Sixteenth Century France," *Past and Present* 50 (1981): 49–74; Bristol, *Carnival and Theater*, 162–79.

22. On cross-dressing, see, for example, Howard, *Stage and Social Struggle*, 93–128; Natalie Z. Davis, "Women on Top: Symbolic Sexual Inversion and Political Disorder in Early Modern Europe," in *The Reversible World: Symbolic Inversion in Art and Society*, ed. Barbara Babcock (Ithaca: Cornell University Press, 1978), 147–90; Laura Levine, "Men in Women's Clothing: Antitheatricality and Effeminization from 1579 to 1642," *Criticism* 28 (1986): 121–43.

23. Darko Suvin, *Metamorphoses of Science Fiction: On the Poetics and History of a Literary Genre* (New Haven: Yale University Press, 1979), 14 ff.

24. Steven Mullaney, *The Place of the Stage: License, Play, and Power in Renaissance England* (Chicago: University of Chicago Press, 1988), 26–60.

25. Agnew, *Worlds Apart*, 101 ff.

26. Mette Hjort, *The Strategy of Letters* (Cambridge, Mass.: Harvard University Press, 1993), 160–88.

27. Stanely Cavell, *Must We Mean What We Say?* (New York: Scribner, 1969), 277 ff.

28. Orgel, *Impersonations*.

29. Wofford, "'To You I Give Myself,'" 163–69.

30. J. L. Austin, *How to Do Things with Words*, 2d ed. (Cambridge: Harvard University Press, 1962), 22.

31. On speech act theory more generally, see Austin, *How to Do Things with Words*; Mary Louise Pratt, *Toward a Speech Act Theory of Literary Discourse* (Bloomington: Indiana University Press, 1977); Joseph A. Porter, *The Drama of Speech Acts: Shakespeare's Lancastrian Tetralogy* (Berkeley: University of California Press, 1979).

Contributors

RANDALL ANDERSON (Lawrence University) has completed a dissertation at Yale on Tudor verse miscellanies. He is the author of a chapter, "Typographic Expression in Early Printed Books," in vol. 4 of *A History of the Book in Britain*.

MICHAEL D. BRISTOL (McGill University) is the author of *Carnival and Theater: Plebeian Culture and the Structure of Authority in Renaissance England*, *Shakepeare's America, America's Shakespeare*, and *Big-time Shakespeare*.

DOUGLAS BRUSTER (University of Texas, Austin) is the author of *Drama and the Market in the Age of Shakespeare*.

MARGARET J. M. EZELL (Texas A&M University) is the author of *Writing Women's Literary History*, *The Patriarch's Wife: Literary Evidence and the History of the Family*, and *Social Authorship and the Advent of Print*.

ALEXANDRA HALASZ (Dartmouth College) is the author of *The Marketplace of Print: Pamphlets and the Public Sphere in Early Modern England*.

F. J. LEVY (University of Washington) is the author of *Tudor Historical Thought* and of numerous articles on early modern English history, including "How Information Spread among the Gentry," *Journal of British Studies* (1982). He is working on a book on the dissemination of news in seventeenth-century England.

JOSEPH LOEWENSTEIN (Washington University, St. Louis) is the author of *Responsive Readings: Versions of Echo in Pastoral, Epic, and the Jonsonian Masque* and of articles on early print culture, including "The Script in the Marketplace," *Representations* (1985). He is finishing a book on early modern print culture and the origins of concepts of intellectual property.

HAROLD LOVE (Monash University) is the author of *Scribal Publication in Seventeenth-Century England*. He has edited *The Works of Thomas Southerne* and the Oxford Critical Edition of the works of the Earl of Rochester.

LEAH S. MARCUS (Vanderbilt University) is the author of several books, including *Unediting the Renaissance: Shakespeare, Marlowe, Milton* and *Puzzling Shakespeare: Local Reading and Its Discontents*.

ARTHUR F. MAROTTI (Wayne State University) is the author of *John Donne, Coterie Poet* and *Manuscript, Print and the English Renaissance Lyric*. He has edited or co-edited several collections of essays, including *Catholicism and Anti-Catholicism in Early Modern English Texts*.

STEVEN MULLANEY (University of Michigan) is the author of *The Place of the Stage: License, Play, and Power in Renaissance England*. He is currently at work on a book dealing with English colonialism.

Index

Achinstein, Sharon, 84 n. 46
Acts and Monuments (Foxe), 22–23, 181, 235–51; and affect, 239, 247, 249 n. 3; the Canterbury martyrs, 243, 248; and class, 242–48; contents, 238; and Foxe's imagined community, 23, 237, 238, 242–44, 247; ideological values, 239; and the theatrical, 242, 246–47, 248; and women, 237, 242–48
Addison, Joseph: *Cato,* 209
Aetius (Æcius) (literary character), 204, 205, 206, 211
Aetius, Flavius (Roman general), 201–2
Aldis, Harry G., 226, 228
Allen, William: *A Briefe Historie of the Glorious Martyrdom of XII. Reverend Priests,* 175
Alley, William, 107, 108
Almond, John, 183
Anderson, Andrew, 226; Anderson family, 226, 227, 228
Anderson, Randall, 15
Anderton, Laurence, S.J., 173
anonymous poems: "He fell of consanguinetye," 137–38; "In vaine it is my carefull cares," 139; "It was an oulde sayenge of S*i*r John Kettels," 148; "Nay, Phewe nay pishe?," 145–47; "A secret murther hath bene done of late," 143–44, 145; "Sing gentll Swa*nn,*" 142–43, 145; "A sylence seldome seene," 136; "To the Reader," 137; "When first of all dame nature wroughte," 136
anthologizing, 15, 134–35, 151–53; and the canon, 152
antitheatricalism, 19–20, 300, 302
Aquaviva, Claudio, 191–92, 199 n. 66
Arbor of Amorous Devices, The, 134
Archbishop of Canterbury, 51
Archer, Thomas, 266
Aretus, 204
Arminianism, 257, 258, 259
Arundel, Countess of, 176
Ascham, Roger, 42
Askew, Anne, 244
As You Like It (Shakespeare), 25, 279–81, 296–304
Augustine, St.: *Confessions,* 19
Augustus, 69, 272
Ault, Norman, 135
Austin, J. L., 302
authorial rights, 7, 12–13

309

INDEX

authorship, 10, 12, 18, 69–72, 104–5, 116, 117, 130–31, 215; and attribution, 115; and authorial labor, 92–96, 99, 111–12; and the "best-seller," 59, 63; and copyright, 12, 105, 107, 110; and entrepreneurism, 12; and literary property, 12, 14, 105, 107, 109, 111–17; multiple, 130–31; and style, 71–73

Bacon, Francis (Lord Chancellor), 72–73, 252; *Apology*, 72
Bacon, Nicholas, 35, 36
Ballard, George: *Memoirs of Eminent Ladies*, 216
Bampfield, Colonel, 223
Barber, Tom, 270
Barnavelt, Sir John Van Olden, 257, 258, 259
Barrington, Lady Joan, 269
Barrington, Sir Thomas, 270
Bathampton, Somerset, 281–82, 286, 291, 292
Battle of Turnholt (lost play), 259
Bayfield, Richard, 241
Beal, Peter, 14, 160 n. 4, 164 n. 36
Beaumont, Francis, 17
Beaumont and Fletcher: folio of 1647, 205, 206
Bednarz, James, P., 80 n. 13
Beesley, George, 182
Bell, Robert (Speaker of Parliament), 44–45, 122 n. 45
"best-sellers," 11, 56–59, 74; and authorship, 59; definition of, 56; and "embodied writing," 50–52, 63, 73
Bikerdike, Robert, 177
Bishop of London, Richard Bancroft, 51, 53
Bishops' Ban (1599), 51, 64, 75, 77, 80–81 n. 16; and mixing of sacred and profane, 53–54
Black, L. G., 163–64 n. 31, 165 n. 46, 167–68 n. 70
Blackfan, Father, 183
blazon, the, 50, 54–55, 136, 147–49, 170 n. 93

Bodey, John, 176, 186–87, 188
Bodleian Library MS Rawlinson poet. 85 (RP 85), 15, 133–59; compared to other miscellanies, 134–35, 148, 151, 154–59; compiler of, 138–40; contributors, 134; and coterie, 136, 138–42; general contents, 134–35, 136, 139, 148; genres in, 135–38; modern editors of, 135; physical description, 133–34; and poetic style (tone), 136–51; the sonnet in, 143–45; summary of contents (table), 154–59; and women poets, 148–50. *See also* miscellanies
Bodleian Library MSS Eng.th.b.12, 176
body, the. *See* "embodied writing"
Book of Martyrs (Foxe). See *Acts and Monuments*
Boose, Lynda E., 80–81 n. 16
Borgmann, Albert, 3–4, 20, 280
Bourdieu, Pierre, 225
Bourne, Nicholas, 265
Bowes, Marmaduke, 176
Braithwaite, Richard, 267–68, 271
Brayne, John, 246
Breitenberg, Mark, 238
Breton, Nicholas, 131, 134; *Old Mad-Cap's New Gallimaufry*, 62; *Pasquil* series, 58, 62, 64
Bright, Timothy, 107
Bristol, Michael, 24–25
British Library MS Harley 6910, 134, 165 n. 41
British Library MS Harley 7392, 134, 165 n. 40
Brittons Bowre of Delights, 128, 134
Brown, Nancy Pollard, 176
Brown, Sally, 160 n. 4
Browne, William, 104
Browning, Robert, 146
Bruster, Douglas, 10, 24
Buc, Sir George, 258–59, 260
Bucer, Martin, 250 n. 14
Bullacker, Thomas, 182
Burbage, Richard, 66–67
Burnet, Elizabeth, 219
Bush, Douglas, 152

INDEX

Butter, Nathaniel, 265
Byrd, William, 176

Calley, William, 269
Caltha Poetarum (T. Cutwode), 55, 74
Calvinist Remonstrants, 257, 259, 260
Cambridge University, St. John's College, 15, 37, 60, 75, 136, 138, 139–41, 168 n. 71, 169 n. 77, 210, 264–65
Cambridge University MS Dd.5.75, 134
Campion, Edmund, S.J., 174, 178, 182, 189, 190, 191–92, 194–95 nn. 3, 12; "Brag," 172; *Two Books of the Histories of Ireland*, 172
Canarie, James: *A discourse. . . . manifestation of the will of God*, 227
Canterbury, Archbishop of, 183
Capp, Bernard, 95, 100 n. 3, 101–2 n. 13
Carleton, Sir Dudley, 258, 264, 266
carnivalesque, 19–20, 25, 283, 290
Catholicism (England), 15–16, 172–78, 181, 187, 191–92, 224, 242, 255; in the provinces, 183; reduction in persecution of, 192. *See also* martyrdom accounts
Caxton, William, 6
Cecil, Sir Robert, 34, 35, 37, 39
Cecil, Sir William, Lord Burghley, 35, 38, 39, 45
censorship, 17, 24, 64, 211, 255–57, 258–61, 266, 272–73; self-, 10, 224
Chaffinch, William, 211
Challoner, Bishop Thomas, 191
Chamberlain, John, 106, 253, 258, 259, 262–63, 264, 266, 268
Chambers, E. K.: *Oxford Book of Sixteenth Century Verse*, 135
Chapman, George, 53; *All Fools*, 52; *Biron*, 260
Charles I (king of England), 113, 138, 192, 205, 223, 252, 262, 268, 272, 273
Charles II (king of England), 192, 207
Charnberne (Chamberne), James, 285, 286
Charnberne, Sarah, 285–86
Chartier, Roger, 132, 218
Chaucer, Geoffrey, 137

Chettle, Henry: *Greene's Groatsworth of Wit*, 67–68, 70, 72
Chilax (Chylax), 207, 212
Chiver, Oliver, 291, 292, 294–95
Chomley, Sir Roger, 245–46, 247
"Church Papists," 177, 192
Clegg, Cyndia Susan, 81 n. 16
Clerk, Sir John, 217
Clitherow, [Saint] Margaret, 178; John Mush's life of, 176
Cogswell, Thomas, 262
Cohen, Walter, 21
Coke, Sir Edward, 109
Colling, Henry, 167
Collinson, Patrick, 249 n. 2
commonplace compilation, 28 n. 42, 206
Coningsby, Humphrey, 165 n. 40
Connerton, Paul, 23
Constable, Henry, 168 n. 71
Convocation of 1624, 105, 109–10
Cooper, Thomas, Bishop of Winchester, 52
copyright, 12, 105, 107, 110, 215; and Statute of Anne of 1709, 105. *See also* authorship; literary property
Corbett, Richard: "Iter Boreale," 66
corantos, 265–68, 269, 272, 273. *See also* news; newsletters
Countercuff Given to Martin Junior, 52
Counter-Reformation, 54, 191
court, 15, 113, 139, 206, 207–8, 211, 264, 270
Court of Venus, The, 128
Crane, Mary Thomas, 28 n. 42
Croft, Pauline, 82 n. 25
Crofts, Catherine, 211
Cromwell, Oliver, 206
Crosse, Robert, 120 n. 23
Crosseman, Emanuel, 288–90, 291
Crowne, John: *Calisto*, 208
Cummings, Laurence, 138–39, 143, 168 nn. 73, 74, 170 nn. 86, 90
Cust, Richard, 28 n. 37

Dallington, Robert: *Survey of the Great Dukes State of Tuscany*, 255

Dangerfield, Joan, 243
Daniel, Samuel: *Delia*, 57; *Historie of England*, 107
Darcy v. Allen, 122 n. 37
Davenant, William: *News from Plymouth*, 273
Davies, John: *Epigrams and Elegies*, 58; *Hymns of Astrea*, 58; *Nosce Teipsum*, 58
Davison, Francis, 140
Day, John, 119 n. 18
Dekker, Thomas, 61; *The Gull's Horn-Book*, 52–53
de Vere, Edward, Earl of Oxford, 134; "My mynde to me a kingdom is," 135, 145; poetry, 148
Devereux, Robert, Earl of Essex, 14, 37, 72, 260; revolt of, 183
Dickenson, Arthur, 62; *Arisbas: Euphues Amid His Slumbers*, 59
Dickenson, Roger, 190
Diehl, Huston, 22
Dinghurste, John, 288, 289
Dinghurste, William, 288
discourse, as commodity, 12
Dodd, Richard, 287–90, 291, 292
Donaldson, Ian, 201
Donne, John, 5, 182, 256; sermons, 9
Dort, Synod of, 255
Drayton, Michael, 160 n. 2; *England's Heroical Epistles*, 57
Dryden, John, 209
Duckett, James, 175, 177–78
Dutton, Richard, 29 n. 55, 260
D'Urfé, Honoré, 209; "Histoire d'Eudoxe, Valentinian, et Ursace," 16, 200, 201–4
Dyer, Sir Edward, 134, 140, 164 n. 36; poetry of, 131, 143, 145
Dymock, Sir Edward, 255

East Brent, Somerset, 287, 290, 291, 292
Edward I (king of England), 237
Eikon Basilike, 192
Eisenstein, Elizabeth, 1, 5, 9
Elderton, William, 255
Eliot, T. S., 116
Elizabeth, Princess (daughter of James I), 254
Elizabeth I (queen of England), 9–10, 11, 33–48, 72, 73, 148, 164 n. 34, 172, 180, 185, 237, 238, 255
  speeches of, 9–10, 33–48; criticism of law and lawyers in, 41–42; editing of, 46; on the execution of Mary, Queen of Scots (1586), 34–35, 38–39, 47 nn. 11, 12; extempore, 37–38, 44; "The Golden Speech," 34, 43; in Latin, 37; malleability of, 33, 38; manuscript vs. printed versions of, 35–36, 43, 46; orality vs. written forms of, 33–38, 40–41, 44–45; before Parliament on 2 Jan. 1567, 35; and presence, 33–34, 46; and *prototypon*, 10, 35, 38, 46; reply to parliamentary delegation of 5 Nov. 1566, 43–44, 45; reply to parliamentary petition of 12 Nov. 1586, 38–43; revisions of, 39, 42–45; and uses of memory, 37–38, "When I was fayre and younge and fauour graced me," 148
"embodied writing": and authorship, 59, 69, 77; and the "best-seller," 56–59, 63; and Bishops' Ban, 53; and the blazon, 50, 55; the body and the book, 10, 49–50, 80 n. 13; definition and examples of, 50; genres of, 55–56; and the *hos ego* myth, 69–71, 73; and Lyly, 59–62, 64; and the Marprelate controversy, 51–56; and print, 50–52, 78 n. 2; and the public sphere, 63–65; reasons for rise of, 73–77; and style, 60–61, 69, 86 n. 62; and theater, 76–77; and the younger Elizabethans, 75–76
Emerford, Thomas, 174
England's Helicon, 128–29, 130, 134
Enright, B. J., 164 nn. 33, 37
entrepreneurism, 12, 93–96. *See also* subscription; "subscription scenario"
Erasmus: *The Praise of Folly*, 283
erotica, 54–55, 73

INDEX

Esler, Anthony, 75–76
Eudoxia, 201–2, 204
Euphuism (Euphues), 60–62, 65, 67, 68, 73
Exclusion Crisis, 223, 225
Ezell, Margaret J. M., 18

Fagius, Paul, 250 n. 14
Fawkes, Guy, 256
Fenn, James, 174
Filcock, Roger, 176
Finch, John, 184
Finet, John ("I. F."), 138–40, 169 n. 77
Fitzherbert, Thomas, 189
Fletcher, John, 16–17, 200–210, 212; *Valentinian*, 16–17, 200, 203–8
Florio, John, 75
Folger Shakespeare Library MS V.a.89, 134
Ford, Thomas, 188
Foxe, John, 74–75, 235–39, 241–44, 246–48. See also *Acts and Monuments*
Foxon, D. F., 105
Frederick (king of Bohemia, elector palatine), 254, 266
freedom of speech, 252
Freeman, Thomas, 55
Freeman, William, 189

Gainsford, Captain, 267
Garnet, Henry, S.J., 176, 183, 184, 185, 196 n. 25; "Treatise of Equivocation," 172
Gennings, Edmund, 175, 180, 182, 184, 185, 190
Gibbons, John: *Concertatio Ecclesiae Anglicanae*, 175
Gibbons, Orlando, 107
Gibson, William, 177
Gild, William: *Moses unveiled*, 227
Glasier, Robert, 289, 290
Golding, Arthur, 107
Gondomar, Don Diego Sarmiento de Acuña, Conde de, 261–62
Gorgeous Gallery of Gallant Inventions, A, 128
Gosson, Henry, 90, 100–101 n. 4

Gosson, Stephen, 143
Gottschalk, Katherine K., 165 n. 41
Gouldner, Alvin, 1
Greg, W. W., 118 n. 7
Greenblatt, Stephen, 242
Greene, Robert, 60–62, 65, 67, 69; cony-catching pamphlets, 62, 64; *Euphues His Censure to Philautus*, 59; *Greene's Groatsworth of Wit*, 67–68, 70, 72; *Menaphon*, 59; *Quip for an Upstart Courtier*, 58
Greenfield, Matthew, 75
Grimston, Harbottle, 115
Grimston, Ralph, 177
Guillory, John, 225
Gunpowder Plot, 192, 256

Habermas, Jürgen, 11, 65
Haigh, Christopher, 238
Halasz, Alexandra, 11, 85 n. 46
Halkett, Ann, 18, 215–51; anticipating readership, 219–23, 229; and authorship, 215, 217–21, 223, 228–29; biography, 216, 218, 224–25; and the Civil War, 216, 223; and cultural capital, 225; and devotional practices, 219, 221, 223, 228; and gender, 223–24; *Instructions for Youth*, 218; manuscript collections of, 216–17, 223; *Meditations and Prayers Upon the First Week*, 218; *Meditations on the Twentieth and Fifth Psalm*, 218; and politics, 223–25, 228; posthumous publication, 222–25, 228–29; "public" vs. "private" texts, 217, 220, 228; relation to print culture, 217, 219–23, 225–29; and religion, 224, 228; and "S.C.," 218, 220–23
Halkett, Sir Charles, 225
Halkett, Robert, 224
Hall, John, 293
Hall, Joseph, 55, 70, 71; *Virgidemiae*, 54, 70
Hall, Mary, 293
Hanse, Everard, 189
Harbage, Alfred, 21, 22
Harding, Thomas, 237–38

Harington, John: *Apology*, 58; the *Ajax* books, 62, 64; *The Metamorphosis of Ajax*, 58
Hart, William, 175
Harvey, Gabriel, 60–61, 62, 64, 65, 69, 72, 255; *Four Letters*, 60; *Have With You to Saffron-Walden*, 49
Hay Any Work for Cooper, 51–52
Haydock, George, 174
Hazlitt, William, 152
Hebel, J. William, 135
Hemerford, Thomas, 181
Henri de Navarre (King Henry IV of France), 259–60
Henry VIII (king of England), 255–56
Heracle, 203, 204
Heyward (Haywood), John: *. . . Life and Reign of King Henry the IV*, 87 n. 65
Hill, Christopher, 74
Hill, Curate Thomas, 287–88, 289, 291
Hobbs, Mary, 14, 161 n. 17
Hoby, Sir Edward, 47 n. 12
Hodgson, Sydney (alias Robert Sidney), 180
Holinshed, Raphael: *Chronicles*, 39, 85 n. 47
Holles, Denzel, 263
Holles, Sir John, 256, 261–65
homosexuality, 17, 212
Honigmann, E. A. J., 59
Hook, Robert, 229
Hopkins, John, 106–7
Horner, Nicholas, 184, 188
House of Commons, 109–10, 253, 268, 272
House of Lords, 105
Howard, Henry, Earl of Surrey, 134; "The longer lyfe the more offence," 150–51
Howard, Mall, 211
Howard, Philip, Earl of Arundel, 172, 191
Howard, Sir Robert: *The Conquest of China*, 210, 211
Howard-Hill, Trevor, 260
Hudson, Hoyt H., 135
Hume, David: "Of the Standard of Taste," 151

Humphrey, Laurence, 185
Hunter, G. K., 62
"imagined community," 23, 237, 238, 242–44, 247
Innis, Harold, 3, 4, 8
Inns of Court, 75, 210
Irish Rebellion of 1641, 192
Isle of Rhé expedition, 205, 269

James I (king of England), 56, 106, 109, 117, 192, 253, 255, 256, 258, 261–62, 266, 268, 290
James II (king of England), 223, 224, 226, 227
James, Francis, 290
Jaques, 279, 299–300
Johnson, Robert, 188
Jollette, Thomas, 176
Jones, Emrys, 15; *New Oxford Book of Sixteenth-Century Verse*, 135, 143, 152
Jonson, Ben, 16, 20, 21, 25, 53, 62, 69, 95, 105–6, 204, 208, 254, 270–72, 273; *Bartholomew Fair*, 246; *Cynthia's Revels*, 67; "Epistle Answering to One That Asked . . . ," 272; "Execration upon Vulcan," 62; *The New Cry*, 256; *News from the New World Discovered in the Moon*, 253–54, 270, 272; *The Poetaster*, 53, 67, 68–69, 272; *The Staple of News*, 24, 254, 270–72; *Time Vindicated*, 105–6; *Works* of 1616, 206
Jores, David, 249 n. 6
Joyner, Robert, 62

Kelliher, Hilton, 130, 160 n. 4, 168 n. 71
Kemp, Will, 67
Kendrick, Christopher, 116
Kent, Earl of, 256
Kernan, Alvin, 1
Kettle, Sir John, 148
King, Bishop John, 258, 260
King's Men, the (the King's Company), 205, 207, 210, 211, 262
Kinnoul, Earl of, 224
Knight, Mary, 211

INDEX

Knight, William, 177
Knott, John R., 251 n. 23
Knowles, Toby, 120 n. 23
Knox, Henry, 227, 228
Kyd, Thomas: *The Spanish Tragedy,* 57

Lacey, Brian, 184
Lachmann, Karl, 132
Lake, Bishop Arthur, 287
Lake, Sir Thomas, 263
Lamb, Charles, 104
Lander, Jesse, 82 n. 27
Latham, Agnes, 134
Latimer, Hugh, 236, 241, 242
Latin, importance of, 88 n. 77
Laud, Archbishop, 291–92, 294–95
Leavis, F. R., 116
Lee, Nathaniel, 209
Leicester's Commonwealth, 172
L'Estrange, Roger: *A popish priest at his execution at Tyburn,* 193
letters, 174, 256, 264, 266; interception of, 256, 257
Levin, Carole, 244, 250–51 nn. 14, 20
Levy, F. J., 24, 25
Lewis, C. S.: Drab verse vs. Golden lyrics, 128–29
libel, 82 n. 25, 137, 138, 172
Life and Death of Mr. Edmund Geninges, Priest, The, 175
Lincoln, Earl of, 255
Line, [Saint] Anne, 176, 178
literary labor, 92–96, 99, 103–4
literary (authorial, intellectual) property, 12, 14, 105, 107, 109, 111–17. *See also* plagiarism
Livy, 209
Locke, Thomas, 258
Lodge, Thomas, 58, 62; *Euphues' Shadow,* 59; *Rosalind,* 57, 59; *Scilla's Metamorphosis,* 54
Loewenstein, Joseph, 12–13
Loftis, John, 216, 219
Lord Keeper, 256
Love, Harold, 5, 14–17, 41, 26–27 n. 16, 28 n. 40, 132–33, 162 n. 22, 164 n. 32, 217

Lucina (Isidore), 201–4, 209, 212; compared to Lucretia, 201, 202
"Lucina legend," 200–214; relation to media, 203–4; sources in Procopius, 201–2
Lucina's Rape (Rochester), 16–17, 200, 207–11; ideological implications of, 207, 210; and media-related changes, 208–11; as "revision" of Fletcher's *Valentinian,* 207–8; and stagecraft, 208; sources, 200; venue for performance, 207
Lycias, 212
Lyly, John, 74; *Endymion,* 55; *Euphues* texts, 56, 59–62; *Euphues, the Anatomy of Wit,* 59; *Euphues and His England,* 59; *Midas,* 55

M. R., Mrs.: "Howe can*n* the feeble forte butt yeelde att last," 149–50
MacKenzie, Sir George, 225; *Laws of Scotland,* 227
MacPherson, C. B., 115
Manningham, John: *Diary,* 66
manuscript culture: and canon formation, 15, and circulation (transmission), 13–17, 172–77, 190, 200, 210–12; features of, 5, 13, 14, 27 n. 33; and martyrdom accounts, 15–16, 172–99; and orality, 5–6, 13; and print culture, 6–7, 9, 13–18, 22, 33–38, 40–41, 44–45, 73, 200; studies on, 14; and women, 17–18. *See also* miscellanies; print culture; printing
Marcus, Leah S., 9–10, 24
Markham, Gervase, 55; *The Poem of Poems, or Sion's Muse,* 54
Markley, Robert, 205, 207
Marlowe, Christopher, 20; *Hero and Leander,* 54, 55; *Massacre at Paris,* 259–60
Marotti, Arthur F., 14, 15–16, 28 n. 49, 57, 130–31, 163 n. 29, 217
Marprelate controversy, 51–56, 64, 71–74, 78 n. 2; *An Almond for a Parrot,* 51–52; *An Answer unto a Certain Calumnious Letter. . . . ,* 71–73; *Countercuff Given to Martin Junior,* 52; and "embodied writ-

Marprelate controversy (*continued*)
ing," 51–52; *Hay Any Work for Cooper,* 51, 71, 72; *Martin Mar-Sixtus,* 75; and printers, 71; and the public sphere, 74; and stylistic identification, 67, 72, 86 n. 62; *A Summons for Sleepers,* 56; and Job Throckmorton, 71
marriage ceremony, 303
Marriott, John, 114
Marsh's Library (Dublin) MS Z3.5.21, 143, 165 n. 46
Marston, John, 34, 69
Martial, 136, 146
Martyr, Catherine, 250 n. 14
Martyr, Peter, 250 n. 14
martyrdom accounts
  Catholic, 15–16, 172–99; and canonization of saints, 191; and Catholic ceremony, 186–87; compared to Protestant accounts, 180–81; devaluation of, 192; features, 173, 177, 181–82, 186; and gallows humor, 184–85, 186; and last words, 185–86, 193; and lay martyrs, 178–80, 188; in manuscript, 174, 177–91; and the miraculous, 187–90; and places of execution, 183–84; printed, 172, 174, 175, 177; as propaganda, 173, 174, 191; recontextualization of, 192–93; and relics, 182, 187, 188, 189–91; religio-political functions, 177; and sympathy for martyrs, 182–83, 185; and torture, 181–82; Westminster Diocesan Archives booklet, 176–79; and witnesses, 189–90; and women, 176, 178, 190
  Protestant, 23, 180–81, 236–51; and affect, 236–37, 251 n. 24; Catholic readings of, 237–38; and heresy, 239–41; and humiliation, 239–41; ideological meaning, 236; and Perotine Massey, 235–38, 241–42; as official ritual, 239–41; and the theatrical, 240–42, 246; and torture and execution, 239–41, 249–50 n. 12; and women, 239, 242
Marx, Karl, 8, 96, 98; *Grundrisse,* 91

Mary, Queen of Scots, 34, 38–44
Mary I (queen of England), 225, 235, 237, 238, 240–42
Maslen, Keith, 101 n. 11
Massey, Perotine, 235–38, 241–42; woodcut of, 236, 237, 248–49 n. 2
Massinger, Philip, 205
Maurice, Prince of Orange, 257–59
Maximus, Petronius, 200, 201–4, 206
May, Bab, 211
May, Steven, 131–32, 145, 160 nn. 1, 3, 166 n. 51
McKenzie, D. F., 206
McKerrow, R. B., 59
McLuhan, Marshall, 2, 3, 5
Mead, Rev. Joseph, 264–65, 268
media, early modern, 1–26; of communication, 34; mixing of and "The Rapes of Lucina," 16–17, 200–214; relation of to artistic rendering, 203–4, 212; stage vs. page, 206, 209; and style, 206–7
Melville, Elizabeth, Lady Culross: *A Godly Dream,* 227
Meres, Francis: *Palladis Tamia,* 59
middle-class writers, 65
Middleton, Anthony, 184
Middleton, Thomas: *A Game at Chess,* 6, 24, 77, 254, 260–63; *Microcynicon, or Six Snarling Satires,* 77; *The Peace-maker,* 107
Miller, Ralph, 182
Mills, Robert, 138, 140–42; "Ad te saepe venit mea chartula," 141; "farewell to his freend," 140; "Finnet, Amice, vale, fugit hinc tuus ecca," 141; "To a feygned faythless and vngrateful frende," 141–42
Milner, Ralph, 190
Milton, John, 192; *Areopagitica,* 105, 111, 116
miscellanies
  manuscript, 15, 128, 130–71; and authorship, 130–32; Bodleian Library MS Rawlinson poet. 85 (RP 85), 133–71; British Library MS Harley 6910, 134, 165 n. 41; British Library MS Harley 7392, 143, 165 n. 40; Cambridge Uni-

versity MS Dd.5.75, 134; community vs. society of readers, 132–33; compared to printed miscellanies, 131, 151; features of, 130, 131; Folger Shakespeare Library MS V.a.89, 134; and genealogy of tastes, 132–35, 140; malleability, of, 131; Marsh's Library (Dublin) MS Z3.5.21, 143, 165 n. 46; and New Historicism, 132
  printed, 15, 127–71; *The Arbor of Amorous Devices,* 134; *Brittons Bowre of Delights,* 128, 134; *The Court of Venus,* 128; and "editorial" processes, 128, 135; *England's Helicon,* 128–30, 134; *A Gorgeous Gallery of Gallant Inventions,* 128; and the lyric, 128–30; *The Paradise of Dainty Devices,* 128, 139, 164 n. 39; *The Phœnix Nest,* 128–29, 130, 134, 143, 161 n. 12; *A Poetical Rhapsody,* 128, 130, 140, 150–51; and poetic style, 129; social features of, 130; *Songs and Sonettes* ("Tottel's Miscellany"), 128–29, 137, 150, 164 n. 39; and taste, 151–52

Moggs, Reginald, 292–93
Moggs, Samuel, 291–92, 294–95
monopolies, 116; Act of Monopolies, 109; and royal prerogative, 109, 110; Statute of Monopolies, 110
More, Thomas, 172
Moreton, Peter, 265
Moretti, Franco, 115
Morgan, Edward, 182, 184, 186
Morton, Sir Albertus, 263
Moulton, Ian Frederick, 53
Mountford, Susannah, 212
Mueller, Janel, 48 n. 16, 249–50 n. 12
Mullaney, Steve, 22–23, 25, 299
Mumford, Lewis, 2, 9
mummery, 280, 282–87, 291, 292, 296, 300; social function of, 286–87
Mush, John, 176

Nashe, Thomas, 58, 60, 64, 74, 76, 255; *An Almond of a Parrot,* 51–52, 54; "The Choice of Valentines," 54; *Pierce Penniless,* 57; *Pygmalion's Image,* 55; *Salmacis and Hermaphroditus,* 55
news, 24, 252–78; and censorship, 255–57, 258–61, 266, 272–73; as commodity, 270–71; and the diary, 268–69; and foreign policy, 255, 258, 261, 262, 266; and manuscript form, 253, 270; and martyrdom accounts, 174; the "news" play, 257–63; and print, 254, 270; and the provinces, 268–70; relation to theater, 254, 263
newsletters, 210, 253, 271; amateur writers of, 264–65; and corantos, 265–68, 269, 272, 273; and the familiar letter, 263–65; and foreign policy, 255, 258, 261, 262, 266; professional writers of, 264–65
Nichols, John, 216
Norbrook, David, 15, 63, 84 n. 46; as editor of *Penguin Book of Renaissance Verse,* 152
Norden, John: *Speculum Britaniae,* 107
Norris, Lord, 256
Northampton, 105
Northbrook, Lord: *A Treatise wherein Dicing . . . Are Reproved,* 19
Norton Anthology of English Literature, 216
Nuttall, Geoffrey, 178, 183
Nutter, Robert, 174

Oates, Titus ("Popish Plot"), 17, 192, 193, 210
Ong, Walter, 1, 4
Onslow, Richard, 36–37
orality, 1, 4–5, 33–38; types, 18–19
Osbaldson, Edward, 176
Ovid: *Metamorphoses,* 54
Oxford University, 37, 75, 168 n. 71, 210

Pallicer, Thomas, 176
pamphlets, 8, 11, 51–52, 62, 67, 68, 71, 100–101 n. 4, 259, 262, 265; and Catholic works, 172, 193; and pamphlet culture, 75; and John Taylor, 90–102; travel pamphlets, 91, 92, 93, 94

Paradise of Dainty Devices, The, 128, 139, 164 n. 39
Parkes, Malcolm, 169 n. 77
Parliament, 35, 36, 38, 110, 111, 254, 255, 263, 265
Parnassus trilogy, 65; *The Return from Parnassus,* 70
Parr, Katherine, 244
Parsons, Philip, 209
Parsons, Robert, 74; *Directory,* 56
Passionate Pilgrim, The, 58
pastoral, 103, 104, 111, 114, 115, 136, 296–99
patents, 12–13, 106–11; and decorum, 257; royal, 13, 106–10, 112–14, 226, 254, 255
patronage, 5, 76, 95, 117
Patterson, Annabel, 85 n. 47
Patterson, Lyman Ray, 105
Peele, George, 134
Pembroke, William Herbert, Earl of, 106, 262
Penry, John, 72
Pepys, Samuel, 219
Percy, Bishop, 130
performance, 18–26
Perkins, William: *Armilla Aurea,* 56, 74; *The Foundation of Christian Religion,* 57; *A Treatise Tending unto a Declaration . . . ,* 56
personal, the (personalism), 49–50, 56, 64, 65
personalization of texts, 10–11, 50–51, 63, 77
Persons, Robert, S.J., 174, 191, 192–93, 194 n. 3; "A Memorial for the Reformation of England," 172
Petrarch, 71
Phaer, Thomas, and Thomas Twynne: *The Whole XII Books of the Æneidos,* 70
Phœnix Nest, The, 128–29, 130, 134, 143, 161 n. 12
Pilcher, Thomas, 189
Pincus, Steven, 84 n. 46
Pitfirrane, Lady, 222
plagiarism, 12, 70–72, 104, 114. *See also* literary property

Plasden, Oliver, 185
Playfere, Thomas: *A Most Excellent and Heavenly Sermon,* 56
Plomer, 227, 228
Plutarch, 209
Poetical Rhapsody, A, 128, 130, 140, 150–51
"poetomachia." *See* satire wars
Pole, Margaret, Countess of Salisbury, 178
Pole, Reginald, Cardinal 178
Poole, Kristen Elizabeth, 78 n. 78
Popham, Sir John, Judge, 179
popular festivity (folk ritual), 19–21, 25, 279–81, 284, 286, 287, 296. *See also* skimmington; mummery
Pormort, Thomas, 184
Pory, John, 264, 265, 268
possessive individualism, 115–16
postal service, 28 n. 40, 210
posthumous publication, 18, 215–51
Powle, Mrs., 284–86
Powle (Poale), Thomas, 282–87, 296
Pribush, John, 183
print culture: and centralization, 6; and "embodied writing," 50–54, 58–63, 73–74; features of, 5; and manuscript culture, 6–7, 9, 13–18, 22, 33–38, 40–41, 44–45, 73, 200; and news, 24; and orality, 5–6, 9, 13; and the personal, 49, 56; and the public sphere, 63–65; and theater, 18–26, 76–77, 200
printing, 1–11, 13; collateral development of, 3, 9; as communications medium, 2–3, 10–11; cultural authority of, 1; and cultural change, 7–13; of dramatic scripts, 65–66; and gender, 18; habituation to, 74–75; and market relations, 11; and mass production, 7–8; and orality, 1; social power of, 3, 8; structural transformation of, 49–89; and technological determinism, 2; as technology, 7–9
Pritchard, Allan, 117 n. 2
private sphere, 11, 18, 64
Privy Council, 24, 110, 226, 228, 252, 255–56, 260–61

INDEX

Proby, Peter, 264
proclamations, royal, 252, 253, 256, 261–62, 269, 273
Procopius: *History of the Wars*, 201, 203; sources for Lucina legend, 201–4
Proculus, 211
Protectorate, 192
Protestantism, 16, 178, 181, 187, 191, 236, 238, 247. See also *Acts and Monuments*
Protestant Reformation, 22–23, 50, 74, 238, 239, 242
prototypon, 10, 35, 38, 46
public sphere, 10–11, 12, 18, 24, 51, 63–65, 74, 98; definitions of, 63–64, 84–85 nn. 45, 46; and print culture, 63–64; and the theatrical, 65–66, 76
Puckering, Sir John, Lord Keeper, 183
Puttenham, George, 139; *Arte of English Poesie*, 69–70

Quarles, Francis: *Enchiridion*, 227; *Psalms of David in metre*, 227

Ralegh, Sir Walter, 14, 134, 140, 185, 273; "In vayne my eyes . . . ," 139; poetry of, 131, 171 n. 96
Rawlinson, Richard, 133
Reshoulde, James, 138, 140, 168 n. 73, 169 n. 79
Revels Office, 19, 280
Reynolds, E. F., 193
Reynolds, Thomas, 182–83
Ringler, William, 134, 143, 170 n. 88
Roberts, John, 182, 184, 191
Rochester, John Wilmot, Earl of, 200–201, 204; and British Library manuscript, 211–12; *Lucina's Rape*, 16–17, 200, 207–12; circulation of work of, 210–12; "revision" of Fletcher's *Valentinian*, 207–8; "Scæna," 210, 211; and Yale Library MS Osborn fb 334, 210, 211
Roe, Bartholomew, 183
Rollins, Hyder E., 134, 160 n. 3
Rome, 15, 174, 261, 266
Rosalind, 279, 280, 302–4

Rose, Mark, 105
Rossingham, Edmund, 264
Rous, John, 257, 269
Rowsam, Stephen, 187–88
Rudyerd, Sir Benjamin, 263
Rutland, Earl of, 268

Saintsbury, George, 160 n. 5
Sandys, George, 113
Sargent, Ralph, 143
satire wars ("poetomachia"), 51–53, 67, 73, 76
Satiromastix (Dekker), 67
Scarry, Elaine, 249–50 n. 12
Scott, Montford, 182
Scott, Thomas: *Second Part of Vox Populi*, 262
scribal publication, 14–15, 17, 132–33, 211, 217, 254; types of, 14
Seres, William, 119 n. 18
Seymour, Thomas, 113, 114
Shaaber, M. A., 266
Shakespeare, William, 16, 21, 62–63, 66–68, 69, 72, 204, 205, 208; *As You Like It*, 25, 279–81, 296–304; father of, 172; First Folio (1623), 206; *Henry VI* plays, 52; *1 Henry VI*, 58; *3 Henry VI*, 68; *Love's Labor's Lost*, 298; *The Merry Wives of Windsor*, 52; *A Midsummer Night's Dream*, 19, 298; *The Rape of Lucrece*, 58, 62; *Richard III*, 66; *Romeo and Juliet*, 58; *The Tempest*, 20; *Venus and Adonis*, 49, 54, 55, 57, 58, 62
shame, 281, 286, 291, 293–96; and the theater, 298, 299, 300–301
Shapiro, James, 67
Sherwin, Ralph, 182
Sherwood, Thomas: "A Relation written by his Brother for his Nephews," 175
Shirley, James, 205–7
Shirt, John, 188
Sidney, Sir Philip, 74, 134–36, 140, 147, 161 n. 12, 168 n. 73, 255; *Arcadia*, 14, 57, 61, 134, 149; *Astrophil and Stella*, 76, 130, 134, 144, 146–47, 168 n. 73; *Certain Sonnets*, 134; "Her lose hears be the

Sidney, Sir Philip (*continued*)
shot," 149; influence of, 130; poetry of, 130, 131, 133, 143, 149
Sidney (Sydney), Sir Robert, 14, 256, 264
Sir John Van Olden Barnavelt (Fletcher and Massinger), 24, 254; background to, 257–58; and censorship, 258–59; as "news" play, 257–60
skimmington, 280, 292–94; as social protest, 294–96
Skryne, Elizabeth, 283, 284
Skryne, John (and as James Charnberne), 282–86
Smith, Bruce, 26 n. 12
Smith, Henry, 56–58, 74; *A Sermon of the Benefit of Contentation*, 57; *The Sermons of Henry Smith*, 57; *Six Sermons Preached by Master H. Smith*, 57; *The Trumpet of the Soul*, 57; *The Wedding Garment*, 57
Smith, Richard, Bishop of Chalcedon, 175, 177
Snow, Peter, 176
Somers, Thomas, 182, 184, 191
Somerset, Robert Carr, Earl of, 25
Songes and Sonettes ("Tottel's Miscellany"), 128–29, 137, 150, 164 n. 39
Sophocles: *Oedipus Rex*, 42
Southerne, John: *The Fate of Capua*, 209
Southwell, Robert, 56, 58, 172, 174, 181, 185; *A Humble Supplication to the Queen*, 179; manuscript collections of, 194 n. 9; *Mary Magdalens Funeral Teares*, 54, 57, 74; *St. Peter's Complaint*, 54, 57, 74
Southworth, John, 16, 192–93
Spanish Infanta, 192
Spenser, Edmund, 134; *Amoretti*, 144, 164 n. 36; *The Faerie Queene*, 49, 74, 75
Spiera, Francesco, 251 n. 24
Spinola, Cardinal, 267
Sprague, Arthur Colby, 209
Star Chamber, 256, 263
Stationers' Company, 8, 12–13, 19, 90, 93, 96, 97, 105, 107–15, 117, 266, 280; *Stationers' v. Carnan*, 122 n. 41

Sternhold, Thomas, 106–7
Stokes, James, 25, 282, 285, 291, 296
Strange, Ferdinando, Lord, 147–48; "My mistress in hir brest dothe were," 147
Stubbes, John, 255
Stuteville, Sir Martin, 264–65
subscription, 11, 90–102, 264; as "bill," 94, 97–98; as "expense account," 95; and production and consumption, 91, 96, 98–100; and the public sphere, 98–100; social dynamics of, 91; as wager, 94
"subscription scenario," 11–12, 90–102; breakdown of, 96, 98–99; as capitalism, 93, 99–100; and economic, cultural capital, 95–96, 99; and labor, 92–96, 99; and the marketplace, 92, 97; as patronage, 95; and relationship between reader and writer, 96, 98; social dynamics of, 91–96; and surplus, 96–97, 98–99; and John Taylor, 90–102; as wager, 94
Sullivan, Ernest, 130–31
sumptuary legislation, 257
Sutcliffe, Matthew: *An Answer unto a Certain Calumnious Letter . . .* , 71–73
Sutton, Abraham, 190
Sutton, Robert, 189
Sympson, Andrew, 218; *Tripatriarchicon*, 227–28

Tarlton, Richard, 60–61, 65, 72, 83 n. 34
Taylor, John (the Water Poet), 11–12, 90–102; and authorial labor, 92–96, 99; as "creditor," 97–98; folio works of 1630, 90; *Kicksey-Winsey: or a Lerry cometwang*, 93–95; *A Pennilesse Pilgrimage*, 93–94, 95; *A shilling, or travailes of twelve-pence*, 92; *Taylors Travels and Circular Perambulations*, 91–92; *Taylors Travels from London. to the Isle of Wight*, 97; *Taylors Travels to Prague in Bohemia*, 94
technological determinism, 1, 2, 24, 26 n. 5
technology, 2–4; and culture, 2, 218; and news, 24; and women writers, 215–16

theater: and art, 22; and the carnivalesque, 19–20, 25; as commodity, 280–81; compared to the printed book, 11, 16–17, 280, 281; and early modern culture, 18–26; and "embodied writing," 51–52, 65–70, 77; features of, 4, 19; and ideology, 21–22; and "imagined community," 23; and the marketplace, 300; and modernity, 25–26; and news, 24; and orality 4, 18; and the performative, 302–3; and the satire wars, 51–52; social character of, 21; and social space, 25; as technology, 19–20, 280
theaters (commercial, public, court), 9, 11 17, 18–19, 50, 65, 68, 76–77, 207, 209, 246, 260, 270, 279–80, 297, 298; and commodification, 20, 24–26
theatricality, 279, 303, 304
theatrical space, 296, 298, 299, 301
Thirty Years' War, 254, 266, 267
Thomas, John, 187–88
Thomas, William, 287
Thomson, James, 176
Thoreau, Henry David, 4
Throckmorton, Job, 71
Thulis, John, 173
Tönnies, Ferdinand, 132, 162 n. 25, 163 n. 28
Topcliffe, Richard, 180, 181, 184–86
torture and execution, public: and heresy, 239–41; and the theatrical, 240–41
Tottel, Richard, 128; "Tottel's Miscellany" (see *Songs and Sonnets*)
Touchstone, 298, 299, 301
traditional community, 300–302
True Report (Alfield), 174, 178

Ulysses Upon Ajax, 58

Valentinian (Fletcher), 16–17, 200, 203–8; media history of, 205–8; ideological implications of, 205–6
Valentinian III, 200–204, 210; as Charles II, 207
Vaux, Lord, 176
Vavasour, Anne, 148

Vergil (Virgil), 69–70, 71, 272
Verstegan, Richard, 174; *Theatrum Crudelitatem Haereticorum nostri temporis,* 175
Villiers, George, second duke of Buckingham, 105, 205, 207, 210, 262, 268, 269, 272
Vorstius, Conrad, 259

Wake, Sir Isaac, 265
Walpole, Henry, 183
Ward, [Saint] Mary, 178
Wardroper, John, 146
Warner, Michael, 2
"War of the Theaters." *See* satire wars
Watson, Agnes, 226
Watson, James, 226, 227
Weever, John: "*Ad Gulielmum Shakespear,*" 62; *Epigrams,* 59, 62; *Faunus and Melliflora,* 54
Weimann, Robert, 21–22, 74, 280
Wells, Swithen, 175, 180, 184
Whyte, Rowland, 14, 256, 264
William of Orange (King William III of England), 225, 227
Williams, Michael, 177
Williams, Raymond, 21, 249 n. 3
Willoby His Avisa, 55
Wilmot, John. *See* Rochester, John Wilmot, Earl of
Wilson, Arthur, 253
Wilson, John: *English Martyrologe,* 175
Wilson, John Dover, 52
Windebank, Sir Francis, 120 n. 23
Winters, Ivor, 129–30, 153
Winwood, Sir Ralph, 259
Wither, George, 12–13, 103–22; *Abuses Stript and Whipt,* 103, 117; audience of, 106; and authorship, 104–5, 115, 117; and book monopolies, 105, 108, 110–13; compared to Milton, 116; *Faire-Virtue,* 114–15; *Hymn and Songs of the Church,* 12, 106–9, 116; imprisonment, 104–6, 117, 117 n. 2; *Juvenilia,* 104; and literary labor, 103, 111–12, 115; and monopolies, 109–11; as poet-prophet, 104, 111; *Prepa-*

Wither, George (*continued*)
ration to the Psalter, 106; Psalter of, 106–8; royal patent of, 106–12; *Satire to the King,* 104, 106; *The Schollar's Purgatory,* 104–5, 108–17; *The Shepherd's Hunting,* 103–4, 114–15; *Wither's Motto,* 104–5
Wofford, Susanne, 302
Wood, George, 109, 121 n. 27
Wooden, Warren, 101 n. 12
Woodes, Nicholas: *The Conflict of Conscience,* 251 n. 24
Worthington, Thomas: *A Relation of Sixtene Martyrs,* 175

Wotton, Sir Henry, 263
Woudhuysen, H. R., 14, 15, 27 nn. 30, 33, 133, 164 n. 38, 168–69 nn. 71, 77, 195–96 n. 20
Wright, Leonard: *A Summons for Sleepers,* 56

Yachnin, Paul, 21
Yale Library MS Osborn fb 334, 210–11
Yonge, Walter, 256, 268–69
Young, Elizabeth, 23, 244–45, 247–48; learning of, 245–46
Young, James, 180